NEW TALES FOR OLD

Folktales as Literary Fictions for Young Adults

Gail de Vos

Anna E. Altmann

1999
Libraries Unlimited, Inc.
and Its Division
Teacher Ideas Press
Englewood, Colorado

To Peter, for his support and love.
GdV

To my mother, who told us the stories,
and to the memory of my father, who lived them.
AEA

LIBRARIES UNLIMITED, INC.
and Its Division
Teacher Ideas Press
P.O. Box 6633
Englewood, CO 80155-6633
1-800-237-6124
www.lu.com

Library of Congress Cataloging-in-Publication Data

De Vos, Gail, 1949-
    New tales for old : folktales as literary fictions for young
adults / Gail de Vos, Anna E. Altmann.
    xxi, 408 p. 19x26 cm.
    Includes bibliographical references and indexes.
    ISBN 1-56308-447-3
    1. Literature and folklore. 2. Young adult fiction--History and
criticism. 3. Tales--Adaptations--History and criticism. 4. Young
adult fiction--Themes, motives. 5. Young adults--Books and reading.
6. Folklore in literature. I. Altmann, Anna E. II. Title.
PN56.F58D48   1999
398.2'083--dc21   99-33150
                                                                CIP

EPIGRAPH

It is the particular beauty of fairy tales that no one interpretation is the true one, no one version is correct. The ingredients of the tale can be simmered and stirred, flavored and served up in a thousand different ways. Each author begins with common fairy-tale characters, dilemmas, dangers, riddles, and enchantments. Yet with this common straw they make *gold*, and language is the wheel on which they spin. It is through the language of the tales, and not the plot, that each retelling becomes unique, adding the voices of a new generation of storytellers to the voices of centuries past (Datlow and Windling, *Ruby Slippers, Golden Tears*, 6).

But a close look at the stories reveals much more than a simple formula of abuse and retribution. The trials our heroes encounter in their quests illustrate the *process* of transformation: from youth to adulthood, from victim to hero, from a maimed state into wholeness, from passivity to action. As centuries of artists have known, this gives fairy tales a particular power: not as a quaint escape from the harsh realities of modern life, but in their symbolic portrayal of all the dark and bright life has to offer (Datlow and Windling, *Black Swan, White Raven*, 4).

Contents

ACKNOWLEDGMENTS

Over the past 10 years I have had many long conversations with my companion, David Goa, about the nature and meaning of myth and folktale. Those conversations significantly shaped my understanding of this material.

AEA

I wish to acknowledge the vision and effort of Ellen Datlow and Terri Windling, two people I have not met but have come to appreciate in regards to the shaping of this book. Without their anthologies and editorial comments, this book would be a great deal less. Thanks also to my daughters, Esther and Taryn, for all their support. An extra thanks to Taryn, who has read almost as many of these reworkings as Anna and I have. The book would also not have been as complete without my colleagues Merle Harris and Margaret Mackey. Thanks for letting me bend your ears, and thanks, Margaret, for your insight and research into *Wolf*.

GdV

INTRODUCTION

The Authors' Perspectives on Folktales

Anna:

When I was a child, my mother told us folktales whenever one of my sisters or I was sick. They were stories from the Grimms' *Kinder- und Hausmärchen* and, although we had brought a copy of that collection with us when we emigrated to Canada from Germany, the stories were always told, never read, and always in German. Rapunzel, Snow White, Cinderella, Rumpelstiltskin, Briar Rose, the boy who wanted to learn how to be afraid, Rose White and Rose Red, the Devil's grandmother, Hans in Luck, the Hare and the Hedgehog—all were early familiars of mine in the world of enchantment offered by fictional narrative. They belonged to the landscape we had left (and which my mother missed so sorely), not only because their language was German but also because my grandmother kept two spinning wheels in the attic, where apples and mushrooms were hung to dry, and hens in a green garden enclosed by rosy brick walls that might have belonged to the sorceress who took Rapunzel. My grandfather and uncles were huntsmen, with green hats and long boots, who brought rabbits home for dinner. My father, who brought us and the stories to a different, emptier country, embodied the truth of the tales for me. The youngest of three sons, he set out penniless to meet adventure with blithe courage, always ready to share what little he had, open to wonder and good fortune.

When I was 10 or 11 years old, I discovered that there were other versions of these tales. I spent a week at a church camp, and after lights-out in our cabin I told the story of Cinderella as my contribution to the mildly illicit entertainment. My bunkmates were enthralled. They all knew the story, of course, but had never heard about the tree on Cinderella's mother's grave, the stepsisters cutting off their heel or toe, the blood in the shoe, the doves pecking out the stepsisters' eyes at the wedding. I became a minor celebrity for the week, and every night told another of the grim/Grimm tales. With childish chauvinism I assumed I had the real stories, the originals, and that they were better than the watered-down, prettied-up Disney versions my friends knew. I held this conviction until, at the age of 40, I began to teach children's literature to university students and had to think my way through questions about the nature of oral traditions, what happens to oral tales when they become part of a literary tradition, and the interpretation and literalization of folktales and myths.

Gail:

Unlike Anna, I grew up as part of the North American landscape, a second-generation Jewish Canadian living on the prairies. While my childhood was filled with stories, they were not the German tales or even the Russian folktales from my grandparents' homeland. No, they were all survival stories, stories of pioneers making a home for themselves in a new environment. Unlike Anna's stories, they did not hark back to the place and people left behind.

Strong female characters battling mothers-in-law, government officials, the landscape, the climate, and other dragons peopled the stories I remember best. My father taught and sang with us story-songs, but my grandmother's stories of the early days fascinated me more than anything else. It wasn't till I went to school that I became familiar with the canon of folktales, and my first recollection is of rebellion. I was the eldest child of three but not, in my mind, destined to fail in favor of my younger brother, and, even more important, my hair was not golden! The only heroine that I could physically identify with was Snow White—but my skin was too dark even for that. So I went searching further to find the tales that did speak to me, and I became intrigued by both their similarities to and differences from the tales referred to in school.

I became a secondary school history teacher and traveled, gathering other people's experiences and histories along with my own. Eventually I went back to university to become a research librarian, but the first course I took at library school derailed my plans somewhat. It was a course on storytelling! All of my early marvel came flooding back, and I needed to know more about folktales and their adaptability and roles in popular culture. But even more important, I wanted to be able to tell them to the appropriate audience: young adults. (Hence my first book, *Storytelling for Young Adults: Techniques and Treasury* [Libraries Unlimited, 1991].) The degree finished, I became a professional storyteller, but I also became the instructor for that very same course that changed my life. Now I could legitimately feed my curiosity.

How the Book Came About

Both of us work with folktales. We also read a great deal of fantasy. Because part of our work has to do with books for teenagers, we are in the enviable position of being professionally obliged to keep current in a genre we personally enjoy. At the beginning of the 1990s we noticed that an increasing number of new fantasy novels were book-length reworkings of folktales we knew well. Each of us already had on our list of all-time favorite books a fantasy novel that was based on a well-known folktale. Anna's was Robin McKinley's *Beauty*, a novel published for young adults that Anna first read at the age of 41. She can remember coming to the end of the book and being so unwilling to leave the world within its covers that she immediately turned back to the first page and began the story all over again—the only time she's ever done that, although she is an inveterate re-reader of books she's enjoyed.

Gail's was Diana Wynne Jones's *Fire and Hemlock*. Tam Lin was one of the first stories she had told professionally; it has all aspects of a story that she considers important: a strong female character, decisive action, magic, and a historical foundation. This young-adult novel unveiled more and more layers of the ballad for her each time she returned to it, and she returned to it often. She also went looking for more and more information about the ballad itself and, because of her research, that first story she told has undergone considerable metamorphosis. (*Beauty* and *Fire and Hemlock* are included in a forthcoming companion volume to this book.)

Because of our reading histories and professional preoccupations, we have a particular interest in fantasy by contemporary writers that is recognizably based on folktales. We began to keep track of the new novels that were written for or would be accessible to teenage readers and, with the idea that we would write about this phenomenon, to search for older ones. The number of titles on our list grew and soon included realistic fiction and science fiction as well as fantasy, short stories as well as novels, and picture books complex enough to be of interest to young adults. We proposed a book on the subject to Gail's editor at Libraries Unlimited, and at his suggestion expanded the scope of our project to include poems, films, and music. This book is the result of our explorations.

Scope and Organization of the Book

We have restricted ourselves to reworkings of folktales written in English, with their sources in the European folk tradition, because the bulk of current publications falls into this category and because of the limits of our own expertise. Reworkings of the stories by Hans Christian Andersen have been excluded because they are literary folktales rather than folktales from the oral tradition. The first chapter of this book should make that distinction clear. (Andersen's stories are included in the companion volume.) By "reworkings," we mean versions of a folktale that are more than straightforward retellings or adaptations of the tale for children.

The first chapter looks at the nature of folktales, their place in contemporary North American culture, and the characteristics of these tales that make them appealing to adolescent readers (or would make them appealing if adolescent readers knew about them). The following chapters each focus on a particular tale, giving the tale type and its motifs, a synopsis of the tale, an overview of critical interpretations of the tale, and a summary and discussion of each reworking that we have included. The overview of critical interpretations is arranged by date of publication. The summaries of the reworkings are arranged by format and, within each format, by date of publication. Suggestions for use of this material by teachers and librarians working with young adults come at the end of each chapter. Web sites in this book were last checked in September 1998.

The terms "tale type" and "motif" need some explanation. In 1910 Antti Aarne, a Finnish folklorist, published a classification scheme for folktales collected in Finland and northern Europe. His classification scheme established tale types, basic patterns underlying different tales that allowed variants of the same tale to be grouped together. Stith Thompson defines a type as follows: "A type is a traditional tale that has an independent existence. It may be told as a complete narrative and does not depend for its meaning on any other tale. It may consist of one motif or many." (1977, 415) Each tale type is assigned a number, and if there are subdivisions with their own variants within a given type, these subdivisions are given a letter designation. So, for example, "Rapunzel" is tale type AT 310, *The Maiden in the Tower*, while "Beauty and the Beast" is tale type AT 425C, *Beauty and the Beast*, within tale type AT 425, *The Search for the Lost Husband*. (The prefix "AT" before the number stands for Aarne-Thompson.)

Aarne's classification scheme has been revised twice by Stith Thompson. The second, and current, edition was published in 1961 in Helsinki. Thompson expanded the classification to include folktales from Europe and West Asia and added a list of the motifs that commonly occur in each tale type. Thompson defines a motif as "the smallest element in a tale having a power to persist in tradition" (1977, 415). A motif has power to persist because there is something memorable about it. Thompson identifies three classes of motifs: the actors in a tale, such as witches, fairies, the youngest child, or the cruel stepmother; items in the background of the action, such as magic objects or particular customs or beliefs; and single plot incidents, which make up the largest class by far. A tale that is made up of a single incident is both a type and a motif.

While we have tried to locate and include as much critical discussion and as many reworkings for each tale as we could, we do not claim that our lists are exhaustive. To avoid duplication, major issues that are relevant to a number of tales are addressed fully only once. For example, the general discussion of Disney's reworkings of tales comes in the chapter on "Snow White" because *Snow White* was the first of the Disney folktale films.

Because we expect a diverse audience for this book, we have included elements that may not be of interest to everyone. The tale type numbers and motifs are essential information for storytellers and are included to satisfy that need. The classroom extensions are merely suggestions to provide some direction for teachers of both young adults and university students. Many of these extensions can easily be adjusted from one tale to another and adapted for further study or comparisons between tales. The book is arranged to allow the user to dip into it at any point.

We decided that each of us would write in her own voice, dividing the book between us by chapters according to our own interests. The book as a whole is our joint responsibility, and we hope that it will give its readers something of the interest and delight that working with these texts has given us. If we have missed one of your favorite reworkings of these folktales, please let us know where we can find it.

References

Thompson, Stith. 1961. *The Types of the Folktale: A Classification and Bibliography. A Translation and Enlargement of Antti Aarne's Verzeichnis der Märchentypen.* 2d revision. Helsinki: Suomalainen Tiedeakatemia.

Thompson, Stith. 1977. *The Folktale.* Berkeley: University of California Press. [1946. Holt, Rinehart and Winston.]

CHAPTER 1

FOLKTALES AND LITERARY FICTIONS

Standing firmly on the <u>terra</u> of literacy, we can see two episte-mological chasms. One of these chasms cuts us off from the domain of orality (Illich and Sanders, x–xi).

Oral cultures indeed produce powerful and beautiful verbal per-formances of high artistic and human worth, which are no longer even possible once writing has taken possession of the psyche (Ong, 14).

Folktales as Oral Narrative

Folktales come from oral cultures, cultures without a written form of language. We are accustomed to thinking of such cultures as primitive, preliterate, in the early stage of a development that naturally progresses to literacy. There is, of course, a progression from orality to literacy in that all languages, except artificially constructed ones, are spoken long before a written form of them is devised. And once a system of writing exists, the culture that has previously had only spoken language makes a gradual transition to dependence on written texts. But there is a huge dif-ference, Illich and Sanders's "epistemological chasm," between what Walter J. Ong calls the "thought world" of an oral culture and that of a cul-ture that has interiorized literacy. The difference isn't one of worse and better, primitive and advanced, but of apples and oranges. It is difficult for people like ourselves, whose culture is deeply literate (whether members can read and write or not), to understand the way words and memory work when writing is completely unknown. But some grasp of the thought world of oral cultures is essential to any useful discussion of folktales and their literary versions.

A primary oral culture is one in which the notion of recording sound is completely unknown. Words vanish as soon as they are spoken. There is no possibility of "looking something up"—that phrase illustrates our own thorough dependency on visually accessible distributed knowledge, knowledge stored outside our own heads. The instructions for hooking up a VCR, the wattage on a light bulb that needs replacing, lecture notes, mathematical formulas, a recipe for cranberry muffins, Walter Ong's thoughts about the differences between literacy and orality, a poem or novel or article that we intend to read or reread, my outline for this chapter in a computer file—all are recorded sounds that we can recall because they are stored in conventional symbols, frozen in time, static and passive, to be activated and given meaning by being turned into sounds again in our minds. Sound is still fundamental to language in chirographic or typographic cultures, those with handwriting or print, but thought, through the words that express it, can be kept in lasting, visual form: as text, to be read for the first time or checked again.

We literally *see* words as discrete units, made up of individual letters, strung together in a particular order into phrases or sentences, the building blocks of text. Words for us are reified, thing-like, separate, because they are seen rather than only heard. But if thoughts are always only sound and therefore vanish the moment they are spoken, in the mind or aloud, then words are continuous action, and thought and speech cannot be separated.

Written words, however, are concrete traces of thought that can be reproduced exactly by reading or memorization. Good teachers of storytelling in our culture have their students learn to remember the shape and content of a story when telling it, rather than recite it word-for-word. But, even so, they necessarily think of memory as a deposit that we can draw on, a concept that does not exist in oral cultures but that we find very difficult to think our way past. Illich and Sanders differentiate between *mnemosyne*, the Greek word for memory and the name of the mother of the Muses, and *memoria*, the Latin word from which our word *memory* comes. Memoria, our notion of memory, is a storage room from which we can retrieve things. "Like words and text, memory is a child of the alphabet" (Illich and Sanders, 15). But prealphabetic mnemosyne "is a streamful of treasures," and pieces of a story are like driftwood fished from the stream, "something cast off in the beyond that had just then washed up onto the beaches of the mind" (Illich and Sanders, 16). Mnemosyne is memory that is born at the same time as thought. This sort of memory implies a notion of storytelling very different from ours. No story is ever repeated, and none is completely original. The teller improvises with the driftwood of stock themes and phrases, original in the momentary linking of them.

Thinking from within literacy, equating memory with mnemosyne, we make what seem to be sensible assumptions about the nature of folktales that are, in fact, profound misunderstandings. For example, one well-known textbook on children's literature states that folktales are short because short stories are easier to remember than long stories for tellers in an oral culture who cannot record or consult a written text. And it follows from this, suggests the textbook, that the characters in folktales are types because a short story doesn't have room for the development of round characters. Such an explanation seems reasonable from a literary perspective, a generous exoneration of what might seem to us to be a shortcoming of the folktale. But it is completely off the mark because it maps onto oral tales the expectations and values of readers and writers, leaping across the epistemological chasm between literacy and orality in a single, impossible bound. The term *oral literature* itself embodies this leap. Ong calls it a monstrous concept, a "strictly preposterous term" that "reveals our inability to represent to our own minds a heritage of verbally organized materials except as some variant of writing, even when they have nothing to do with writing at all" (11).

Ong's book *Orality and Literacy: The Techologizing of the Word* gives a very helpful introduction to the noetic economy,[1] or organization of thought, in a primary oral culture. What follows is a summary of the main points in Ong's third chapter, "Some Psychodynamics of Orality," that establish a context for the folktale as oral narrative.

When words are always only sounds, thoughts must be put together in a memorable way if they are to be recalled. All the narratives of oral cultures that have been preserved as texts, whether they are grand epics like *The Iliad*, *The Odyssey*, and *Beowulf*, or folktales, myths, and legends, are marked by *mnemonics and formulas*.[2]

> In an oral culture, to think something through in non-formulaic, non-patterned, non-mnemonic terms, even if it were possible, would be a waste of time, for such thought, once worked through, could never be recovered with any effectiveness, as it could be with the aid of writing (Ong, 35).

Rhythm, pattern, repetition, formulaic phrases, and standard settings for certain themes are mnemonic (from the word *mnemosyne*) devices that allow poets and tellers of prose tales to compose as they speak, stitching together communally known, prefabricated story elements that come readily to mind. The same devices allow the audience to follow the story, to remember what has gone before and anticipate what is to come. As listeners rather than readers, they can't check back for something they've missed or pause to think about a passage that confuses them. In a literary narrative, commonly known phrases and stock situations are dismissed as clichés, hackneyed and trite. In oral narrative, they are the necessary repertoire of both teller and listener and have the beauty of the perfectly apt, polished and refined by frequent use. They carry in a compact bundle a wealth of associations and are a shorthand that listeners can expand according to their own experiences.

Oral tales don't have to be short to be remembered: think of *The Iliad* or *Beowulf*. The tellers didn't reproduce them from rote, text-based memory, but recreated them each time from the familiar formulas of stock phrases, situations, characters, and themes. We literate folk primarily value originality of expression. But the audience for an oral tale would have recognized the formulaic phrases and story elements with pleasure and appreciated the skill of the teller who used them effectively.

Some of the characteristics of oral thought and expression that Ong explains have largely vanished from the tales we know best because they have been retold in written form so many times. One of these characteristics is the *additive rather than subordinative* structure of oral thought and expression. In oral narrative, ideas are connected by "and" rather than by "but," "therefore," "thus," "while," "when," or "then." They follow along like equal beads on a string, one after the other. Relationships of cause and effect and within time are not spelled out. Using simply "and" as a link between events or units of the story makes it easier for storytellers to compose as they speak, and the nature of the relationship between the ideas can be indicated during the telling by gesture, facial expression, pauses, and tone of voice, or supplied by the knowing audience. But someone writing a story for readers has to replace these contextual cues with more complex grammatical structures like subordinate clauses that specify the causal and temporal relationships between narrated events.[3] The string of "ands" has been replaced by other conjunctions and linking phrases in the folktales we know today, from written sources, because additive links sound awkward and archaic to literate ears. But the straightforward laying out of the facts in a folktale, one after the other, without interpretation, reflects its original additive structure.

Another characteristic of oral thought is that it is *aggregative rather than analytic*. Analysis breaks up thought into its separate parts for examination. In oral thought, words clump together and, if the aggregation is a memorable one, they stay clumped. The formulas that are essential tools of oral memory are such aggregations, clusters of words that stick together in a single unit of thought, as if they were a single word. Proverbs, like "a stitch in time saves nine" or "pride goeth before a fall," are examples of such clusters. So are epithetic formulas like the beautiful princess, the shining sword, the wicked witch, the wine-dark sea. They are stable word groups that are kept intact so that the ideas they hold remain available.

Oral cultures are *conservative or traditionalist* because knowledge that is not frequently repeated aloud is lost. Conserving what is already known takes up a great deal of time and is much more important than continuous innovation, which would be evanescent. So the same stories are told over and over again. New elements are constantly added because the story is told slightly differently every time, to fit the particular audience and the particular situation, and with variations that depend on the skill and repertoire of the teller. Therefore, each telling of a given story produces a new version. But the core and shape of the tale remain the same.

According to Ong, oral expressions of thought are *agonistically toned* and he describes oral cultures as agonistically programmed. ("Agonistic" comes from the Greek word *agon*, which means contest.) Verbal contests in the form of riddle games, bragging, and name-calling are common oral art forms. The characters in stories embody opposing extremes: power and helplessness, cleverness and stupidity, evil and goodness, kindness and cruelty. There are no gray areas or ambiguity. And oral tales frequently describe gruesome physical violence although they contain much less, if any, description of inner (psychological) struggles. Ong suggests that this agonistic tone comes partly from the fact that life in pretechnological societies is a daily struggle for survival, full of physical hardship. And physical violence in such societies is never indirect: Fighting is an immediate, hand-to-hand business rather than a matter of bombs dropped by the push of a button on some city continents away. If you kill or wound someone, the blood splashes on your hand and your enemy dies in front of your eyes. But the agonistic tone of oral tales isn't explained only by the physical demands of existence. Ong points out that the very structure of orality is contestative or agonistic, in the sense that verbal communication is always face-to-face, without the detachment made possible by written words on the neutral space of a page. Speaker and listener are physically opposed, that is to say, facing each other.[4]

And the communication is immediate, between two present and separate speakers, whether the exchange is friendly or hostile. (The slang
expression "in my face" gives a good sense of the immediacy I am trying
to explain.) This point about the agonistic tone of oral narrative is a very
important one because it explains the strong polarities found in the
themes and characters of folktales, polarities that have given rise to literate criticism of the tales for their so-called stereotypical characters and
violence.

What Ong calls the noetic role of *heroic 'heavy' figures and the bizarre* is
related to the agonistic programming of oral cultures, but is also an important aid to memory. Heroic figures in oral tales are generally marked
by one dominant, exaggerated characteristic that makes them "heavy"
and memorable. That is to say, they are types. We find them still in the
folktales we know: "the overpowering innocence of Little Red Riding
Hood, the unfathomably wicked wolf, the incredibly tall beanstalk that
Jack has to climb—for non-human figures acquire heroic dimensions,
too" (Ong, 70). Bizarre characters, though the reverse of typical, are similarly memorable because of an outstanding characteristic. The gingerbread house Hansel and Gretel find in the forest and Baba Yaga's cottage
that moves on chicken legs stick in our minds, even if we forget all the
other details in the story.

Ong adds that "formulary number groupings" of characters, often
seven or three,[5] are another mnemonic aid. Number distinguishes and
certainly adds weight simply by multiplication. There are seven dwarfs
living seven mountains away, seven little kids, three blind mice. In these
three examples, the number has the function that Ong identifies, as a
memorable, weight-giving tag. But number groupings can serve a structural purpose in the story as well, and it is important to distinguish between their two different functions. Some groupings, especially of three,
set up a pattern of repeated action. One such group is the three sons, in
"The Water of Life," for example, or "The Three Little Pigs," who set out
one after the other on the same quest. The number three is also formulaic
in these cases, but here it is more than a weight-giving mnemonic label. It
is a cue for the repetition that gives the teller a breathing space, helps
the audience to keep on track, and strengthens the difference between
the hero and her unsuccessful sisters or the hero and his unsuccessful
brothers.[6] If the first brother, and then the second, arrogantly pass by the
dwarf who asks for bread or offers advice, the openness and compassion
of the third brother becomes that much more significant.

In summary, then, I have drawn on Ong for the context we need to
appreciate the characteristics of folktales that mark them as coming from
oral cultures. On our side of the epistemological chasm, we look for

subtlety and originality in modern literary fictions. But formulaic elements and the patterns of antithesis and repetition, the pure opposition of polarized extremes, the lack of overt interpretation and psychological complexity, are essential parts of oral narrative. When we find them in literary tales, they either strike us as a failure of skill and creativity on the author's part or seem deliberately used to call up memories of folktales that contribute to our reading of the text. In oral tales, we must understand them differently to recognize their beauty and function.

Is a Folktale a Fairy Tale?

The terminology used in discussion of oral tales has not been standardized. Folktale (or folk tale, folk-tale), fairy tale (or fairytale), märchen, wonder tale, myth, legend, fable, are all jumbled together, with no universal agreement about which term means what. Maria Tatar, in her book *The Hard Facts of the Grimms' Fairy Tales*, offers a schema for distinguishing between these labels that we have found very useful. To begin with, a primary division is made between myth, legend, and fable on one side and folktale on the other. Myths and legends are culturally specific stories that tell about origins. In societies where the symbolic language of myth and legend is still meaningful, these stories have a teaching function and the authority of truth, telling a people how they came to be and setting out exemplary patterns of how to live in the world.[7] It must be understood, however, that they were never meant to be taken literally. Too many writers about myth, especially those who write about children's literature, accept the thinking of nineteenth-century mythographers who explained myths as the best a primitive people could do by way of science and history. Myths are told in the picture language of metaphor and make their meaning symbolically. Fables are also teaching tales and, therefore, also culturally specific. They are intended to impress upon listeners the morals and values of a particular society. Folktales, as distinct from myths, legends, and fables, are stories that are intended to entertain. They may be very serious stories from which we can learn a great deal, but they are regarded as fiction and often flagged as such by opening formulas like "Once upon a time" and closing formulas like "and they lived happily ever after." These opening and closing phrases separate the story from the lived experience of the teller and audience. Folktales are more universal than myths, legends, and fables. Although culturally specific details do embellish particular tellings, the core of a given tale is the same across cultures and centuries: Cinderella is recognizable, whatever name she has, whether the story is told in China, Africa, the British Isles, or North America.

Tatar further divides folktales into folk tales (written as two words) and fairy tales. Folk tales are set in a naturalistic world. They may contain improbabilities such as talking wolves that can swallow a person whole or blow down a house built of straw or sticks, but there is no magic in them. Fairy tales do have magic in them, a power greater than and very different from the powers of human beings. The term "fairy tale" is misleading, because many such stories have no fairies in them. They may have wise women, magical fish, ogres, sorcerers, genies, or witches instead. "Wonder tale" is a much more accurate label for the folktale with magic, but "fairy tale" is so widely used that it will have to stand.

Of course, all categories leak, but Tatar's schema works reasonably well. If we apply it to the so-called fairy tales we know best, "Little Red Riding Hood" and "The Three Little Pigs" turn out to be folk tales, not fairy tales at all. In this book, we have adopted Tatar's terminology and use "folktale" to include both "folk tales" and "fairy tales." One more distinction must be made: between literary *versions* of folktales, like those of the Brothers Grimm and Charles Perrault, and original literary fictions that draw on or imitate traditional folktales, like those of Hans Christian Andersen. For the former, we borrow Max Lüthi's term "book folktale" (or "book fairy tale" where appropriate). The latter we refer to as "literary folktales" (or "literary fairy tales") .

The Art of the Folktale

The literature on the style and composition of folktales is substantial. A good place to begin is Benton and Fox's *Teaching Literature: Nine to Fourteen*. Although the book is written for teachers of readers mostly younger than those we are concerned with here, a short section in chapter 3, "Narrative Lines," gives a good introduction to the way tales from the oral tradition work for readers of any age.

A folktale has no identifiable author, so the narrative voice within the story is without individual personality, never self-conscious. In the literary folktales of Hans Christian Andersen, we are always aware of Andersen's unique voice. His life experiences and way of seeing the world have shaped every story: The ironic humor; the themes of steadfast, unrequited love and inherent worth unappreciated by grosser natures; the nineteenth-century Protestant conviction that happiness is not to be found in this world but only in the afterlife; are all distinctively Andersen's. Folktales don't give us this sense of an individual author behind the story who has a particular understanding, shaped by circumstance and historical context, of what it is to be human and live in the world. A folktale is told much more plainly, almost as a statement of simple facts, with no persuasion toward a particular interpretation of those facts. In this respect, Charles Perrault's book folktales, *Histoires, ou Contes du temps passé*, are much more like traditional tales than Andersen's stories are. Perrault did add explicit morals to his versions of the folktales that he rewrote, but he tacked them on at the end rather than build them into the story, and often offered a choice between two very different morals, thus acknowledging that the tale was open to various interpretations.

Although folktales in the oral tradition do not have identifiable authors, in some folktales we can trace the influence of a particular writer or written version. For the movement from oral tale to book folktale is sometimes reversed, and a book folktale or literary folktale that has become very popular makes its way back into the oral tradition. Perrault's versions of the tales he rewrote influenced the oral versions of the same stories, and "Beauty and the Beast" as we know it began as a novel written by Madame Gabrielle de Villeneuve and published in 1740.

All of the force of a folktale is in the plot, which is laid out as a straightforward, linear string of events. The characters have no inwardness or complexity. They are types—of goodness, beauty, wickedness, sloth, cleverness, power, or innocence. The settings are as little elaborated as the characters. The story happened once upon a time in an unspecified kingdom or in an unnamed great forest. The one thing the listeners know for certain is that the story is set in a place and time other than their workaday reality. "The secondary worlds of traditional stories are governed not by the surface features of time and place, cause and effect, imported from the primary world, but by the conflicts of human experience" (Benton and Fox, 40). And these conflicts of human experience are the grand themes of folktales. These are stories of fundamental human wishes and fears. In "Hansel and Gretel" and "Jack and the Beanstalk" we can see the need for enough to eat and the fear of being eaten, both constant in hunting and gathering cultures and those in the early stages of the development of agriculture, where people lived surrounded by wild animals. The fear of starvation is still very real, even in our industrialized cities, and so is the fear of being killed, swallowed up by untimely death. Equally timeless are the destructiveness of vanity and jealousy that motivates the plot in "Snow White," and the greed and selfish arrogance that push Cinderella into the ashes of the hearth where she longs for comfort and beauty, and to be recognized.

Fairy tales, the folktales with magic in them, also show another deep human need: the need to embody our sense of the numinous, "the unseen forces and powers that lie behind the realities we live by" (Benton and Fox, 42). We cannot satisfactorily explain the world to ourselves in entirely human terms. Our sense of something transcendent, something other and larger than our human limitations, takes form as the magical helpers or opponents of the hero in fairy tales. The magic is not necessarily intentionally helpful or inimical to humans, like the watchful fairy godmother in "Cinderella" or the witch in "Hansel and Gretel" who makes a gingerbread house to lure children into her trap. It can also just be there, with its own place in the world, and when human characters stumble into its sphere the magic responds to them according to its nature. The sorceress in "Rapunzel" is simply the neighbor of Rapunzel's parents and demands their child only as compensation when they trespass into her garden. The king in "Sleeping Beauty" invites the fairies (or wise women) to the christening feast, and one of them curses rather than blesses the baby only because she has been slighted, either by having been left out of the invitation or by being given inferior tableware.

Benton and Fox suggest that "the direct, unelaborated style" (41) of the folktale, its short length and lack of psychological exploration, make its timeless themes both immediate and concrete, and that this immediacy and concreteness is one of the main attractions of the folktale. Where literary fictions may use details of verisimilitude and originality of style, situation, characters, or insight to catch and hold their audience, the folktale offers instead a familiar style, well-known motifs,[8] and universal themes. But the style, motifs, and themes of folktales have long delighted and continue to delight both listening and reading audiences. As Max Lüthi points out, "Fairytales have been told time and again not because they are so easy to tell, but because they have provided pleasure" (1984, ix). Folktale audiences don't wonder what's going to happen next. The tale will be familiar to them, and the happy ending is guaranteed. The same is true of book folktales. What holds the listeners and readers, Lüthi suggests, is that the tale "sets in motion a pattern of internal experience, sets off a sequence of tension and relief of tension . . . similar in effect to that of a musical work . . . which one needs to hear time and again, since the effect is deepened through repeated listening" (1984, 73).

Lüthi, one of the most insightful of the scholars who have written on folktales, analyzes these tales as an artform, considering "mnemetic technique, the technical basis of oral narration," also as "a means to artistic effect" (1984, 44–45). I argued at the beginning of this chapter that we must know something of the context, primary orality, in which the folktale developed in order to understand it on its own terms. Awareness of the cultural conditions in which the folktale came to be helps us avoid assumptions or expectations based on our deeply interiorized literacy that may skew critical approaches to any folk narrative. But historical explanations for the shape the folktale takes are not enough. They do not account for the enduring popularity of folktales, the pleasure they give and fascination they hold for listeners and readers who may be centuries and continents removed from their point of origin. Lüthi's analyses acknowledge that an oral thought world determined the folktale's narrative form. But his comparison of, for example, the folk legend and the fairy tale reminds us that oral storytellers, like writers, made artistic choices in exercising their creative imagination and craft, and that distinct genres of oral narrative developed out of such choices, each with its own internal rules and particular aesthetic appeal to an audience.[9]

In his writings about folktales (*Märchen*), Lüthi focuses mainly on the fairy tale, or *Zaubermärchen*, the folktale with magic. But what he has to say, other than considerations of magical elements, applies to the folktale generally. And with one exception, the folktales we are discussing in this book are fairy tales, so Lüthi's work is entirely relevant.

Lüthi describes the folktale as a highly stylized narrative form marked by depthlessness, linearity, isolation, one-dimensionality, and abstraction. "In several senses, the art of the folktale is an art of surfaces" (1961, 14). But it is definitely not superficial, nor does its simplicity of style make it simplistic. The folktale paints a clear picture on a flat plane. It seems to avoid depth, limiting any description of character, state of mind, object, or setting to a word or two, as if intentionally staying clear of complexity that could lead to confusion. The folktale is a tightly controlled composition. In it, the mnemonic devices characteristic of oral narrative seem as much required by the genre's drive for strict clarity as for their mnemonic function. The exactly repeated formulaic epithets, number groupings, and opening and closing phrases; the sharp polarities; and the simple sequencing of the additive narrative style seem essentially part of the tale's spare precision.

The folktale has a preference for hardness or rigidity, itself a type of clarity: objects, often even clothing and trees, are made of gold or silver, glass, crystal, jewels, wood, or stone. Things made of metals and minerals have definite contours that resist change, and hard, shining surfaces that keep us from investigating what's inside. The glitter of gold and silver has the glamour of riches, but it is also as impenetrable as a mirror, showing us only our own reflections. Folktale props are sharply outlined, and closed and enclosing rather than open: tiny boxes, nuts, eggs, cities and castles with their walls (Lüthi 1984, 40f).

The folktale plot, too, is strongly linear. Like the additive style of the narration, the action follows a simple line, moving surely and rapidly forward through a sequence of equally weighted and isolated adventures. Each plot episode stands alone because the characters, who are really only carriers of the action, do not connect them by learning from their own experience or the experience of others. This is not a sign of stupidity but of the isolating style of the folktale. Learning from experience is change through time, and the folktale lacks the dimension of time almost completely (Lüthi 1961, 33). In it, change is never gradual but always instantaneous. Three or seven or a hundred years may go by, but the interval is collapsed into one point on the line of the plot. In this aspect, too, the folktale operates on a single plane.

The plot of the folktale focuses entirely on the single quest of the hero, and other characters appear in the story only to act on the hero as either helpers or opponents. What Lüthi calls "the law of threeness" (Lüthi 1961, 15), Cinderella's three balls, the three attempts on Snow White's life, governs the episodes of the plot: Their number is never random. Extremes also give sharpness and precision to the shape of the action: The reversals of powerlessness and power, the polarities of hero and opponent or rich reward and gruesome punishment, the strict conditions of the tests that lead to success or failure, the rescue only and always at the very last moment, are absolute. There is no flexibility, no give or tolerance in the plot. The height of this stylization, writes Lüthi, is the element of wonder (1961, 15). Instead of slow development and change that are part of everyday life, there is instant, marvelous transformation.

Folktale characters, whether human or supernatural, are without depth. They have no inner struggles, no emotional ambiguities. They are like papercuts, cleanly outlined but flat. In fact, they are actants, merely carriers of the action, rather than characters. Their qualities, abilities, emotions, and relationships enter into the story only as part of the action of the plot. Affection, envy, or whatever impulse or imperative motivates the supernatural helpers is often represented as an object. The relationship between two figures that emotion entails is expressed by the giving of a red hood, a poisoned apple, or a cloak that makes the hero invisible. Relationships externalized and encapsulated in an object do not create emotional depth in a story; they exist beside the characters on the same plane rather than on a deeper level within them (Lüthi 1961, 30).

Falling in love at first sight is as common in folktales from the oral tradition as it is in literary folktales. But the folktale never dwells on love nor describes the joy or the anguish that it can bring. Andersen's little mermaid and steadfast tin soldier suffer deeply for unrequited love. Disney characters dream of love, longing for the right prince or princess to come along. In these stories, relationship, even if it is only adolescent fantasy, is a central preoccupation. But in the folktale, love has significance only as a single action that furthers the plot: the falling in love that sets off the search for the woman whose foot fits the slipper, or that leads to the stumble with the coffin that jolts the piece of poisoned apple from Snow White's throat.

In Trina Schart Hyman's picture book version of Snow White, the illustrations show the stepmother-queen sinking into anguished madness as the story progresses: Her envy of Snow White's beauty is an illness that devours her and leads to her death. Hyman's pictured interpretation of the story is psychologically compelling. It does not contradict anything in the core tale, the folktale, but it does go well beyond it for folktale characters don't truly suffer: Because they are depthless, they are soulless (Lüthi 1961, 31). For that reason, physical violence and suffering in folktales are abstract rather than real, and the audience is distanced from it. The hero may have her hands cut off by her incestuous father, or cut off her own finger to unlock the glass mountain, but nothing is said about pain. The gruesome punishment that befalls the villain at the end of a folktale exacts vengeance for the hero, but the hero is completely detached from it, neither desiring nor delighting in vengeance. Putting the wicked queen into a barrel into which spikes have been driven from the outside, and rolling the barrel down the long hill from the castle into the town, gives the audience great satisfaction, but it doesn't matter to the queen's former victim. The vengeance is demanded not by the hero but by the tale's balancing of polarities: The completely satisfactory ending for the hero is matched by the most severe punishment for the villain.

Folktale characters are also without depth because they are isolated. They have only as much background or history as is required to motivate the action. How it comes about that the woodcutter and his wife live next door to a sorceress, or whether the wolf had eaten other grandmothers in Little Red Riding Hood's neighborhood, simply isn't a question. The characters are not embedded in a community with its intricate web of multilayered connections. As a result, they are all isolated figures, but that isolation sets them free. Folktale heroes are the most thoroughly isolated: orphaned, disregarded, scorned, or abandoned in some other way. Therefore they are free to move through their sharply delineated world, responsible only for their quest and open to engage the wondrous when they encounter it, even though it may be disguised. The characters in competition with the hero, arrogant brothers and selfish sisters who are less isolated because a parent loves them, are not open, as the hero is, to the world around them.

The magical figures, too, are isolated, in their case from a numinous otherworld. No explanations are given for their presence or of the unknown laws that govern their actions. Lüthi suggests that in the folktale, though not in other genres of oral tales, the supernatural is naturalized into the secondary world of the story by detachment. Although it is entirely mysterious, it evokes no shudder or dread, often not even surprise. The kind sister accepts supernatural help with gratitude, but without awe; the lazy, greedy sister simply ignores or scorns it, and suffers the inevitable punishment. Hansel and Gretel fear the witch because she wants to eat them, not because they are in the presence of a supernatural power. Within the folktale, the numinous and magical become a matter of course, and for this reason Lüthi calls the folktale one-dimensional. There is no gap between the sphere of the otherworldly and the sphere of the human; they exist in the same spiritual dimension.

Lüthi points out that the folktale sublimates the numinous, magical, and mythical, just as it does the erotic, living, and real, into weightless pictures that reflect our world as a mirror does—from a flat, shining surface. Whatever is dark, heavy, confused, or uncertain in real life is light, clear, and sure in the folktale. The polarities within the story's subject matter are paralleled by polarities in the form. The detached, freely moving characters stand out against the fixed solidity of the props.

The strong tendency of the folktale style to isolate all elements of the story (characters, episodes, objects) has fundamental significance. Where no connections are expected, any connection is possible. Within the folktale, no explanations are given for the wondrous or improbable things that happen. A miller's daughter may marry a king, and helpers with magical powers come out of nowhere exactly when they are needed, without question (Lüthi 1961, 40). There is no need in the folktale for a complex substructure that would ground the development of the story in the apparent logic of realism. And it is the absence of such a substructure that gives the folktale its lightness, in the sense of freedom of movement within the story, and its clarity.

The folktale is indeed an art of surfaces. But, as Lüthi repeatedly points out, that does not mean that it is in any way superficial. Nor does the simplicity of its cleanly drawn outlines make it simplistic. The sharp-edged delineation of its style gives the folktale a spare elegance and also makes it strongly suggestive (Lüthi 1961, 15). And what it is that the folktale suggests is open to many different interpretations.

The Interpretation of Folktales

The style of the folktale makes it porous to meaning. This brilliant term for the almost infinite adaptability of the folktale is Marina Warner's. In *From the Beast to the Blond* she refers to "the porousness of stories to their tellers' temper and beliefs" (255). When I first read this phrase I thought of the porousness of a coral reef, a stiff skeletal structure in which multitudes of small sea creatures dart about or make their homes. But after having worked with Warner's word for a while, I decided that the right metaphor is a sponge. The living animal, harvested from its aquatic home, is dried out and cleaned. Its tough, elastic skeleton can be squeezed in any kind of liquid, which it absorbs as it expands to its original shape. Squeeze it again, and the liquid runs out. Release it, and the sponge expands again, full of empty spaces but always recognizably itself. The folktale has this spongelike hospitality and resilience. Its economical style easily accommodates embellishment. The depthless, typical characters and undeveloped settings allow writers to elaborate their particular version of a tale, just as readers or listeners will fill in details meaningful to themselves. The spaces between the extremes and among the isolated elements, like the additive style, are open to the creation of variously nuanced connections. The universal themes and spare, clean outlines of the folktale have a springy strength that supports interpretation without being bent permanently into a different shape by its weight.

Interpretations of individual folktales are inevitably made by readers or listeners, who make their own meanings of them. Each writer who makes an adaptation or a new version necessarily gives an interpretation. Single tales and the overarching meanings of entire groups of tales are explicated by various kinds of scholars and critics. The serious folktales—that is to say, those that are not primarily humorous—have attracted the largest number of interpretations. These are the folktales that are generally called fairy tales, whether they have magic in them or not. They seem to invite exploration within many different frameworks of meaning, and can carry the ideological or psychological preoccupations of a broad spectrum of interpreters. In *The Hard Facts of the Grimms' Fairy Tales*, Maria Tatar points out the impossibility of arriving at the one true or fundamental meaning of any folktale. The first problem is establishing a definitive text of the tale. Obviously, no original version can be identified for any tale from an oral tradition. Because each telling or writing of a tale is a new version, carrying the "temper and beliefs" of its teller, all existing versions would have to be overlapped and only those elements that are common to all of them kept if a single, universal meaning is to be drawn from the story. Tatar gives two very funny examples of interpretations that have gone awry because they depend on variants. One is Bruno Bettelheim's and Stephen Jones's reading of the significance of frogs waiting to be disenchanted. Frogs, they point out, arouse "clammy sensations," and therefore there must be a symbolic connection between frogs and the male sexual organ. Unfortunately for their analysis, there are many stories in which the frog is an enchanted princess. The other example is Erich Fromm's reading of "Little Red Riding Hood," which depends on the bottle of wine in Little Red Riding Hood's basket as a symbol for her virginity. This interpretation collapses in the face of the many versions of the tale that don't include a wine bottle at all.

The second problem that stands in the way of a universally valid interpretation is the influence a reader's background and intention have on the meaning the reader takes from a story. The frog and wine bottle, read from particular psychological perspectives, show this second pitfall, too, and our following chapters on individual folktales give many more examples. Any interpretation of a folktale or a group of folktales tells us as much about the interpreter as it does about the story. This warning shouldn't lead to the conclusion that interpretation is therefore useless and shouldn't be attempted. There is no point in reading any text if we don't make sense of it. But we must realize that no single meaning can be the only true one, and that any meaning is shaped by the context in which a story is written and read or told and heard.

Any given interpretation can seem spot-on to those who share the outlook and purpose of the interpreter, and totally misguided to those who don't. For example, when I ask my students to read the chapter in Bruno Bettelheim's *The Uses of Enchantment* on "Cinderella," most of them are shocked by Bettelheim's interpretation and dismiss it scornfully. Bettelheim, a developmental psychologist, is widely known among people who work with folktales as children's literature. His name is usually the first to be mentioned in almost any discussion of the psychological significance of folktales. But, new to the field and without any background in Freudian psychology, my students find Bettelheim's reading of the tale farfetched. I assign it, however, to give them some idea of how seriously folktales can be taken and how wide open the interpretive possibilities are, to get them thinking. Reading Bettelheim is, at the least, provocative!

Interpretations of the entire folktale genre, or of its subgenres, are likely to be more widely accepted than interpretations of individual tales. This makes sense, because the search for meaning depends on common features among a large group of tales rather than on elements that vary in particular versions. For instance, while I have difficulties with Bettelheim when he writes about individual folktales (and more of this later), I agree with his notion that all folktales, in one way or another, teach the same thing: that one must leave home to find one's kingdom; that the kingdom cannot be found at once; that tests and trials must be undergone on the journey; that one needs helpers to succeed; and that the helpers must be given something that they want (Bettelheim, 133). Bettelheim is describing the elements of a quest, and it is generally agreed that folktales are quest tales.

A quest is a process of initiation. Mircea Eliade, in an appendix to *Myth and Reality* on myths and fairy tales, writes that the folktale "presents the structure of an infinitely serious and responsible adventure, for in the last analysis it is reducible to an initiatory scenario" (201). This serious and responsible adventure, the quest (or initiation), has a paradigmatic form that can be found in many different narrative genres, both oral and literary.[10] The pattern varies in its details, but the main outline is constant. The hero is somehow isolated or different from family and community. He or she sets out on a journey that can be literal or symbolic. The journey may be undertaken to achieve something for the sake of others (e.g., to find the water of life for a dying father; to find and break the spell on six brothers who have been turned into swans) or to escape the misery or danger of the hero's present life (e.g., Snow White running away into the forest after the huntsman spares her life). During the journey the hero undergoes tests and trials that may be physical or psychological or both. Typically, the most demanding of these tests is met in a descent to the underworld, an encounter with death itself or, symbolically, the hero's own dark side. If the quest is successful, the hero returns from the journey as if reborn into the world, with a boon for the community in which she or he will now take a proper place. The search of the quest, whatever its physical object, is for the discovery and integration of the self (for self-knowledge) and for the reintegration of the self into society.

The "infinitely serious and responsible adventure" of the quest is, as Eliade points out, "an initiatory scenario." The hero's journey, symbolic or actual, is a leaving behind of the structures and roles of the social order and a move into liminal space, the space of initiation where the self may be developed.[11] The word "liminal" comes from the Latin *limen*, threshold, so liminal space is a threshold space. Candidates for initiation, in a group or individually, are temporarily isolated from society, removed to a special place or sent alone into the wilderness. For a time they remain separate, free from their former place in the world and not yet entered into their new place. They stand on the threshold between two stages of life. The candidates prepare and prove themselves ready to cross the threshold by undergoing tests and trials that usually involve hardship or pain, initiatory ordeals such as fasting, and confrontations with terrifying manifestations of the spirit world. In this state of passage between one stage of individual and social life and the next, they are taught what they need to know by a figure who is permanently outside the social structures of the community: a priest, shaman, or spirit guide. Those who pass the tests and successfully cross the threshold, often with a new name to signify that they are changed, are welcomed back into their community with celebrations that recognize their new status and role. The boon they bring is their own newly discovered powers and gifts.

The initiatory scenario of the quest is easily recognizable in folktales. The hero is usually isolated by difference or abandonment at the beginning of the story. Cinderella loses her mother and is banished to the cinders of the kitchen hearth; Beauty is kinder and more bookish than her sisters, and poverty exiles her with her family from society; the old soldier who discovers the secret of the dancing princesses is wounded and of no use as a soldier any more. Even the hero who is cherished, like Little Red Riding Hood or Jack of beanstalk fame, sets out on a journey into the unknown, the dark woods or up the beanstalk into the clouds. The folktale helpers are from the otherworld: fairy godmothers, wise women, the giant's wife, a magic tree. Snow White's helpers are dwarfs who live permanently outside society, and whose cottage, far away over seven hills, is Snow White's liminal space. The difficult trials, too, are usually set by otherworldly figures: a sorcerer, witch, ogre, giant, or troll. The happy ending of the folktale always involves a celebration of the hero's reintegration into society. Beauty breaks the enchantment that separates the Beast from the world, and all the world comes to their wedding. Hansel and Gretel return home with pockets full of riches to begin a new life with their father. When Sleeping Beauty wakes up, the hedge around the castle vanishes, the court comes back to life again, and there is a wedding. Little Red Riding Hood and her grandmother, reborn from the belly of the wolf, eat the good food in the basket.

No paradigm fits every case perfectly, or in the same way, and that is why any description of one is riddled with the word "usually." For example, because the folktale of Little Red Riding Hood is not a fairy tale in the strict sense, the wolf isn't from the otherworld, but he is a creature of the forest rather than the village, and certainly outside of human society. Neither the Grimms' nor Perrault's Little Red Riding Hood has a supernatural helper. But the Grimms' huntsman, who pursues his occupation hunting beasts in the forest, in a sense belongs in that liminal space. And the isolating journey, the test, the meeting with death in the dark underworld of the wolf's stomach, a helper, and the rebirth into the world are all there. Cinderella's journey isn't to some place far away: She only goes to a ball. But the palace is certainly a world different from her own, and she is disguised, not her usual self, completely unrecognized even by her family, and so it fits the notion of liminal space. Sleeping Beauty's journey is even shorter—up the tower stairs—but she is exploring unknown territory, all alone, and meets a danger that sends her into a death-like sleep. It must also be noted that the hero's quest is often a spiral rather than a straight line, so an element of the initiatory scenario may occur more than once, especially in folktales with their formulaic sets of three. The hero of the "Twelve Dancing Princesses" is on a journey to begin with, and undertakes another one, three times, down into the magic underworld where the princesses go to dance every night.

Because the folktale avoids psychological exploration, the quest and its trials are always externalized into the physical world. The heroes never struggle with their own dark sides, acquire self-knowledge, or change in any interior way. Only their place in the world changes: they become prosperous shoemakers again, marry a king, or gain a princess and half a kingdom. The benefit to society, the boon they bring back from the quest, is therefore also outside themselves: the breaking of an enchantment, the water of life, a hen that lays golden eggs, or the death of an evildoer. Sometimes the heroes of folktales succeed through cleverness. Sometimes they pass the tests and get the help they need simply because they are good or steadfast. Sometimes they are simply lucky. But they are what they are from the beginning of the story to the end. The inner significance of initiation, the recognition and integration of the self, is coded in the picture language of the folktale. In Max Lüthi's words, "Folktales want to be explicated." And because a picture or symbol carries manifold meanings, the witch, ogre, or dragon can be at the same time the natural environment against which human beings feel they struggle for survival, and the dark or unconscious side every person has within her- or himself (1961, 3).

Lüthi, like most other scholars who have written about folktales, thinks that recognizably similar folktales with the same motifs have been told in very different cultures all over the world because the tales express something fundamental about what it is to be human and live in the world—about universal experiences, struggles, and desires. They are much deeper than moral tales setting out rules for good behavior, although their porousness allows them to be reduced to that. The heroes of folktales are not always moral or ethical ideals. The princess breaks her promises to the frog that retrieves her golden ball from the well, and throws him against the wall out of revulsion and anger, not compassion. But the spell is broken nonetheless. The supernatural in folktales is free of human morality and has its own standards for reward and punishment. Generally, goodness is rewarded and badness punished, but folktales aren't stories about justice, or about the battle between cosmic good and evil, either. Just as the hero is not always good, the hero's opponent is not always evil. Cinderella's stepmother and stepsisters are bone selfish and inconsiderate, but they aren't evil. The fairy who curses Sleeping Beauty with death and the sorceress who takes Rapunzel from her parents aren't gratuitously nasty. They are responding, appropriately according to their ways, to insult or injury. Nor are folktales about simple wishes for more money and lasting prosperity, although the picture language of the folktale often represents the hero's gain of the happy ending in those images. The hero's path isn't an easy one, and the struggles have meaning.

Lüthi links his analysis of the form of the folktale to a consideration of its meaning. The style of the folktale isolates the figures in it. The other side of isolation is openness, and the hero is both the most isolated figure and the one who is truly open to the world and to the gifts it offers not as reward but as grace. Because folktale heroes are open both to what is familiar and to what is strange, they meet and accept the helpers who give them the strength or tools they need to fulfill their quest. Jack Zipes writes that

> In the oral wonder tale, we are to wonder about the workings of the universe where anything can happen at any time. . . . The tales seek to awaken our regard for the miraculous condition of life and to evoke in a religious sense profound feelings of awe and respect for life as a miraculous process. . . (1988, 11).

He goes on to say that enchantments stop the process of life, freeze whatever is enchanted into a fixed state so that it can no longer change and respond to life and grow. That is why enchantments must be broken, as one would break the ice on a river or lake to reach the living water underneath. Zipes's large body of work on folktales is primarily concerned with the social functions of book folktales and literary folktales, the way the stories have been written and rewritten to express and influence the ideologies of particular cultures at particular times.[12] But in the passage just quoted, he considers the oral folktale, the resilient, porous, stylized skeleton of this spongelike narrative genre, and the meaning he makes for it is much like Max Lüthi's. The meaning of the folktale is not life as it should *be* (the conditions of life) but life as it should be *shaped* (the way we live our lives). The point of the tale is the movement within it, the pursuit of the quest, the journey of initiation, with its necessary stages and conditions. Folktales take us through that journey in its proper form.

We don't have many formal rituals of initiation left in our secularized society to guide and celebrate the transition between one stage of life and another, so the purpose and steps of initiation are not part of our everyday awareness. We have to study them as part of anthropology or comparative religion. Of course, the preparation and ceremonies for transitions like bar and bat mitzvahs, confirmation, and marriage do retain elements of initiation ritual, whether we are conscious of them or not. Novels and movies have given us some idea of initiation rites in traditional societies, especially, here in North America, of the spirit quest of Native North American religions. But, as Eliade points out, initiation is not "a type of behavior peculiar to the man of the traditional societies." Whether we recognize it or not, "what is called 'initiation' *coexists with the human condition*, [and] *every existence is made up of an unbroken series of 'ordeals,' 'deaths,' and 'resurrections'* " (Eliade, 202, emphasis added). According to Eliade, folktales have no "initiatory responsibility," that is, no institutionalized role in bringing about the changes that take place in the liminal space of initiation. They are seen as only a diversion for children and an escape for adults. But they do work those changes on the level of the unconscious, "recreating the 'initiatory ordeals' on the plane of imagination and dream" (202). Within the world of the story we may cross thresholds of initiation as they should be crossed, setting out on the journey, braving the ordeals, accepting the help that is offered, and arriving at a new stage of life more completely ourselves. Initiation, as Eliade points out, occurs not only between childhood and adolescence, or between adolescence and adulthood. The initiatory scenario plays itself out throughout our lives.

The Folktale Audience

Folktales are not children's stories. In the oral cultures in which these tales were told, children weren't tucked away in nurseries and schools. They played and worked among the adults. When folktales were told in taverns and at social gatherings, in the kitchens of great houses and spinning rooms, by the fireside at night and wherever else hands were busy with work but minds free to imagine, children were undoubtedly listening. But the subject matter of folktales was not tailored to children. For 200 years and more, adults who write, publish, and choose stories for children have worked hard to make sure that those stories are psychologically appropriate for young readers, free of sex and bad language, packed with edifying themes or good clean fun. Folktales, before they became children's stories read in books, showed no such concern for innocent ears. Many of them contained bawdy and scatological humor, violence that didn't contribute to moral teachings, and heroes who were less than exemplary—clever thieves, liars, braggarts, lucky lazybones.

Early literary versions, or book folktales, weren't intended for children, either. Jones gives a chronology of the fairy tale in the literary tradition from the Renaissance onward (p. xv), and the first three books listed—Boccacio's *Decameron* (14th cent.), Straparola's *The Pleasant Nights* (16th cent.), and Basile's *Pentamerone* (1634)—were certainly not children's stories. The fourth book, Perrault's 1697 *Histoires, ou Contes du temps passé*,[13] is often mistakenly claimed as the first book of folktales published for an audience of children, but it was nothing of the kind. Jack Zipes, in the first chapter of *Fairy Tale as Myth, Myth as Fairy Tale*, gives an excellent overview of the development of the book folktale and literary folktale. As he states, "Perrault never intended his book to be read by children but was more concerned with demonstrating how French folklore could be adapted to the tastes of French high culture and used as a new genre of art within the French civilizing process" (1994, 17). The adaptations made by Perrault and the other French writers (mostly women, interestingly) who turned folktales into literary tales at the end of the seventeenth century were certainly a factor in making folktales the children's story *par excéllence*, but that was not their original purpose.

Perrault's is one of the two collections that have most strongly influenced the form of book folktales as we know them today. The other is the *Kinder- und Hausmärchen* of Jacob and Wilhelm Grimm. The first volume was published in 1812, the second in 1814. The Grimms' title does have the word "children" (*Kinder*) in it, but it was not intended to suggest the audience for whom they wrote the book. Theirs was a scholarly collection, a pioneering work of folklore studies, originally published for the information and pleasure of other scholars. The Brothers Grimm called the stories they collected "Children's [or nursery] and Domestic Tales" because that was what folktales had largely become in Europe from the eighteenth century on. They were stories uneducated folk told among themselves, and in the houses of the well-to-do they were told to middle- and upper-class children by the servants (uneducated folk) who looked after them because these were the stories the servants knew. When the Grimms' book unexpectedly became a bestseller that parents read to their children, the brothers, especially Wilhelm, made changes, over seven editions, that made the stories more suitable for children. Maria Tatar's *The Hard Facts of the Grimm's Fairy Tales* examines in a well-balanced and very readable way the changes the Grimms made from their field notes to the first published edition and in each successive edition of the collection. Reflecting the values and educational models of nineteenth-century bourgeois Germany, they took out the sex, especially any suggestion of incest, turned cruel mothers into stepmothers, added Christian piety, heightened the sufferings of the hero and the punishment of the villain, and generally strengthened the movement of the tales from victimization to revenge.

Folktales do make marvelous children's stories. They are short, with a straightforward narrative line, and all the force of the story is in the eventful plot. They have patterned repetition, strong contrasts, very little description, and unambiguous characters. They are also a superb playground for the imagination, full of wonders and the bizarre, free from the limitations of everyday reality, with layers of meaning that the conscious or unconscious mind may discover according to its readiness or need. And their porousness and resilience lets them survive a great deal of pasteurization, homogenization, and the addition of whatever the currently approved moral equivalents of supplementary vitamins and minerals for children might be. Their shift into the nursery did not happen without some protest. The redoubtable Mrs. Sarah Trimmer, for example, who produced stacks of improving literature for children in the early nineteenth century in England, held out against folktales, arguing that they were full of all the worst passions of which children should be innocent. But from the 1720s on, folktales rewritten for children (cleaned up and with improving messages added) were being produced in print; in 1729, a translation of Perrault's *Histoires* was published in England as a book for children; and folktales, endlessly adapted, rewritten, and reillustrated, remain firmly established as children's stories.[14]

Literature intentionally produced for children has seldom been entirely free of the adult need to shape our young so that they may grow and flourish as we think is best. This need informs not only the writing but also the adult reading of children's stories. The widespread notion that folktales are preeminently children's stories has been reinforced by the many literary and social critics and psychologists who read book folktales and literary folktales to find what they may teach children. My quarrel with Bruno Bettelheim is on this ground. Anyone who reads his *The Uses of Enchantment* is likely to get the impression that the sole purpose of folktales since time immemorial has been to guide children through the developmental stages identified by Sigmund Freud. Maria Tatar's book *Off with Their Heads: Fairy Tales and the Culture of Childhood* examines Bettelheim's interpretations of the canon of children's folktales and is a useful corrective to widely accepted assumptions about the meaning of these stories as children's texts.

While we are most aware of folktales as children's stories, we must also realize that they have never stopped being stories for adults and adolescents. Book folktales and literary folktales for teenage and adult readers have appeared as short stories, poems, novels, plays, and films. The recent boom in these reworkings of folktales for an older audience gave rise to this book, and many of them are works enjoyed by teenagers and adults both. Folktales have their place in current nonfiction as well. Jack Zipes points out in *Happily Ever After: Fairy Tales, Children, and the Culture Industry* that in the 1990s, a number of bestselling adult books have used folktales "to raise highly significant questions about social and political conditions, which reach broad audiences throughout the world" (9). Among his examples are Robert Bly's *Iron John* and Clarissa Pinkola Estés's *Women Who Run with the Wolves*, which have been read by men and women, singly and in book groups, all over the North American continent.

Stephen Jones, in *The Fairy Tale: The Magic Mirror of the Imagination*, published in 1995, identifies three subcategories of folktales: "tales for young children; tales for developing adolescents; and tales for relatively mature adults" (22). He establishes these categories on the basis of the age of the protagonists and the kind of problems they face. According to Jones, tales for young children deal with the difficulties of family life: Oedipal conflicts, sibling rivalry, the fear of being unloved and unwanted. Tales for developing adolescents form the largest group and are concerned with leaving one's parents' home, finding a mate, and establishing a home of one's own. Tales for mature adults "concern moral and philosophical dilemmas, such as fidelity in a marriage, communication between partners, or adjusting to the birth of children" (Jones, 25). Jones's analysis is flat and concentrates in such a literalistic and pedestrian way on what he calls the functionality of fairy tales that one would expect all folktales to be shelved with the self-help literature crowding our bookstore shelves. He conveys almost no sense of the folktale's resilient porosity, multilayered symbols, and sense of wonder that give the tales their durable charm. His categories ignore the different levels of meaning that any one tale offers. But I quote him here because he does recognize, although in a very limited way, that folktales are stories for all ages, and that many of them can have significance for young adults. The initiatory scenario of the folktale has particular resonance for teenagers, who face a number of high thresholds all at once: leaving home, choosing a trade or profession, entering into adult sexuality, taking on responsibility for themselves. They are preoccupied with who they are and who they will become, with choosing a path into the unknown. In the folktale they can follow the clear path of the hero's quest with the necessary focus and courage, overcoming difficult obstacles and surviving dangerous tests because they are open to the help and opportunity offered by the wonder-filled world.

Filling the Oral Folktale's Sponge

Unless it is simply a transcript of a story told within a still-living oral tradition, any written version of a folktale is necessarily an interpretation because the thought world of a literate culture is so different from that of an oral culture.

The additive structure becomes subordinative, and as connections are established the situations and characters may become more complex. Some written versions of folktales do little more than make the story sound right to literate ears. The clear, sharp outlines and flat surfaces are preserved. In others, the writer has embellished and filled in the gaps created by the folktale style with a personal interpretation that may include the tone of voice of the narrator, physical and psychological details about the characters, motivations for the events of the plot, and descriptions of the setting.

Any picture-book version of a folktale cannot help but fill some of those gaps because graphic images are directly referential and necessarily explicit about all sorts of details that the writer of the text may choose not to mention. Pictures tell us the ages of the characters, their physical appearance from hair color to height, and their personalities and relationships to other characters as shown by facial expressions and posture. If the text says that the miller had a beautiful daughter, a picture of the daughter will have to show us the illustrator's notion of her beauty—apple-cheeked or ethereal, earthy or aristocratic, blond or brunette. To a greater or lesser extent, the buildings, furniture, and clothing in the pictures will suggest a time and place in which the story is set. The colors and style the illustrator uses will also set the overall tone of the story, a visual equivalent of the storyteller's tone of voice and relationship to the audience: humorous, whimsical, romantic, tragic, didactic, cozy, and so on. All of these decisions by artists follow from their own interpretations of the story, the way they fill the folktale's spare outline in their imagination.

Trina Schart Hyman's picture books, for example, are rich and subtle visual interpretations. In her *Snow White* she plays with time in an unusual way. The clothing of the characters and domestic objects such as eyeglasses, toothbrushes, teapots, and mugs come from a range of historical periods, suggesting the no-time or transcendent time setting of the folktale. But within the story we see time moving forward normally as the great tree by the dwarfs' cottage changes with seasons and the queen's black kitten grows into a cat. In *Rapunzel*, Hyman shows us why the sorceress took the child: We see her love of living beauty in the picture that shows her bringing flowers from her lush, tangled garden into the house, and her love for Rapunzel in the picture of the two winding wool together, the sorceress bent toward the happy child with an expression of deep tenderness. Like many other picture books, Hyman's have a complexity that can easily engage the imagination of young adult and adult readers.

Novels and films, because they are so much longer than a folktale, necessarily offer a great deal of interpretation to flesh out the story. Films, of course, have in addition the visual explicitness of a picture book, to which they must add interpretation expressed through sound and movement. When a folktale is transplanted from fantasy to realistic fiction or science fiction, a fundamental change has to be made. The wondrous must be replaced by the rational, grounded in the observable facts of every-day. Poems like those by Anne Sexton and Gwen Strauss make perhaps the most radical shift from the oral folktale. While the folktale is a narrative of surfaces that avoids complexity, the lyric poem is all inwardness and emotional depth, tangled and allusive.

Many new versions of folktales are written to explore particular meanings that the porousness of these tales makes possible. Others are written deliberately to change an ideological perspective that earlier versions of the tales seem to carry. The role of girls and women in the folktales we know best is the ideological issue that has raised the most discussion and led to many socially conscious revisions. Much feminist criticism of folktales seems to assume that folktales are inherently patriarchal, necessarily relegating women to the role of passive princesses and helpless victims. Because this critique so strongly informs the current popular understanding of folktales, its basis is worth investigating here briefly. First, Maria Tatar and other scholars have pointed out that gender is not a fixed attribute of particular folktale roles. For example, there is a Russian folktale with a male Sleeping Beauty and a Turkish variant of Cinderella in which the main character is male. A look at Aarne and Thompson's *The Types of the Folktale: A Classification and Bibliography* reveals beast brides as well as beast bridegrooms. Second, the folktales we know have been selected for publication over roughly three centuries by writers and editors who quite naturally chose those which pleased them best, and those were likely to be the tales that corresponded most closely to their understanding of the world. Our canon of folktales is made up of those that most easily reflected the world view of the (mostly male) anthologists, writers, illustrators, and filmmakers. Third, because oral tales need to be changed to make them enjoyable reading, and because their spare style invites elaboration, these same anthologists, writers, illustrators, and filmmakers made their own interpretations explicit in the versions they produced. Therefore, the patriarchal social forms that our well-known folktales mirror are not inherent in the folktales themselves but are a production of selection and revision of the tales over time. The canon or repertoire of well-known folktales changes, and reading the tradition on the basis of what is popular in our own time is a huge error. Finally, readers who do not understand the mnemonic and stylistic functions of the flat characters and strong opposites of the oral folktale are likely to misread the characters as stereotypes in a negative sense rather than as types.

Book folktales and literary folktales that can be called feminist are only as good as the writer's craft and creative imagination. The same holds true for every other -ism that folktales have been used to carry. Some positively creak with didacticism and good intentions, while others, like Katherine Paterson's picture book *The King's Equal* and Jane Yolen's stories, have a beauty, strength, and charm equal to those of the oral tales that have been winnowed by much time and telling. But it must be noted that one popular type of revisionist folktale is not a folktale at all, and that is the parody. The main point of parody, and usually the main joke, is to overset the readers' previously formed expectations, and in the process challenge the inevitability of those expectations. That is, parody looks back, plays with a particular genre or narrative form to comment on that form and on the meaning that has already been made with it.[15] Its most pronounced characteristic is self-conscious and pointed reference to another text or body of texts. Parodies of folktales, feminist and otherwise, are everywhere these days. They range in length from single cartoons to comic strips to short stories and novels. Some are parodies of particular tales, while others parody the whole genre. The humor can be caustically critical or gently playful. Clever parodies, like Patricia Wrede's *Dealing with Dragons* and its sequels, William Goldman's book and film *The Princess Bride*, Babette Cole's *Prince Cinders*, Jon Scieszka's *The Stinky Cheese Man and Other Fairly Stupid Tales*, and Fiona French's *Snow White in New York* delight us by their wit. But they are commentary on folktales, not folktales themselves. They have a different function, and their gift to the reader is a different one.

Folktales in Postmodern Times

Book folktales and literary folktales have never gone out of fashion. But the increase of reworkings of folktales for young adults and adults in the past 15 years or so strikes us as unusual. Ace Books, a major mass-market fantasy publisher, began "The Fairy Tale Series," full-length paperback novels based on classic folktales and commissioned from well-known writers of fantasy, in 1986. (The series, created by Terri Windling, is now published by TOR.) Ellen Datlow and Terri Windling edit occasional anthologies, published by Avon, of newly commissioned adult fantasy and horror stories based on traditional folktale themes. Scholastic puts out a teenage romance series called Once Upon a Dream, in which each novel is based on a traditional folktale. Robert Bly's *Iron John* and Clarissa Pinkola Estés's *Women Who Run with the Wolves* brought large numbers of men and women to think about their lives in the symbol language of folktale. Walt Disney Studios' *Beauty and the Beast* was a *succès fou* in movie theaters in 1991 and is a video bestseller with adults as well as children, and the 1998 Disney remake of the made-for-television musical *Cinderella* aired on Sunday night prime time.

Cartoons for sophisticated adults in magazines like *The New Yorker* and popular comic strips in the newspapers call on our repertoire of folktales with striking frequency. What's happening here?

My own speculation has been that this current reflowering of folktales has three roots. One is a sort of *fin de siècle* decadence. Our imaginative creativity has become tired and limp under the constant pressure to produce something new for the market, so writers and artists are searching through the trunks in our cultural attics for inspiration, gladly rediscovering the durable muse of the folktale, who has the added commercial advantage of being free of copyright. The second is a shortage of wonder in a world dominated by speed, money, materialism, and a reliance on applied science for all the answers to life's big questions. It seems to me that this root, the sensed lack of the numinous and transcendental in our lives, also feeds the New Age phenomena, the powerful interest in goddesses, and the search for spirituality in religions that seem exotic and therefore seem to offer something different. Established religious traditions that shape the world for a community make demands on members of that community. Folktales don't make demands. They give a sense of the numinous without hedging one in or tying one down.

The third root is a sense of rootlessness, brought about by the bewildering challenges of increasing diversity and globalism. Many of us face the postmodern confusion and profusion of truths and values without the grounding of a tradition that can serve as a base from which to think things through and sort them out. We don't know who we are or where we belong. Folktales, with their patina of age, give us a sense of continuity with a deep-rooted past and of community with tellers, listeners, writers, and readers who share that past.

Jack Zipes, in *Fairy Tale as Myth, Myth as Fairy Tale*, considering the books of folktales that fill the windows of bookstores at Christmas time, suggests that folktales offer hope for richer lives than the ones we lead in our everyday world. He goes on to ask whether there is any basis for such hope: "Are the fairy tales in America mere commodities that compensate for the technological evolution that has narrowed the range of possibilities for developing the imagination and humane relationships in reality?" (139) The answer is yes and no. Some of them are mere commodities. But some are more than that. In Zipes's view, "the major characteristic of the best of contemporary American fairy tales [is] the self-reflective search for a fantastical form that will recuperate the utopian function of the traditional fairy tale in a manner that is commensurate with the major social changes in the postindustrial world" (159). J. R. R. Tolkien wrote in *Tree and Leaf* that fantasies ("fairy-stories") new and old have three functions: recovery of the freshness and wonder of the world around us; legitimate escape from the ugly brutality of our times and the limitations of being mortal humans; and the consolation of the happy ending, which does not deny the existence of sorrow and failure but does deny universal final defeat, "giving a fleeting glimpse of Joy, Joy beyond the walls of the world, poignant as grief" (62).

Some of the writers, illustrators, and filmmakers whose work we include in the following chapters have always known that folktales offer us recovery, escape, and consolation. Terri Windling has explained in her introductions to The Fairy Tale Series novels and the Avon anthologies that she herself has loved and felt the transformative power of these tales all her life. Jane Yolen's book folktales and literary folktales spring not from social consciousness or ideological intention but from a profound appreciation of the nature and function of the traditional folktale as an expression of what it is to be human and live in the world. Others have reworked the old tales because their strong symbols and plots are so deeply embedded in our culture that they offer richly allusive and intertextual possibilities. Some have produced what will sell, or played off our common knowledge of folktales to make a point that matters to them.

But the pleasure any piece of fiction gives depends both on the craft and imagination of its creator and on the skill, repertoire, and expectations of the reader. We have not set out to evaluate the reworkings of folktales included in this book. Our opinions undoubtedly show through in places, but our purpose is to present rather than to judge.

Endnotes

1.   I find the very unfamiliarity of Ong's term *noetic economy* a useful reminder of the strangeness and complexity (to us) of oral culture. I decoded it with my *Concise Oxford Dictionary* as follows. "Noetic"—"of the intellect" from the Greek verb "noeo" to apprehend. "Economy"— "(administration or condition of) concerns and resources of a community"; archaic use, "organized system; literally, management of a house" (the Greek "oikos" and "-nomos" from "nemo" to manage). Therefore, *noetic economy* can be thought of as the administration or condition of the intellectual or thought resources and concerns of a community, or organized system of thinking, or organization of thought. Working my way through these definitions let me adopt the term comfortably with a much deeper understanding of Ong's explanations. Using it puts me inside layers of meaning.

2.   A formula is a fixed phrase, a combination of words that is repeated as a unit. It functions in an oral culture as a single word. The term can also be expanded to refer to fixed combinations of story elements.

3.   The additive structure of oral tales is paratactic (*para-* beside, *taxis* arrangement), an arrangement of events side-by-side, as if on a straight horizontal line. Subordinative structures, also called hypotactic (*hupo-* under), could be represented by a diagram like a family tree, showing vertical as well as horizontal relationships.

4.   It is instructive, in considering the agonistic tone of oral narrative, to look at the etymology of the word *oppose*. The Latin prefix *op* or *ob* means openness or facing or opposition. *Pose* is from the Latin verb *ponere*, to put or place. The opposing entities need not be hostile to each other—the notions of openness or simply facing are present in the root prefix. But they are discrete entities, quite separate, one or the other, rather than part of a continuum. And a contest always has at least two opponents or sides facing each other. There is no gray area, no continuum of interests between them. The issue is black and white, win or lose.

5.   The significance of the numbers that turn up so often in folktales is beyond the scope of this chapter. But it is a fascinating subject for investigation. About the number three, Max Lüthi writes:

> In the western world the number three is woven in many ways into the general cultural structure. It is a mythic number. . . . The three stands between singularity and amorphous multiplicity. . . . The three is not only the first but also the most impressive representative of plurality. (*The Fairytale as Art Form and Portrait of Man*, p. 44f.)

6.   I will use the word "hero" for both male and female protagonists of folktales, designating the role rather than gender of this figure. "Heroine" has its own particular literary implications about the nature of female roles in fiction that do not apply in the context of folktale, as I have argued at length elsewhere (Altmann 1992).

7.   The first chapter of Northrop Frye's *The Secular Scripture* gives a good description of the differences between folktale and myth.

8.   A motif is "a plot kernel, a concrete pattern of events, in contrast to a *theme*, where a conception is involved (an idea, principle, or belief; a hope, a fear, an illusion, etc.). . . . It can be the carrier of various themes." This definition comes from the "Glossary" in Lüthi's *The Fairy Tale as Art Form and Portrait of Man*.

9.   The comparison mentioned here comes from Lüthi's 1975 *Volksmärchen und Volkssage*. Three of Lüthi's books are available in English translation: *Once Upon a Time: On the Nature of Fairy Tales* (Bloomington, IN: University of Indiana Press, 1976); *The European Folktale: Form and Nature* (Philadelphia: Institute for the Study of Human Issues, 1982); and *The Fairytale as Art Form and Portrait of Man* (see Bibliography). In this chapter I have drawn on *Volksmärchen und Volkssage: Zwei Grundformen erzählender Dichtung*, and *The Fairytale as Art Form and Portrait of Man*. All translations from *Volksmärchen und Volkssage* are my own.

10.   Joseph Campbell's *The Hero with a Thousand Faces* is probably the most well-known of the descriptions of the quest paradigm. For the constant elements of the paradigm I have used the summary by Lee Edwards in her "The Labors of Psyche," p. 34.

11.   For an extended analysis of quest as initiation see Altmann, "Welding Brass Tits on the Armor." Victor Turner's *The Ritual Process: Structure and Anti-Structure* (Ithaca, NY: Cornell University Press, 1977) is an excellent source on the structure and meaning of initiation rites.

12.   The article by Zipes quoted here, which is from an issue of *The Lion and the Unicorn* entirely on fairy tales, is a very good introduction to Zipes's approach to and thinking on folktales. I recommend it to readers who want a place to start, or have only enough time to read a little Zipes.

13.   Jones's dates are correct, but the title he gives for Perrault's 1697 publication is wrong. "Contes de [not du, as Jones has it] ma Mère l'Oye" comes from the frontispiece of the book, not the title page.

14.   The fact that folktales are in the common domain, and therefore do not require copyright permission or fees, must to some extent be a factor in their perennial popularity with publishers and illustrators.

15.   For a more thorough examination of parody and feminist folktales see Altmann's "Parody and Poesis in Feminist Fairy Tales."

Bibliography

Altmann, Anna E. "Welding Brass Tits on the Armor: An Examination of the Quest Metaphor in Robin McKinley's *The Hero and the Crown*." *Children's Literature in Education* 23: 3 (1992), 143–56.

———. "Parody and Poesis in Feminist Fairy Tales." *Canadian Children's Literature* 80 (1994), 20–33.

Benton, Michael, and Geoff Fox. *Teaching Literature: Nine to Fourteen*. New York: Oxford University Press, 1985.

Bettelheim, Bruno. *The Uses of Enchantment: The Meaning and Importance of Fairy Tales*. New York: Vintage Books, 1976.

Edwards, Lee. "The Labors of Psyche: Toward a Theory of Female Heroism." *Critical Inquiry*, Autumn 1979, 33–49.

Eliade, Mircea. *Myth and Reality*. New York: Harper Torchbooks, 1975.

Illich, Ivan, and Barry Sanders. *ABC: The Alphabetization of the Mind*. New York: Vintage Books, 1989.

Jones, Stephen Swan. *The Fairy Tale: The Magic Mirror of Imagination*. New York: Twayne, 1995.

Lüthi, Max. *Volksmärchen und Volkssage: Zwei Grundformen erzählender Dichtung*. Bern: Francke, 1961.

———. *The Fairytale as Art Form and Portrait of Man*. Translated by Jon Erickson. Bloomington, IN: Indiana University Press, 1984.

Ong, Walter J. *Orality and Literacy: The Technologizing of the Word*. New York: Methuen, 1982.

Tatar, Maria. *The Hard Facts of the Grimms' Fairy Tales*. Princeton, NJ: Princeton University Press, 1987.

Tolkien, J. R. R. *Tree and Leaf*. London: Unwin Paperbacks, 1988.

Warner, Marina. *From the Beast to the Blonde: On Fairy Tales and Their Tellers*. London: Chatto & Windus, 1994.

Zipes, Jack. "The Changing Function of the Fairy Tale." In *The Lion and the Unicorn* 12:2 (1988), 7–31.

———. *Fairy Tale as Myth, Myth as Fairy Tale*. Lexington, KY: University of Kentucky Press, 1994. (Thomas D. Clark Lectures, 1993.)

———. *Happily Ever After: Fairy Tales, Children, and the Culture Industry*. New York: Routledge, 1997.

CHAPTER 2

CINDERELLA

There is a general consensus in the folktale literature that "Cinderella" is the most widely known folktale of all. More than 700 variations of it have been collected from around the world (Thomas, 145). The oldest datable version was found in a Chinese book written around 850–860 CE (Opie, 157), but there is evidence that motifs special to the Balkan "Cinderella" are 2,000 years old (Philip, 7). Sorting out the different tale types that are linked together in what Rooth calls the Cinderella cycle is a very complicated task, and analyses of "Cinderella" sometimes treat as variants of the same type two tales that actually don't belong together. This chapter focuses on the Cinderella tale proper, tale type AT 510A. Its place in the larger Cinderella cycle is discussed under the heading "Cinderella in Oral Tradition."

Throughout this chapter I will refer to the tale and its protagonist as "Cinderella." The Grimms' "Aschenputtel" is kept as the title of many English translations although it is sometimes anglicized as "Ashputtle." Perrault's "Cendrillon" is usually translated as "Cinderella." Both the German *Asche* and the French *cendre* mean "ash," while cinders are actually slag residue of wood or coal, hard lumps that can be raked out of the ashes and used again for fuel. Because several interpretations of "Cinderella" rely heavily on the symbolic significance of ashes, "Cinderella" is actually a misnomer. But popular usage and literary warrant have established "Cinderella" so firmly that there is no point in arguing etymology.

Tale Type: AT 510A

Tale type 510 is *Cinderella and Cap o' Rushes*. It has two subtypes: 510A, *Cinderella*; and 510B, *The Dress of Gold, of Silver, and of Stars (Cap o' Rushes)*. Type 510A is summarized as: "*Cinderella*. The two stepsisters. The stepdaughter at the grave of her own mother, who helps her (milks the cow, shakes the apple tree, helps the old man). Three-fold visit to church (dance). Slipper test" (Thompson, 177). The analysis of 510A is the following:

I.   *The Persecuted Heroine.* (a) The heroine is abused by her stepmother and stepsisters and (a^1) stays on the hearth or in the ashes and (a^2) is dressed in rough clothing—cap of rushes, wooden cloak, etc.

II. *Magic Help.* While she is acting as servant (at home or among strangers) she is advised, provided for, or fed (a) by her dead mother, or (b) by a tree on her mother's grave, or (c) by a supernatural being, or (d) by birds, or (e) by a goat, a sheep, or a cow.

III. *Meeting the Prince.* (a) She dances in beautiful clothing several times with a prince who seeks in vain to keep her, or she is seen by him in church.

IV. *Proof of Identity.* (a) She is discovered through the slipper-test.

V.   *Marriage with the Prince.*

Motifs:

S31: Cruel stepmother

L55: Stepdaughter heroine

L102: Unpromising heroine

L131: Hearth abode of unpromising hero (heroine)

E323.3: Dead mother returns to aid persecuted daughter

E631: Reincarnation in plant (tree) growing from grave

N810: Supernatural helpers

F311.1: Fairy godmother

N815: Fairy as helper

D1473.1: Magic wand furnishes clothes

D1050.1: Clothes produced by magic

F861.4.3: Carriage from pumpkin

D411.6.1: Transformation: mouse to horse

D315.1: Transformation: rat to person

B450: Helpful bird

B313.1: Helpful animal reincarnation of parent. The dead mother appears to the heroine in the form of an animal.

D1658: Grateful objects

D1658.1 Objects repay kindness

N711.6: Prince sees heroine at ball and is enamored

C761.3: Tabu: staying too long at ball. Must leave before certain hour

R221: Heroine's three-fold flight from ball

K2212.1: Treacherous stepsisters

H36.1: Slipper test. Identification by fitting of slipper

K1911.3.3.1: False bride's feet mutilated

F823.2: Glass shoes

J1146.1: Detection by pitch trap. Pitch is spread so that shoe is left behind as clue

L162: Lowly heroine marries prince

℘

A girl's mother dies and her father marries again. The stepmother is a cold and haughty woman with two daughters of her own, who are fair to look at but black of heart. The new wife mistreats her stepdaughter, turning her into a servant in her own home. Because she sleeps on the hearth she is often dirty and covered with ashes, so she is called Cinderella. One day the father goes to a fair and asks his three daughters what they would like him to bring back for them. The stepsisters ask for jewels and dresses, but Cinderella asks for the first branch that brushes against his hat on the way home. He gives her a hazel twig that knocked his hat off, and she plants it on her mother's grave. The twig, watered by her tears, grows into a tree. A white bird comes to perch on the tree whenever Cinderella visits her mother's grave, and whatever Cinderella wishes for, the bird throws down to her.

The king announces that a ball will be held on three successive days so that the prince may choose a bride. Cinderella begs to go, and her stepmother says she may if she can pick a bowlful of lentils out of the ashes in less than two hours. Cinderella calls the doves and turtledoves and all the birds of the air to help her, and the task is done. Then the stepmother says she must pick two bowlfuls of lentils out of the ashes in one hour. Again the birds help. At that the stepmother tells her she can't go because she has nothing to wear. Cinderella goes to the hazel tree on her mother's grave and says "Shake and shiver, little tree/shake gold and silver down on me" and the bird throws down a gold and silver dress and slippers embroidered with silver. Cinderella goes to the ball and dances with the prince until evening, and then she wants to go home. The prince wants to see her home to find out who she is, but she gives him the slip. He follows her and sees her hide in the dovecote. When her father comes home, the prince tells him about the girl who hid in the dovecote. The father wonders whether it might be Cinderella, gets an ax, and breaks into the dovecote, but no one is there. Cinderella has slipped out the back and returned her beautiful clothes to the bird in the hazel tree, and is lying in the ashes in the kitchen. The same thing happens the next day, except that Cinderella hides in the pear tree, which her father chops down. On the third day of the ball, the prince has had the staircase spread with pitch, and one of Cinderella's golden slippers sticks to it.

The prince declares he will marry only the girl whom the shoe fits. When the eldest stepsister tries it on in her room and the shoe is too small, the stepmother gives her a knife and tells her to cut off her toe. She does, and the prince puts her on his horse and rides away with her. But the two doves sitting in the hazel tree call out "Cooroo, cooroo, there's blood in the shoe, this is not the bride for you." The prince looks at her foot, sees the blood gushing, and takes her home again. The second stepsister cuts off her heel with the knife her mother gives her, the prince rides away with her, and again the doves point out the blood. He takes her home and asks whether there isn't another daughter in the house. The father answers that there is only the little kitchen maid his dead wife left him, and the stepmother adds that she's much too dirty to be seen. The prince insists she be called and puts the slipper on her foot. It fits perfectly, and when he looks at her face he recognizes his true bride. He rides away with Cinderella and the two doves go with her, one on each shoulder. The two stepsisters go to the wedding, and on the way into the church the doves come and pick out one eye of each of them. And on the way out of the church the doves pick out the other eye, so that they are blind for the rest of their lives as a punishment for their wickedness and falseness.

A History of Cinderella

In North America, most popular versions of the tale are based on Charles Perrault's "Cendrillon," published in his *Histoires, ou contes du temps passé* in 1697. The other dominant version is "Aschenputtel" by the Brothers Grimm. I have based the synopsis that precedes this introduction on the Grimms' version, in part because the Perrault story is the one most readers will already be familiar with. Also, the Grimms' version, although it reflects the nineteenth-century Protestant German background of Jacob and Wilhelm Grimm just as "Cendrillon" does Perrault's late seventeenth-century French milieu, is closer to the folktale variants within this tale type than Perrault's version is. I think "Aschenputtel" is a more interesting and stronger story than "Cendrillon."

Cinderella in Oral Tradition

Two major studies have been done of Cinderella variants. The first, by Marian Cox, was published in 1893. The second, by Anna Birgitta Rooth, published in 1951, builds on Cox's work. Cox and Rooth have mapped for us the development of the Cinderella cycle in oral traditions around the world. Cox established five groupings of Cinderella tales that Rooth links to four types in the Aarne-Thompson classification (Rooth, 14):

Table 2.1

Cox	Aarne-Thompson
A. Cinderella	510A
B. Cat-skin	510B
C. Cap o'Rushes	510B
D. Indeterminate	511
E. Hero Tales	511B

Cox's category E, Hero tales, is composed of tales in AT 511 that have male protagonists. Because it has no number of its own in the Aarne-Thompson classification, Rooth has called it 511B.

Rooth's Cinderella Cycle

Tracking the historical development of the oral Cinderella cycle, Rooth found five types: A, AB, B, B1, and C. Rooth's Type A is the oldest type of the tale and developed in the East. It spread from there and is also found in Eastern Europe. Rooth's Type AB developed in the Near East from Type A and another motif complex, that of the object found and lost by chance (like Cinderella's slipper in Perrault). It was brought to southeastern Europe and spread west to Italy, Spain, and Portugal and north to the Slavonic and Baltic areas. From the Slavonic area it reached Scandinavia and the British Isles. Rooth's Type B (AT 510A), the Cinderella tale proper, crystallized from AB in southeastern Europe and spread throughout Europe. Type B1 (AT 510B), "Cap o' Rushes," borrowed the motif-complex of the protagonist's visits to the ball or feast in the magically acquired lovely dresses from Type B, Cinderella. That is the only relation between the two types. But the borrowing has created confusion between Types B and B1 in Scandinavia and in the critical analysis of the two types. Rooth's Type C, the tale with a male protagonist, apparently evolved early in the Near East as an equivalent of Type A. It migrated to southeastern Europe and from there to Ireland and Scandinavia. In Scandinavia it has been confused with Type AB (Rooth, 236). A summary of each of these types follows.

A

(AT 511): The heroine is abused by mother (or stepmother and sisters [or stepsisters]). While she is acting as a servant she is advised, provided for, and fed by a supernatural being or by a goat, a sheep, or a cow. When the goat (cow) is killed, a magic tree springs up from her remains. The heroine alone is able to pick the fruit of the tree. She marries a prince. (Summary taken from Thompson 1964, 175 and 178.)

AB

(AT 511 & 510A): A teacher with a daughter of her own inveigles her pupil into killing the pupil's mother. The girl's father takes the teacher as his second wife. The dead mother turns into a cow who helps the girl when her stepmother mistreats her. Following her mother's advice she gets a special gift from a supernatural being: a moon on her forehead and a star on her chin. The stepsister discovers the gift and is sent by her own mother to the supernatural being to get the same for herself. She does the wrong things and is given monkey's ears on her head and a monkey's tale on her chin (in some variants donkey ears and donkey penis).

Later, a princess is to be married and everyone is invited to the wedding. Fatima is commanded to sort beans and lentils and fill a trough with her tears before she can go to the feast. From the cow's horn come a cock and a hen to sort the grain and a stream of salt water to fill the trough. From the other horn she gets fine clothes. She goes to the feast. The prince falls in love with her and follows when she leaves. She drops her shoe. Shoe test. Fatima is hidden by her stepmother, but a cock crows and reveals her presence and that she is the owner of the shoe. The girl and the prince marry and live happily ever after. The stepmother and stepdaughter die of annoyance. (Summary taken from Rooth, 17–18.)

B

(AT 510A): The Cinderella tale proper (see synopsis at beginning of chapter).

B1

(AT 510B): A girl flees in disguise from her father, who wants to marry her. She dances in beautiful clothing several times with a prince who wants to marry her. She is discovered through a ring that she throws into the prince's drink or bakes in his bread. Marriage with the prince.

C

(AT 511B): A young man gets a stepmother with several daughters of her own. He is mistreated by the stepmother. He is fed by an ox. The stepsisters spy on him and tell their mother about the ox. The stepmother orders the ox killed. The ox flies away with the boy. They ride together through a forest of copper, a forest of silver, and a forest of gold. In each the boy picks a flower although the ox warns him not to. Each time he picks a flower a different animal appears to ask why the forest is damaged. The ox fights the animal and kills it. In a fourth battle the ox is killed and the boy keeps his right horn as the ox told him to. The horn feeds him. A flock of sheep emerges from the horn and a witch helps him get them back into the horn on the condition that he promise to marry her. Afterwards he meets a miller's daughter and falls in love with her. They marry. When the witch comes the miller's daughter puts a broom and a fire rake upside down by the door and bread and water on the table. When the witch asks to be let in the objects speak. The witch thinks that inside the house there is a greater witch than she is and becomes so angry that she bursts. (Summary taken from Rooth, 20–22.)

Influences from Other Sources

Some oral variants of Rooth's Type B, "Cinderella," show the influence of the literary tradition. A tale collected by Cox in Martinique contains a fairy that changes different things into a carriage and servants. This motif comes originally from Perrault's "Cendrillon" (Rooth, 95). The glass shoe that appears in several variants is probably Perrault's invention as well. Two of Cox's Italian variants have been influenced by Basile's "Cat Cinderella," and two Danish and a German variant appear to be offshoots of the Grimm tale (Rooth, 99 n.10).

According to Rooth, the slipper motif, which occurs in Type AB and Type B, has a Chinese origin. The "ash" nickname that comes from the protagonist's place at the hearth occurs only in Type B and only in the European tradition. Type B1, with the motifs of the unnatural father and the visit to the feast or ball, appears only in the European tradition. Rooth stresses the fact that "Type B1 has no original affinity with Types AB or B either through style or content" (119).

Cinderella in Print

Like many of the familiar folktales, the tale of Cinderella also has an established history as a literary tale.

Basile

The earliest European version of "Cinderella" to appear in print is Giambattista Basile's "The Cat Cinderella," the Sixth Diversion of the First Day in his *Pentamerone*, published in 1634. The Cinderella figure is named Zezolla. She is the daughter of a prince who remarried after her mother died, and her stepmother mistreats her. Zezolla's governess persuades the girl to kill her stepmother. The girl does so and then persuades her father to marry the governess, who has promised to treat the girl kindly when she becomes her stepmother. The prince marries the governess, and after a short time the new stepmother brings six daughters of her own, whose existence she had kept secret, into the family. The stepmother alienates the prince's affection from his daughter, and Zezolla is reduced to sitting in the kitchen by the fire. She is nicknamed the Cat Cinderella. The prince goes to Sardinia, and before he leaves he asks all his daughters what he should bring back for them. The stepsisters ask for various luxuries, but Zezolla asks "that thou recommend me to the pigeon of the fairies, bidding her tell them that they would send me somewhat" (Basile, 55). A fairy sends her a date tree and a mattock to plant it, and a golden bucket and a silken napkin to cultivate it. In four days it grows to be the size of a woman, and a fairy steps out of it and asks her what she wants. Zezolla tells her she would like to leave the house to enjoy herself. The fairy teaches her a verse that will make the tree give her fine clothes.

The king gives a festival, and Zezolla gets fine clothes, a horse, and 12 pages from the date tree and goes. The king falls in love with her and sends a servant to follow her home, but Zezolla throws down a handful of gold coins the tree had give her and escapes. On the next day much the same happens. On the third day Zezolla goes to the festival in a golden carriage. The servant of the king sticks to the carriage, and Zezolla makes the coachman drive so quickly that one of her slippers flies out of the carriage. The servant takes it to the king, who invites all the women in the kingdom to come to a banquet to try on the slipper. It fits none of them and the king commands them to come again the next day, leaving not a single female at home. The prince explains that he has a daughter who sits by the fire in the kitchen and isn't worth bringing. The king commands that she must come before all the others. When Zezolla is brought to the banquet, the king recognizes her at once but pretends not to until she tries on the slipper. Then he puts his arms around her and a crown on her head and tells everyone to bow to her as their queen. The stepsisters are very angry and envious and go home to their mother's house (Basile, 53–59).

Perrault

The first of the two most influential print versions of Cinderella to be published in Europe is Charles Perrault's "Cendrillon," which appeared in his *Histoires, ou contes du temps passé* in 1697. It was first published in an English translation in 1729. It is in many ways an untypical "Cinderella," although it is the standard version in North America. The story is so widely known that it does not require a summary here, but a few particulars must be pointed out. Perrault invented the fairy godmother as a replacement for the magic tree or magic animal and added the pumpkin turned into a coach, the mice turned into horses, the rat into a coachman, and the lizards into footmen. He also probably invented the glass slippers, although agreement on this point is not universal. Cinderella's "gentleness and goodness were without parallel," while the stepmother is "the haughtiest and proudest woman in the world," and her daughters are just like her (Perrault, 25). About the appearance of the three girls we are only told that "Cinderella looked a thousand times more beautiful in her shabby clothes than her stepsister, no matter how magnificent their clothes were" (25). Perrault's story contains a great deal of description of clothing and frequent references to female psychology (Morgan, 94–95). Perrault adds two morals at the end that mark his story quite clearly as a literary revision rather a folktale. The first is straightforward:

> A woman's beauty is quite a treasure
> We never cease to admire.
> Yet graciousness exceeds all measure.
> There's nothing of virtue higher.
> The fairy, according to our story,
> Contributed it to Cinderella's glory
> And taught her what becomes a queen,
> (Left in a moral to be gleaned.)
> Beautiful Ladies, it's kindness more than dress
> That wins a man's heart with greater success.
> So, if you want a life filled with bliss,
> The truest gift is graciousness. (Perrault, 29–30)

The second moral is much more cynical and, in fact, undercuts the first one:

> No doubt it is a benefit
> To have strong courage and fine wit,
> To be endowed with common sense
> And other virtues to possess
> That Heaven may dispense.
> But these may prove quite useless—
> As well may many others—
> If you strive to gain success
> And neglect godfathers or godmothers. (Perrault, 30)

There is humor in this second moral, "which takes an objective look at what actually happens in the tale, stripping away the idealized sentiment, and interpreting the situations described according to real life experience" (Morgan, 98). In other words, anyone who takes the story as a serious lesson should think again. Unfortunately, modern versions of "Cinderella" based on Perrault seem to be the work of persons who either didn't know or chose to ignore the second moral.

The Brothers Grimm

The second of the two most influential print versions of Cinderella to be published in Europe is Jacob and Wilhelm Grimm's "Aschenputtel," which is number 21 in their *Kinder- und Hausmärchen* published in 1812–1814. (The collection was published in England in translation as *German Popular Stories* in 1823–1826.) The Grimms' tale undoubtedly came indirectly from a French source. Ruth Bottigheimer describes the "Aschenputtel" of 1812 as "a German-language carbon copy of Perrault's sparkling tale" (1988, 197). But this seems to be an egregious overstatement, for while the Grimms made numerous and significant changes in "Aschenputtel" over the six editions that followed the first one, the pattern of the tale was not changed. The table below summarizes the differences between the first (1812) and the second (1819) edition. In the table I have drawn on differences noted by Ellis, Bottigheimer (1987), and McGlathery (1991).

Table 2.2

"Aschenputtel" 1812 Text	"Aschenputtel" 1819 Text
Dying mother tells Cinderella to plant hazel tree on grave and shake it when she needs help.	Cinderella asks father for first hazel twig that brushes his hat, plants it on grave.
One sister cuts part of her toes off.	One sister hacks her toes off.
False bride's stockings stained red and the blood had penetrated up through them.	The prince looked at her foot and saw the blood gush out.
Stepmother and stepsisters are shocked and turn pale when the slipper fits Cinderella, but the prince leads Cinderella away.	The stepsisters go to the wedding to ingratiate themselves, but the two doves peck out one eye of each on the way into the church, and the other eye on the way out as a punishment for being so wicked and false.

The differences are characteristic of Wilhelm Grimm's editing of the second and later editions. He intensified the mistreatment of the protagonist as victim and strengthened the revenge. Bottigheimer demonstrates that he also consistently silenced the "good" women in the tales and gave more speech to the "bad" women and any men in the stories (Bottigheimer 1987, 59).

Generally, the Grimms' tales are grimmer than Perrault's versions of the same stories, which is undoubtedly why the Perrault versions have been chosen as the basis of modern retellings for children. The Grimm tales are also less embellished. John Ellis, Ruth Bottigheimer, and other critics have established that the Grimm tales are not the oral tales from the German folk tradition that the two brothers claimed to have collected. But they are, nonetheless, closer to the folktale in style and content than the unashamedly literary tales of Perrault.

Table 2.3
A Comparison of Perrault's and Grimms'
Versions of Cinderella

Perrault	Grimm
Stepsisters not as beautiful as Cinderella: beauty and goodness equated.	Stepsisters beautiful: beauty may be only skin deep. Cinderella's appearance not described.
	Father offers gifts and Cinderella asks for hazel twig.
Cinderella prevented from going to ball because of clothes.	Cinderella given two impossible tasks and then no clothes.
Fairy godmother gives her what she needs.	Cinderella asks tree on mother's grave for clothes.
Glass slippers.	Silver and gold slippers.
Pumpkin coach, etc.	Transportation not mentioned.
Midnight curfew.	No curfew.
	Prince follows Cinderella, and father cuts down dovecote and pear tree.
Cinderella loses shoe.	Prince puts pitch on stairs on third night, and one shoe sticks fast.
Gentleman of the court comes with the slipper, and only Cinderella can wear it.	Prince comes with slipper; stepsisters cut off toe or heel to get slipper on; doves point out blood.
Cinderella finds husbands for stepsisters.	Doves peck out stepsisters' eyes at wedding.

Overview of Critical Interpretations of Cinderella

Trina Schart Hyman has never illustrated "Cinderella" because she never particularly liked the tale. To her mind, "it's all about clothes and girls being mean to each other" (298). Hyman's characterization of the tale could stand as a succinct summing up of some of the views expressed by the critics in this section of the chapter. But other readers have made very different meanings of it.

1974: Julius Heuscher points to themes in "Cinderella" that bear out Freudian theories of childhood development. For example, the good, dead mother and the wicked stepmother represent "the earliest ambivalence of the child towards the mother" (224). The father is also an ambivalent figure, and the hazel twig he brings his daughter is a phallic symbol; it grows into a tree that provides her with everything she wishes. The twig pushes the father's hat from his head, and "hat and head could—psychoanalytically—be construed as symbols and representation by displacement, of the male genitals" (224). When the father cuts down the dovecote and the pear tree it may be a jealous castration.

But Heuscher is more interested in what he calls a phenomenologic approach to the tale. He suggests that three main phases of human development can be seen in many folktales, phases related to Joseph Campbell's three divisions of the hero's quest as departure, adventure, and return (195). Heuscher's three phases are a prematerialistic period, a long period oriented toward the material world of sensory perception and physical space, and a (future) post-materialistic period (195). In "Cinderella," the actual story covers the materialistic period, one of hard work, deprivation, and concern with external circumstances. Her happy childhood while her mother was still alive was the prematerialistic period, and the memories of her mother are Cinderella's sense of a spiritual origin of her being (225). During the materialistic period, "the human being, alone and covered with the dirt of the physical world, still tries to separate the nourishing lentils and peas from the worthless ashes" (208). That is, during this period Cinderella strives for authenticity, struggling to integrate her spiritual longing with her earthly existence. The three balls are moments of temporary escape for the soul, anticipation of the third stage in which Cinderella will be accepted for what she truly is. Each of her excursions to the ball strengthens her consciousness, until she is ready to meet the prince, not dressed up in unaccustomed finery but as her everyday self. According to Heuscher, a properly fitting slipper "allows a harmonious balance of the human being between his erect posture that points upward and the horizontal earth that he must not ignore" (157). The fitting of the slipper signals the beginning of the future post-materialistic period. The prince's castle "represents a meaningful world and body in which spirit and matter are integrated" (208).

1974: In their introduction to "Cinderella," the Opies make sense of the tabu that makes Cinderella leave the ball early, whether she does so of her own accord or is warned by her fairy godmother that the magic will vanish at midnight. It is a common folktale motif that the hero cannot be won by a suitor until she or he is recognized in her "mundane, degraded state" (158). This theme is obvious in "Beauty and the Beast," for example. So Cinderella must remain the beautiful unknown at the balls and cannot allow the prince to catch her as she escapes. The prince must follow the clue of the lost slipper (or ring) to find the woman he thinks he loves in rags and ashes as a kitchen maid. The Opies cite Mme d'Aulnoy's version as the only one that omits this imperative, but Perrault's "Cendrillon," a translation of which follows their introduction, also does so. In Perrault's story, a court gentleman, not the prince himself, goes around the town with the slipper, and the fairy godmother magically dresses Cinderella in magnificent clothes again before she is taken to the prince. Perhaps the court gentleman with the shoe, who finds Cinderella "very handsome" and insists that she try on the slipper, serves as proxy for the prince.

1975: Bettelheim reads "Cinderella" partly as a story about sibling rivalry, which has its source in the child's feeling that she is less loved by the parents than the sibling, and in the child's fear of rejection by the parents. There is also a connection to toilet training and the whole process of teaching children to be clean and neat. Children may feel worthless because they can never meet their parents' standards in this regard, and the despised Cinderella is both dirty and ragged. The child may also feel that her Oedipal wishes are dirty and relegate her to the dirty ashes of the hearth. But the hearth is also a symbol for the mother, the center of the home. "Seen in this light, at the story's beginning Cinderella mourns not only the loss of the original mother, but also grieves at the loss of her dreams about the wonderful relation she was going to have with her father" (248). Her mother (and Oedipal rival) is dead, but her father has supplanted Cinderella by remarrying.

The hazel twig Cinderella asks for and receives from her father is a sign that their relationship is being reestablished. The tree on the mother's grave, planted by Cinderella and watered by her tears, "symbolizes that the memory of the idealized mother from infancy, when kept alive as an important part of one's internal experience, can and does support us even in the worst adversity" (257).

Modern, popular versions of the story, based on Perrault, conceal Cinderella's Oedipal conflict behind the sibling rivalry and Cinderella's incomparable goodness. The nastiness of the stepmother and stepsisters is more than enough explanation for Cinderella's situation. Because Perrault's Cinderella is much kinder and much more passive than the Cinderellas of other versions, the theme of maturation, which requires becoming independent of one's parents, is obscured. Perrault's story also leaves out the self-mutilation of the stepsisters common to most other versions. According to Bettelheim, this cutting off of toe or heel is an expression of the castration anxiety felt by both male and female children. The stepsisters cut off a part of their bodies to become more feminine and worthy of marriage. On the other hand, the famous slipper is a symbol of the female vagina. In offering Cinderella the slipper, although she is still dressed in her dirty rags, the prince "symbolically offers her femininity" (271) and signals his acceptance of her vagina/female sexuality. Cinderella, in taking the slipper and putting it on herself, welcomes her own femininity. The prince selects Cinderella "because she is the uncastrated woman who relieves him of his castration anxiety." "She selects him because he appreciates her in her 'dirty' sexual aspects, lovingly accepts her vagina in the form of a slipper, and approves of her desire for a penis, symbolized by her tiny foot fitting within the slipper-vagina" (271). In sum, the Cinderella story represents the stages of self-development: basic trust in the good mother, autonomy, initiative, industry, and identity. At the end, Cinderella is ready for true intimacy with another.

1977: The Meinhardts find in "Cinderella" a record of the transition from matriarchal tribal society to the patriarchal merchant society of the late seventeenth century. The tale also forecasts the problems created by the development of the nuclear family as the social norm. Cinderella is isolated, demoralized, devalued by the drudgery of housework, and imprisoned in the nuclear family. The fairy godmother is the female power of creation, all the goddesses, witches, and wise woman figures of the Old Religion.

Cinderella, with the help of the fairy godmother, takes control of her household power, which is the power of household creation.

1980: Derek Brewer produces a very funny literalistic and literary reading of Perrault's "Cinderella" that makes Cinderella and the prince a very stupid pair, justifies the stepmother's behavior, and turns Cinderella into the villain of the tale. His point is that any useful interpretation of a story must meet the story on its own ground. In the case of Perrault's "Cinderella," readers and interpreters must identify themselves with the protagonist and realize that everything in the story is seen through her eyes. Like any child, she knows that she has good qualities that no one recognizes, that she is treated unfairly by her parents and sisters, and that her parents would help her if they knew what the trouble was. But they don't know, and she can't tell them. The inability to tell one's parents things, the gulf between child and parents, "is a fundamental *donnée* of the whole Cinderella complex, because it is also inevitable in the process of growing up" (21).

Brewer goes on to suggest that both the stepmother and the godmother are versions of the mother figure, the former the aspect that reproaches the child, the latter the aspect that is the all-powerful, benevolent source of everything the child wants. The stepsisters belong on the stepmother's side through most of the tale, but at the end Cinderella lovingly forgives them. They may, therefore, be projections of Cinderella's unconscious contempt for herself. Once she is truly recognized and truly accepts herself, she has forgiven herself and no longer needs to sit and sulk in the ashes.

Other versions of Cinderella, among which Brewer includes stories belonging to tale type 510B, have a larger role for the father. In these, Cinderella's ambivalent feelings for her father have a correspondingly larger place in the story. In the stories of tale type 510B, which have incestuous fathers, the father's desire for his daughter is a projection of her desire for him. Cinderella flees from him because she doesn't really want to marry her father; she wants to marry a younger man outside the family. The father may be a helper as well as a focus of his daughter's resentment. In the Grimms' tale, for example, he brings her the hazel twig. Brewer argues that "Both other people and helpful animals, magic trees, etc., are 'splits' of parent-figures and thus aid in the working out of the set of tensions set up in the family drama in an entirely convincing yet completely non-naturalistic way" (27–28).

1982: Aarland Ussher reads "Cinderella" as "a very sensitive allegory for the Soul's discovery of its Image—that Image which lives hidden, like an invisible spark among the ashes, in the humdrum hours and tasks" (195). By "Image," Ussher seems to mean the creative idea or insight that can be apprehended only by intuition or spiritual vision, not produced by rational thought. The hazel twig is the Tree of Life, and the lentils in the ashes represent Cinderella herself, "a seed of imaginative life amid the cold ash of dead and self-glorifying mental concepts" (196). The axes and hammers the father and prince use to break down the dovecote and cut down the tree are will and reason, tools that are useless in the pursuit of "fleeting inspiration" (197). The third day of the ball is the third day of resurrection. The pitch on the stairs is "the dense, dark stuff of our subconscious," "the element of the toiling earth" in which Cinderella has lived (198). The blinding of the stepsisters reminds us that "imagination . . . is nothing but the deeper apprehension of reality—the conventional valuations are blinded because they are already blind" (199).

1982: According to Jane Yolen, "The wrong Cinderella has gone to the American ball" (297). The American image of Cinderella, loved by millions and criticized by feminists, is a mixture of Perrault's selfless, feminine Cendrillon, "spun-sugar caricatures" of tougher European and Asian Cinderellas, and the Disney Cinderella who is "a coy, helpless dreamer, a 'nice' girl who awaits her rescuer with patience and a song" (297). The true Cinderella is "a shrewd, practical girl persevering and winning a share of the power" (296). She is tough and resilient and hasn't a trace of Perrault's gentility or Disney's dreamy cuteness. She doesn't go from rags to riches but from riches to rags to riches, getting back what was hers to begin with. She doesn't wait to be rescued by fairy godmother, mice, or prince, but plants and cultivates her own source of help. She outwits stepmother, father, and prince as she chooses. She may well wish, but she also takes proper action. "To make Cinderella less than she is, then, is a heresy of the worst kind. It cheapens our most cherished dreams, and it makes a mockery of the true magic inside all of us—the ability to change our own lives, the ability to control our own destinies" (299).

1983: Ann and Barry Ulanov use the story of Cinderella to explore envy from Jungian psychological and Christian theological perspectives. Cinderella and her sisters are the two sides of the envy complex most of us harbor. They explore psychologically what it feels

like to envy and be envied, the central role of the mother, envy between the sexes, and envy that attacks the very good that it longs
for. In the second part of the book, they explore envy theologi-
cally: as a major sin, its effect on spiritual integrity, and its effect
on our sexual identity. Cinderella is read as a female Christ figure, refused and attacked by envy.

1987:   Ruth Bottigheimer points out that in the Grimms' version Cinderella herself works magic. She makes use of two spells. The first is
the verse with which she calls the doves, the turtledoves, and all
the birds of the air to her aid. The second is the verse she speaks to
the tree to get her fine clothes. Cinderella gets her power from her
mother, who transmits it to her daughter through the twig Cinderella plants on her grave (42–45). Although Bottigheimer does
not explicitly draw my conclusion, it seems to me that being able
to command the birds of the air and the tree makes Cinderella a
forceful and active character.

1987:   Maria Tatar notes that Cinderella, like so many of the Grimm
heroines, gets her man and social promotion through a combination of hard domestic labor and supernaturally enhanced beauty
(118). Equally typical are the passive or absent father and the
complete villainy of the stepmother (who is a stand-in for the
mother). The Grimm tales, with the exception of "Thousandfurs"
("Allerleirauh," Grimms' number 65), "dramatize female Oedipal conflicts in unique fashion" (155). Maternal malice is heightened, and paternal erotic pursuit of the daughter is suppressed.
Although folktales are enduringly popular because they mirror
inner realities, not social realities, "they are nonetheless reshaped
and modified by the cultural setting in which they are told and
retold" (155). The Grimms reshaped and modified their tales to
make them acceptable as stories for children at the beginning of
the nineteenth century.

1988:   In *The Brothers Grimm,* Jack Zipes marks the changes over time in
the Cinderella type of heroine. In some of its earliest forms, the
"Cinderella" tale type reflects a matrilineal society (circa 7000
BCE) in which the young woman at the center of the story actively
completes her quest with the help of her dead mother. By approximately 3000 BCE, Cinderella had become "a helpless, inactive
pubescent girl, whose major accomplishments are domestic, and
who must obediently wait to be rescued by a male" (141).
The tale, therefore, was already patriarchalized within the oral

tradition. There are still traces of matrilineal elements in two of the first three important literary versions of "Cinderella." Basile's Zezolla kills her first wicked stepmother, and the Grimms have the dead mother who guides Cinderella and helps her in the form of a dove and a tree. Perrault cuts all matrilineal connections by inventing the fairy godmother. All three of these versions insist that Cinderella must be domesticated before she can marry and that she be rescued from misery by a king or prince. The Perrault and Grimm versions came to dominate the literary tradition of "Cinderella." As a result, "An oral tale (without illustrative frills) that once celebrated the ritualistic initiation of a girl entering womanhood in a matrilineal society had been transformed within a literate code that prescribed the domestic requirements in bourgeois Christian society necessary for a young woman to make herself acceptable for marriage" (142).

1988:   Jack Zipes, in his article "On the Use and Abuse of Folk and Fairy Tales with Children," challenges Bettelheim's analysis of folk-tales, using his chapter on Cinderella as an example. Any folktale Bettelheim deals with is "transformed into a symbolic parable of self-realization and healthy sexuality" (66). Zipes argues that any psychoanalytic approach to "Cinderella" must take into account the social context in which it is told. He summarizes August Nitschke's investigation of the oldest traceable context of the tale to make his point. According to Nitschke, "Cinderella" can be dated back to the late Ice Age. The hero is a woman who receives help and gifts both from her dead mother living on as a tree and from animals. The story reflects a hunting and grazing society in which women were at the center, honored as the nurturing element.

In today's society, Zipes goes on, "instead of doing homage to women, we have a tale which is an insult to women" (68). The insult lies in the following elements of the story: The stepmother is wicked, but the father isn't; Cinderella is essentially industrious, dutiful, virginal, and passive; girls quarrel over a man; all men are handsome; marriage is the goal of life; and it is important to marry a rich man. This list suggests that "the ideological and psychological pattern of and message of *Cinderella* do nothing more than reinforce sexist values and a Puritan ethos that serves a society which fosters competition and achievement for survival" (68).

1989: Joyce Thomas writes about Cinderella's shoe as the object that in effect defines the tale. The shoe functions "as the physical nexus of the tale's action and theme" (196). At the beginning of the story Cinderella is covered by ashes and rags. Then she is dressed by magic in a regal dress and shoes that reflect her inner purity and foreshadow her transformation into a princess at the end of the tale. The contrast between Cinderella's two states of appearance raises a question: "[I]s Cinderella the future princess *despite* her physical appearance and lowly state, or is she the princess *because* of that appearance and state?" (201). The symbolic meaning of the ashes from which she gets her name suggests that she is both the princess and the ragged, overworked stepchild, not just a princess in disguise. Ashes belong to the hearth, the center of the home. As well, they signify purity, are used for ritual cleansing, and mark the initiate in initiation rites. They are also a sign of mourning, in this case Cinderella's for her mother. The ashes themselves are not degrading, but the way the stepmother and stepsisters see them is. Cinderella acts as a princess all along. The main theme of the story is not reversal of fortune but "the inability to apprehend appearance's reality, reality's appearance" (203). The lost shoe stuck in the pitch the prince has spread on the palace steps is a dual image that captures this theme. The golden shoe is properly part of the prince's world. The black, dirty pitch is properly part of Cinderella's world. Yet the shoe is Cinderella's and the pitch is spread by the prince. "In actuality, appearance and reality are one, are not at odds with each other except as other people choose to see them that way" (278).

1991: Considering the relationships between fathers and daughters in romantic folktales, McGlathery concludes that fathers are usually devoted to their children but are hindered in acting on that devotion by their second wives, the stepmothers. In Basile's "The Cat Cinderella" and the Grimms' "Cinderella," the father brings his daughter the instrument of her escape from the tyranny of her stepmother. According to McGlathery, in the Grimm tale the hazel twig that will be planted on Cinderella's mother's grave "may suggest that he secretly harbors a devotion to the dead wife that has transferred itself to the daughter" (92).

In the chapter on "Hags, Witches, and Fairies," McGlathery compares Cinderella's helpers in the Basile, Perrault, and Grimm tales. In Grimm, the magic—tree and birds—comes from the dead mother's grave and is her agent. In Perrault, the fairy is a magical substitute for the mother: Cendrillon's godmother. In Basile's

"The Cat Cinderella," Zezolla's mother has nothing to do with it. The doves, the date twig, and the fairy come directly from the magic island of Sardinia, and the tree is a projection of the girl's own secret and only half-conscious romantic desire. In all three versions of the story, though, Cinderella is not a passive figure like Sleeping Beauty. McGlathery sees her "as a maiden engaged in skillfully fetching herself a prince" (188).

1992:   Maria Tatar points out the contrast between tale type 510A, "Cinderella," and tale type 510B, "The Dress of Gold, of Silver, and of Stars" in their representation of Oedipal conflict. She notes that the latter, which she calls "Catskin," has a stronger resemblance to tale type 706, "The Maiden Without Hands," because both are stories about girls who are victims of a father's incestuous desire. Their fathers love them too much and inappropriately. Cinderella, on the other hand, has a mother who doesn't love her (step)daughter enough. "The two stories ['Cinderella' and 'Catskin'] give us different aspects of one plot—each demonizing only one of the two parental actors in that drama of family conflict" (127).

1994:   Marina Warner writes that "Fairy tales like 'Cinderella' bear witness against women" (210). She finds explanations for the absent mother and cruel stepmother both in social history and in the literary and interpretive traditions of the folktales. Warner argues that the absent mother in folktales is a historical reality that analysts like Bettelheim wrongly ignore. Many children grew up with stepmothers because death in childbirth was the most common cause of female mortality before our modern era. When resources were scarce, the stepmother and her children could well feel that they were in competition with children from the first marriage. The Grimms did change mothers into stepmothers to tone down the harshness of the material they were working with. The natural mother, safely dead, could continue to represent the essential goodness of the ideal. This editing of their material by the Grimms fueled Bettelheim's theory of the split image of the parent: the stepmother on whom the child can safely pin resentment and anger, and the dead natural mother as a different person who provided the first and most fundamental security for the child (212).

Warner describes the silence of and about Cinderella's father as "a lost piece of the puzzle" (347). In modern versions of the tale, he too is dead and therefore cannot control his women; or he is hen-pecked into submissiveness, a second victim of the wicked stepmother. But in the Grimms' "Cinderella," the father who does nothing to defend his daughter from her stepmother and stepsisters is violent in helping the prince pursue her. He smashes the dovecote and cuts down the pear tree in which she hid on the first and second nights of the ball. "This Cinderella hides from both prince and father, though why the latter should pursue her so savagely has been scrambled and fallen out of the tale" (348). With her usual good sense, Warner continues: "Such silences help the stories to reverberate, however, as the father's crazed conduct sends shivers through the listener or reader" (348). Taking history and the complexities of transmission into account, Warner reminds us that a folktale is more powerful than any explanations of it.

1996: Nicole Lehnert looks at the female characters in the Grimms' collection of tales and finds that they predominantly correspond to the ideal of womanhood held in early nineteenth-century Germany. She describes that ideal as having the following characteristics: childlike naiveté; beauty; silence (keeping silent may even be one of the tests the folktale heroine must pass); modesty and humility; empathy, selflessness, and helpfulness; renunciation of revenge (punishment for the wicked is meted out by magical powers like Cinderella's doves or by the heroine's rescuer); faithfulness (to father, brothers, or bridegroom); diligence and domesticity; and a close connection with nature (Cinderella's doves and hazel tree) (25–31). Lehnert uses "Little Red Riding Hood," "Snow White," "Cinderella," and "Rumpelstiltskin" as examples.

Cinderella has all of these characteristics and is by far the most hardworking of the protagonists studied. Lehnert notes that Cinderella becomes increasingly silent in the successive editions of the Grimms' tales. She is given less and less direct speech, while the stepsisters, stepmother, father, and prince are given more. Silence is a characteristic of a *good* woman. Looking at the three most influential early literary versions of the tale, Lehnert points out that a progressive change in Cinderella from active, independent young woman to a domestic, obedient, and passive one can be tracked over time without going back as far as hypothetical matrilineal societies during the Ice Age. Basile's protagonist kills her stepmother and therefore can be counted as emphatically active. Perrault emphasizes marriage as a necessary end more strongly than Basile does, and his Cinderella is helpless, diligent, and modest. The Grimms' "Cinderella" demonstrates the additional virtues of self-denial and obedience.

1997:   Margery Hourihan suggests that " 'Cinderella' depicts the desperate struggle of young women to secure an appropriate husband" (201). In "Cinderella," as in other folktales that feature a relationship between women, that relationship is a hostile one. Young women are in competition with each other, and mothers make their daughters suffer as they suffered themselves in order to please men. The stepsisters are made to mutilate themselves in the hope of winning a prince. Guilt and resentment make a mother into a folktale stepmother: Mothers feel guilty for what they do to their daughters and resent the daughters for making them feel guilty. Daughters resent their mothers for robbing them of their freedom and feel guilty because their resentment makes the mother unhappy.

Reworkings of Cinderella in Novel Form

Two of these novels are new, and two are old. The recent reissuing in paperback of the two old ones is undoubtedly due to the swelling popularity (whether among publishers or readers) of reworkings of folktales. None of these four would interest older adolescent readers, although perhaps Baker's book could attract inveterate readers of teenage series romances.

Silver Woven in My Hair

1992: Murphy, Shirley Rousseau. **Silver Woven in My Hair**. New York: Aladdin Books. [First published in 1977.]

Thursey is the daughter of an innkeeper in a medieval village surrounding the king's castle. Her father was killed in a great battle to rescue the queen and young prince, and Thursey does all the work of the inn under the bullying of her selfish stepmother and stepsisters. She listens to the travelers telling wonderful tales at night in the common room.

All these stories are variants of the same tale—Cinderella. Thursey has a friend, a monk who stays at the inn occasionally, who teaches her how to mix color and to paint. She writes the stories down and illustrates them as she sees them in her mind.

One day it is announced that the queen and prince are finally coming home to the palace, and a ball will be given. Thursey, watching the royal entourage like the rest of the village, meets the young man who herds the special goats that give the milk the prince needs to recover from his wounds and illness. They become close friends. For the ball Thursey secretly makes a dress for herself from beautiful fabric that the goatherd brought her as a gift. But the stepmother and stepsisters find it and tear it to shreds. She does go the ball in the end, though, in a muslin slip covered with roses from a legendary magical bush that grows in a swamp. She rides the inn's bony old work horse. At the ball she discovers what readers will already have guessed—that the goatherd is the prince.

At Midnight: A Novel Based on Cinderella

1995. Baker, Jennifer. **At Midnight: A Novel Based on Cinderella**. New York: Scholastic.

This book was published in the Scholastic series of teenage romances based on well-known folktales. The series is called Once Upon a Dream, and the back cover says: "Once Upon a Dream . . . where wishes really do come true." The series title is an accurate signal of the book's content, for while the phrase "Once upon a time" is mythic, "Once upon a dream" is simply wish fulfillment. This novel has only one piece of magic in it—the fairy godmother who magically fixes the dress the stepmother had torn and the (plexi?)glass slippers she had broken to stop Ella from going to the dance. The rest is relentless romantic "realism."

Ella is a high school girl whose beloved father dies of a heart attack just after he marries Lucinda, the stepmother. At their wedding, Ella fantasizes about the man she will marry some day. The prince has been sent by his royal parents to be educated at an expensive American prep school for boys. (The small kingdom he comes from is unnamed.) He spends a lot of time alone in his room surfing the Internet, because all the girls he meets only like him because he's royalty. The fairy godmother (named Fay) first appears as a woman in a shabby van who collects things for the needy. The ball is a party the prince and his friends throw so that they can meet some girls. And at the end, the prince's parents will look after Ella until the prince finishes school and they get married. They think she's a good influence on the prince because she has already helped him to set up a foundation for the needy that is getting their little kingdom a lot of great publicity.

The Glass Slipper

1995. Farjeon, Eleanor. **The Glass Slipper**. New York: Harper Trophy. [First published in 1955.]

This is the Perrault story, with some additions. Cinderella's father loves her dearly and knows there is something wrong with the way she is treated, but he is terrified of his wife. Cinderella wins the help of the fairy godmother in a traditional folktale way. In the snowy forest, gathering sticks for the fire, she gives what little food she has to the hungry birds and helps an old crone with a huge bundle of firewood. The crone, of course, is the fairy. This is the only one of the versions discussed in this chapter to use the motifs of the grateful objects that repay kindness. The kitchen things that Cinderella tends try to help her when the stepmother wants to stop her from going to the palace to try on the glass slipper. They don't succeed, but the fairy does. Cinderella gets to try on the slipper, in rags and with tangled hair, and the prince recognizes her even before she puts the slipper on.

There are a great many pleasant rhymes in the book and a good deal of humor. The back cover says it is for all ages, but the cheerful simplicity of the story would be most attractive for readers 10–14 years old.

Ella Enchanted

1997: Levine, Gail Carson. **Ella Enchanted**. New York: HarperCollins.

This novel answers the question many readers of "Cinderella" have asked: Why is she so hopelessly good and obedient? Why doesn't she stick up for herself? Ella was given a gift on the day of her birth by a fairy whose magic gifts always go hopelessly wrong. In Ella's case, the fairy had announced that Ella will always be obedient. And so she is. She can't disobey an order to save her life. The story is set in a fairy-tale kingdom with elves, ogres, and other strange creatures. Ella has two fairy helpers, not one. The first is the hapless Lucinda, who made her obedient but is of some help with the pumpkin coach for the three balls. The other is the cook, Mandy, who looks after her like a mother and will only do small magic because it's dangerous to meddle with the large.

Ella's father has little affection for her. He is only interested in marrying her off to a rich man to recoup his fortunes. Ella is sent to boarding school with the two nasty girls who will become her stepsisters. However, she runs away and gets caught up in a grand and dangerous adventure with the prince, whom she first met at her mother's funeral. The two soon fall in love. He's a very nice young man with a sense of humor as well as a sense of responsibility, but Ella can't marry him because she carries a curse that would cause his death. In the end, of course, she does. Mandy comes to live with them to be cook and godmother to their children. Ella refuses to become a princess, though. Instead, she adopts the title of Court Linguist and Cook's Helper. She and her prince live happily ever after because her contrariness keeps him laughing, and his goodness keeps her in love.

The reading audience suggested by the publisher is grades three to seven. Because this book is so metafictional, I think grades four to nine would be more appropriate.

Short Stories

Several of the stories listed here are very good indeed. But one stands out above them all: Jane Yolen's "The Moon Ribbon."

1976. Yolen, Jane. "**The Moon Ribbon**." In *The Moon Ribbon and Other Tales*. New York: Curtis Brown, 1–15. Also in *Don't Bet on the Prince: Contemporary Feminist Fairy Tales in North America and England*, edited by Jack Zipes. New York: Methuen, 1986, 81–87.

"The Moon Ribbon" is a Cinderella story without the ball, the slipper, and the prince but with all the magic and high seriousness of the wonder tale. This is how the story begins:

> There was once a plain but good-hearted girl named Sylva whose sole possession was a ribbon her mother had left her. It was a strange ribbon, the color of moonlight, for it had been woven from the gray hairs of her mother and her mother's mother and her mother's mother's mother before her. (81)

Sylva, the Cinderella figure, acts to save herself from the misery of life with her stepmother and stepsisters. Her courage comes from despair, but it is courage. Her helper, a numinous female figure whom Sylva is invited to claim as both mother and sister, teaches her that there is always a choice, and that the jewel of one's heart, oneself, can only be given with love, never under coercion. There are no men in this story, except for the father who dies on the first page "in order to have some peace" (81).

1985: Binchy, Maeve. **"Cinderella Re-Examined."** In *Rapunzel's Revenge: Fairytales for Feminists*. Dublin: Attic Press, 57–64.

Cinderella's father has given her sister Thunder the money to open a boutique and her sister Lightning the money to open a beauty parlor, but he won't give Cinderella the money to buy a franchise for a fast food chain. She stays home, keeps house, and takes correspondence courses. Six weeks before the ball Cinderella finds out that she's won the Amazing Charm Course. She would rather have the money, but that's not an option, so she agrees to do the course because she figures she can sell some of the stuff that comes with it. It turns out that part of the prize is going to the ball in rented finery that has to be given back at midnight. The prince is a drunken bore, but Cinderella enjoys herself with the king, going around the palace and pointing out all the ways in which the palace could be run more cheaply and efficiently. The prince wants to marry her, but she turns him down because "her post as Chief Executive of Palace Enterprises was going to keep her busy and very happy ever after" (64).

1990. Brooke, William J. **"The Fitting of the Slipper."** In *A Telling of the Tales: Five Stories*. New York: Harper & Row, 51–74.

The story begins at the point where the prince is trying the slipper on the feet of the stepsisters. They make a fuss; he's been at this for a long time; his Lord Chamberlain tries to move him on to the next house; and it is suddenly all too much for him. He goes through the nearest door and locks it behind him. He finds himself in a dark room with a small fire at the far end and a shadowy figure by it. Frightened, he grabs for the rough door and runs a painful sliver into the palm of his hand. The figure comes forward at his cry.

As we know but he doesn't, he is in the kitchen and the figure is Cinderella. Her voice seems familiar to him, but she keeps her face hidden. After she has first spoken, the prince tells her, "I believe that you have the most awful grammar that I have ever heard" (58). Her grammar is awful, but it's not put on as a disguise. It is the only way of speaking she knows. She said very little at the ball and carefully avoided words she knew she would mispronounce. Cinderella doesn't want to marry this prince because he isn't real; he lives in a dream world. As for herself, she thinks her stepmother will clean her up and marry her off one day to a rich merchant's son for the business connection. She will keep her house tidy and her kitchen cozy and smile when she thinks about her prince. The issue hangs fire for some time. Each of them is tempted to marry the other, but each has doubts. In the end, they take the risk and try on the slipper. It doesn't fit. But the prince declares that he will summon the royal glassblower to make her shoes that fit. "The shoe must fit the foot. It's madness to try to make the foot fit the shoe" (73).

The cover suggests a reading audiences of ages 8–12. My suggestion would be 12–16.

1990. Carter, Angela. "**Ashputtle: Or, the Mother's Ghost.**" In *The Year's Best Fantasy and Horror, 4th Annual Collection,* edited by Ellen Datlow and Terri Windling. New York: St. Martin's Press, 408–14.

The story is divided into three progressively shorter sections. The first, "The Mutilated Girls," has a narrator reflecting on the Cinderella story and its horrors. The two stepsisters are mutilated by their mother, and when Ashputtle puts on the shoe and walks around, "squelching [in the blood of her sisters] but proud," the turtledove, her mother's ghost calls out: "Her foot fits the shoe like a corpse fits a coffin! See how well I look after you, my darling!" (414).

The second section, "The Burned Child," contains the folktale motifs of the helpful animals. The mother's ghost goes into a cow, and Ashputtle thrives and grows up on the cow's milk. A man comes courting the stepmother, and Ashputtle tells the cow she wants him for herself. So the cow gives all her milk for Ashputtle to wash in. Then the mother's ghost goes into the cat, who combs Ashputtle's hair with her claws until they are all pulled out. Then the mother's ghost goes into a bird that sticks its beak in its breast and covers Ashputtle with blood that becomes a red silk dress. Ashputtle shows herself to the man, and he takes her away and gives her money and a house. " 'Now I can go to sleep,' said the ghost of the mother. 'Now everything is all right' " (415).

In the third section, "The Traveling Costume," the girl weeps on her mother's grave because her stepmother had burned her with the poker. The mother climbs out of the grave, kisses her daughter so that the scar vanishes, gives her a red dress ("I had it when I was your age, I used it for traveling"), and gives her worms from her eye sockets that turn into jewels she can sell if she needs to (415). Finally they go together to the grave, and the girl steps into her mother's coffin. It turns into a coach and horses. The last words of the story are the mother's: "Now go and seek your fortune, darling."

1996. Walker, Barbara. "**Cinder-Helle.**" In *Feminist Fairy Tales*. San Francisco, CA: HarperSanFrancisco, 189–96.

The introduction explains that "This version of the Cinderella story may be traced back to religio-political allegory, satirizing the feudal church and state (Ecclesia and Nobilita), and recalling northern Europe's indigenous worship of the Goddess Helle, or Holle, or Ella, or Hel" (189).

Cinderella's name is Helle. She is the daughter of a priestess of the Goddess who married a wealthy man. Her stepmother, "an arrogant and greedy woman," (191) is named Christiana, and the stepsisters are Ecclesia and Nobilita. Helle goes for comfort to the tree on her mother's grave, and on Hallow Eve she makes a harvest charm as her mother had taught her, a hollowed pumpkin with a candle inside it, and takes it to her mother's grave. The tree gives her directions for turning the pumpkin and other things into what she needs to go to the ball. The spell will work for her because she is "in her moon time" (i.e., menstruating) and therefore has magic. Menstrual blood is part of the charm. After she marries the prince, she reforms both of her stepsisters by making them live up to their pretensions. But Christiana dies unsatisfied.

This mixture of Perrault, folktale, and goddess lore is far too didactic to make a satisfying story.

1997: Donoghue, Emma. "**The Tale of the Shoe.**" In *Kissing the Witch: Old Tales in New Skins*. New York: Joanna Cotler Books/HarperCollins, 1–11.

Cinderella is tormented by her grief over her mother's death, not by a stepmother. "Whatever I put on my back now turned to sackcloth and chafed my skin" (1). There are only two characters in the story, Cinderella and the fairy godmother. Whether the fairy godmother really is magical is not clear. She is a woman who breaks into Cinderella's grief and gives her mother back again by showing the girl the hazel tree on her mother's grave. Cinderella asks to be taken to the ball because that's what girls are supposed to want. She is looking to make her fortune as society expects her to. On the third night, when the prince is about to propose, she runs away, leaving one shoe behind. The fairy godmother is waiting for her, as she waited the other two nights. Cinderella realizes she had got the story all wrong. It is her godmother she wants, not the prince. She tosses the other shoe into the bushes and goes away with the fairy godmother. A powerful psychological reading of "Cinderella" that turns it into a story about grief and a girl's discovery of her love for another woman.

1997. Lee, Tanith. "**The Reason for Not Going to the Ball (A Letter to Cinderella from Her Stepmother).**" In *The Year's Best Fantasy and Horror, 10th Annual Collection*, edited by Ellen Datlow and Terri Windling. New York: St. Martin's Griffin, 45–49.

This is the stepmother's explanation of the story, and a grimly interesting one. She married Cinderella's father because Cinderella reminded her of herself as a girl and because she knew Cinderella's father was cruelly deviant. As Cinderella's stepmother, she could protect the girl from being raped by her father. To that end she kept her dirty and dressed in rags and out of sight in the kitchen. The stepmother tried to keep Cinderella from going to the ball because she had the prince investigated and knew he was abusive and a sadist. But she failed. Now she writes to offer Cinderella help: a trusted servant to take her away and a house she has bought for her as a refuge. She hopes Cinderella will read this letter rather than throw it in the fire because her stepmother hid her in cold cinders.

We have only the letter. What Cinderella did, we will have to imagine.

Feature Films

Although two of the three films in this section are Disney products, their effect is very different. Because *Snow White* was the first of the Disney animated films based on folktales, the chapter on "Snow White" contains an extended examination of the Disney Studio's approach to and impact on folktales.

1950: **Cinderella**. Produced by Walt Disney. Directed by Wilfred Jackson, Clyde Geronimi, and Hamilton Luske.

The Disney *Cinderella* is based on Perrault's version of the tale. The film exonerates the father from any responsibility for Cinderella's misery by having him die right at the beginning. The comically plain stepsisters are petty and mean to Cinderella, but the stepmother truly hates her. We are told that she is a cold, cruel woman who is jealous of Cinderella's charm and beauty; Disney has stepped up maternal malice and the rivalry between mother and daughter a notch further. Cinderella is so completely the victim that she is harassed even by Lucifer, the cat.

Cinderella is lovely, good, nice, patient, and forgiving. She is also hardworking, and clean and neat no matter how hard she works. There are no ashes on *her*. She is very kind to animals but not much use to herself. Even when her stepmother manages to break the glass slipper just before Cinderella is to try it on, Cinderella offers the slipper she has in her pocket—not with any air of triumph or self-vindication, but just to be helpful. She only dreams and sings of being rescued and is instantly discouraged by any setback. Her animal helpers are cute mice with nothing magical about them; they have no more power than Cinderella does. They play a pivotal role, however, in a moment that is entirely Disney's invention. When the Grand Duke comes to the house with the glass slipper, the stepmother locks Cinderella in her garret. The mice steal the key from the stepmother's pocket and with enormous exertion and courage free Cinderella so that she may have her chance to try on the slipper.

Animals have a large part in this film, but they have nothing to do with natural forces. Nicole Lehnert has pointed out that the folktale heroine is close to nature. Cinderella de-natures the animals she loves. She recommends to Bruno, the dog, that he learn to like cats for the sake of peace in the household. The first thing she does when a new mouse is added to her substitute family of furry and feathered friends is dress him in shirt, shoes, and hat and give him a human name—Gus.

The fairy godmother is a cuddly, plump little old lady. She does her job, after some confusion about where she put her wand, and gets Cinderella to the ball, but as a fairy she is a disappointment. She is cozy rather than numinous, and the key words in her magic spells are not words of power but the comical refrain "Bibbity Bobbity Boo." When she notices, at the last minute, that Cinderella is in rags, she sets to work like a good dressmaker, checking measurements with her wand and taking into account the color of Cinderella's eyes. The ball gives the film an unparalleled opportunity to emphasize beauty as a woman's salvation. As Maria Tatar points out, "the amount of footage devoted in 'Cinderella' to the perennially 'female' problem of what to wear is extraordinary" (1992, 138).

1990: **Ashpet: An American Cinderella**. Davenport Films. Directed by Tom Davenport. Delaplane, VA.

Another in Tom Davenport's series *From the Brothers Grimm*, this version of "Cinderella" is set in the Appalachians in the early 1940s. The ball is a "victory dance" for soldiers going overseas. The part of the fairy godmother was written for the African American storyteller Louise Anderson, who added her own lines to the screenplay (Davenport, xi). According to Zipes, "*Ashpet* is about a young white woman's reclaiming her proper heritage through the help of a wise black woman, whose sense of history and knowledge of oppression empowers the enslaved 'Lily' to pursue her dreams" (Davenport, vii).

Lily's father and mother are dead, and her stepmother and stepsisters make her do all the work to "earn her keep." They call her Ashpet because she has to sleep in the chimney corner and always has ashes in her hair and on her face. Lily tries to run away and get a job at the nearby army base, but the stepsisters find out her plan and stop her. When a dance is announced for soldiers going overseas, the stepsisters go to Dark Sally, the old washerwoman, for love charms. But they can't answer her riddles (a classic folktale test) and don't get the charms, so they send Lily to ask Dark Sally again. Lily answers the riddles and gets a charm for herself. After Lily is left at home alone, Dark Sally shows Lily her dead mother's clothes in the attic, and Lily goes to the ball in her mother's gown and silver dancing shoes, riding her father's old horse. She dances all night with a soldier named William, and when she has to rush off to get home before her stepmother and stepsisters, she loses one of her shoes. The next morning, William arrives with the shoe to find his partner of the night before. William can see at once that neither of the stepsisters is the one he's looking for. They deny that there's any other young woman living in the house, but when he turns to go, he sees Lily standing outside in her old tattered dress, holding a suitcase. He claims her immediately, kisses her, tells her he'll be back, and has to leave to join his troop. Lily goes to live with Dark Sally.

1997: **Rodgers and Hammerstein's Cinderella**. The Wonderful World of Disney and Whitney Houston.

This musical was commissioned as a movie for prime time television and first broadcast on CBS in 1957. It was produced and filmed again in 1965, and for a third time in 1997.

The very first thing one notices about this film is the marvelous disregard of race and color. Whitney Houston plays the fairy godmother, Brandy plays Cinderella with her hair in hundreds of thin braids, and Whoopi Goldberg is the prince's mother; all three are African Americans. The prince, a new actor named Paolo Montalban, is an extraordinarily handsome product of a mixture of races. His father, the king, Victor Garber, is white, as is the stepmother, Bernadette Peters. One of her daughters is white, the other African American. The crowd scenes also show a fine mixture of skin colors. The genetic logic is no doubt faulty, but the effect is a complete delight. A change in the trying on of the slipper is less obvious but equally revolutionary. It still fits only Cinderella, but several of the many feet that we see trying on the slipper are too small for it rather than too large!

The plot line is Perrault's with one exception. In the opening sequence, Cinderella and the prince wander around a crowded marketplace singing the same song about waiting for love. (The prince is incognito, mingling with his people.) They pass close by each other several times but don't meet until she is knocked over by a passing carriage and he helps her up. He is instantly smitten, and in a short chat they discover that they have a lot in common. The point is that the prince is first attracted to Cinderella in her everyday clothes, as she really is, rather than in her finery for the ball. It's too bad that when he sees her at the ball he doesn't recognize her at once, as Basile's king recognizes his Cinderella. But that would have brought the story to an end too soon.

Hammerstein introduced a number of other new wrinkles in expanding the Perrault tale to the length of a musical film. All of them are amusing, but perhaps the funniest is the scene in which the stepmother insists on trying on the slipper too. The general tone of the film is humorous. The stepmother is cynical and silkily sardonic, and ridiculous in her desperation to get her daughters married off. The queen is just as desperate to arrange a marriage for her son. The fairy godmother is powerful but hip. Everybody gets clever lines except for the prince and Cinderella. Cinderella innocently asks her stepmother: "Shouldn't a man love you for who you are in spite of everything?" and the stepmother replies, "This isn't about love, it's about *marriage!*" And when Cinderella protests that her dead father is still alive in her heart, the stepmother answers softly, "*Don't* cling to the past. It's not very attractive." Cinderella and the prince have to play it straight as dreamy, soulful young lovers. The quirky, funny supporting cast make them look like paper dolls—beautiful but flat. The fairy godmother does have to spell out the moral message that nothing is holding Cinderella back but her own fears: "The music is in you, deep down in your soul, and when you find it, nothing will be able to keep you from walking out that door."

Poetry

Both men and women seem to find in "Cinderella" dark meanings that contrast sharply with the highly colored, hopeful novels and films made of this story. Most of these poems speak of anguish and despair, and almost none has a happy ending.

1925. Reid, Dorothy E. "**Coach into Pumpkin.**" In *Coach into Pumpkin*. New York: AMS Press, 40. Also in *Disenchantments: An Anthology of Modern Fairy Tale Poetry*, edited by Wolfgang Mieder. Hanover, NH: University Press of New England, 73.

A woman named Ellen sat by the fireside as a girl and read the story of Cinderella. She is now a farmer's wife who has given up her dreams. But her daughter, Eleanora, now sits by the fire, dreaming. Ellen, her husband Elmer, and young Eleanora all have names with part of Cinderella in them. Do all young people see themselves as fairy-tale heroes when they are young, and lose something by settling for everyday reality when they grow up?

1946. Roberts, Elizabeth Madox. "**Cinderella's Song**." In *A Pocket Full of Rhymes*, edited by Katherine Love. New York: Thomas Y. Crowell, 54. Also in *Disenchantments: An Anthology of Modern Fairy Tale Poetry*, edited by Wolfgang Mieder. Hanover, NH: University Press of New England, 74.

In this apparently simple and childish poem of four verses Cinderella speaks to her little cat. She tells the cat that it is she whose foot the slipper fits and that her dress was gold. But then she says the dress was blue and that it will come to her again. A number of meanings could be made out of the poem depending on how one reads the last two verses.

1947. Weaver, Edith. "**Lost Cinderella**." In *Poetry* 70:2, 69–70. Also in *Disenchantments: An Anthology of Modern Fairy Tale Poetry*, edited by Wolfgang Mieder. Hanover, NH: University Press of New England, 76.

A wealthy child lives a privileged life, protected from inconvenience and danger. But something has changed, and she sits by the fire crying over the dead sparrow she holds. What that something is, is left for the reader to puzzle out.

1960. Pickard, Cynthia. "**Cinderella**." In *Poetry for Pleasure: The Hallmark Book of Poetry*. Garden City, NJ: Doubleday, 59. Also in *Disenchantments: An Anthology of Modern Fairy Tale Poetry*, edited by Wolfgang Mieder. Hanover, NH: University Press of New England, 79.

Cinderella is overworked and trapped in her life with the stepmother. Her godmother gave her rest, beauty, and the standing of a queen. In exchange for a bucket of water she gave her the freedom of a running stream.

1969. Jarrell, Randall. "**Cinderella**." In *The Complete Poems*. New York: Farrar, Straus & Giroux, 217–18. Also in *Disenchantments: An Anthology of Modern Fairy Tale Poetry*, edited by Wolfgang Mieder. Hanover, NH: University Press of New England, 77–78.

There's an imaginary fairy godmother in this poem, and a prince, and an unhappy marriage. More than that I find difficult to work out.

1974. Ahmed-ud-Din, Feroz. "**Cinderella**." In *This Handful of Dust*. Calcutta: Writers Workshop, 16. Also in *Disenchantments: An Anthology of Modern Fairy Tale Poetry*, edited by Wolfgang Mieder. Hanover, NH: University Press of New England, 82.

The pumpkin carriage and the ball become a metaphor for death.

1974. Hussey, Anne. "**Cinderella**." In *Best Poems of 1974*, edited by Waddell Austin et al. Palo Alto, CA: Pacific Books, 71. Also in *Disenchantments: An Anthology of Modern Fairy Tale Poetry*, edited by Wolfgang Mieder. Hanover, NH: University Press of New England, 83.

Cinderella is a phoenix rising from the ashes. The prince has only the glass slipper and a note from her addressed to Dear Sir.

1975. French, Mary Blake. "**Ella of the Cinders**." In *Convocation! Women in Writing*, edited by Valerie Harms. Tampa, FL: United Sisters, 98. Also in *Disenchantments: An Anthology of Modern Fairy Tale Poetry*, edited by Wolfgang Mieder. Hanover, NH: University Press of New England, 83.

A six-line declaration of independence by Cinderella. She rejects society's image of women.

1977. Broumas, Olga. "**Cinderella**." In *Beginning with O*. New Haven, CT: Yale University Press, 57–58. Also in *Disenchantments: An Anthology of Modern Fairy Tale Poetry*, edited by Wolfgang Mieder. Hanover, NH: University Press of New England, 85–86.

A woman speaks of the bitterness of her success in a man's world. Playing by men's rules, she is isolated from other women and feels she has betrayed her sisters. She longs to return to them again, even though it means giving up the physical comforts of the prosperous life that is killing her spirit.

1980. Fisher, Aileen. "**Cinderella Grass**." In *Put in the Dark and Daylight*. New York: Harper & Row, 114. Also in *Disenchantments: An Anthology of Modern Fairy Tale Poetry*, edited by Wolfgang Mieder. Hanover, NH: University Press of New England, 91.

An ice storm has coated the grass, twigs, weeds, and clover with glass like Cinderella's slippers. At first reading this description seems simply to be a charming simile, but it could have a darker meaning.

1980. Mitchell, Roger. "**Cinderella**." *Poetry* 137:3, 149–50. Also in *Disenchantments: An Anthology of Modern Fairy Tale Poetry*, edited by Wolfgang Mieder. Hanover, NH: University Press of New England, 87–90.

The four parts of this poem trace the stages of Cinderella's life. 1. She is mad, or seems mad. She is punished for what others find unnatural, an intimate connection with the natural world. 2. She runs away like a hunted fox, carrying a knife to defend herself from her oppressors. 3. When she knocks on the door of her sisters' house they give her a shoe and a cinder instead of the food she asked for. 4. She finds a common man, a woodcutter who drinks, nothing like a prince, but her life gives her what she needs: nature, free and in its own place.

1981. Plath, Sylvia. "**Cinderella.**" In *The Collected Poems*, edited by Ted Hughes. New York: Harper & Row, 303–4. Also in *Disenchantments: An Anthology of Modern Fairy Tale Poetry*, edited by Wolfgang Mieder. Hanover, CT: University Press of New England, 80.

Plath's poems are impossible to paraphrase. The setting is the prince's ball, and Cinderella hears the clock ticking.

1982. Hay, Sarah Henderson. "**Interview.**" In *Story Hour*. Fayetteville, AR: University of Arkansas Press, 32. Also in *Disenchantments: An Anthology of Modern Fairy Tale Poetry*, edited by Wolfgang Mieder. Hanover, NH: University Press of New England, 81.

The stepmother gives an interview to a journalist writing a story about girls who have won the Miss Glass Slipper of the Year title. The stepmother hasn't changed any, and her daughters still aren't married.

1982. Viorst, Judith. "**. . . And Then the Prince Knelt Down and Tried to Put the Glass Slipper on Cinderella's Foot.**" In *If I Were in Charge of the World*, 29. New York: Athenaeum. Also in *Don't Bet on the Prince: Contemporary Feminist Fairy Tales in North America and England*, edited by Jack Zipes. New York: Methuen, 73.

The citation and title are longer than the poem itself. In four lines Cinderella has second thoughts about the prince and decides she'll pretend the slipper doesn't fit.

1990. Strauss, Gwen. "**Cinderella.**" In *Trail of Stones*. New York: Alfred A. Knopf, 18.

Cinderella wishes she could go back to the moment when the doves brought her the golden dress on her mother's grave. The prince is looking for her with the slipper, and she is afraid, unprepared for what is coming, desiring but doubtful. Anthony Browne's illustration on the page facing this poem shows Cinderella, her face on her knees, sitting on the floor in front of the fire. The fire is a blaze of light, and above her head is a strong, sharp hook.

1991. Kushner, Ellen. "**Sonata: For Two Friends in Different Times of the Same Trouble**." In *The Year's Best Fantasy and Horror: Fourth Annual Collection*, edited by Ellen Datlow and Terri Windling. New York: St. Martin's Press, 166–67.

The speaker imagines what it would have been like for Cinderella if she had not left the ball at midnight. The result must have been like the end of a romantic relationship—to see oneself rejected, the beautiful image changed to shabbiness, the only hope another chance at another ball, the likelihood of it happening all over again. The speaker concludes that there's no comfort in real life; a traditional folktale ending would have been much better.

1993. Yolen, Jane. "**Knives**." In *Snow White, Blood Red*, edited by Ellen Datlow and Terri Windling. New York: Avon Books, 357–58.

The editors call this "a dark, unsentimental, and thoroughly adult look at the story of Cinderella" (356). Yolen plays with the images of glass and shoe to talk about the complexities of language, love, and marriage. She makes use of both Perrault's glass slipper and the Grimms' knife that the stepsisters use to cut off a part of their feet.

1995. Bull, Emma. "**The Stepsister's Story**." In *The Armless Maiden and Other Tales for Childhood's Survivors*, edited by Terri Windling. New York: Tor, 85–86.

One of the two stepsisters recognizes Cinderella at the ball because she truly loves her. She wants to call Cinderella "sister" and to rescue her. She is afraid of her own mother.

1995. Vande Velde, Vivian. "**Evidence**." In *Tales from the Brothers Grimm and the Sisters Weird*. San Diego, CA: Harcourt Brace, 107–8.

This poem poses a question about the glass slippers that many readers have asked themselves: Why didn't they vanish with the rest of the magic at midnight? The suggested answer is that the stepmother may have secretly given them to Cinderella because she wants to get rid of the girl and her irritating perfection. The last line, about Cinderella's singing, may be aimed at the Disney animated film.

Opera

1817. Rossini, Gioacchino. **La Cenerentola**. Libretto by Jacobo Ferretti. Naples, Italy.

In this version, Cinderella is persecuted by her stepfather rather than a stepmother. The issue is providing dowries for the three girls. He plans to marry off his own two daughters but ignores Cinderella, and even says she is dead. When she protests, he threatens her with violence. This is the only version I have come across in which the father is the stepparent.

The Metropolitan Opera Association staged and filmed this opera for television in 1998 in New York. The conductor was James Levine, and la Cenerentola was sung by Cecilia Bartoli. The film, a Metropolitan Opera Television Production, was directed by Brian Large.

Picture Books

1983. Perrault, Charles. **Cinderella**. Illustrated by Roberto Innocenti. Mankato, MN: Creative Education.

The text of this book is straight Perrault, but Innocenti's illustrations set the story in England in the 1920s. Cinderella's brown hair is bobbed, and her stepsisters are fashionable flappers. The royal family is a creative anachronism: Queen Victoria is still on the throne, and the prince looks a great deal like the present Charles, Prince of Wales. The pictures are full of subtle extensions of the text. For example, the first double spread shows a blind man with a guide dog walking past Cinderella's house. He could be a commentary on the father (standing behind the stepmother at the door of the house) who is blind to his new wife's mistreatment of his daughter. A blackbird watches Cinderella when she is left at home alone while the others go off to the ball; a white dove and a pigeon sit on the wall when the godmother is at work with her magic; and a peacock watches Cinderella and the prince dance at the ball. The picture on the last page shows the fate of the stepmother, bored, alone, empty bottles and fading flowers beside her on the floor, her hair dyed blond, looking out at the bare branches of wintry trees.

1988. Cole, Babette. **Prince Cinders**. New York: G. P. Putnam.

"Prince Cinders was not much of a prince. He was small, spotty, scruffy and skinny." Cole reverses the gender of Cinderella, her sisters, and the prince. The fairy is a little girl in school uniform who gets her spells wrong. The princess that marries Prince Cinders is called Lovelypenny, and instead of a slipper Cinders loses his blue jeans.

1994. Ellen Jackson. **Cinder Edna**. Illustrated by Kevin O'Malley. New York: Lothrop, Lee & Shepard.

Cinderella and Cinder Edna are neighbors. Both have a stepmother and stepsisters that make them do all the work, but Edna doesn't waste time sitting in the ashes. Instead, when her housework is done she mows lawns and cleans parrot cages for the neighbors for $1.50 an hour. Cinderella is beautiful while Cinder Edna isn't "much to look at," but she is "strong and spunky" and knows a lot of good jokes. Cinderella gets to the ball in pumpkin coach and glass slippers. Edna doesn't believe in fairy godmothers. She buys her own dress, wears comfortable loafers for dancing, and takes the bus. Cinderella marries the narcissistic prince. Edna lives happily ever after with his younger brother Rudolph "in a small cottage with solar heating," playing duets for accordion and concertina. The comment on the traditional Cinderella story is impossible to miss.

1994. Mintera, Frances. **Cinder-Elly**. Illustrated by Brian Karas. New York. Puffin.

The ball is a high school basketball game, and Cinder-Elly goes in glass sneakers. She waits for Prince Charming, the star of the team, after the game, but he takes so long blow-drying his hair and signing autographs that her ten o'clock curfew (so much more reasonable than midnight for a schoolgirl!) comes and she has to leave. The story is written in four-line verses of doggerel. *Publishers Weekly* calls this an "ultracool version of the fairy tale [that] updates the classic with singular flair" (back cover). I think that despite the presence of the fairy godmother, the story has lost all its magic.

1996. Buehner, Caralyn. **Fanny's Dream**. Illustrated by Mark Buehner. New York: Dial Books for Young Readers.

Fanny Agnes is a Wyoming farm girl who believes the story of Cinderella and confidently expects to marry a prince, or at least the mayor's son. The night of the mayor's grand ball, she waits for her fairy godmother to come and do what's necessary, but Heber Jensen shows up instead. He points out that Fanny Agnes isn't really suited for life in a castle and asks her to marry him instead. "I need a wife who will work by my side, through thick and thin, sweat and joy, and be glad for good food and great company. Will you, Fanny?" After thinking it over for an hour, Fanny says yes. The fairy godmother does come, several years and three children too late, on a night when the mayor is giving another grand ball. She wants to send Fanny, but Fanny thinks it over for a minute and says no. Text and illustrations make a beautiful picture of a good marriage.

1997. Alan Schroeder. **Smoky Mountain Rose: An Appalachian Cinderella**. Illustrated by Brad Sneed. New York: Dial Books for Young Readers.

Perrault's Cinderella is translated into Appalachian dialect and a Smoky Mountain setting. The text is a joy to read aloud, with the cadences and pacing of an oral tale. Rose gets her ball dress from a hog who knows magic: "First of all, we gotta get ye out o' them rags. Now stand up and turn around real fast, like ye got a whompus cat bitin' at yer britches." Seb, the rich "hog an' grits feller" who gives the ball, insists on trying the slipper on Rose. " 'Come over here and stick out yer foot,' Seb told her. He watched as Rose came a-walkin' toward him. 'You look mighty familiar, missy. Come on now, just set yerself down on this here bucket and stick out yer tootsie.' " The last picture shows them living happily years later, an elderly couple sitting on a porch swing, holding hands, with a contented hog lying at their feet. This reworking has all the power and delight of a traditional folktale because it seems completely unselfconscious and because the author and illustrator have respected the integrity of the tale.

Internet Resources

The Cinderella Project, found at http://www-dept.usm.edu/~engdept/cinderella/cinderella.html, was established in February 1995 and updated in December 1997. It is a text and image archive containing 12 English versions of the tale, dating from a translation of Perrault (1729) to an early American publication of 1912. These tales, according to the introduction to the project, "represent some of the more common varieties of the tale from the English-speaking world in the eighteenth, nineteenth, and early twentieth centuries." The texts may be compared horizontally or vertically or linked through the nine episodes that comprise the tale. Materials were drawn from the de Grummond Children's Literature Research Collection at the University of Southern Mississippi.

Classroom Extensions

The following suggestions may be adapted for use with other tales.

Feminist Readings

Jane Yolen's "The Moon Ribbon" and Barbara Walker's "Cinder-Helle" could both be described as feminist reworkings of the Cinderella story. Walker announces her feminist agenda in her introduction, while

Yolen lets her story stand on its own. Compare the way these two stories are told and the meanings they make of the traditional tale. Then decide which you prefer, and why. Which resonates more clearly with your own experience?

Films

The two Disney films of Cinderella were made almost 50 years apart. What does each of them have to say about the world in which we live? Has that world, or the filmmakers' view of it, changed in the years between the two films?

Perrault and the Brothers Grimm

One kind of magic is understood to come from outside oneself and one's normal experience. Another kind of magic is bound to the mystery of one's own experience, an opening to the sources of meaning within one's own experience. Perrault has a fairy godmother who makes the magic that takes Cinderella to the ball. Magic in the Grimms' tale is in the tree on her mother's grave and the doves in the tree. Cinderella speaks the spells that bring the birds to help her and that make the tree give her what she needs for the ball. Does the meaning of the magic differ in the two stories? Which of the two forms of magic do you prefer, and why?

Picture Books

Compare *Smoky Mountain Rose* by Alan Schroeder with *Cinder-Elly* by Frances Minters. Both set the story in the United States in the twentieth century. But Schroeder's story is considered a much more satisfying version of the tale than Minters's. Why?

The most frequent complaint about "Cinderella" is that the story teaches girls to be passive beauties waiting for a fairy godmother to come along and help them find a prince to marry. Is this a fair criticism of the tale itself, or should it be leveled at the writers and filmmakers who have retold the tale according to the meaning they want to make of it? Babette Cole's *Prince Cinders* is a parody and therefore a comment on the Cinderella story. Using Cole's book as a starting point, consider whether gender is crucial to the story of Cinderella. Does the protagonist have to be a young woman, and do the three characters who mistreat the protagonist have to be a stepmother and stepsisters?

Pictures and Words

Gwen Strauss writes in her introduction to *Trail of Stones* that she and illustrator Anthony Browne hoped that the collection "might open a small door into the quieter moments of transformation and reveal those dark and startling events that lie buried within the stories." Read the poem and look at the picture that faces it very carefully. How do you put the poem and the picture together? What do they reveal that lies buried within the story?

Repetition

The Grimms' "Aschenputtel" has three visits to the ball, Perrault's "Cendrillon" two, and many modern versions only one. Read the Grimm story, the Perrault story, and a modern version with only one visit to the ball. One of the Disney films would do. What function and significance does the repetition of the balls have in the tale? What difference does changing the number of the balls to two or one from three make in the story?

Bibliography

Basile, Giambattista. "The Cat Cinderella." In *The Pentameron*, translated by Sir Richard Burton. London: Spring Books, 1952, 53–69.

Bettelheim, Bruno. *The Uses of Enchantment: The Meaning and Importance of Fairy Tales*. New York: Vintage Books, 1977.

Bottigheimer, Ruth. *Grimms' Bad Girls and Bold Boys: The Moral and Social Vision of the Tales*. New Haven, CT: Yale University Press, 1987.

———. "From Gold to Guilt." In *The Brothers Grimm and Folktale*, edited by James M. McGlathery. Urbana, IL: University of Illinois Press, 1988, 192–204.

Brewer, Derek. *Symbolic Stories: Traditional Narratives of the Family Drama in English Literature*. Cambridge, England: D. S. Brewer, 1980.

Cox, Marian. *Cinderella: Three Hundred and Forty-Five Variants of Cinderella, Catskin, and Cap O'Rushes*. London: Folklore Society, 1893.

Davenport, Tom, and Gary Carden. *From the Brothers Grimm: A Contemporary Retelling of American Folktales and Classic Stories*. Fort Atkinson, WI: Highsmith Press, 1992.

Ellis, John M. *One Fairy Story Too Many: The Brothers Grimm and Their Tales*. Chicago: University of Chicago Press, 1983.

Grimm, Jacob, and Wilhelm Grimm. "Ashputtle (Cinderella)." In *Grimms' Tales for Young and Old: The Complete Stories,* translated by Ralph Manheim. Garden City, NY: Anchor Press, 1977, 83–89. [Based on the 1819 ed. of *Kinder- und Hausmärchen*]

Heuscher, Julius E. *A Psychiatric Study of Myths and Fairy Tales: Their Origin, Meaning, and Usefulness.* 2d ed. Springfield, IL: Charles C. Thomas, 1974.

Hourihan, Margery. *Deconstructing the Hero: Literary Theory and Children's Literature.* London: Routledge, 1997.

Hyman, Trina Schart. "Cut It Down and You Will Find Something at the Roots." In *The Reception of Grimms' Fairy Tales: Responses, Reactions, Revisions,* edited by Donald Haase. Detroit: Wayne State University Press, 1993, 293–300.

Lehnert, Nicole. *Brave Pinzessin oder freie Hexe? Zum bürgerlichen Frauenbild in den Grimmschen Märchen.* Münster: Professur für Frauenforschung der WWU Münster, 1996.

McGlathery, James M. *Fairy Tale Romance: The Grimms, Basile, and Perrault.* Urbana-Champaign, IL: University of Illinois Press, 1991.

Meinhardt, Lela, and Paul Meinhardt. *Cinderella's Housework Dialectics: Housework as the Root of Human Creation.* Nutley, NJ: Incunabula Press, 1977.

Morgan, Jeanne. *Perrault's Morals for Moderns.* New York: Peter Lang, 1985.

Opie, Iona, and Peter Opie. *The Classic Fairy Tales.* New York: Oxford University Press, 1974.

Perrault, Charles. "Cinderella, or the Glass Slipper." In *Beauties, Beasts and Enchantment: Classic French Fairy Tales,* translated and with an introduction by Jack Zipes. New York: New American Library, 1989.

Philip, Neil. *The Cinderella Story.* London: Penguin, 1989.

Rooth, Anna Birgitta. *The Cinderella Cycle.* Lund, Sweden: C. W. K. Gleerup, 1951.

Tatar, Maria. *The Hard Facts of the Grimms' Fairy Tales.* Princeton, NJ: Princeton University Press, 1987.

———. *Off with Their Heads! Fairy Tales and the Culture of Childhood.* Princeton, NJ: Princeton University Press, 1992.

Thomas, Joyce. *Inside the Wolf's Belly: Aspects of the Fairy Tale.* Sheffield, England: Sheffield Academic Press, 1989.

Thompson, Stith. *The Types of the Folktale: A Classification and Bibliography. A Translation and Enlargement of Antti Aarne's Verzeichnis der Märchentypen*. 2d revision. Helsinki: Academia Scientiarum Fennica, 1964. (FF Communications, no.184).

Ulanov, Ann, and Barry Ulanov. *Cinderella and Her Sisters: The Envied and the Envying*. Philadelphia: Westminster Press, 1983.

Ussher, Aarland. "The Slipper on the Stair." In *Cinderella: A Casebook*, edited by Alan Dundes. New York: Garland, 1982, 193–99. [First published in *World Review* 25 (March 1951), 50–52.]

Warner, Marina. *From the Beast to the Blonde: On Fairy Tales and Their Tellers*. London: Chatto & Windus, 1994.

Yolen, Jane. "America's Cinderella." In *Cinderella: A Casebook*, edited by Alan Dundes. New York: Garland, 1982, 294–306. [First published in *Children's Literature in Education* 8 (1977), 21–29.]

Zipes, Jack. *The Brothers Grimm: From Enchanted Forests to the Modern World*. New York: Routledge, 1988.

———. "On the Use and Abuse of Folk and Fairy Tales with Children: Bruno Bettelheim's Moralistic Magic Wand." In *How Much Truth Do We Tell the Children: The Poetics of Children's Literature*, edited by Betty Bacon. Minneapolis, MN: Marxist Editions Press, 1988, 59–73.

CHAPTER 3

THE FROG KING OR IRON HENRY

The tale of the frog, the golden ball, and the beautiful princess is known as KHM 1, the first tale in the Grimms' collection.

The youngest daughter of the king drops her golden ball into the well. The frog retrieves it after she promises that it can be her companion and playmate and to eat and sleep with her. The princess promptly forgets the promise as soon as she has her ball and returns home, leaving the frog behind. The next evening, however, when the princess is dining with her father, the frog knocks on the door and reminds the princess of her promise. The princess tries to ignore this call, but her father insists she lives up to her promise. She reluctantly allows the frog to enter the palace and to sit beside her at the table. With further urging by her father, the princess begrudgingly allows the frog to share her meal. Again, at her father's urging, the princess takes the frog up to her bedroom, but when the frog requests that he be allowed to sleep in her bed, the princess reacts with rage and throws the frog against the wall. The frog immediately is transformed into a handsome prince, and the princess is now quite pleased to be able to keep her promise. The next morning, the prince's carriage and his faithful servant arrive. As the prince and princess ride away to his kingdom, the three iron bands around the servant's chest break, one by one. These bands were applied to keep Henry's heart from breaking while his master had been under the spell.

Tale Type: AT 440

The Frog King or Iron Henry. A maiden promises herself to a frog in a spring. The frog comes to the door, the table, the bed. Turns into a prince.

I. *Promise to Marry the Frog.* (a) To the youngest of three sisters a frog in a spring gives clear water (a ball thrown into the water). (b) In return he exacts a promise that the girl shall marry him.

II. *Reception of the Frog.* (a) Though the girl has forgotten her promise, the frog appears at her door and requests entrance. (b) He then sleeps at the door, on the table, and finally in her bed.

III. *Disenchantment.* The frog is disenchanted and becomes a prince (a) by being allowed to sleep in the girl's bed, (b) by a kiss, (c) by decapitation, (d) by being thrown against the wall, or (e) by having his frog-skin burnt.

IV. *Iron Henry.* His faithful servant has three iron bands around his heart to keep it from breaking; at his master's rescue the bands snap one by one.

Motifs:

L50: Victorious youngest daughter

C41.2: Tabu: letting ball fall into water

G423: Ball falling into water puts person into ogre's (witch's, water spirit's) power

B211.7.1: Speaking frog

S215.1: Girl promised herself to an animal suitor

D195: Transformation: man to frog

K1361.1: Transformed person sleeps before a girl's door, at the foot of the bed, in the bed

B654.1.2: Marriage to person in frog form

D734: Disenchantment of animal by admission to woman's bed

D735.1: Disenchantment of animal by being kissed by a woman

D711: Disenchantment by decapitation

D712.3: Disenchantment by slinging against something

D721.3: Disenchantment by destroying skin (covering)

L162: Lowly heroine marries prince (king)

F875: Iron bands around heart to keep it from breaking. When master is disenchanted, bands around heart of faithful servant snap one by one (Thompson, 149–50).

A History of the Frog King or Iron Henry

The history of the tale has not survived in any great detail. The best-known rendition of it was the one captured in print by the Brothers Grimm.

The Frog King in Oral Tradition

The Opies state that the tale has long been known in England, but no satisfactory text has been preserved. It appears to have been listed in the *Complaynt of Scotland* (1549) but not recorded in narrative form until 1842 by Robert Chambers. He apparently learned it from Charles Kilpatrick Sharpe, who had learned it from his Annadale nurse about the year 1784. This fragmentary tale was put together by Joseph Jacobs for his *English Fairy Tales* (1890) (Opie, 239). The Opies state that when Sir Walter Scott saw the tale in the Grimms' collection, he remembered it as a tale he heard in his childhood (he was born in 1771) (238). However, "despite the fact that the story . . . had . . . been common property in Scotland for three hundred years, and that it was known, also, in Ireland and in Somerset . . . the Grimm brothers in Hesse were the first to set down a complete telling of the tale" (239).

The Frog King in Print: The Brothers Grimm

The setting for this tale in the 1810 manuscript is simple and lacking in frills; there is no castle, the incident seems to take place on a large estate, and the king's daughter could be the daughter of a peasant. The frog has no desire other than to sleep with the girl, and this is made clear in the narrative, which is sexually explicit and contains allusions to universal initiation and marital rituals (Zipes 1983, 50). In both the 1812 and 1857 editions, the king's daughter "provides more of an identification basis for a bourgeois child" as she is unique, wealthy, and somewhat spoiled (51). She offers material rewards to the frog and treats it as a servant or member of a lower class, an attitude not evident in the original version. The addition of ornate description serves to camouflage the sexual elements, and the frog is less direct. He now wishes to be a companion and playmate to the girl. "Sex must first be sweetened up and made to appear harmless since its true form is repulsive" (51). There is no evidence of the exact wording of the 1810 manuscript in reference to the frog, after his transformation, falling into the bed, and the princess laying with him. However, the original draft, which was sent to the Grimms' friend Clemens Brentano and recovered years later, is explicit about the "princess's alacrity" in joining him where he has fallen (Tatar 1987, 8). Maria Tatar points out that when Wilhelm Grimm was preparing the 2d edition of the tales, he added a second line of dialogue for the king: "[The frog] helped you when you were in trouble and you mustn't despise him now." "But," Tatar continues, "the father's pronouncements on the importance of keeping promises and remaining loyal move against the grain of the story itself. The Frog King is not released from his enchanted state until the princess displays her contempt for him through an act of physical violence. Passion rather than compassion leads to a happy ending" (Tatar 1988, 143).

The first English translation of the Grimms' folktale into English, published in 1823, was written by Edgar Taylor. He departed from his source in a number of ways. He changed the title from "The Frog King" to "The Frog Prince," and he completely altered the violent breaking of the spell by having the frog sleep with the princess for three nights until the spell was broken. As D. L. Ashliman states, "it appears, in his judgment, the English readers of the 1820s, unlike their German counterparts, would not accept a heroine who throws her frisky bed companion against the wall" (1986).

Table 3.1
Adaptations Made by the Brothers Grimm in the Frog King

For further comparison on the changes in this tale, go to D.L. Ashliman's Internet site where he has provided an in-depth comparison of the Grimms' 1812 and 1857 versions. The address is http://www.pitt.edu/~dash/frogking.html.

1810 Manuscript	First edition (1812)	Second edition (1819)	Third edition (1837)
When the youngest daughter loses the ball, she is nasty to the frog but promises to take him home with her if he fetches the ball.	The princess, after losing the ball, begins "to weep and lament pitifully: Oh! If I had my ball again, I would give everything for it, my clothes, my pearls, and anything else in the world" (Ellis, 127).	No change.	Beginning becomes more poetic: "then she began to weep, and wept louder and louder and was inconsolable. And as she lamented so, someone cried out to her, What are you doing, king's daughter, you're crying so much that a stone would take pity" (Ellis, 132).

1810 Manuscript	First edition (1812)	Second edition (1819)	Third edition (1837)
Frog initiates discussion.	Frog responds to her crying. He asks to be taken as her beloved companion, to sit near her and eat from her golden plate, and to sleep in her bed.	No change.	The frog stretched his fat ugly head out of the water; she calls him "old water splasher." He refuses her material bribes: "If you will love me and I can be your companion and play-mate, sit near you at your little table, eat off your little golden plate, drink out of your little goblet, and sleep in your bed" (Ellis, 132).
Frog fetches the ball, princess takes it and leaves the frog behind.	Princess agrees but cannot believe the frog is serious. Takes the ball and leaves the frog behind.	No change.	No change.
Frog knocks on door during the evening meal. Princess slams the door in his face.	The next evening, the frog knocks on the door. She slams the door in fear.	No change.	No change.
Father asks her for ex-planation, which she gives. She now has to open the door for the frog.	Father asks about cause for fear. She tells him and is told, "What you have promised, you must do"(Ellis, 128).	No change.	No change.
Frog asks to eat be-side her; she refuses, but the king orders her to allow it.	Frog demands to be put on a chair next to her and to eat off her plate. King orders her to do so.	Princess and frog are eating off the same plate. "Full of annoy-ance she did this too, and the frog enjoyed it very much, but every mouthful stuck in her throat" (Ellis, 130).	No change.
Frog asks to sleep be-side her; she refuses. "She didn't want to do that at all, because she was very much afraid of the cold frog" (Ellis, 126).	Frog asks to sleep with her. "The king's daughter was alarmed when she heard that, she was afraid of the cold frog, she didn't think she could touch him, and now he was to lie beside her in her bed, and she began to cry and didn't want to do it at all" (Ellis, 128).	"The king's daughter began to cry most bit-terly and was afraid of the cold frog, she did not think she could touch him and now he was to sleep in her beautiful clean little bed."	"The king's daughter began to cry and was afraid of the cold frog whom she did not dare to touch."

1810 Manuscript	First edition (1812)	Second edition (1819)	Third edition (1837)
King orders her to do so.	King becomes angry and "ordered her on pain of his displeasure, to do as she had promised. It was no use, she had to do as her father wished, but she was bitterly angry in her heart" (Ellis, 128).	No change.	"The king looked angrily at her, and said, 'What you have promised, you must do, and the frog is your companion.' "
She takes the frog to her room and "full of anger she seized him and threw him with all her strength against the wall in her bed."	She seizes the frog with two fingers, carries him to her room, gets into bed and throws him crash! against the wall: "Now you'll leave me in peace, you horrid frog!"	No change.	No change.
"As he hit the wall, he fell down into the bed and lay there as a handsome young prince, and the king's daughter lay down with him" (Ellis, 126).	When the frog hit the wall he was transformed into a handsome prince. "He now became her dear companion, and she cherished him as she had promised and they went to sleep contentedly together" (Ellis, 128).	"What fell down was not a dead frog but a living, young king's son with handsome and friendly eyes. He now became rightfully and with her father's approval, her dear companion and husband. They now fell asleep contentedly together" (Ellis, 131). Maria Tatar explains that the 1819 revision "deprived the frog of his soft landing spot [the bed] and simply observed that the transformation took place as soon as the frog hit the wall (1987, 8). The couple do not retire for the night until they receive her father's blessing and exchange marriage vows.	No change.
Next morning, the prince's faithful servant brings the coach to take them home. He had suffered so much that three iron hoops formed over his heart; the hoops crack as they journey homeward.	No change.	No change.	No change.

Overview of Critical Interpretations of the Frog King or Iron Henry

1948: Bruno Jockel states that the tale represents the transition between childhood and maturity for the girl (McGlathery 1993, 63).

1968: Joseph Campbell considers three signals heralding the oncoming of adolescence for the girl: the disappearance of the ball, the frog and "the call to adventure," and the unconsidered promise (51).

1974: Julius Heuscher refers to a paper, read by C. Simburg in 1961 at the Northern and Central California Psychiatric Meeting, that discussed the phallic nature of the frog in some of the tales. "The innocent young girl's fear of and repugnance toward the male genitals and the transformation of this disgust into happiness and sanctioned matrimony can hardly be symbolized better than by this transformation of the frog into a prince" (234). According to Heuscher, the story symbolizes the transition from childhood to a spiritual awakening and maturity during puberty.

1974: The Opies assert that the idea that a kiss, or the marriage bed, could release the curse of monstrousness, was an ancient one in which the cursed person was most often a young female (239) They offer early analogs to this type of tale in "The Wedding of Sir Gawain and Dame Ragnell," first published in 1390, and the magic tale told by the wife of Bath in Canterbury Tales (240). They also state that although the story has a long history in Scotland, Ireland, and Somerset, the Grimms were the first to set down a complete retelling of the tale. "It is deserving of notice that in the German text, as in the Scots, the frog speaks in rhyme" (240).

1976: Bruno Bettelheim claims that the servant, Iron Henry, was not part of the original tale but was a later addition to contrast his extreme loyalty to the disloyalty displayed by the princess. Because Bettelheim felt this element did not add anything to the story's meaning, he would not include it in his discussion (286). He offers symbolic interpretations for many of the other elements, however. The ball represents the yet undeveloped narcissistic psyche that contains all of the potentials but remains in a unrealized state (287). As the ball falls, so does the princess's childish innocence, and only the ugly frog can restore it for her. "Life has become ugly and complicated as it begins to reveal its darker sides" (288). Because she is "still beholden to the pleasure principle," she makes meaningless promises to retain her ball. When faced with the consequences of this action, the princess slams the door on them. Her father embodies her superego, and the more she tries to go against the demands of the frog, the more her father insists she keep her promises. "What started playfully becomes most serious: the princess must grow up as she is forced to accept the commitments she has made" (288). Bettelheim also sketches the steps the princess takes towards intimacy. Initially, she is alone. The frog initiates conversation at the well and then comes to visit her at her home, first at the dinner table and then in her bedroom and bed. The closer the frog gets to the princess physically, the more anxious and fearful she becomes. The awakening to sex is not free of fear, disgust, or even anger (288). To Bettelheim, the story tells the reader that to be able to love, one must be able to feel first, even if those emotions are negative. The princess has not the capacity for feeling at the beginning of the tale; her self-centered self easily makes empty promises. The closer the frog approaches, however, the stronger her feelings become; she is becoming more of a person. And with the breaking of the spell, she becomes herself, just as does the frog prince (288). Thus, the story tells us that we cannot expect our first erotic encounters to be pleasant; they are too difficult and fraught with anxiety. However, if we persevere, we will "experience a happy shock of recognition when complete closeness reveals sexuality's true beauty" (288). The princess's perseverance was advocated by her father; "parental guidance which leads to superego formation develops a responsible conscience," necessary for a happy personal and sexual union (289). Her disgust with the frog, according to Bettelheim, conveys to the child that there is no need to be afraid of the (to him) repugnant aspects of sex because this feeling will evolve when the time is ripe. "By using the frog as a symbol for sex, an animal that exists in one form when young—as a tadpole—and in an entirely different form when mature, the story speaks to the unconscious of the child and helps him accept the form of sexuality which is correct for his age, while making him receptive to the idea that as he grows up, his sexuality too must, in his own best interest, undergo a metamorphosis" (290). This necessary message of sex education, concludes Bettelheim, "is delivered without ever directly mentioning anything sexual" (291)

1978: Roger Sale discusses the "unfairness" of the story. "Why should a princess who seems petulant and spoiled, who doesn't want to keep her end of the bargain, be rewarded precisely at the moment when she is being most petulant and insistently breaking her bargain, when she picks up the frog and smashes him into the wall?" (37). This sense of unfairness, Sale continues, is exactly what is required for the princess to overcome her fear and revulsion as the frog becomes increasingly more intimate. "Thinking of it that way—as the story of a girl forced by her father and her own past consent to let a repulsive creature come to her bed, as the story of a girl gripped by a fear that is understandable and stronger than any bargain . . ." makes the tale much more understandable (38). Sale contends that the fear represents not intimacy and sex, but fear of ugliness and revulsion, and while fairy tales rarely concern themselves with ugliness, this one proves an exception to the rule (60).

1980: Derek Brewer claims that this tale has been known in the British Isles from the sixteenth century. He states that in these early versions, it is clear that sexual intercourse has taken place and the frog asks that his head be chopped off in order to break the enchantment (37). The Grimms prettified the text and, as well, modified the reason for the girl's appearance at the well from the mundane chore of fetching water to playing with her golden ball (38). Brewer insists the tale is about love and especially sex. The tale is told from the female perspective. "The acceptance of love, and the giving of love, is a way of taming male sexual aggression. . . . The frog represents those sexual desires in oneself that seem nasty and aggressive. Accepted and loved they became manageable" (38). Brewer also feels that there is a complete lack of parental involvement and includes no mention of the father's role in having his daughter keep her promises.

1980: Wolfgang Mieder examines how the Grimms' fairy tales, and "The Frog Prince" in particular, are the basis for ironical and satirical comments about our modern society. The bedroom scene is "of particular interest to writers and cartoonists of today, since the preoccupation with sexual implications is evident even in the Grimm tale" (1980, 125).

1983: Jack Zipes demonstrates the changes made by the Grimm brothers in their various editions to show "how different types of changes relate to gradual shifts in the norms and socialization process reflecting the interests of the bourgeoisie" (1983, 49). All three versions examined "suggest a type of patriarchal socialization for young girls that has been severely criticized and questioned by progressive educators today, but the final version is most consistent in its *capacity* to combine feudal folk notions of sexuality, obedience, and sexual roles with bourgeois norms and attirement" (1983, 51).

1985: Maria Tatar explores the role of the wicked witch in fairy tales, including the woman responsible for turning the prince into a frog. While the transformation is often attributed to an evil woman, the "source of the prince's bewitchment does not constitute a part of the tale's plot and is mentioned more in passing than as a significant episode from the prince's past . . . there is clearly a story behind it and a history to it" (1985, 33).

1986: D. L. Ashliman contends that the most significant symbolic element in the story is the throwing of the frog against the wall. However, most of the interpretations of this passage focus on the evolution of the girl's attitude toward sex from one of revulsion to that of pleasure instead of paying any attention to the *timing* of the change. "It is not her acceptance of traditional values, but rather her violent assertion of sexual independence, that brings her satisfaction" (194).

The princess, therefore, is not remade by her husband but indeed remakes him, transforming him from an ugly, repulsive creature into a handsome, desirable prince. Ashliman considers this a fairly clear-cut expression of the female storyteller's desire for some power, authority, and independence in the marriage partnership (194).

1986: Lutz Rohrich concludes that "without a doubt, in the case of the "Frog King" we are dealing, at the bottom, with a decidedly erotic tale, not with a story for children" (McGlathery 1993, 63).

1987: Ruth Bottigheimer analyzes the Grimms' tales and connects "The Frog King" to the rest of the unfortunates in the collection, "not [because of] his frogginess, but the fact that the well is the unlucky location of his enchantment" (33). She reminds us that at the end of the tale, the frog-prince explains that a wicked witch bespelled him into a frog; the listener is not given a reason for either this action or the reason why he was transformed into a frog rather than any other creature. Bottigheimer examines the nonspeaking roles of female characters in some of the tales, including "The Frog King."

> Alongside the frog's curt command to the princess, "Be quiet" (Sei still) . . . the reader sees the princess' numerous complaint reactions to the frog's imperious commands: to lift him to the table, to eat from her golden plate, and to take him to rest. Only when he adds that he expects to share her bed does the princess respond with spirited outrage, which turns out in fact to be Wilhelm Grimm's rather than hers" (52).

1987: Wolfgang Mieder contends the tale deals with transformation, obligation, maturation, sex, and marriage, with the focus of the tale on the fear of sexuality. He repeats his earlier findings that the popularity of this tale in the adult world is based on the possibility of a sexual interpretation (1987, 17). Mieder discusses modern adaptations, cartoons, and other satirical and humorous allusions based on the basic motifs in this tale.

1987: In discussing the revisions made by the Grimm brothers, Maria Tatar claims, "What the brothers found harder to tolerate than violence and what they did their best to eliminate from the collection through vigilant editing were references to what they coyly called 'certain conditions and relationships' "—pregnancy, hints of premarital activity, and incest and incestuous desire (1987, 7). Their revisions of "The Frog King" reveal their tactics for doing this. "[The] Grimms' transformation of the tale replete with sexual innuendo into a prim and proper nursery story with a dutiful daughter is almost as striking as the folkloric metamorphosis of frog into prince" (1987, 8). Tatar considers that the acts of violence in the tale may initially have been motivated by compassion rather than fear and revulsion. The girl may "simply be displaying her spontaneous reaction to the unending importunities of a 'disgusting frog' when she hurls him against the wall, but she may also have behind her act the weight of folkloric traditions that require an act of physical violence for love to flourish in its most human and humane form" (1987, 175).

1988: Madonna Kolbenschlag considers this story to be a parable of puberty and the first experience of a sexual encounter (205). The golden ball represents the higher, spiritual aspect of the personality, acting also as an emblem of youth, innocence, and virginal freedom, while the frog is "symbolic of the impatient manifestation of physical instincts and temporary submersion of the spiritual aspect in adolescence" (205). The initial meeting of the story, therefore, is a meeting of the physical and spiritual aspects of the character. Kolbenschlag also addresses feminist concerns when she states, "Feminists might well object that the conventional interpretation of the tale is a cautionary message to females to bear with the atavistic aspects of the male personality, to accommodate themselves to the abrasive, exploitive demands of the male partner" (206). She recognizes in the girl's behavior "the all-too familiar pattern of the battered woman"; she is a prisoner of male dominance (206). The faithful male servant Henry, therefore, is introduced as a foil for the deceitful female who makes false promises. This tale is also described as "a metaphor of the crisis of identity" between the genders (207). As women shed the "feminine mystique" and become aware of their own identity, they become repulsed by the macho (froglike) aspect of the male. "The more a woman is liberated from stereotypical roles, the more unacceptable he becomes" (208).

1988: Lutz Rohrich, in his discussion on meaning in folk narrative research, points to the erotic metaphors of Freudian interpretations of the tales. "The slippery, slimy frog-prince in the fairy tale, whom the princess does not want to take to bed with her, embodies her still-unconscious rejection of sexuality. Breaking the spell symbolizes the change from rejection to acceptance of love" (1988, 9).

1988: Jack Zipes notes several motifs introduced or emphasized by the Grimm brothers during their 42 years of reshaping the tale: the paternal authority of the king, and the resistance of the princess, who is rewarded for her negative and destructive action. Zipes offers the notion that whether this is actually a reward or not is open to question! (1988, 115)

1989: Joyce Thomas asserts that the bargain made by the king's daughter constitutes all the progressive elements necessary for the frog to become humanized. The frog first wishes to be a playmate, then a companion and guest in her home, and finally a lover in her bed, encapsulating, in an abbreviated form, the stages of intimacy, relationships, and courtship (158). Much of the tension in the tale is derived from the fact that no one knows the frog is enchanted; he is thought of as a repulsive, disgusting, and loathsome creature throughout the tale. The girl's rebellion against the demands of her father and the frog demonstrate that "one's sense of self-worth and esteem matter more than keeping a promise or obeying one's parent as guarantor of that promise; neither promise nor obedience can justify an unacceptable demand such as the frog's [obviously sexual] bed request" (159). Symbolically, the frog functions as a reminder that what is, at first, perceived to be negative, repulsive, and threatening, can, in time, be experienced as positive, desirable, and fulfilling (159). The tale functions as a lesson for women: "As long as she sees him (or sex) as an animal, he is one; as soon as she sees him as human, he is disenchanted" (159). The cracking of the three iron bands around Henry's chest represents the chain reaction of release and newfound freedom for all three characters: the girl, the frog prince, and the loyal servant (258).

1990: Boria Sax discusses the historical connections between people and animals, stating that in early times, people were afraid that intimate contact with animals could dehumanize them (42). Frogs and toads were particularly suspect; they were considered to be witches' familiars, and the sudden appearance of a frog or toad heralded a summoning of a demon (47). This tale, therefore, in the oral tradition, is an erotic tale meant for adults and not children because the sexual dimension is essential to the tale (54). Both the German and English versions are explicitly set in ancient mythic times by their retellers (60). The Grimms, in fact, placed this tale at the beginning of their collection, and it is still regarded as the "quintessential fairy tale, though not necessarily the best" (61). Sax discusses the fact that while the tale is well known and is retold and parodied as often as any of the other "popular" tales, it has not aged as well. "It retains a certain charm but little pathos. What makes it somewhat anachronistic is not changes in our understanding of human society. It is the change in our understanding of frogs. They have gone from being mysterious and formidable creatures, who might indeed enter into an equal partnership with human beings, to dumb little balls of protoplasm. While they may still suggest sexuality, this quality is emptied of powerful emotions such as love and fear" (63).

1991: James McGlathery maintains that the princess's adventure "projects not only initial abhorrence at the thought of marriage and loss of virginity and of losing her position as the pampered youngest daughter of an evidently widowed father, but also revulsion at the thought of becoming intimate with a young man" (1991, 58). The fact that she plays with toys and is so frantic at the loss of one toy demonstrates her unwillingness to mature. The intensity of her emotional crisis is heightened by her father's insisting the promise to the frog be kept, "an insistence that may echo the girl's own feeling that the time has come when she must abandon her filial attachment and cleave to a spouse" (1991, 59). However, regardless of her initial revulsion and fear, the princess is not prudish once the transformation from frog to handsome prince takes place, and her father does not seem to mind that the couple consummated their union prior to the wedding (1991, 89).

"The most intriguing aspect of the tale is the fact that the girl does not recognize—consciously, at least—that her magical adventure has placed her on the road to marriage" (1991, 64).

1992: Maria Tatar articulates that this tale is rich in opportunities for risqué humor as the tale issues "stern warnings about the importance of keeping promises—even when it means sharing your bed with an amorous frog" (1992, 4). Modern revisions often do nothing to improve the tale because many do not eliminate the father's intervention and warnings about keeping promises, but do abolish the princess's act of frustration and fear, replacing it with the transformation of the frog after he spends three nights in the princess's bed. The jokes and cartoons usually revise the transformation as well; the disenchantment is broken by a kiss (1992, 20). In her discussion on the role of the father, Tatar asserts, "It is telling that in the earliest version of the Grimms' tale the king does nothing but issue orders; by the time the *Nursery and Household Tales* reached print, however, he was teaching lessons to readers as he was telling his daughter what to do" (1992, 62). Tatar also refers to the similarities between this tale and that of "Beauty and the Beast." Both tales are classified as tale type AT 425C, "The Search for the Lost Husband," but the former is delineated by the subheading "transformation through an act of violence" rather than compassion, as it is for Beauty's tale (1992, 151). Both heroines are similarly rewarded for their actions, whether they be compassionate or violent. "Much as the Grimms tried to rewrite this tale with paternal promptings about the importance of keeping promises and showing gratitude, they could not succeed in camouflaging the way which the tale rewards indignant rage" (1992, 154).

1995: Jack Zipes asserts that "The Frog King" is an important tale for today's children to understand. It, along with "Cinderella," concern damsels in distress. "The young 'heroines,' obviously ready for marriage, are humiliated, degraded, and besmirched. Their major value is patience and, to a certain extent, opportunism" (1995, 39). These tales repeat the message about the need for a man to make them worthy and whole. The essentially passive but frustrated princess does fling the frog against the wall in some of the versions, but most people are more familiar with the motif of kissing the frog to end the enchantment and to provide her with eternal happiness. Zipes alludes to some of the "hidden symbolism" in the tale by stating, "Given the abundance of inexplicable symbols and their profound layers of meaning, there is no "correct" way to interpret a fairy tale" (1995, 39). He reminds readers that the tales were not necessarily told the way they have been frozen in print and on the screen, which are "specific to a male, middle-class ideology" exemplified in this tale, in which "the frog and the father 'collaborate' to blackmail and humiliate the princess until she is ready to do what they want" (1995, 39).

Reworkings of the Frog King or Iron Henry in Novel Form

Two highly divergent but amusing reworkings of this story have appeared in novel form. They are aimed at the two poles of young adult readers but can be enjoyed by good readers of any age.

The Prince of the Pond Otherwise Known as DE Fawg Pin

1992: Napoli, Donna Jo. **The Prince of the Pond Otherwise Known as DE Fawg Pin**. Illustrated by Judith Byron Schachner. New York: Dutton Children's Books.

The summary of this novel states, "Having been turned into a frog by a hag, a frog prince makes the best of his new life as he mates, raises a family, and instills a new kind of thinking into his frog prince." While intended for a younger audience, this novel is still suitable for young adults, particularly those who are interested in puns, parody, satire, and nature. Told in first person, from the viewpoint of a female frog, the story follows the adventures of the male frog from his moment of transformation (including his first awkward movements in his new body and his anguish at his new status) through to his re-transformation. Because he still has human tendencies, the frog takes Jade (the narrator) to the well at the palace in order to protect the eggs she will be producing. After another dangerous interlude with the hag, the family retreat to the same well where they face another danger: a young woman preparing to "eat" favorite son Jimmy. The frog prince jumps up, pushes Jimmy safely away, and accidentally receives the kiss that was to be bestowed on his son. The spell is broken, and Jade is confused about the disappearance of her mate. This circular tale is continued in the sequel, *Jimmy: The Pickpocket of the Palace*, published in 1995, which follows Jimmy's subsequent adventures at the palace.

Fair Peril

1996: Springer, Nancy. **Fair Peril**. New York: Avon.

In direct contrast to the above novel, Nancy Springer spins a tale for an adult audience in which a middle-aged storyteller discovers a talking frog. Recognizing the tale from which he has sprung, she decides to keep him a frog for financial gain. Her plans are pulled asunder by the "princess," her 16-year-old daughter Emily; Prince Adamus (the frog prince himself); her former mother-in-law Fay (the Fairy Godmother); and various other players in this comical exploration of family relationships, friendship, love, and the unknown.

The story begins with Buffy (the main character) discovering an indignant and highly vocal frog who is not impressed with her avaricious response to his presence. He manages to evade Buffy and convince daughter Emily to kiss him and free him from his spell. Together they head out to the Mall (Fair Peril). With the help of librarian and friend LeeVon, Buffy combs both "levels" of the mall and the dangerous characters that populate the "other" level. The story is peppered liberally with allusions to the tale of the Frog Prince and other traditional tales, familiar characters such as Thomas the Rhymer and the Faerie Queen, poet Anne Sexton, and storytelling as a whole. Springer beguiles her reader as Buffy and LeeVon rush to save both the princess and the impetuous frog prince. It would not be fair to divulge too much of this plot as it dashes along the roller coaster of mother-daughter relationships, divorce and trophy wives, and the other world. Although this work is classified as light fantasy, Springer manages at the same time to ponder the physical and symbolic implications of being transformed into a frog, the power to cast spells, and the power of storytelling. Several other questions are raised as well. What would happen if the Wicked Stepmother and the

Fairy Godmother are the same person? What ramifications occur if the frog under the spell is gay?

A finalist for the 1997 Mythopoeic Fantasy Award, *Fair Peril* offers "an oral tale" that is a fast-paced and satisfying read for young adults.

Short Stories

While the critical interpretations have largely focused on the sexual connotations of this tale, the reworkings in short-story format do not concentrate on any one image. The stories are told from varied viewpoints (including male and female frogs) and range from humorous satires to chilling explorations of human nature and psychology. All of these tales are accessible for young-adult readers.

1981. McKinley, Robin. "**The Princess and the Frog.**" In *The Door in the Hedge*. New York: Greenwillow, 81–103.

Told in three parts, the story revolves around the relationship between a young princess and a neighboring prince whom is she is to marry. He gives her a gift of a necklace that reeks of magic and power. She takes it to a nearby pool where, surprised by the croaking of a frog, she drops the necklace into the water. She promises the frog a home if he rescues it. He gladly does so, and when the necklace emerges from the pool, its power is gone. Her fiancé (and sorcerer) flies into a rage when he discovers the power is gone, and he leaves the area. The frog arrives at dinner time and quickly becomes the confident of the girl. She explains her predicament and her sadness that her childhood friend, the older brother of the sorcerer, has disappeared. By this time she realizes that he is not a real frog and must be under a spell. " 'Of course,' snapped the frog. 'Frogs don't talk.' " (97) Part 3 brings the three characters together. The sorcerer mocks the girl's choice of a pet, and when enraged, "he seized the frog by the leg and hurled it against the heavy stone wall opposite the thrones." (99) This of course breaks the spell, and the frog regains his true form as the sorcerer's older brother. After a watery defeat, the sorcerer is gone forever. The future looks peaceful and happy, "and her father smiled." (103)

McKinley uses the basic elements of the tale to tell her story of sibling rivalry, sorcery and empowerment, and the ironic denouement of the sorcerer himself accidentally breaking his spell.

1983: Lee, Tanith. "The Princess and Her Future." In *Red as Blood (or Tales from the Sisters Grimmer)*. New York: DAW, 82–90.

The monster Hiranu sits patiently waiting in the cistern in the Asian jungle. He has been subjected to this binding for such a long duration that stories about the demon shapechanger haunting the temple grounds have grown and circulated widely. Jarasmi, the ruler's 16-year-old daughter is given a golden glass ball that will show her the future. All she must do is smash it to the ground. Because she does not want to share this important moment with anyone else, Jarasmi makes her way to the temple grounds. She has long dismissed the stories of the demon as foolish tales to frighten children. When she throws the ball, her aim is bad, and the ball lands in the cistern. It seems lost, but then it magically seems to resurface. When she reaches for it, it bursts upon contact and her hand is caught by another hand, slimy and cold, under the water. It was as if her hand disappeared. Finally, her hand released, Jarasmi flees to the safety of her home. This safe haven is breached when the door is opened later that evening to a imperative voice stating, "The princess has summoned me." No one seems to be at the door, but the princess's plate and cup are emptied, and the unseen presence follows her to her bed chambers. She finally looks at him and sees a handsome prince. She has broken the spell and he will love her for all her life. They are married, and his coach and faithful servant arrive to take her to her new residence. In the carriage, the prince assumes his true form. It's too bad that the princess's life is so short!

1992: Brooke, William J. "A Prince in the Throat." In *Untold Tales*. New York: HarperCollins, 1–47.

Suitable for the younger young-adult reader, the story follows the former frog and his wife several decades after their famous romance and wedding. The queen is celebrating her forty-fifth birthday, and her gallant husband is giving a speech filled with, according to the good woman, rhymes just like those he had made when he was courting her. He stems the rhymes, and she quickly loses interest in the proceedings but bursts into tears when he chokes and the Lord Chamberlain announces that "His Majesty just had a frog in his throat." (7) Life remains constant. The queen is distant and her husband distracted until he meets the palace cook, who is quite distraught. Apparently, the queen would like to feast on flies! His majesty convinces the cook that she meant fried potatoes but "he hated fried potatoes. Almost as much as he had hated flies." (15) The situation continues to deteriorate. The queen becomes more and more unhappy and the king more and more bewildered, until the king has a plan. Unfortunately his plan backfires, but after some time, and no kisses, the two of them live happily ever after.

A light-hearted and fairly detailed tale filled with puns, action, and humor.

1993: Wilson, Gahan. "**The Frog Prince.**" In *Snow White, Blood Red,* edited by Ellen Datlow and Terri Windling. New York: William Morrow, 80–88.

The introductory comment preceding this tale states that Wilson was "inspired perhaps by Bruno Bettelheim's use of Freudian psychoanalysis of fairy tales" (Datlow and Windling, 80). The story is told from the point of view of a frog, lying on the coach and speaking to his psychiatrist! The patient tells of his dream: of the pool and his happiness there, of the arrival of the "great, bright pinkness" (84), his falling in love with the female who takes the ruby necklace he has rescued and puts it on. In her delight, she picks up the frog and brings him closer to her lips. But things in life, and dreams, are not all light and happiness! " 'And this is where you always wake up,' sighed Doctor Neiman. . . . 'Yes,' he croaked. 'Always.' " (88)

1994: Garner, James Finn. "**The Frog Prince.**" In *Politically Correct Bedtime Stories: Modern Tales for Our Life & Times.* New York: Macmillan, 63–66.

When the politically correct young womyn drops her ball into the pond, she has no desire to force the frog to find it for her. But the frog has other ideas and wishes to make a bargain with her. He fetches the ball and then explains his present state of "frogginess" and the antidote for his problem. The princess kisses the frog, who is instantly transformed into "a man in a golf shirt and loud plaid pants—middle-aged, vertically challenged, and losing a little bit of hair on the top." (65) She is surprised that a witch would waste a spell on such an ordinary specimen but, as the man informs the princess, he is a real-estate developer who did not waste his time as a frog. Yes indeed, why he could transform the area into a resort or golf course. The princess shoves the ball back into the man's mouth and holds him under the water. "And while someone might have noticed that the frog was gone, no one ever missed the real estate developer." (66)

A tongue-in-cheek (or ball-in-mouth) reworking of the tale with no redeeming qualities other than that it is funny!

1994: Quinn, Daniel. "**The Frog King, or Iron Henry.**" In *Black Thorn, White Rose,* edited by Ellen Datlow and Terri Windling. New York: William Morrow, 87–97.

A circular tale, told almost entirely in dialogue between a prince suffering from amnesia and his faithful servant Iron Henry. In his attempts to jog the prince's memory, Iron Henry tells and retells elements of the story to the prince, but to no avail. A disquieting tale, as the reader never knows where exactly the dialogue is taking place, but the clues are most ominous. "A rectangle of moonlight blazes on the floor like a shield. . . . Beside the window, a shadow stirs in the darkness, and it is he. . . . 'It will soon be dawn,' he says, 'and the queen will be sighing in her bed.' " (87)

1995: Foster, Alan Dean. "The Kiss." In *The Book of Kings*, edited by Richard Guilliam and Martin H. Greenberg. New York: ROC, 155–58.

In this contemporary urban horror tale, Jenny leaves work in a hurry trying to make her transportation connections on a cold January evening. As she crosses the bridge she hears the croaking of a frog and investigates. She picks up the frog, her hands protected by her gloves, and is startled by the anger in its eyes. "After that the voice was almost anticlimactic." (156) She kisses the frog as directed and returns him to its rock. When she reaches the apex of the bridge, she is confronted by a man with a knife and knows the knife is for her. In answer to her question, the man replies, "Never kiss a dark frog. . . ." (158) After his murderous deed, the man heads deeper into the city "knowing there would be other princesses. Real and true." (158)

A chilling tale that assumes the reader knows the traditional tale and plays with those expectations.

1995: Vande Velde, Vivian. "Frog." In *Tales from the Brothers Grimm and the Sisters Weird*. Orlando, FL: Harcourt Brace, 27–35.

This is the story of Prince Sidney, a middle son, who knew his fairy tales but still got turned into a frog. In his quest to have the spell broken, he finds a princess who promises him that he can eat off her plate and put his head on her pillow. True to form, she breaks her promises, is forced to accept the frog by her father, and throws the frog against her wall. When the princess sees how handsome he is in his true form, she immediately makes future plans. However, Sidney has seen *her* true form and makes his escape.

A droll reworking of the tale from the frog's point of view. Suitable for the younger spectrum of young adults.

1996: Walker, Barbara G. "The Frog Princess." In *Feminist Fairy Tales*. San Francisco, CA: HarperSanFrancisco, 35–45.

Walker introduces this tale with an anecdote about her positive feelings towards frogs. "When I read the story of the frog prince," she tells the reader, "I couldn't understand the heroine's frenzied reluctance to kiss the frog. Personally I wouldn't have objected" (35). In her version of the tale, the frog is a female who becomes enchanted with a prince who spends time at the pond. Like all frogs, she knows the classic story of the frog prince and goes on a quest to the nearest fairy who lives a distance away. She becomes dehydrated and requests the help of several birds and animals. The crow and owl refuse, but the doe helps her willingly, and the frog tells her, "When I become a princess, I'll make permanent laws against deer hunting." (39) For the promise of the largest diamond the frog can find, the fairy comes out of retirement to help the frog. The fairy reminds her of the "essential drawback in all frog-to-human enchantments . . . the kiss!" (39–40) Making her way back to the pond, the frog must now convince the prince to kiss her, and in her own way manages the task. The prince is enchanted with the princess who knows so much about the natural world and marries her. She soon becomes pregnant but is not completely happy and cannot entirely forgo some of her former ways. Things come to a head when she appropriates the largest jewel in the kingdom and uses it to pay her debt. Her life is spared until the birth of her child, but the child is deformed, resembling a large tadpole, and does not live. Her grieving husband grants her a final request, taking her back to the pond where they first met. The frog returns to her original form and once again is happy and at peace. The prince eventually finds another princess, gets married, has a growing family, and no longer has any time for fishing at the pond.

Walker has woven other motifs into her reworking to produce a tale of romance and strength of purpose.

Short Films

There have been no full-length retellings of this tale in the film medium, but two significant shorter films have been popular.

1980: **The Frog King**. Retold and directed by Tom Davenport. Delaplane, VA: Davenport Films. Starring Ann Clark.

This 27-minute film uses a real frog instead of a puppet. The setting has been changed to an upper-class, late-nineteenth-century American dining room at the home of a wealthy industrialist and his family. Other than this change in setting, there is very little difference in the storyline from Grimms' 3d edition of the tale on which it is based. Gary Arnold of *The Washington Post* wrote, in his February 15, 1981, review of the film, "Grown-ups may feel more amused by the aplomb of Ernest Graves in the role of the host and by the implications of the heroine's discomfort, which wittily evokes a good deal of the social and erotic panic associated with adolescence." The film was a CINE Golden Eagle Winner and the American Film Festival Blue Ribbon winner. To accompany the film, a documentary about the making of this film was produced highlighting the basics of filmmaking, including acting, illustrations, and the manipulation of time. It also shows the special problems of working with live animals such as frogs. A teaching guide accompanies the entire Davenport series of remakings of the Grimms' tales.

1982: **The Faerie Tale Theatre: The Tale of the Frog Prince**, written and directed by Eric Idle, produced by Jonathan Taplin. Starring Robin Williams and Teri Garr. Livonia, MI: Playhouse Video.

This 55-minute parody relates the tale of the bespelled prince who is befriended by a self-centered princess who eventually saves him with a kiss. The sets and costumes are based on the illustrations by Maxfield Parrish. While viewers have applauded the Faerie Tale Theatre approach to these tales, critics have been less impressed. Ursula Beitter claims that "the biggest threat to the traditional fairy tale comes from the made-for-T.V. video-tales, produced by Shelley Duvall's Fairy Tale Theatre" (277) In her article, Beitter examines this film in great detail. The first 20 minutes are dedicated to explaining how the prince came to be a frog, which includes an interesting connection to the well-known curse in "Sleeping Beauty." In this case, the angry witch, when not invited to the christening, turns the baby into a frog. The scene shifts to the household of another royal couple and their extremely spoiled daughter, played by Teri Garr, who is to meet Hal, the frog prince's younger brother. The original meeting does not come to pass and, to make amends, Hal sends the princess a "huge golden sphere that has the magic property of being able to float" (Beitter, 278). She takes the toy into the garden where she meets, and has an argument with, the frog, played by Robin Williams. When the sphere falls into the well, she tries to bribe the frog with material goods but eventually promises, begrudgingly, to befriend him. Beitter points out that 35 minutes of the video have lapsed by this point. This is followed by a five-minute digression at the castle kitchen in which the cook wishes to serve frog legs but the "uncooked" escapee impresses the royal court with his song-and-dance routine at the banquet table. Another five minutes passes while the princess's father explains the necessity of keeping promises, particularly if one is royal. The royal princess keeps her promise and allows the frog to sleep in the same bed as her. During the night, "a scorpion is about to attack the princess and (while dramatic music is playing in the background) the frog, armed with a needle, kills the scorpion" (Beitter, 279). The frog is rewarded by a kiss, transforms into a prince, and is immediately discovered in the princess' bed by her irate father. The prince is thrown into a dungeon, the princess is sent away to boarding school, and the father turns to drink! However, the witch, appearing in a golden floating sphere, explains the situation to the king and all is well—or perhaps not, as, at the wedding, the groom is still furtively snatching at flies. Beitter concludes her discussion by stating that Faerie Tale Theatre, intended for adults, no longer deals with fairy magic tales, but with a new genre of TV entertainment: the fairy tale situation comedy (281).

Poetry

In spite of the frequent sexual images that surround this tale in popular culture, the poetic reworkings tend to ignore them and focus instead on relationships and the effects of the transformation/rebirth process.

1969: Hill, Hyacinthe. "**Rebels from Fairy Tales**." Reprinted in *Disenchantments: An Anthology of Modern Fairy Tale Poetry*, edited by Wolfgang Mieder. Hanover, NH: Published for University of Vermont by University Press of New England, 1985, 27.

A chorus of frogs proclaims their desire to remain frogs. Why would they even deign to transform themselves to such creatures as men; after all, "frogs wouldn't even eat men's legs." A poetic look at the havoc man has performed on nature.

1969: John N. Miller. "**Prince Charming**." Reprinted in *Disenchantments: An Anthology of Modern Fairy Tale Poetry*, edited by Wolfgang Mieder. Hanover, NH: Published for University of Vermont by University Press of New England, 1985, 29.

Told in the first person, the poem explores the thoughts of a young male, eager to be kissed but nervous about the possibility that the person who kisses him may not be the right one.

1969: Thompson, Phyllis. "**A Fairy Tale**." Reprinted in *Disenchantments: An Anthology of Modern Fairy Tale Poetry*, edited by Wolfgang Mieder. Hanover, NH: Published for University of Vermont by University Press of New England, 1985, 28.

Using the image of the frog prince, the first-person female narrator discusses sexual congress.

1971: Sexton, Anne. "**The Frog Prince**." In *Transformations*. Boston: Houghton Mifflin, 93–99. Also in *Disenchantments: An Anthology of Modern Fairy Tale Poetry*, edited by Wolfgang Mieder. Hanover, NH: Published for University of Vermontbu University Press of New England, 1985, 30–34.

Sexton examines traditional superstitions and beliefs about frogs before retelling the story of one particular frog. After his transformation, the prince makes sure his bride will never meet another "frog." The poem illustrates the situation of women in general. "Her [Sexton] bias is clear: she is constantly concerned with the manner in which women are *obliged* to internalize conventional norms and values not of their own making which prevent them from pursuing their own desires" (Zipes 1986, 20).

1972: Pettingell, Phoebe. "**Frog Prince**." Reprinted in *Disenchantments: An Anthology of Modern Fairy Tale Poetry*, edited by Wolfgang Mieder. Hanover, NH: Published for University of Vermont by University Press of New England, 1985, 35.

This poem contains the musings of a mother after the birth of her child.

1972: Smith, Stevie. "**The Frog Prince**." Reprinted in *Disenchantments: An Anthology of Modern Fairy Tale Poetry*, edited by Wolfgang Mieder. Hanover, NH: Published for University of Vermont by University Press of New England, 1985, 25–26.

This poem explores the thoughts of a frog as he awaits his disenchantment. Although he is happy and has waited over a century in his present form, he knows that one day he will meet with a princess who will transform him and that too, will be fine, even "heavenly."

1973: Brewster, Elizabeth. "**The Princess Addresses the Frog Prince**." In *Mountain Moving Day: Poems by Women*, edited by Elaine Gill. Trumansburg, NY: Crossing Press, 36. Also in *Disenchantments: An Anthology of Modern Fairy Tale Poetry*, edited by Wolfgang Mieder. Hanover, NH: Published for University of Vermont by University Press of New England, 1985, 36.

The princess explains to the frog in the pond that she had no ulterior motive in dropping the golden ball into the pond, but now that he has rescued it, she is willing to have him as her "ugly pet."

1975: Graves, Robert. "**The Frog and the Golden Ball**." Reprinted in *Disenchantments: An Anthology of Modern Fairy Tale Poetry*, edited by Wolfgang Mieder. Hanover, NH: Published for University of Vermont by University Press of New England, 1985, 24.

The princess, in love with her newly transformed prince, is in panic at the thought of the reactions of her parents, who "had promised her in marriage to a cousin. . . ." The frog prince is surprised that the "magic of love" is not as powerful as successful financial mergers between two families.

1975: Jones, Paul R. "**Becoming a Frog**." Reprinted in *Disenchantments: An Anthology of Modern Fairy Tale Poetry*, edited by Wolfgang Mieder. Hanover, NH: Published for University of Vermont by University Press of New England, 1985, 37.

Images of an amphibian transformation fill this first-person narrative about relationships.

1978: Mitchell, Susan. "**From the Journals of the Frog Prince**." Reprinted in *Disenchantments: An Anthology of Modern Fairy Tale Poetry*, edited by Wolfgang Mieder. Hanover, NH: Published for University of Vermont by the University Press of New England, 1985, 38–39.

Happily ever after is not necessarily a consistent state, as the transformed frog soon discovers. Discontented with his human lifestyle, he surrounds himself with dreams and images of his former life. Told in the first person.

1980: Kinnell, Galway. "**Kissing the Toad**." Reprinted in *Disenchantments: An Anthology of Modern Fairy Tale Poetry*, edited by Wolfgang Mieder. Hanover, NH: Published for University of Vermont by University Press of New England, 1985, 41.

Included in the collection of "Frog Prince" poetry because of the intertwined images of kissing the toad and sexual union, this poem does not refer to the traditional tale at all.

1980: Pack, Robert. "**The Frog Prince (A Speculation on Grimm's Fairy Tale)**." Reprinted in *Disenchantments: An Anthology of Modern Fairy Tale Poetry*, edited by Wolfgang Mieder. Hanover, NH: Published for University of Vermont by University Press of New England, 1985, 40.

The narrator in this short poem speculates on the princess's mother's reaction to the two transformations that took place in the princess's bedroom that evening: that of frog to man and that of girl to woman.

1982: Hay, Sara Henderson. "**The Marriage**." In *Story Hour*. Fayetteville, AR: University of Arkansas Press, 11. Also in *Disenchantments: An Anthology of Modern Fairy Tale Poetry*, edited by Wolfgang Mieder. Hanover, NH: Published for University of Vermont by University Press of New England, 1985, 23.

This is a short poem from the young princess's mother's point of view. Although her son-in-law may not be the enchanted frog his wife likes to think he is, they are happy together. And, after all, is that not what every parent wants for their child?

1990. Strauss, Gwen. "**The Frog Princess**." In *Trail of Stones*. New York: Alfred A. Knopf, 24–26.

The young princess has always disliked frogs, and the fact that she must allow it to sleep on her pillow fills her with rage. She manages to control herself for three weeks, but finally casts the creature against the wall, and that is how she got her prince "to explode from a frog." The poem contains powerful images and use of language.

1992: Yolen, Jane. "**Frog Prince**." In *The Storyteller*. Cambridge, MA.: NESFA Press, 143.

A mother ponders about potential husbands for her daughters and laments that "it is so hard these days to find a proper prince." A note from the author explains that this is a biographical poem written for her daughter Heidi (and influenced somewhat by popular culture: a button stating *You Have to Kiss a Lot of Frogs Before You Find a Prince*).

Picture Books

While there are various illustrated editions of this tale on the market, only two reworkings of this tale stand out. Both of these stories consider the fact that the frog may not be fully satisfied in his human form or with his princess bride.

1989: Berenzy, Alix. **A Frog Prince**. New York: Henry Holt.

The tale begins with the Grimms' version of the traditional story of a frog rescuing the princess's golden ball from the pond and her keeping her promise only in obedience to her father. But instead of the spell being broken by the actions of the princess, the rather large frog decides to go on a quest to find a true princess who will appreciate him for himself. The king, appalled at his daughter's petulant behavior, outfits the noble frog as befits a prince and gives him a horse. While on his journey, the frog rescues a dove from two trolls and a turtle from a witch casting spells. He finally comes to a castle containing the most beautiful princess he could ever imagine. The frog awakens her with a kiss and marry to live happily ever after—both still frogs!

Ammon and Sherman include this title in their compilation *Worth a Thousand Words*, citing references to fractured folktales, themes such as honor and kindness, and transformation. It was the winner of the Bologna Book Fair Critical Erba Prize.

1991: Scieszka, Jon. **The Frog Prince Continued**. Illustrations by Steve Johnson. New York: Viking.

As the title implies, this picture book challenges the happily-ever-after ending of the traditional folktale. Plagued by the nagging princess, the Frog Prince cannot help but wonder if he was indeed happier before the day of the fateful kiss. As the satire plays out, the frog prince confronts familiar witches from "Sleeping Beauty," "Snow White," and "Hansel and Gretel." And, in the end, the prince and princess do indeed live happier ever after, after!

Graphic Novels

Although the Frog Prince is not an active character in any graphic novels at this point, his faithful servant, Iron Henry, is a mysterious character in the ongoing comic-book series *Castle Waiting* by Linda Medley. The graphic novel and subsequent issues of the comic book are discussed in the chapter on "Sleeping Beauty."

Internet Resources

There are several significant resources on this tale available on the Internet. The most useful site, particularly for the history of the tale, is D. L. Ashliman's Folklore and Mythology Electronic Texts. "Frog Kings: Folktales about Slimy Suitors" can be found at http://www.pitt.edu/~dash/frog.html. The contents are constantly being updated as variants are translated and posted. Full-text manuscripts are available for the Grimms' final version as well as the first English version of the Grimms translated and adapted by Edgar Taylor. At the same site, Ashliman provides a comparison of the Grimms' 1812 and 1857 versions, word by word.

A secondary site (http://www.northsouth.com/Bios/FrogPrince.html) is provided by the illustrator Binette Schroder discussing her approach when illustrating her 1985 picture book *The Frog Prince, or Iron Henry*. She explains how she had problems with illustrating these characters, characters whom she had loved as a child but loathed as an adult. "The only lovable and positive figure in the whole story is Iron Henry. And his role is not integrated into the story, but simply acts as a postscript tacked on at the end." Schroder explains how she looked to literary criticism and analysis for inspiration. "I do not normally have much respect for the psychological interpretation of fairy tales. But in the end, the work of a psychologist and marriage guidance counselor which [sic] made this story accessible to me and enabled me to relate to the main character."

The Frog King is also a character in a comic strip titled "Happily Ever After." The strip, background notes and archives are available at http://www.concentric.net/~doodlesb/biomain.html. The strip features Queen Maggie and King Rupert. "Maggie kissed a frog and turned him into a prince, but it's been 15 years now, and, well . . . have you ever heard of a relapse?" The strip also features other fairy tale characters such as Rapunzel and the wolf and his three nemeses.

Classroom Extensions

Many of the following suggestions may be easily adapted to discuss other fairy tales.

Antecedents

Compare the stories of "Dame Ragnell or the Loathly Lady" from King Arthur with Chaucer's "The Wife of Bath." What do these stories have in common with "The Frog King or Iron Henry?"

Cartoons

Find as many cartoon and comic-strip versions of this tale as possible. Do they, as Wolfgang Mieder suggests, focus on the bedroom scene to the exclusion of all of the other elements? Discuss your findings.

Character Analysis

What are the major character traits of the princess, her father, and the frog? Are any of them really likable? Trustworthy? How would the story change if the frog was telling the tale? The princess or her father? An observer?

Endings

Which ending of this tale were you most familiar with before discussing this tale? Does the frog get dashed against the wall, disenchanted by a kiss, or transformed patiently over three days of sleeping in the princess's bed? Does the overall tone of the story change with these divergent methods of transformation? Why or why not?

The Ethics of Promises

The Grimms adapted the older story to reflect their idea of paternal obedience and the importance of keeping promises. Is there any time when the keeping of promises is not a good idea? What of the future happiness of the princess and her transformed suitor? Does a relationship based on the outside imposition of keeping promises have a good chance for survival?

Fair Peril at the Mall

How and why does Nancy Springer incorporate modern mall culture to represent the faerie world? Is it an apt analogy? Discuss.

Frog Princesses

There is another group of folktales based on the idea of a bespelled female frog. How would the tale of "The Frog King" change in meaning if the gender was reversed? Find copies of "The Frog Princess" and discuss the differences in the scope and meaning of this tale compared with the one we have been discussing.

Iron Henry

Bruno Bettelheim decided that he could not fathom a purpose for this faithful servant and so ignored him completely. The Grimms obviously thought him important, however, as he is cited in the title of the story. What role does he play in the traditional tale? Were you aware of this character in the version you remember?

Popular Culture and the Tale

Jane Yolen, in her poetic reworking of this tale, credits a popular saying on a button for some of her inspiration. Have you seen other examples of this tale in popular culture? What are they, and what do they tell us about our present society?

Bibliography

Ashliman, D. L. "Symbolic Sex-Role Reversals in the Grimms' Fairy Tales." In *Forms of the Fantastic: Selected Essays from the Third International Conference on the Fantastic in Literature and Film*, edited by Jan Hokenson and Howard Pearce. New York: Greenwood Press, 1986, 193–98. (Contributions to the Study of Science Fiction & Fantasy, no. 20).

Beitter, Ursula E. "Identity Crisis in Fairy-Tale Land: The Grimm Fairy Tales and Their Uses by Modern-Day Imitators." In *Imagination, Emblems and Expressions: Essays on Latin American, Caribbean and Continental Culture and Identity*. Edited by Helen Ryan-Ransom. Bowling Green, OH: Bowling Green State University Popular Press, 1993, 274–82.

Bettelheim, Bruno. *The Uses of Enchantment: The Meaning and Importance of Fairy Tales*. New York: Vintage Books, 1976.

Bottigheimer, Ruth B. *Grimms' Bad Girls and Bad Boys: The Moral and Social Vision of the Tales*. New Haven, CT: Yale University Press, 1987.

Brewer, Derek. *Symbolic Stories: Traditional Narratives of Family Drama in English Literature*. Cambridge, England: D. S. Brewer, 1980.

Campbell, Joseph. *The Hero with a Thousand Faces*. 2d ed. Princeton, NJ: Princeton University Press, 1968.

Ellis, John M. *One Fairy Story Too Many: The Brothers Grimm and Their Tales*. Chicago: University of Chicago Press, 1983.

Heuscher, Julius E. *A Psychiatric Study of Myths and Fairy Tales: Their Origin, Meaning, and Usefulness*. 2d edition. Springfield, IL: Charles C. Thomas, 1974.

Kolbenschlag, Madonna. *Kiss Sleeping Beauty Good-Bye: Breaking the Spell of Feminine Myths and Models*. San Francisco: Harper & Row, 1988.

McGlathery, James M. *Fairy Tale Romance: The Grimms, Basile, and Perrault*. Urbana-Champaign, IL: University of Illinois Press, 1991.

———. *Grimms' Fairy Tales: A History of Criticism on a Popular Classic*. Columbia, SC: Camden House, 1993.

Mieder, Wolfgang. "Modern Anglo-American Variants of the Frog Prince (AT 440)." *New York Folklore*. 6: 3–4 (Winter 1980): 111–35.

———. *Tradition and Innovation in Folk Literature*. Hanover, NH: University of Vermont Press, 1987.

Opie, Iona, and Peter Opie. *The Classic Fairy Tales*. New York: Oxford University Press, 1974.

Rohrich, Lutz. "The Quest of Meaning in Folk Narrative Research." In *The Brothers Grimm and Folktale*, edited by James M. McGlathery et al. Urbana-Champaign, IL: University of Illinois Press, 1988, 1–15.

Sale, Roger. *Fairy Tales and After: From Snow White to E. B. White*. Cambridge, MA: Harvard University Press, 1978.

Sax, Boria. *The Frog King: On Legends, Fables, Fairy Tales and Anecdotes of Animals*. New York: Pace University Press, 1990.

Tatar, Maria. "From Nags to Witches: Stepmothers in the Grimms' Fairy Tales." In *Opening Texts: Psychoanalysis and the Culture of the Child*, edited by Joseph H. Smith and William Kerrigan. Baltimore, MD: John Hopkins University Press, 1985, 28-41. (Psychiatry and the humanities, vol. 8).

———. *The Hard Facts of the Grimms' Fairy Tales*. Princeton, NJ: Princeton University Press, 1987.

———. "Beauties vs. Beauties in the Grimms' Nursery and Household Tales." In *The Brothers Grimm and Folktale*, edited by James M. McGlathery. Urbana-Champaign, IL: University of Illinois Press, 1988, 133–45.

———. *Off with Their Heads! Fairy Tales and the Culture of Childhood*. Princeton, NJ: Princeton University Press, 1992.

Thomas, Joyce. *Inside the Wolf's Belly: Aspects of the Fairy Tale*. Sheffield, England: Sheffield Academic Press, 1989.

Thompson, Stith. *The Types of the Folktale: A Classification and Bibliography. A Translation and Enlargement of Antti Aarne's Verzeichnis de Märchentypen*. 2d revision. Helsinki: Academia Scientiarum Fennica, 1964. (FF Communications, no. 184).

Zipes, Jack. *Fairy Tales and the Art of Subversion: The Classical Genre for Children and the Process of Civilization*. New York: Methuen, 1983.

———. *Don't Bet on the Prince: Contemporary Feminist Fairy Tales in North America and England*. New York: Methuen, 1986.

———. *The Brothers Grimm: From Enchanted Forests to the Modern World*. New York: Routledge, 1988.

———. *Creative Storytelling: Building Community, Changing Lives*. New York: Routledge, 1995.

CHAPTER 4

Hansel and Gretel

Thus even the witch of "Hansel and Gretel" has been tugged in new directions by our demands, our desires, just as she was once shaped by the fantasies of early modern women. Those earlier fantasies are still present in vestigial form, but without further knowledge of the early modern context, they are no longer readable, and are liable to be recuperated as psychic symptoms or as inscrutable historical darkness. This process of transformation, which is not without its contestations, involves a series of noticeable losses. For the essence of the early modern witch is fear, and we no longer find the witch frightening. . . . The real terror of the witch lies in this mixture of familiarity and unbearable strangeness. She represents what we cannot bear to acknowledge as ours, the feelings, violence, dirt and filth that we cannot own without destroying our pleased sense that we are good and kind and clean (Purkiss, 281–82).

The witch and her gingerbread house, along with the two young abandoned children in the forest, are the most frequent images of this tale displayed in such popular culture media as cartoons and advertisements. What is it about this tale that fascinates the modern reader, listener, and reteller? And how much of the traditional tale is even remembered? The story, as set down by the Brothers Grimm in their final rendition, is about . . .

℘ ————————————————————————————

A man, his wife, and his two children who lived in a cottage by the woods. The man was a woodcutter and, times being hard, not a very successful man. His wife, afraid of starving, came up with a plan. They would take the children out into the woods and leave them there to their fate. The father was horrified at the idea but, as a weak and ineffectual man, did nothing to stop his wife. The children had been listening to their conversation, and the boy comforted his younger sister saying that he, too, had a plan. Hansel gathered pebbles and left a trail for them to follow back home on the first attempt to abandon them. But on the second attempt, he had been unable to leave the house and thus used the only material he had available: bread crumbs. Unfortunately for the children, these crumbs proved to be as ineffectual as their father, and they were lost for several days in the woods. A bird directed them to a cottage in the woods, a cottage made entirely of eatable materials, and the hungry children feasted without thought until the owner of the house showed herself. The woman was at first helpful and friendly, but it soon developed that she was a wicked manipulative witch who had trapped the children (and previous ones?) with her delectable house. For four weeks, Hansel was locked in the stable and fattened while Gretel cooked and slaved for the witch and received very little food. Hansel managed to fool the witch into thinking that he was not gaining weight, but she soon was too greedy to care and had Gretel prepare the oven and fire to bake the bread and cook the boy. Gretel, realizing that no one would save either one of them, managed a trick of her own and shoved the witch into the oven, condemning her to the flames. Gretel freed Hansel, and they immediately plundered the house for wealth (and there was a great deal) before catching a ride on a nearby duck to get them safely home. When they arrived at their father's house, they discovered that the wife had died and the home was now truly safe. The three of them lived happily with their newly gained riches (and freedom?).

———————————————————————————— ♌

Tale Type: AT 327

The Opies state that this tale type was well known throughout Europe before the Grimms set the tale down in their collection. The children's contact with the ogre or witch in this tale type "is involuntary, unlike the youthful heroes of the 'Jack' tales, whose great object is to make contact with uppish monsters whether to win glory, obtain loot, or indulge in their love of blood sports" (Opie, 308).

The Children and the Ogre

I. *Arrival at Ogre's House*: (a) Children are abandoned by poor parents in a wood, (b) but they find their way back by cloth shreds or pebbles that they have dropped; (c) the third time birds eat their breadcrumbs, or grain clue, and (d) they wander until they come to a gingerbread house which belongs to a witch; or (e) a very small hero (thumbling) and his brothers stay at night at the ogre's house; or (f) the ogre carries the child home in a sack; (g) the child substitutes a stone in the sack twice but is finally captured.

II. *The Ogre Deceived*: The ogre smells human flesh and has the children imprisoned and fattened. (b) When the hero's finger is to be cut to test his fatness, he sticks out a bone or piece of wood. (c) The exchange of caps, (d) the ogre's wife or child burned in his own oven (Type 112), or (e) the hero by singing induces the ogre to free them; or (f) the hero to be hanged feigns ignorance and has ogre show him how; or (g) hero feigns inability to sleep until ogre brings certain objects and escapes while ogre hunts the object.

III. *Escape*: (a) The children are carried across the water by ducks (or angels), or (b) they throw back magic objects that become obstacles in the ogre's path, or (c) they transform themselves, or (d) the ogre (ogress) tries to drink the pond empty and bursts, or (e) the ogre is misdirected and loses them.

Motifs:

S321. Destitute parents abandon children

S301. Children abandoned (exposed)

S143. Abandonment in forest

R135. Abandoned children (wife, etc.) find way back by clue (breadcrumbs, grain, pebble, etc.)

R135.1. Crumb (grain) trail eaten by birds

F771.1.10. Gingerbread house. House made of cake

G412.1. Ogre's gingerbread house lures child

G10. Cannibalism

G82. Cannibal fattens victim

G82.1. Cannibal cuts captive's finger to test fatness

G82.1.1. Captive sticks out bone instead of finger to test fatness

G526. Ogre deceived by feigned ignorance of hero. Hero must be shown how to get into oven (or the like). Ogre shows him and permits him to be burnt

G512.3.2. Ogre burned in his own oven (Thompson, 116–19)

History of Hansel and Gretel in Print

When asked about the story of "Hansel and Gretel," very few people consider any antecedents or variants of this tale. It is strongly identified as a German tale, a tale from the Brothers Grimm. However, as the discussion on the changes the Grimms made to this tale reminds us, there is indeed a previous history to the story. The theme of child abandonment, omitted in Humperdinck's opera and thus from many modern interpretations of the story, and the laying of the trail have long been features of the tale type, and they occur in the story of "Finetta Centron" by Madame d'Aulnoy, which was published in English in 1721 as "Finetta the Cinder-Girl" (Opie, 308). Other similarities include the house made of treasure (more delectable to the lost but well-fed princesses of the story) and the cooking of the giant in the oven by the same manner of reasoning.

Basile

"Ninnillo and Nennella" (Day 5, tale 8) features the motif of the trail used in a survival attempt when the two children are abandoned by their father at their stepmother's request. But in this case, it is the father himself who first leaves the trail of ashes and, on the second attempt, a trail of bran that is consumed by an ass (Opie, 167).

Perrault

There are considerable similarities between the first part of "Little Thumb" or "Le Petit Poucet" and "Hansel and Gretel." The catalyst for both tales is imminent starvation, and both stories celebrate a child's ingenious means of thwarting the intentions of the parents. Both stories also contain a dangerous encounter with a predatory adult in the forest (Hallett and Karasek 1996, 78). The Opies state that the theme of child abandonment in times of trouble is an old theme, as is the secret laying of a trail in dangerous territory to find oneself home to safety (Opie, 167). In the first English translations of the story, the hero is called Little Poucet, but by the 6th edition, the name had been changed to "Little Thumb." The name "Hop o' My Thumb" was a common phrase 400 years ago to refer to a tiny person and was first given to the hero by Mary

Jane Goldwin in *Tabart's Collection of Popular Stories for the Nursery*, published in 1804 (Opie, 169). The French version is less fanciful than its better-known cousin. Robert Darnton stresses that, in opposition to many of the other tales such as "Cinderella," the Grimms' version has more fanciful and poetic touches and the mysterious forest and the naïveté of the children in the face of inscrutable evil are emphasized. "Unlike their German relatives, the French ogres appear in the role of *le bourgeois de la maison* (burgher head of the household) as if they were rich local landowners" (Darnton, 21–22).

Darnton assesses Perrault's tone in his version as a matter-of-fact acceptance of how commonplace the death of children had become in early modern France. Perrault wrote this tale at the height of the worst demographic crisis in the seventeenth century, "a time when plague and famine decimated the population of northern France, when the poor ate offal thrown in the street by tanners, when corpses were found with grass in their mouths and mothers "exposed" the infants they could not feed so that they got sick and died" (Darnton, 30).

The Brothers Grimm

The importance of being aware of the history of any folktale is born to us when we realize how often theories formed without background knowledge are easily discredited and discounted. For example, the opening theme of the "famine" was introduced by Wilhelm Grimm in the fifth edition (1843). When scholarly critics use this theme as the starting point for their interpretation, they are definitely on the wrong track (Rolleke, 108).

Jack Zipes agrees, stating that most of the interpretations of this tale are fallacious because these interpretations do not consider the changes that were made by the Grimms in their various editions of the tales. Zipes points out that these changes were based on the readings of previous literary texts. The Grimms knew the versions by Perrault and Basile and "the most dramatic changes occurred in the fifth edition of 1843, after Wilhelm had read Stober's Alsatian tale 'The Little Pancake House.' " (Zipes 1997, 43).

Zipes points to an irony here. Stober collected his tale from an informant who was probably familiar with the Grimms' version and adapted it for his or her own purpose. Stober credits the Grimms' collection as his literary source (Zipes 1997, 44). Diann Rusch-Feja refers to the changes made to the text that were directly derivative of Stober's tale. These include Hansel's wish to say goodbye to the cat, the white bird that led the children to the gingerbread house, the verse forms used to request the duck to carry them over the water, and the closing verse as well. (Rusch-Feja, 41).

According to Zipes, the embellishment of the text was done at first to make the tales more palatable to the younger audience the collection was beginning to attract. Dialogue was introduced to deepen the characterization of the parents: The father became more caring and concerned about the children (although he remains amazingly weak for such a "caring" father!) while the (step)mother becomes even more cold-hearted and cruel (Zipes 1997, 47). John Ellis credits the changes made in the subsequent editions of this tale as resulting in major changes in family relationships and therefore, "since family relationships are a large part of the content of the tales, the brothers were in this respect interfering in an important way with the basic material available to them" (Ellis, 64). Changes were made to present the father as a basically good man who, although he loves his children, is also weak and easy to manipulate by his evil wife. In this way, he is almost deserving of the fortune his children bring to him at the end of their journey. "This change also has the effect of reducing emphasis on the conflict between parents and children—a persistent tendency of the Grimms" (Ellis, 66). The Grimms reduced the number of malevolent parents from two (in the manuscript) to one (in the first edition) and then to none in the 4th edition by simply and casually making the natural mother into a stepmother (Ellis, 73). By the time the story was rewritten for the 5th edition, the stepmother's wickedness becomes the sole source of the children's problems. But because the father still must acquiesce, the brothers introduce even more material in the 5th edition to demonstrate his "innocence of wrongdoing." His wife's pressure to abandon the children becomes more severe, and the father still feels sorry for the poor children! (Ellis, 73). Zipes goes even further than Ellis in condemning this progression of adaptations.

> Aberrant actions are made rational, but in the process there is a rationalization of the father's deed that reinforces a patriarchal social and symbolic order. In the rational structure of the text, abuse takes place on two levels: the children, Hansel and Gretel, are abused by having nourishment withheld from them and eventually are drawn into accepting the rule of the father as more benevolent than that of the mother; and children as young readers are abused by following the rational order of the text and being misled to conceive that order will always be restored through the intervention of God the father and a resolution that restores faith in the good father (Zipes 1997, 50).

Zipes attempts to rationalize these changes from the personal history of the two brothers. It is possible, he states, to consider the two children as representations of the brothers themselves. The early death of their father was considered as abandonment in their autobiographical writings. Their embellishments made the story more charming, quaint, and comforting to the readers as well as more rationally based according to the ideological perspective of the brothers. "The 'evil' in the tale is shifted from the bad actions of a father and stepmother to a female witch, the opposite of the male Christian God" (Zipes 1997, 47). This shifts the focus of the tale from surviving abandonment to overcoming abuse in the form of the witch. There are now three distinct times at which the children call upon God for help. The first two times are offered by Hansel to console his sister when they are still at home. The third time is a plea by Gretel as she is ordered to help the witch cook her brother. These changes transform the pagan children of the manuscript into good, Christian, God-fearing children, and it is this goodness and faith in God that help them overcome the evilness of the witch. Zipes also contends that "abandoned by one father, they must appeal to another, divine father, who will not desert them. Fathers are continually extolled in the tale, whether they be biological or divine" (Zipes 1997, 49). Social reality is evidenced by the extreme poverty and the deprivation of spiritual, psychological, and physical nourishment that the children (and numerous peasant households in Germany during the first half of the nineteenth century) undergo. Wilhelm's changes to the text bring a dual identification of the stepmother and witch-figure, both demonized and both duplicitous in their initial friendly appearance while inwardly plotting the destruction of the children.

Marina Warner concurs, asserting that the Brothers Grimm, while not making it disappear entirely, did indeed soften the harshness in the tales involving family dramas. "On the whole, they tended towards sparing the father's villainy, and substituting another wife for the natural mother, who had figured as the villain in the versions they had been told: they felt obligated to deal less harshly with mothers than the female storytellers whose material they were setting down" (Warner, 211).

Wolfgang Mieder discusses these changes by concentrating on the use of proverbs in Wilhelm Grimm's editing process. He demonstrates how the use of these proverbs alters the meaning of the tale. Regarding the changes from the manuscript through the 7th edition in 1857, it is easy to see how folk speech was employed in making the (step)mother's second plan more palatable for his child audience. Both the manuscript (1810) and the first edition (1812) do not contain any proverbial materials (Mieder 1988, 125). "The most significant stylistic change between these two versions consists of the move from indirect to direct speech, the detailed account of the impoverished home, the precise description of the bread, the stones . . . [and] . . . the names Hansel and Gretel" (Mieder, 125). The proverb "whoever has begun a thing must go on with it," added in 1843, convinces the father to be an active, if unwilling, participant once again in abandoning his children in the woods. "He cannot stand up against the proverbial and therefore 'justified' argument of his wife since he had already taken part once before . . ." (Mieder 1988, 126).

Table 4.1
Changes Made by the Brothers Grimm

Manuscript	First edition (1812)	Second edition	Fifth edition
"The Little Brother and the Little Sister" (A notation in Jacob Grimm's handwriting was placed beneath this title in the manuscript: "alias Hansel und Gretchen" and immediately below this, "cf. Perrault petit Poucet") (Rusch-Feja, 40).	"Hansel and Gretel"	No change.	No change.
Both the mother and father wake the children on the first attempt to abandon them.	The mother is the one who wakes them with "get up, you children, we will go into the forest" (Ellis, 64).	No change.	The first time the famine is mentioned as a reason for distress.
Both parents are involved in the second attempt as well.	The mother is the sole parent involved in waking the children.	No change.	Stepmother (changed in the 4th edition). She tells the children to "get up, you lazy-bones."

Manuscript	First edition (1812)	Second edition	Fifth edition
The decision to carry out the second attempt to abandon the children is quickly passed over.	An elaborate account of the father's reluctance to do so is included in the text.	No change.	The scene of the parents' further cruelty in the woods is added to the first attempt. "And because they heard the blows of the axe, they believed that their father was nearby. But it was not the axe, it was a bough which he had tied to a dead tree and which the wind blew back and forth. And when they had sat in this way for a very long time, their eyes fell shut in tiredness, and they fell asleep, when they woke up it was already black night." When the children arrive safely at home, they are scolded by their stepmother for being an inconvenience. However the father is secretly pleased to have them return.
No religious statements.	Comments on the reliance on the good Lord have been added to Hansel and Gretel's dialogues.	No change.	Proverbial phrase added to bolster stepmother's pleas to her husband. The white bird makes an appearance to lead them to the house of the witch.
House made of bread; the roof was covered with cake and the windows are sugar.	House built completely of bread and covered with cake, and the windows were of pure sugar.	No change.	No change.
Brother ate some of the roof and the little sister, some of the window.	"We'll sit down there and eat our fill," said Hansel; "I'll eat some of the roof, you eat some of the window, Gretel. That is deliciously sweet for you."	No change.	"We'll start on that," said Hansel, "and have a good meal. I'll eat a piece of the roof, Gretel, and you eat some of the window, it's sweet."

Manuscript	First edition (1812)	Second edition	Fifth edition
Delicate voice called out from the house. The children were badly startled.	Delicate voice called. Hansel and Gretel were so frightened that they let fall what they held in their hands.	Delicate voice called. The children answered: "The wind! The wind! The heavenly child!" and continued eating. Gretel broke out a whole round windowpane for herself, and Hansel tore off a mighty piece of cake from the roof for himself.	Delicate voice. The children answered and continued eating without letting themselves be put out. Hansel, who liked the taste of the roof, pulled down a large piece of it, and Gretel picked out a whole round window pane, sat down with it, and enjoyed it.
Soon after a small old woman came out.	Immediately afterwards they saw a small, old woman creep out of the door. The Grimms establish her identity early as a cannibalistic witch by clarifying, once the children were fed and tucked into bed. "The old woman, however, was a wicked witch, who lay in wait for children and had built her little house of bread to tempt them, and whenever one of them got into her power, she killed it, cooked it, and ate it, and that was a day for her to celebrate" (Ellis, 182).	Then the door opened, and a very old woman came creeping out. Hansel and Gretel were startled so badly that they let fall what they had in their hands.	Then suddenly the door opened and a very old woman who leaned on a crutch came creeping out.
The next morning she put the little brother in a little stable, he was to be a little pig, and the sister had to bring him water and good food.	She seized Hansel and put him in a little stable, and when he awoke there, he was surrounded by iron bars, just as young chickens are penned in, and could only walk a few steps. Gretel was shaken awake: "Get up, you lazybones."	No change.	She seized Hansel with her thin hand and carried him into a little stable. No matter how he screamed, it didn't help him; she locked him in with an iron-barred door, and then went to Gretel, jolted her awake and cried "Will you get up, lazy-bones?"

Manuscript	First edition (1812)	Second edition	Fifth edition
After four weeks, boiling water and heating oven. "She said to her: sit on the board, I will push you into the oven, see if the bread is already done; but she wanted to leave the little sister in there and roast her."	Hansel always stuck out a bone for her to feel; she was puzzled that he would not put on weight. Plans to cook him do not change. Gretel told to check to see if bread was brown enough, but old witch wanted to cook Gretel as well. Further elaboration about the witch's evil intents. "She wanted to eat her up too: that was what the wicked witch was thinking, and that is why she had called Gretel" (Ellis, 183).	No change.	Gretel is to find out if the oven is hot enough to cook the bread.
Little sister uses her natural cunning to understand the woman's intention and pretends she does not understand what is expected of her. "The witch burned to death."	"God inspired Gretel" to show her ignorance. "The old woman began to scream and wail in the hot oven."	No change to the oven scene, but when Gretel frees Hansel he "jumped out like a little caged bird" from his cage.	"Whoo! Then she began to howl, quite horribly; but Gretel ran off and the godless witch had to burn to death wretchedly."
The children return to their father and bring him jewels that will make him rich. The mother is dead.	Father expresses regret over what he had done. Ellis feels that this change was in response to the Grimms being offended by this undeserved fortune on the father's part after his behavior to his children (Ellis, 65).	Before they reach their home, they have to cross the water with the aid of a duck that carries Gretel over first and then Hansel. In Germanic tradition, the duck is related to the goose and to the swan and represents a distinctly feminine, motherly aspect or helpful mother replacement (Rusch-Feja, 159).	Verse added to summon duck. Hansel immediately gets on it and tells Gretel to join him, but she tells him that they would be too heavy for the duck and waits for the second trip.

Overview of Critical Interpretations of Hansel and Gretel

1974: Julius Heuscher considers this tale as one depicting the stages of maturation for very young children. These stages include repression that is displaced by regression when the frustration level of the children becomes too difficult to comprehend. "They long for a return toward an earlier existence . . . when their existence consisted of eating and sleeping in nice little beds" (Heuscher, 117). It is at this point that they come to the gingerbread house that, at first, fulfills this desire. The witch and her gingerbread house represent a catch in the regression stage: It carries with it the loss of independence, both physical and psychological. "The struggle begins between the two young individuals and the witch (or between the child and what his projection of his wishes has made out of the mother)" (Heuscher, 118). The children, through their experience, have become more aware of what is happening around them and will be better equipped to handle anything life has to offer. Hansel, representing the more conscious, intellectual aspect of the soul (*animus*), is united with Gretel, the feeling aspect of the soul (*anima*), in order to become a fully functional human being (Heuscher, 121). To Heuscher, this tale is about the vicissitudes of the young child in his earliest contacts with the material world and the danger of being swallowed up by that material world (126).

Heuscher assesses the symbolism of (1) the woods: representing losing or abandoning previous values and securities (117); (2) crossing the water: indicating a final process of successful repression of the negative aspect of the ambivalence towards the mother (119); (3) the white kitten: representing home as something you have to stay close to (120); (4) the white dove: symbolizing leaving home without forgetting about it (120); and (5) the witch's house: exemplifying the changed family home upon the second return from the woods (123).

1976: Bruno Bettelheim speaks about the importance of religious themes in the fairy tales such as "Hansel and Gretel," stating that they originated in periods when religion was central to daily life (13). This tale is a projection of the fears and anxieties that beset Hansel and Gretel. "By projecting their inner anxiety onto those they fear might cut them off, Hansel and Gretel are convinced that their parents plan to starve them to death!" (Bettelheim, 159).

Because the mother represents the source of food to the children and no longer is willing to satisfy all the oral demands of her children, she is the person who is blamed for abandoning them. The story exemplifies the debilitating consequences of trying to deal with life's problems with denial and regression. After all, when Hansel used his intelligence to gather pebbles to mark the path, he got himself and his sister home safely. When he did not use his intelligence (anyone living so close to a forest would know that birds ate breadcrumbs), he was lost. "Starvation anxiety has driven him back, so now he can think only of food as offering a solution to the problem of finding his way out of a serious predicament"(Bettelheim, 160). This fixation on food and oral gratification is further evidenced by the children's willingness to greedily destroy the house (their shelter and safety) even though the birds' behavior should have warned them about eating up things. This willingness to devour the house demonstrated their capacity to "eat somebody out of house and home, a fear which they had projected onto their parents as the reason for their dissertation" (Bettelheim, 161). This gingerbread house, a symbol of oral greediness, represents the mother who in fact nurses the child from her own body. The witch is also a manifestation of the same oral greediness and it is, in fact, her evil designs that force the children to recognize the dangers of unrestrained oral dependence and greed (Bettelheim, 162). To survive, they must use their intelligence as Hansel did at the beginning of their adventure. Bettelheim also considers the symbolic significance of the birds in the story. They first prevent the children from returning home by eating the trail; they lead the children to the dubious safety of the witch's house; and in the end, one bird provides them a means to return home. The birds must have known that it would be beneficial for Hansel and Gretel to face the dangers of the world. Because of their experiences with the witch, the children and their parents live happily ever after (163).

In his analysis, Bettelheim has unfortunately disregarded the fact that the (step)mother is no longer alive when the children arrive back home. The journey back home, the crossing of the water, represents a transition and a new beginning on a higher level of existence (as in baptism). This is the first time the children have been separated from each other, claims Bettelheim, and they are now acknowledging the fact that they are each individuals (Bettelheim, 164). This assumes that the separation while Hansel was imprisoned was not as intense as the one experienced during the crossing of the water. They will never encounter or fear the witch again!

1976:   Max Lüthi considers the polarity of the stepmother and the witch. The first wishes to let the children starve so she will not go hungry herself, while the witch lures the children to her in order to eat them. "Concern for their daily bread dehumanizes the parents: the witch's gluttony has the effect of a grotesque echo" (Lüthi, 64). The witch is not a person but rather a personification of evil, which, in the end, consumes itself. The children are less passive than most fairy-tale characters: They eavesdrop on their parents; they plot a way to get home; and first Hansel and then, when he fails, Gretel gets them home with the help of a supernatural helper (added by the Grimms). These child heroes are amazingly independent when compared with their older counterparts in other tales (Lüthi, 65). Lüthi refers affectionately to Hans Traxler's parody of archaeological methods tracing Hansel and Gretel's tale back to its origins. The book *Die Wahreit uber Hansel und Gretel* led many people on a wild goose chase, but Lüthi proclaims that "Fairy tales are experienced by their hearers and readers, not as realistic, but as symbolic poetry" (Lüthi, 66).

Lüthi offers a different vision of the witch in this story. Because she lives in a gingerbread oven and is duped by little children, first Hansel with the bone and then Gretel by crawling into the oven, her death is playful rather than a frightful image for the self-destruction of evil (115).

1979:   Jack Zipes declares this tale to be a story of hope and victory from a plebeian perspective (1979, 32). The struggle is against poverty and against witches who have ample reserves of food and treasure. The witch can be interpreted to symbolize the feudal system or the greed and brutality of the aristocracy who are responsible for the famine and poor living conditions. The killing of the witch represents the "hatred which the peasantry felt for the aristocracy as hoarders and oppressors" (Zipes 1979, 32). This can be seen as well by the fact that the children never place the blame for their situation on their parents (Zipes 1979, 32).

1980:   Derek Brewer professes that Hansel and Gretel, while they are an example of multiple protagonists, are in fact analogous to each other. Greater complexity is the result of the use of dual protagonists, as the children's obvious love for each other adds pathos and a variety of action (Brewer, 52). The dominance of the wicked mother-image suggests to Brewer that the fundamental protagonist is Gretel although Hansel is the stronger character in the first part of the tale. Several other aspects of the tale are articulated to bolster his view of the prominence of Gretel as protagonist: the ending of the story as a return to home, hostility and anxiety against the mother and the ultimate triumph over her, and the womblike oven. Brewer suggests that the oven is both a trap ("The womb will be a tomb if the growing individual is forced back into it") and an ally by making the antagonist ineffective. "When the protagonist has done this, by pushing the maleficent mother-figure into the oven, the main mother-figure is forgiven" (Brewer, 52).

1986: Ruth Bottigheimer briefly explores this tale as an example of "the silenced woman" in German tales as edited by Wilhelm Grimm. "Hansel and Gretel" exemplify the type of tale in which these silences result from the editor's distribution of direct and indirect speech (Bottigheimer 1986, 120). There is a consciously created silence for the female characters of this tale. The pattern of verbalization "undermines and contradicts Gretel's active role in implementing her own and Hansel's escape from the slavering witch" (Bottigheimer 1986, 124). Hansel's first words to her admonish her to silence: "Be quiet Gretel, do not distress yourself, I will soon find a way to help us." He consoles her frequently even when the text provides absolutely no occasion to do so. Bottigheimer suggest that "it is simply assumed that Gretel must be crying or deeply distressed" (1986, 124). The stepmother addresses Hansel and not his sister, establishing the pattern of speech within the tale.

1986: Hans Dieckmann analyzes the elements of this tale to provide a Jungian interpretation. The witch is extremely evil; there is no good in her at all; and she is very clearly and visibly connected to food. Her residence is constructed of it, and it is stressed that she feeds the children when they first arrive. She then fattens Hansel in preparation to boil, roast, and eat her prey (Dieckmann, 34). The oven is considered a womb symbol and a symbol of transformation. "The path from the production of the grain to the bread is a path of transformation of a natural product into a specifically human form of nourishment" (Dieckmann, 37). The role of the white bird is also discussed. Because white is the color of faith, salvation, peace, and joy, the bird illustrates the rightness of the children's meeting with the witch in her gingerbread house. The stones, in the first trail laid by Hansel, represent rigidity and lack of change while the bread, the product of transformation represents action (Dieckmann, 38). He finds it very difficult to rejoice in the ending of the tale, declaring it an unethical ending: "for the father, who was too weak to resist the evil suggestion of his wife and with her abandoned the children in the forest, is not only not punished for his highly immoral way of acting but even gets to enjoy the treasures the children bring back" (Dieckmann, 51).

1986: Gerhard Mueller looks at the criminological significance of selected Grimm tales. The crime of cannibalism, which occurs in "Hansel and Gretel," does not have a counterpart in the law of the Middle Ages and he infers that perhaps that problem had already been solved by society and that legal prohibitions were no longer needed. However, due to the frequent occurrences of cannibalism in the tales, "in the minds of the people, cannibalism lived on, if only as a nightmare" (Mueller, 222). The charge of witchcraft, also a large element in this tale, was punishable by fire, and indeed, the witch is duly incinerated in the oven. Therefore, the violent demise of the witch was entirely in keeping with the process of law.

1987: Ruth Bottigheimer expands on her discussion of silence in the Grimms' tale in her monograph. Gretel, with words put in her mouth by Wilhelm Grimm in the 1819 edition of the story, speaks to the duck. Later this brief command is elaborated into a verse, a quasispell but one that has been invented by someone who did not understand the conventions of true conjurings, "which are always part of a link with nature mediated by a wise woman" (Bottigheimer 1987, 41).

1987: Maria Tatar repudiates Ellis's theory that the Grimms turned what was originally a powerful story of parental malice and family conflict into a mild and harmless tale through all their various editing and adaptations. On the contrary, the mother is indeed the villain regardless of what version of the tale is read. She does become more bad-tempered and her husband more ineffectual during the numerous editing sessions by the Grimms, but there is no fundamental change in these two characters (Tatar 1987, 36). Once that is established, Tatar changes her focus to the setting of the tale, stating that no one has ever succeeded in establishing an approximate time during which the story took place. However, this has not deterred historians from using the tale as a source of cultural data (Tatar 1987, 49). Tatar points out that even as late as 1806, when the Grimms began collecting the tales, infanticide and child abandonment were not uncommon practices among the poor (1987, 49) However, once the children move into the forest, they move into a supernatural world where anything can happen. The witch is invested with symbolic significance open to interpretation beyond the historical realities of witchcraft (Tatar 1987, 51). Therefore, any interpretation of the conquest of the witch must be done on symbolic, rather than realistic, readings of the plot, but the facts of the hero's family life are essential to the ultimate understanding of the tale. "To ignore them is to do violence to the entire text" (Tatar 1987, 52).

1988: James Hoyme, considering Bettelheim's denial of the charge of abandonment of Hansel and Gretel by their parents, asks the question: If this is true, what is the story about? All of Bettelheim's work exhibits these salient features: "[h]is powerful *denial* of actual parental malevolence, his belief that the stories are concerned primarily with the conflicts and developmental tasks of children, and his corresponding faith that the stories actively help children to solve psychological problems and to grow" (Hoyme, 41). Hoyme looked to literature, to problems of child abuse, to clinical experiences in psychiatry, and to personal experiences as a parent in regards to destructive disturbances in the parent-child relationships to find evidence to refute Bettelheim's denial, and he had no shortages of examples. In answer to his own question about whose story/dream Hansel and Gretel is telling, his wry answer is:

> I won't name any names of course, but if I had to chop wood for a meager living and had nothing more to look forward to at the end of each back-breaking day than two gaunt, demoralized children and a nagging, selfish woman, I can imagine that I might wish that they'd all go away, leave me in peace, and fight out their hungry rage elsewhere amongst themselves. I might even wish that my children would someday return . . . fat and rich and smiling, to report their final solution of the greedy witch problem and give me, ungrudgingly, so much money that I'd never have to chop another tree (Hoyme, 45–46).

1989: Joyce Thomas considers the relationship between the two child siblings, in contrast to the pairings within many tales of adolescents and a supernatural or older helper. "The child protagonist is multiplied in the physical sense, but his/her strength is not commensurately doubled; s/he is less two separate beings than a dualistic figure fusing the boy and the girl, male and female— they remain 'the child' " (Thomas, 42).

Thomas regards a charge of sexism for this tale as unfounded because the children fluctuate in their active and passive roles. This alternating pattern of action is reflective of their shared androgynous roles (Thomas, 44). This alternation of roles may reflect their assumption of parental, adult functions as each looks after each other as a parent might. Their stepmother is decidedly not maternal. The witch, on the other hand, displays maternal tendencies when they first are acquainted with her. The witch quickly reverts to her original form as the stepmother, which is clearly indicated by the fact that both characters die at approximately the same time. Hansel and Gretel, on their return home, are now the responsible 'parent' for their ineffectual father and provide for his comfortable future (Thomas, 46). Part of the father's ineffectual role derives from the setting of the story and the identity of the antagonist. The stepmother's "sphere of activity and dominance is the home, whereas his traditionally lies beyond the home, in the outside world of work" (Thomas, 61).

> The very characteristics of maternal care are turned against the children and perverted into the means of their probable destruction. In the same manner, the witch, acting as a kindly grandmother figure, perverts the basic comforts associated with the maternal and the home. No more graphic an illustration of this perversion exists than in the image of her marvelous food-house. The house-home is transmuted into delectable foodstuffs; its cake roof, bread frame and sugar panes epitomize the home's life-sustaining functions and associations (Thomas, 61).

Thomas also focuses on the use of color represented by food, which "is far more the tale's physical landscape than is the woods in which most action takes place" (Thomas, 219). The major image of food, bread, is represented by the pale coloration of flour.

Aspects of irony abound: Hansel, overfed and fattened, tricks the witch by using the image of starvation and deprivation—he uses a bone that "intimates the fate awaiting his flesh (the bone could well be the gnawed remains of the cage's previous occupant)"; and the children, threatened with death because of their parents' fear of starvation, are much closer to death in a house filled, and created, with food. The final irony is the death of the witch herself. "When the witch is baked, the ultimate manifestation of all food imagery is realized, and the tale ceases its explicit use of it" (Thomas, 221).

1991: James McGlathery expounds that this tale centers on the innocent devotion between siblings. The fact that the children are of opposite gender allows their adventure to also be something of an innocent story of love (McGlathery 1991, 28). The evil actions of the two older women provide the challenge for these two children to demonstrate this devotion and cooperation. Both children rescue the other and, along the way, comfort each other as well. The supernatural segments of the story have a dreamlike quality that enhances this innocent love between them. The house of sweets has a threefold purpose: It answers their hunger caused by being lost in the forest for three days; it provides them occasion for a celebration on their closer relationship due to those hardships; and it satisfies a childhood appetite for sweets rather than symbol for a gratification of sexual desire (McGlathery 1991, 28). It also represents the prospect of the two children being able to live together under one roof. The crossing over of the body of water represents a new beginning, "not unlike a bride and bridegroom on their honeymoon" (McGlathery 1991, 28).

1992: Maria Tatar calls attention to flaws in Bettelheim's interpretation that the tale is about children who engage in "denial and regression" in order to remain dependent on their parents. Thus they are the villains of the piece before they ultimately become the agents of rescue for their parents with the witch's treasure. To Bettelheim this tale is not in any way concerned with parents who abandon their children (Tatar 1992, xviii). Tatar then turns her attention to Hoyme's interpretation, which makes it evident that two mutually exclusive accounts can be garnished from this tale:

One "superficial" reading that focuses on the tale's manifest content (parents abandon their children in the woods and leave them at the mercy of a cannibalistic witch) and a second, "deeper" reading that looks for latent meanings by detecting inversions, projections, and enactments of fears and fantasies (children are terrified of abandonment and fear the consequences of their oral greed). Most adult readers are drawn to this second kind of reading, a psychoanalytic interpretation that turns the child protagonists into egocentric villains who are forever projecting the dark side of their fantasy life onto unwitting adults (Tatar 1992, xx).

Tatar submits that adults do not want to face the "unpleasant truths" that may lurk inside these tales. However, in premodern Europe, child abandonment was not all that uncommon ("rates in urban areas probably ranged from 15 to 20 percent of registered births [as compared with a 1.5 percent rate for all recorded births in the United States])" (Tatar 1992, xxi). She turns her attention to the role famine played in fairy tales and in history. "Hansel and Gretel" begins in a realistic world complete with a vivid description of hunger and its consequence (Tatar 1992, 192). However, the witch has no problem accessing the foodstuffs to fatten Hansel up! The witch is obviously driven by more than hunger and the stepmother by more than just survival instincts. "Even when a tale half-heartedly exonerates one or both parents of malice by implying that abandoning children is the lesser of two evils . . . the parents are to blame and begin to emerge at the least as monsters of negligence" (Tatar 1992, 195). The children become the victims of a monster who initially provided them with all the food that their parents did not supply. The children have been starved and left without provisions in the woods, and have walked for several days without nourishment before they come to the witch's house. Is it oral greed that has them eagerly tear pieces of food from the house? Bettelheim's interpretation of the children mastering their oral greed to live happily with their parents can only be produced by ignoring the fact that the children return victorious to their father, who now is alone (Tatar 1992, 197). Nowhere is food endowed with more power than in this tale of death threats revolving around withholding and providing food. And it is easy, in Tatar's estimation, to understand Bettelheim's reaction to the children attacking the witch's house with abandoned gusto (Tatar 1992, 208).

1992: Virginia Walter states that most of the critical commentary on this tale has emphasized its psychological content from the interpretation proposed by Bettelheim, the subsequent criticism by Maria Tatar, and the theories of Jack Zipes and Ruth Bottigheimer on the importance of the forest. She then compares four illustrated versions of the tale, one from each of the last four decades, to discuss the author/illustrators' interpretation of the tale. She then looks at Joan Walsh Anglund ("too sappy"), Adrienne Adams ("emphasizing the symbolic content"), Anthony Browne ("too close to home for many children"), and James Marshall ("right on target for the media-blitzed, sweet, and savvy children of the 1990s").

1995: Steven Swann Jones refers to "Hansel and Gretel" as a primary example of fairy tales that are meant for young children. These tales focus on adjusting to life within the home, and the quest concerns acquiring or demonstrating the social and domestic skills needed to be a valued member of the family. These stories resolve with the successful return to the child's parental home. That this tale is about very young children is evidenced by their lack of awareness that the birds will eat their breadcrumb trail. The lack of food could be interpreted as a lack of love in the parental home (Jones 1995, 23). Jones also maintains that the story illustrates the confrontation of an Oedipal complex. Because Gretel ultimately saves the day, she can be considered the protagonist of this tale, and her conflict between her and her mother overrides the tale. This is exemplified by the fact that the death of the witch coincides with the death of the mother figure. "The evil witch would be an exaggerated representation of the unpleasant aspects of the mother, at least from the young girl's point of view. The correlation between the concern for food on the mother's part and the excessive appetite of the witch is no accident—it is a symbolic connection between the two characters" (Jones 1995, 23).

1995: Diann Rusch-Feja explores the tale in reference to her thesis on the portrayal of maturation of girls in the Grimms' tales. "Hansel and Gretel" is representative of brother-sister tales in which the sister must rescue the brother before she can fully attain her own self-realization (Rusch-Feja, 30). The young age of the children is assessed according to the evidence in the context of the story: They were not yet capable of providing for themselves or contributing to the family coffers. "They are very small children, still at an age where a strong mother-child relationship still exists, with the mother still providing for the children and helping them" (Rusch-Feja, 41). Family relationships are reflected in contrast figures. The weakness of the father is a counterbalance to the heartless domination of the mother, and Hansel's "heroic assurance" towards Gretel contrasts also with the father's weakness.

> Hansel's second attempt to save himself and his sister fails primarily because he wants to insure his way home with precisely the means withheld by the mother, namely the bread. The mother's refusal to provide the children with food, bread, and shelter is symbolic of her denial of love, nutrition, and protection—even if this only represents the superficial level of the real problem and reason for abandoning the children (Rusch-Feja, 43).

Gretel is portrayed as a "little sister" through her fears as a sign of her helplessness and immaturity, in contrast to both the "manly" brother and the overpowering, manipulative, negative mother-figure. Gretel is in a state of inaction, preparing herself for the time when her feminine powers will ripen and she can become active (Rusch-Feja, 44). Rusch-Feja agrees that the witch is an extension of the negative mother-figure. "She symbolizes a danger for the child who has not overcome his attachment to the mother, especially to the loveless mother, but also to the overprotective, consuming and controlling mother" (Rusch-Feja, 46). This figure is threefold: the loveless mother initiates the abandonment because of lack of bread while she is, at the same time, the image of the nourishing source for a small child and the witch who is concerned with the consuming of the children (Rusch-Feja, 47). Gretel proceeds towards maturation with two important initial steps. First, she becomes conscious of the threat of the negative mother-figure, and second, she acts efficiently at the correct time. At this point her maturation ends as, once the danger is past, she returns home to the comfort of the fold. The negative mother-figure has been destroyed in both locations, and the father is released from his overdominating wife. With the help of the treasure brought home with the children, he can now become a more effective and caring father.

1996: Diane Purkiss examines the folktale witch, concentrating on perhaps the most famous one of all time: the witch in her house made of sweets. Purkiss states that the house embodies and represents the witch's magical power in that she can create such an impossible dwelling that, at the same time, is a symbol of plenitude in a time of famine (Purkiss, 278). "It is Gretel's feminine linkage with the kitchen and cooking that allows her to turn the witch from consumer to meal, baking her in the oven she prepares for Hansel" (Purkiss, 278). Purkiss discusses this fact in light of the role of housewives of the time of the witch trial stories; the women understood the witch as a threat to their mastery of the domestic sphere. Gretel, in assuming control over the witch, has also assumed control over her own hearth and child (Hansel). Purkiss examines the function of food in the story and the altered adaptations of the interpretation of its role.

> Serious warnings to be vigilant at the boundaries of the body, anxieties about food and survival in rural subsistence cultures, have become part of narratives which reflect *adult* anxieties about controlling and managing the 'greed' of children. Indicative of these misreadings and rewritings is the alteration of the witch's original bread house to a *ginger*bread house. A simple subsistence food is replaced by a teatime luxury. As a result, the lost children are no longer eating from need but gorge themselves on food which normally would be rationed by caring parents (Purkiss, 280).

The substitution of gingerbread (and later, candies and other luxury sweets) gives some credence to Bettelheim's interpretation of the story as a tale of *children's* oral cravings. However, this aspect is a recent addition by *adults*. Purkiss comments that this change is characteristic of the nineteenth-century adult's desire to manage the drives and desires of children. "In this context, the witch becomes the agent of the adults' wish that greedy children should be punished" (Purkiss, 280). By this manner of retelling, therefore, the children are transformed from subsistence-class peasants to comfortable middle-class children with plenty to eat (Purkiss, 281). The actual role of the witch is modified as well. She no longer is the counterpart of the demon-mother but a dangerous stranger who is a source of temptation of wealth and power. "The motifs of maternity and hunger which had once shaped the tale are disfigured and flattened into psychoanalytic truisms" (Purkiss, 281).

1997:   Margery Hourihan also examines the role and image of the witch in children's stories. "As in most hero tales the opposition between home and wilderness, or the forest, is central but in this story home is not safe for the young hero and his sister because it is dominated by their wicked stepmother whose *alter ego* is the witch who lives in the forest" (Hourihan, 180). She reminds us that the witch and her malevolence are crucial to all the layers of significance of this tale. Hourihan summarizes previous interpretations of this tale by Jack Zipes, Marina Warner, and Bruno Bettelheim. She also states that for modern readers the religious elements and Christian symbols are not all that important. It is the children's relationship with their father and stepmother and the struggle against the witch that is of primary interest (Hourihan, 181). Hourihan claims that a central aspect of this tale is a sense of female power as dangerous and perverse.

1997:   Jack Zipes explores the changes the Grimms made to the tale in great detail but also discusses the relevance of this tale to contemporary children. He points out that the image of the oven became increasingly disturbing to parents and educators since 1945, but he feels that it is a pacifying tale providing hope of surviving a traumatic episode. "But," he continues, "I fear that it is also a tale that reinforces male hegemony and exculpates men from a crime against children, or that rationalizes the manner in which men use the bonds of love to reinforce their control over children" (Zipes 1997, 58).

Zipes states that the theme of abandonment has always been a prominent motif in literature, but the significance of this tale is the "*joyous* overcoming of abandonment and reconciliation with the parents or abusers" (Zipes 1997, 59). He sees this tale as a didactic Christian story with nothing really magical about it, with the exception of the house and the duck, because it appears at a time when people believed that witches did exist (Zipes 1997, 55).

Reworkings of Hansel and Gretel in Novel Form

Two vastly different treatments of this tale are available in novel form. The earliest offering focuses on child abandonment as a way to assure survival of the family; the second "humanizes" the witch figure.

Kindergarten

1980: Rushford, Peter. **Kindergarten**. New York: Alfred A. Knopf.

The story of Hansel and Gretel permeates throughout this dynamic story about a boy, his brothers, and his grandmother. Lilli, the grandmother, is a Jewish refugee from Germany, but this fact the boys (and the reader) only discover in compact segments throughout the novel. Fifteen-year-old Corrie, the strong and silent elder brother, looks after his 11-year-old brother Jo and the baby, three-year-old Matthias. While digesting their newly disclosed heritage, their mother's recent death by terrorists, and an ongoing televised terrorist onslaught at a Berlin elementary school, Corrie becomes captivated by a series of old letters that he finds at his father's school. These letters, from Jewish parents in Germany to a schoolmaster at a boarding school in England during the late 1930s, show the desperation of the parents as they arrange to "abandon" their children in order to assure their survival.

The novel is populated with fascinating characters: Lilli, before her "defection," was a well-known illustrator and painter of works based on the Grimms' fairy tales; Corrie's father, who never has an active role in the story, is the headmaster of the school and is away fundraising for victims of acts of terrorism; and Sal, a friend of the family, is an established author of novels for young people, or "New Adults" as they are "now" labeled. Lilli's illustrations and a wide array of the tales figure largely in the novel, but the tale of Hansel and Gretel takes precedent. Not only is the story told in full in large fragments throughout the novel itself, but Corrie refers to a cartoon version that he has watched on television, the Christmas centerpiece is a gingerbread house, the painting hanging over Corrie's bed is from the story, and the metaphors of being lost in the woods and of ovens are rendered again and again. The situation faced by the Jewish population in Germany is the main concern of the novel, but it is a story made strong by the characterization of Corrie and Lilli as they attempt to understand all three eras that make up their world: the fairy-tale world of the Grimm Brothers; World War II; and the late 1970s in England, which is distorted by terrorist attacks in other parts of the world.

The novel is also filled with references to German composers and music, children's stories such as *Emil and the Detectives*, Anne Frank's house and diary, and the juxtaposition of children's programs on television being followed by graphic live news updates. Rushford's novel is a "journey into woods" and out again that is powerful, memorable, and immediate for both young adults and the intended adult audience.

The Magic Circle

1993: Napoli, Donna Jo. **The Magic Circle**. New York: Puffin.

Kay Vandergrift refers to this novel as one that serves well as a transition between books for young children and those for young adults. "This book is a powerful rendering of an alternative version of the Hansel and Gretel story as told in the first person by the hunchbacked old woman who has become the witch" (Vandergrift, 28). A young mother, motivated by love and the desire to protect her daughter Asa, undergoes a unwilling transformation from midwife and healer to sorceress and then to the "wicked witch" of the traditional tale, one who craves the blood of children. She isolates herself in the woods and vows to resist all temptation. When Hansel and Gretel arrive, she hides their presence from evil demons and battles with her almost overwhelming desire to consume them. Although Hansel and Gretel as characters do not figure into the story until the last third of the book, the novel faithfully follows the story structure and weaves all of the major elements into her rational account: the "gingerbread" house, the confining of Hansel and his trick with the bone, and the fatal encounter with the oven. "In a hauntingly fascinating twist of the old tale, the witch plots her own death and, in death, frees herself from the powers of evil as she frees Hansel and Gretel from the demons who would use her to destroy them" (Vandergrift, 29). This slim novel also explores the history of witches during the Middle Ages. The other women "realize they have been lucky this time— they have not been denounced as witches. All women are in danger of the frivolous denunciation" (61).

Rosie Peasley, in her August 1993 review in *VOYA*, states "this brief novel is beautifully and sensitively written. . . . Napoli presents a powerful, effective alternative to the traditional tale and may tantalize young writers to try their hand at alternative renderings of well-known stories" (169). Reviewer Alison M. Smith, in *Book Report*, is reluctant to recommend the book since "I believe that in many communities it would be considered too instructive about devils, witches, magic and religion" (Smith, 48). The novel, however, was acclaimed an ALA Best Book for Young Adults, a *Bulletin* Blue Ribbon Book, and a *Publishers Weekly* Best

Book of the Year. *VOYA* listed it as both an entry in its 1993 Best Fantasy List and one of the books most likely to be censored!

Short Stories

There are only a few short stories based on the tale published before the 1990s. For some reason, authors became increasingly more "comfortable" with reworking this tale to echo contemporary concerns. Perhaps this coincides with a recent revival of interest in the Holocaust or the increased information available about poverty and child abuse. These stories, however, exhibit as wide a variety of interpretations as did the traditional tale.

1969: Coover, Robert. "**The Gingerbread House.**" In *Pricksongs & Descants: Fictions.* New York: E. P. Dutton, 61–75.

This is a poetic collection of paragraphs illuminating certain attributes of the tale, emphasizing colors, textures, and emotions. The story is only partially told within the 42 numbered segments. The reader is entrusted with aspects of the old man, his son and daughter, and the old and tattered witch. Each of these segments form loosely connected snapshots that, arranged correctly, tells the tale and evokes powerful images that stay long after the book is closed.

Jack Zipes uses this tale as an example of postmodern revision, which, by its very construction, makes the reader aware that there are different ways to shape and view these tales. "The end goal of the postmodernist fairy tale is not closure but openness, not recuperation but differentiation, not the establishment of a new norm but the questioning of all norms" (1992, 33). Coover produces "a trip through the woods filled with tension but never explained" (1992, 33). The hope of the traditional tale has been ripped away, like the heart of the dove, and there is no ending, just a doorway, a threshold, an uncertainty.

1987: Maitland, Sara. "**Angel Maker.**" In *A Book of Spells.* London: Michael Joseph, 1–10.

The witch reminisces about her rapport with Gretel over the many years since she first came to know her. The cottage, still made of spun sugar, has not entirely escaped the benefits of progress, however, as it is now held together by bubblegum. Gretel was but a child and accompanied by her brother the first time she met her. When the witch attempted to show the girl that she could exist quite well without her brother, Gretel, reacting in panic, burned the witch in her own oven. After fleeing home, Hansel and Gretel spread their version of the experience to everyone they could, and thus the witch's reputation was established through their tales. Since that time, and through the following centuries, Gretel has returned again and again to the cottage in the woods to replay that original encounter. Each time the girl is older, and each time the witch seems a little more familiar and Gretel is more at ease with her. This time, Gretel is seeking an abortion. The next time, artificial insemination! Progress and time continues, and soon the "angel maker" is no longer feared or sought out because science has eroded much of her influence and business. But still Gretel returns to eat of the sugar house and seek the magic within. This is a story of strong images, language, and possibilities.

1988: DeMarinis, Rick. "**Your Story**." In *The Year's Best Fantasy. 2d Annual Collection*, edited by Ellen Datlow and Terri Windling, New York: St. Martin's Press, 477–87.

The voice of the narrator in this contemporary retelling of the tale reminds readers that it, and all stories, are the readers' tales and that the readers can take full responsibility for reading the story and the symbolism as they wish to do. The writer will "need your open-minded help to fill in the blanks or to blank out excesses" (478). Gene and Amy decide to rid themselves of their children, Buddy and Jill, by taking them into the woods and leaving them there. Gene is not too keen on this idea, but he does enjoy the physical rewards of making his wife happy, so the two children are abandoned. The speaker, the observer of the action, continually makes comments on the characters, their motivations, and his (her?) own cleverness. This voice not only rides with the family in the truck but also becomes the bear who leads the children to the house in the forest. There the speaker is waiting in its more usual form. Feeding the children, the witch puts Jill to bed and transforms Buddy into a wolf, setting him free to run with the pack. The next morning, the witch puts itself in its customary position of leaning too far into the oven so Jill can lock her inside. Inside the cooling oven, the children now find a perfectly baked angel food cake. Jill is confused and considers that perhaps it was only a dream. The narrator is not impressed. "*It was only a bad dream* are the formulas that have exiled me from the world for several hundred years. Children would have those scoffing catchphrases stenciled into their brains and the useful truth of their dreams would be dismissed time and time again. . ." (486).

An ironic look at truth in stories and the interaction between story (the text) and the reader.

1990: Enger, Leif. "Hansel's Finger." In *The Year's Best Fantasy and Horror: Third Annual Collection*, edited by Ellen Datlow and Terri Windling. New York: St. Martin's Press, 161–67.

Using the strong image of the finger/bone held out to the witch by Hansel in his attempt to keep her at bay, the narrator contemplates a human finger he finds while at Disney World in Florida. In his panic and confusion, the man summarizes a slightly garbled version of the traditional tale, while at the same time he makes a commentary on the way the tales have generally been adapted by the theme park.

Howard's discovery of the finger shows that it is not only a grotesque object but one that shatters an ordinary man's conceptions of the world and himself. "While the tone of the piece is rather cool, the disturbing nature of the disruption of life makes for a neatly horrific, effective tale" (Datlow and Windling, 161).

1993: Goldstein, Lisa. "Breadcrumbs and Stones." In *Snow White, Blood Red*, edited by Ellen Datlow and Terri Windling. New York: William Morrow, 388–406. Also in *Travelers in Magic* by Lisa Goldstein. New York: TOR, 1994, 201–17.

The editorial comment to this tale states, "a powerful, moving story about the metaphysical language of fairy tales and their meaning for one particular family. It takes the symbols to be found in the German tale of Hansel and Gretel and examines them anew" (Datlow and Windling, 388). Goldstein, in her afterword in her own collection states that "as a child I had confused the ovens of the concentration camp with the oven in "Hansel and Gretel" (Goldstein, 217). The realistic story that she ends up telling explores the ways in which parents might abandon children. These include the traditional tale of Hansel and Gretel; the experiences of the narrator's grandparents, who were taken to the concentration camps and died there; and the narrator and her sister, who have never established roots and never knew why. Now that they are ready and anxious to understand, their mother (and some of the answers) is taken by cancer.

Told in first person, this story explores the narrator's mother's early history. Her mother, a blond Jew, was saved during World War II by her appearance and was adopted by a Christian family. She worked in a glass factory. This the narrator already knew, but what she did not know was that her mother had a brother who worked in the same factory. He never reconciled himself to the treatment of the Jews by the Germans and was eventually discovered, arrested, and sent to Auschwitz, where he died. The mother uses the tale of Hansel and Gretel to frame her story . . . to tell it before it is lost forever. And the narrator wonders,

> Had Gretel . . . come back to the forest with her daughter? Many years later, when she was an old woman and tired of secrets, has she taken her daughter by the hand and followed the old path?. . . It seemed to me that all my life my mother had given me the wrong story, her made-up tales instead of Hansel and Gretel, had given me breadcrumbs instead of stones. (Goldstein, 216)

1993: Kronberg, Ruthilde. "Hans and Grete, Nineteen Now: A Drug-Awareness Allegory About the Value of Responsibility and Self-Respect." In *Clever Folk: Tales of Wisdom, Wit, and Wonder*. Englewood, CO: Libraries Unlimited, 35–39.

As the long title of this story implies, this reworking is basically a didactic antidrug treatise aimed at young adults. The protagonists, themselves teenagers, run away to the city as their home life deteriorates. They eventually become involved with a woman who, at their first meeting, saved them from harm. However, as the author points out, "but had Hans and Grete known what was in store for them they would have jumped right off the bus at the next stop and found a police officer" (37). The woman, Crack-Witch, enslaves them: Hans with the free crack she offers, and Grete by her love for her brother. Grete, the only one who is able to think for herself, eventually manages to trap the woman in her basement and call the police. When the woman is led away, her treasure-trove is discovered, but it is not shared with the twins. Grete returns immediately to her home, but Hans must first go to a drug rehabilitation center to become drug-free. A forced and unattractive effort that has offended the young adults to whom I introduced it.

1995: Galloway, Priscilla. "The Woodcutter's Wife." In *Truly Grim Tales*. Toronto, ON: Lester, 107–23.

Narrated by the stepmother/witch, the story revolves around her plans to feast on the children. She has been around for three centuries and is finding that her power has waned somewhat, but she wants to assure her listeners that the tale does not have all the facts correct. Although her sight is failing, she does have a superb sense of smell; the bone did not fool her at all. It was not Hansel's flesh that she wanted but his blood! The children do not push her into the oven but lock her in her own stable. She no longer has the power to bend the bars, but she can transform herself into another shape, a small shape: a child shape, small enough to slip through the bars. She is quite sure the newly reunited family will take her in and take care of her even though the stepmother has disappeared for good.

This reworking takes all the main motifs of the tale and weaves them into a new direction and possible new episodes.

1995: Garner, James Finn. "**Hansel and Gretel**." In *Once Upon a More Enlightened Time: More Politically Correct Bedtime Stories.* New York: Macmillan, 3–14.

Hansel overhears his father, a single parent, discussing his plans with his analyst for abandoning his children. Hansel leaves a trail of granola, but it is eaten greedily by "a cadre of survivalists" who are not interested in sharing their newly found goods. The cottage in these woods is made of sugarless goodies and is (wom)manned not by a witch but a Wiccan. The children are soon caught up in the activities of the woman and her neighbors and become active environmentalists marching to protect their woods and home. During one of these protests they meet with their father, now sporting a suit and a high-profile position in a papermaking factory. When the Wiccan joins forces with the father (for health benefits), the children evoke powers to change the factory into a structure made of candy, the lawyers into mice—hungry mice—and the Wiccan into a weasel. When their father bemoans his new fate, the children transform him into a beaver.

A parody of the traditional tale that takes its own wild path.

1995: Vande Velde, Vivian. "**Twins**." In *Tales from the Brothers Grimm and the Sisters Weird.* San Diego: Harcourt Brace, 88–106.

This story is also narrated by the stepmother, but one of a very different personality! The story follows the first few days of her marriage of convenience to the woodcutter. He needs a mother for his children, but they need nothing but each other. All of her attempts at friendship and mothering are rebuffed by this set of horrific twins. They finally leave home, but the narrator searches for them, thinking them lost. She does find them at the home of a newly deceased neighbor. The children did not like this neighbor, and that was the end of her. But they don't like their new stepmother either. . . .

The children are the agents of evil in this parody of the tale. There is no witch, no danger to the children, and no abandonment. There is only every stepmother's nightmare: what if the children don't like me?

1995: Wilson, Gahan. **"Hansel and Grettel."** In *Ruby Slippers, Golden Tears*, edited by Ellen Datlow and Terri Windling. New York: William Morrow, 225–46.

Datlow and Windling introduce this tale by saying that "Hansel and Gretel are usually seen as poor, helpless innocents (except for devouring a tasty house that doesn't belong to them)—Wilson in his inimitable way, does a little twist" (226).

> Things never really did work out emotionally in the family after the episode, and it was finally arranged that when Hansel and Gretel finished with their education they would receive an enormous amount of money—for you see, darlings, that nasty depression thing had run its course and everyone was rich again—and go off on their own and nobody would ever again mention the unfortunate business about the attempted murder. (230)

The adult Hansel and Grettel leave home permanently and travel the world. They are very rich and psychologically damaged from their childhood experiences. They do not trust anyone but themselves. Eventually, they begin acquiring properties that are, at the same time, sought after and unknown. They discover "King's Retreat," which has a long staircase graced with huge gold statues of famous people. Their guide, Oskar, gives them a tour of these statues and takes them to a room filled with other statues, statues of former owners of the retreat, that have "something disturbing, something sinister, which set them entirely apart from those which stood so proudly in the clean, fresh air and sunlight so high above this dim, dark place" (240). The facial expressions on these statues look absolutely terrified! Hansel and Grettel are given a credible explanation for this and are taken on a confusing route back to the main part of the house. Hansel, however, had been prepared and left a trail of tiny pieces of paper so they could find that secret room and collection again. When they do so, they find out why the statues sport such a horrified look. Hansel immediately and effectively renders the present owner into a statue. Hansel and Grettel happily preside over the retreat with no expectation of anyone knowing how to find the secret chamber and the spell to produce new statues. That is, as the talkative narrator assures his audience, "Not unless they're as well informed as *you*, my darlings!" (246)

Gahan Wilson has created an effective storyteller in his perverse story. And I wonder how the narrator knows as much as he does!

1997: Crowley, John. "**Lost and Abandoned**." In *Black Swan, White Raven*, edited by Ellen Datlow and Terri Windling. New York: Avon, 289–96.

This is a contemporary reworking of this tale, narrated by the father of the children (never named in this story), that, at the same time, makes use of the traditional version within the retelling to ponder on the nature of abandonment. Crowley also briefly explores the structure of story and the art of writing. The narrator, divorced and with custody of his children, undergoes several reversals of fortune: from university sessional to teacher of underprivileged students and, eventually, to the state of unemployment. "I will write my story with a beginning, a middle, and no end. No bread crumbs, no candy, no woods, no oven, no treasure. No who, what, where, when. And it will all be there" (293).

1997: Donoghue, Emma. "**The Tale of the Cottage**." In *Kissing the Witch: Old Tales in New Skins*. New York: HarperCollins, 133–41.

The narrator tells of her experiences as a young girl when she was abandoned in the forest by her parents. The first time she is rescued by her brother, but the second time he is abandoned with her. They find their way to a cottage of sweets and a woman of compassion, but when big brother, growing old enough to sprout whiskers, attempts to get too close to the woman, she locks him in a cage. The girl secretly frees him, gives him a loaf of freshly baked bread, and sends him on his way. She remains in the cottage with the woman, for she has no desire to return to her home. "Home not home if mother not mother" (140).

Written in poetic fragments rather than complete sentences.

1997: Kilworth, Garry. "**The Trial of Hansel and Gretel**." In *Black Swan, White Raven*, edited by Ellen Datlow and Terri Windling. New York: Avon, 104–21.

Two German peasant children are brought before the town judge who, because of his position, feels ultimately superior and impatient with the case. However, he is soon caught up in the tale that the young woman is spinning, although he cannot credit the house of candy or the self-defense plea that the children are putting forth. While he cannot completely credit the charges of sorcery, there have been recent cases of witchcraft placed before the court. The judge knows, however, that the children must be declared guilty in order for the town, and ultimately himself, to gain from the treasure the children brought home to their father, who has since absconded. The judge also has a feeling that the art of sorcery may be one that is possessed by the unlettered girl in front of the court because she insists that the children were aided on their homeward journey by a duck that she obviously controlled. But before the trial continues any further, the children's father and stepmother return to town. The treasure has been put to good use; the town is now part of the father's possessions, and the trial is quickly dismissed And the judge? Let us just say that the judge undergoes a complete transformation as well.

Short Films

Perhaps the stark realities of this story have not attracted people involved in the film world. In this section, we have only one short film to discuss.

Hansel and Gretel: An Appalachian Version. 1975. (From the Brothers Grimm by Tom Davenport and Gary Carden). Delaplane, VA: Davenport Films, 16 minutes.

This adaptation is set in the Depression era, when a poor mountain family abandons the children in the dark forest. It is almost a direct telling from the Grimms, with the exception of not including the duck and the death of the stepmother. The children manage to find their way home by themselves to find that their stepmother had deserted their father. There are no religious references in this retelling. A print version illustrated with stills from the film is available in *From the Brothers Grimm: A Contemporary Retelling of American Folktales and Classic Stories* by Tom Davenport and Gary Carden (Fort Atkinson, WI: Highsmith Press, 1992, 65–72). "Our film followed the story as it appeared in my Pantheon Edition of *Grimms' Fairy Tales*. . . . We did most of the editing without sound as if it were a silent picture, and the dialogue for the whole movie fits on less than a page" (Davenport and Carden, x). Tom Davenport also talks about the reaction to his film, the first one in the series, as it created immediate controversy.

> The realism of the live-action style and the fidelity to the old folktale upset some reviewers who considered the frightening aspects of film inappropriate for children. However, many other children's film specialists recognized the film's overpowering popularity with young children, and saw it as a positive breakthrough in children's films (x).

Davenport states that the plot of Hansel and Gretel, with its dark and frightening elements, is like a modern-day horror film. "Whereas the modern horror film often ends with the evil thing lurking around for a sequel, folktales celebrate the decisive victory of the protagonist over the forces of evil" (Davenport and Carden, xii).

Opera

1893: Humperdinck, Engelbert. **Hansel and Gretel**.

Humperdinck's first and most memorable opera opened on December 23, 1893, with Richard Strauss as conductor and Humperdinck's sister, Adelheid Wette, as the librettist. Wette had first asked her brother to write four songs for an amateur children's production. These were well received, so Humperdinck decided to make a fuller production. Again, this was a success, so he penned a full opera based on the Grimms' tale. Zipes credits the opera with a profound influence on the way the story is perceived in Germany. Many popular editions of the story have been altered to reflect the changes made by Wette. The mother is returned to the story, but as an accidental catalyst for the children's adventures. Both parents are now sympathetic, and the blame for the abandonment has been shifted onto the children.

The first act of the opera takes place within the home of the children and their father, Peter and their mother, Gertrude. Gertrude takes the children out into the forest by herself to pick strawberries, but returns home without the children as they have become separated from her. The forest and the lost children are the focus of the second act, while the third focuses on the children's experiences with the witch and the fairies.

> It is no more a children's opera than *Alice in Wonderland* is a child's book. The absurd simplicity of the story appeals because of its genuine naiveté. . . . The angels would be truly dreadful if they were not seen as the vision of the children, the Witch would be a target for the anti-violence lobby if she was not a fairyland person. Yet Humperdinck is never schmaltzy and presents murder by baking not as an act of violence but as a joke (Forman, 316).

Poetry

While filmmakers may not be too interested in this tale, the same thing can not be said about poets! The images of malevolent gingerbread houses and witches, children abandoned by death and despair, and innocent children filter through these lines of poetry illuminating the power of the tale to incorporate so many different layers. None of these poems are directed at young children, but all can be comprehended by young adults.

1926: O'Conor, Norreys Jephson. **"To a Child (With a Copy of the Author's 'Hansel and Gretel')."** In *The Horne Book of Modern Verse*, edited by Burton E. Stevenson. New York: Henry Holt, 37–38. Also in *Disenchantments: An Anthology of Modern Fairy Tale Poetry*, edited by Wolfgang Mieder. Hanover, NH: University Press of New England, 1985, 59.

While the poem is directed at a specific child, the poet brings attention to the fact that this particular tale was used as a cautionary tale to remind children to mind their parents and that angels watch over them while the children are both awake and asleep.

1949: Richardson, Dorothy Lee. **"Modern Grimm."** In *Poetry* 73:5, 275–76. Also in *Disenchantments: An Anthology of Modern Fairy Tale Poetry*, edited by Wolfgang Mieder. Hanover, NH: University Press of New England, 1985, 60.

While the poem begins and ends with the verse dialogue that is initiated during the first encounter between the witch and the children outside the house, the images evoked are not of the tale but the power and nature of the wind. The most direct references are to the "rich red wind over Hiroshima."

1968: Ray, David. **"Hansel and Gretel Return."** In *Dragging the Main and Other Poems*. Ithaca, NY: Cornell University Press, 43. Also in *Disenchantments: An Anthology of Modern Fairy Tale Poetry*, edited by Wolfgang Mieder. Hanover, NH: University Press of New England, 1985, 67.

David Ray's poem mentions the tale of Little Red Riding Hood as well as Hansel and Gretel when it refers to the child protagonists returning home from their dangerous journeys with a reward and tales for the ones waiting for them "who were neither charming nor caring."

1971: Dickey, William. "**The Dolls Play at Hansel and Gretel.**" In *Disenchantments: An Anthology of Modern Fairy Tale Poetry*, edited by Wolfgang Mieder. Hanover, NH: University Press of New England, 1985, 61–65.

This poem is written in five separate segments. The first poem conjures an image of dolls, discarded after a day of play. The second segment, titled "The Witch's Song," throbs with malevolency, as does "The Gingerbread House's Song," the third segment. "The Oven's Song" continues this theme of indifferent warning and careless danger, while the final segment, untitled, brings the reader back to the image of the discarded (and disgruntled?) toys. Using only slim references to the traditional tale, the poem resonates within readers and leaves them filled with disquiet and tension.

1971: Sexton, Anne. "**Hansel and Gretel.**" In *Transformations*. Boston: Houghton Mifflin, 101–5.

Sexton begins her poem with the visualization of an adult "threatening to eat up" a child because it is "sweet as fudge," before she retells the tale in poetic form. Sexton embraces contemporary images such as Houdini and Coca-Cola and fills her poem with the heady aromas and images of feasting.

1976: Morgan, Robin. "**The Two Gretels.**" In *Disenchantments: An Anthology of Modern Fairy Tale Poetry*, edited by Wolfgang Mieder. Hanover, NH: University Press of New England, 1985, 69.

Hansel remains behind while two Gretels, the internal and external aspects of her personality, wander through the landscape because they have forgotten the breadcrumbs. They are not in danger, however, because they discover the Gingerbread House is inhabited by the "Great Good Mother Goddess." Who needs anyone else?

1979: Ower, John. "**The Gingerbread House.**" In *Disenchantments: An Anthology of Modern Fairy Tale Poetry*, edited by Wolfgang Mieder. Hanover, NH: University Press of New England, 1985, 70.

This poem provides a strong contemporary image of a child caught up in the middle of her parent's divorce as they, in their hate for each other, "gobble up" their child. The child's immediate reaction to the gingerbread house could provide considerable material for classroom discussion.

1982: Hay, Sara Henderson. "**Juvenile Court**." In *Story Hour*. Fayetteville, AR: University of Arkansas Press, 26. Also in *Disenchantments: An Anthology of Modern Fairy Tale Poetry*, edited by Wolfgang Mieder. Hanover, NH: University Press of New England, 1985, 66.

After the body of the witch is discovered burned to a crisp in her own oven, the two children are brought before the court by the police. When they state their examples of the witch's provocation, such as threatening to burn them with boiling water for throwing the cat in the well and drawing pictures on the fence, the court takes their age into consideration and releases them to their parents on probation. The poem is tied into the story through the use of the protagonists' names and the image of the witch's demise in the oven.

1990: Strauss, Gwen. "**Their Father**." In *Trail of Stones*. New York: Alfred A. Knopf, 2–4. Also in *The Armless Maiden and Other Tales for Childhood's Survivors*, edited by Terri Windling. New York: TOR, 192–93.

In this poem are the tortured thoughts of a father who allowed himself to be swayed by his wife to do something he really did not want to do. Passivity seems to be his creed, even after his children return he scatters breadcrumbs for the geese bought by the witch's pearls. The illustrations in Strauss's anthology (by Anthony Browne) are extremely powerful in their contemporary setting, artwork, and sense of neglect.

1995: Burch, Milbre. "**After Push Comes to Shove**." In *Ruby Slippers, Golden Tears*, edited by Ellen Datlow and Terri Windling. New York: William Morrow, 222–24.

Written during the 1993 Los Angeles fires, the poem focuses on the thoughts of the witch from inside the burning oven. She is, naturally, resentful and considers the future of the two greedy children and their ineffectual father. "I take some comfort in this as my organs become ash and I am burned away to what's at my core: a child alone in the woods" (224).

1995: Gluck, Louise. "**Gretel in Darkness**." In *The Armless Maiden and Other Tales for Childhood's Survivors*, edited by Terri Windling. New York: TOR, 227. Also in *Disenchantments: An Anthology of Modern Fairy Tale Poetry*, edited by Wolfgang Mieder. Hanover, NH: University Press of New England, 1985, 68.

Do fairy-tale characters really live "Happily ever after"? What of poor Gretel, who murdered in order to save her brother from certain death? Does anyone consider the pain and guilt that she may carry within herself? And is danger really banished? This short poem embraces numerous philosophical considerations.

1997: Hoffman, Nina Kiriki. "**The Breadcrumb Trail**." In *Black Swan, White Rave*, edited by Ellen Datlow and Terri Windling. New York: Avon, 297–300.

Using Hansel's breadcrumb trail as a metaphor, the poem explores choices and "trails" that one must make along life's journey.

Picture Books

The most effective adaptation of "Hansel and Gretel" in picture-book form has been through the element of setting. Both Anthony Browne and Ian Wallace have moved the traditional tale through time and space to render their own chilling stories.

1981: The Brothers Grimm. **Hansel and Gretel**. Illustrated by Anthony Browne. London, England: Julia MacRae Books.

The text, adapted from the translation by Eleanor Quarrie, faithfully follows the 1857 version as told by the Brothers Grimm. It is through the illustrations that alterations in mood, tone, and story are made. Starting with the cover illustration of the two children huddled beneath a mammoth tree, the reader realizes that this story is contemporary: It could (and perhaps did) happen today! The format of the book is consistent: The left-hand page of text is accompanied by a small illustration, with a full-page illustration on the right-hand page. Browne's illustrations emphasize the modern setting with power poles, television sets, and contemporary clothing.

Virginia Walter proclaims this version controversial. The setting is modern England with a little help from Salvador Dali (Walter, 209). "The title page suggests the central theme of this telling, with its stark typography on a white page with a thin black border. The sole illustration is a square cage containing a white bird on a swing. This is a story about imprisonment, loss of liberty, and betrayal" (Walter, 209). The faces of the children are extremely expressive: "Browne is clearly mining the story for every ounce of psychological gold, with a trace of social commentary as well. It is possible that by placing his story too unambiguously in the present, he is sabotaging his own attempt to emphasize the dark emotional content" (Walter, 210). This story has moved out of the realm of the fairy tale and into the world of social realism, becoming a story about one troubled family rather than a timeless tale of universal truths (Walter, 211). Browne also suggests, through his images, that the stepmother and the witch are virtually the same character. He uses identical shapes such as that of a tall, pointed witch's hat as foreshadowing and identification of character. The stepmother and the witch share the same face "except that the witch is depicted as old while the stepmother is young and beautiful except for her narrow, down-turned red lips" (Hourihan, 181).

A powerful and disturbing reworking of the tale that deserves close consideration.

1994: Wallace, Ian. **Hansel and Gretel**. Based on the tale by the Brothers Grimm. Toronto: Groundwood. (Canadian Fairy Tale Series).

The setting in this picture book has moved to the Atlantic Coast of North America, and the characters consist of the impoverished family of a fisherman residing on the edge of the woods. The text is only slightly altered to encompass this change; otherwise the story line is faithful to the traditional tale as told by the Grimms. The full-page illustrations, facing a full page of text, are dark in both hue and mood. While a full-face portrait of the witch overshadows the front cover, there are no illustrations of the witch's face within the book itself. At times, the woods itself takes on the aspect of the witch, but it is only the rim of her extremely large hat or taloned hands that can be seen in any of the illustrations involving her. The brief passing of time, through autumn with the falling leaves to early winter at the gingerbread house, is subtly demonstrated by Wallace's illustrations. And while the text ends with the words "Their troubles, at last, were over, and they lived together in perfect happiness from then on," the final illustration of the witch arising from the oven may cause a few doubts.

Although the book is part of the Canadian Fairy Tale Series, other than for a few falling maple leaves, this story could be set in any contemporary sea-dependent community.

Classroom Extensions

The following suggestions may be adapted for use with other tales.

Alternative Viewpoints

Kay Vandergrift contends that the alternative perspective offered in many of these contemporary reworkings "encourages young people to look sympathetically at those who have been marginalized or portrayed negatively, an ability that, one hopes, may be transferred from literature to life" (29). Is this truly the case? Do readers of these alternative perspectives look beyond the "cleverness" of the author?

And in the Future?

James McGlathery speculates on what will happen to the innocent devotion between Hansel and Gretel as they grow older and decide to leave home on their own initiative. Comment on the following excerpt.

> The devotion between Hansel and Gretel is perfectly innocent and uncomplicated. They are still young children. What will happen, though, when Gretel becomes nubile? Can we imagine that she will marry? If she does, will Hansel marry too? Whether he does or not, will he live happily ever after with Gretel and her husband, assuming that she does marry? Obviously the Grimms' tale about these still-very-young children does not permit such speculation. Hansel and Gretel go home to their father and live with him happily and forever, as though they will never become adults themselves (1990, 49).

Censorship

Jack Zipes points out that many liberties have been taken with this story by authors and publishers to satisfy various viewpoints. He states:

> Some educators and parents have objected to Gretel's pushing the witch into the oven and have placed pressure on publishers to eliminate this episode. At the end of World War II, some so-called authorities among the Allied Forces of Occupation thought that the cruelty and sadism in the Grimms' fairy tales had contributed to Nazism, and the oven scene in "Hansel and Gretel" was particularly disturbing for many readers after 1945 (1997, 57).

The Opies also mention this in their discussion of the tale. They assert "that the story of 'Hansel and Gretel' was not always regarded as preposterous, that the fantasy was too close to reality, that for some the witch's oven too much resembled the gas chamber at Auschwitz" (Opie, 311). Why would these motifs be considered troublesome? In your opinion, would the reading of fairy tales create a certain mindset in the population? What is it about the power of the written word that seems to frighten people? Are we still censoring our fairy tales (and other literature) because someone is frightened of the power of the images brought to life through words?

Child Abandonment

Martin Hallett and Barbara Karasek, in their first edition of *folk and fairy tales*, ask, "The motif of child abandonment (in one form or another) is also not uncommon in fairy tales; what sociological and psychological realities does this motif reveal?" (1991, 96) Discuss.

Food

"What is the significance of food and eating (in their various manifestations) in this tale?" (Hallett and Karasek 1991, 96) Identify these various manifestations and discuss their role in the story for an eighteenth- and early nineteenth-century audience and a contemporary young-adult audience.

Illustrated Versions of Hansel and Gretel

When comparing the illustrations of the various picture-book versions, look carefully at the way in which the children are portrayed in the forest, the construction and appeal of the witch's house, and the visual aspect of the witch herself. For example, Zelinsky's illustrations for Rika Lesser's retelling set the story in the Middle Ages. How do the artists use light, white space, and composition to help tell the tale? Compare a traditional version of the tale with that of Anthony Browne or Ian Wallace. What happens to the mood and tone of the tale when the story is brought ahead in time?

Illustration History and Isolation

Ruth Bottigheimer proclaims: "What Wilhelm wrote into the tales also emerges clearly in the illustrations he asked his brother, Ludwig Emil, to prepare for the 1825 Small Edition" (1987, 110). Ludwig Emil's early illustration for "Hansel and Gretel" depicted the scene in which Gretel triumphed over the witch and released Hansel from his captivity. This was rejected by Wilhelm in favor of a tearful Gretel standing helplessly near Hansel's cage under the baleful gaze of the witch (Bottigheimer,

1987, 110). This illustration and the other few that were published in this collection "play a particularly large role in how the individual tales were visualized, then and subsequently" (Bottigheimer, 1987, 111). Bottigheimer refers to this as "illustrating of fairy tale heroines," which she maintains has become part of the tradition of illustrating these tales. She continues:

> Isolation in the Grimms' tales, like silence, has a female face, and is most frequently seen in the forest. It was Wilhelm Grimm who edited specifically female isolation into many of the tales whose previous versions had reflected a different and far more sociable ethic for women. The illustration history of *Grimms' Tales* offers vivid confirmation both of the femaleness of isolation and its converse, the isolation of femaleness (1987, 111).

What evidence can you find that either affirms or disputes this position? What, if any, purpose would the isolation of the female characters in these illustrations have for Wilhelm Grimm? For his public at large? For the contemporary public?

The Landscape of Color

Joyce Thomas states that color is the landscape of Hansel and Gretel's story:

> [I]ts spectral paleness conjures up the specter of death which follows the children's footsteps, which haunts the dark woods against which the tale is set. Yet it also provides a whitewash over the tale's most horrific scenes and thus intimates the children's ultimate survival, just as the white flint stones once shone through the wood's shadows and marked the way home (223).

Chart the use of color in this tale, particularly the color of bread or flour that Thomas earlier claims is the strongest image in this tale. Does the use of various shades of white indicate hope for the children throughout their ordeal? How does this image shift with modern adaptations of the tale rendering the house of a less substantial (but more appealing) foundation?

Stepmothers and Weak Fathers

Ruth Bottigheimer makes a passing reference to the amendment of a stepmother figure to the tales of "Hansel and Gretel" and "Snow White." She states "[T]he good biological mothers' early deaths do not alter the fact that succeeding versions of these two tales exculpate the father-figures who remain alive but do nothing to protect their children against the evil machinations of their second wives" (1987, 81). She suggests that this is a general pattern permeating the Grimms' tales. Do you agree? Why or why not?

Witch Pardons

A recent news release (July 12, 1998) stated that the Catholic Church is setting up a commission in the Prague Republic to consider whether pardons should be granted to people burned at the stake as witches. Between the twelfth and eighteenth centuries it was estimated that Church-sanctioned witch hunts resulted in about 100,000 Europeans dying by fire or torture. This commission will examine the Sumperk witch trials of 1679 led by a pub owner who targeted wealthy merchants and seized their property. There is hope that other countries will also follow suit. Germany had the greatest number of witch burnings during this time period but they were also common in England and France. The news item concluded with this statement. "The last known clash between the state and the supernatural came in the German town of Uttenheim in 1925 when a policeman shot a man on suspicion of being a werewolf" (*The Edmonton Journal*, July 12, 1998, A2).

How did these trials and tribulations affect the editing of the traditional tales? What do you think will happen to these stories if the subsequent investigation pardons the witches and werewolves that were tortured and murdered?

Who Are Hansel and Gretel?

In her study of using folktales to help children face their fears, Norma Livo asks her readers to describe the characters in Hansel and Gretel. What did you think of them? How did they show whether they were cruel or kind, selfish or unselfish? Were some of the characters both cruel and kind? Had any of the characters grown and developed as a result of what they experienced? If so, who and why? (Livo, 50)

Bibliography

Bettelheim, Bruno. *The Uses of Enchantment: The Meaning and Importance of Fairy Tales*. New York: Vintage Books, 1976.

Bottigheimer, Ruth B. "Silenced Women in the Grimms' Tales: The 'Fit' Between Fairy Tales and Society in Their Historic Context." In *Fairy Tales and Society: Illusion, Allusion & Paradigm*, edited by Ruth B. Bottigheimer. Philadelphia: University of Pennsylvania Press, 1986, 115–31.

——. *Grimms' Bad Girls and Bold Boys: The Moral and Social Vision of the Tales*. New Haven, CT: Yale University Press, 1987.

Brewer, Derek. *Symbolic Stories: Traditional Narratives of Family Drama in English Literature*. Cambridge, England: D. S. Brewer, 1980.

Darnton, Robert. *The Great Cat Massacre and Other Episodes in French Cultural History*. New York: Basic Books, 1984.

Dieckmann, Hans. *Twice-Told Tales: The Psychological Use of Fairy Tales*. Forward by Bruno Bettelheim. Wilmette, IL: Chiron, 1986.

Ellis, John M. *One Fairy Story Too Many: The Brothers Grimm and Their Tales*. Chicago: University of Chicago Press, 1983.

Forman, Sir Denis. *A Night at the Opera: An Irreverent Guide to the Plots, the Singers, the Composers, the Recordings*. New York: Random House, 1994.

Hallett, Martin, and Barbara Karasek, eds. *folk and fairy tales*. Peterborough, ON: Broadview Press, 1991.

——. *Folk and Fairy Tales*. 2d ed. Peterborough, ON: Broadview Press, 1996.

Heuscher, Julius E. *A Psychiatric Study of Myths and Fairy Tales: Their Origin, Meaning, and Usefulness*. 2d ed. Springfield, IL: Charles C. Thomas, 1974.

Hourihan, Margery. *Deconstructing the Hero: Literary Theory and Children's Literature*. London: Routledge, 1997.

Hoyme, James B. "The 'Abandoning Impulse' in Human Parents." *The Lion and the Unicorn* 12: 2 (December 1988), 32–46.

Jones, Steven Swann. *The Fairy Tale: The Magic Mirror of Imagination*. New York: Twayne, 1995. (Twayne's Studies in Literary Themes and Genres).

Livo, Norma. *Who's Afraid. . . ? Facing Children's Fears with Folktales*. Englewood, CO: Teacher Ideas Press, 1994.

Lüthi, Max. *Once Upon a Time: On the Nature of Fairy Tales*. Bloomington, IN: Indiana University Press, 1976.

McGlathery, James M. *Fairy Tale Romance: The Grimms, Basile, and Perrault*. Urbana-Champaign, IL: University of Illinois Press, 1991.

Mieder, Wolfgang. " 'Ever Eager to Incorporate Folk Proverbs': Wilhelm Grimm's Proverbial Additions in the Fairy Tales." In *The Brother Grimm and Folktale*, edited by James M. McGlathery. Urbana-Champaign, IL: University of Illinois Press, 1988, 112–32.

Mueller, Gerhard O. W. "The Criminological Significance of the Grimms' Fairy Tales." In *Fairy Tales and Society: Illusion, Allusion, and Paradigm*, edited by Ruth B. Bottigheimer. Philadelphia: University of Pennsylvania Press, 1986, 217–27.

Opie, Iona, and Peter Opie. *The Classic Fairy Tales*. New York: Oxford University Press, 1974.

Purkiss, Diane. *The Witch in History: Early Modern and Twentieth-Century Representations*. London: Routledge, 1996.

Rolleke, Heinz. "New Results of Research on *Grimms' Fairy Tales*." In *The Brother Grimm and Folktale*, edited by James M. McGlathery. Urbana-Champaign, IL: University of Illinois Press, 1988, 101–11.

Rusch-Feja, Diann. *The Portrayal of the Maturation Process in Girl Figures in Selected Tales of the Brothers Grimm*. Frankfurt am Main: Peter Lang, 1995.

Smith, Alison M. "Review of *The Magic Circle*." Book Report 12: 4 (January/February 1944), 48.

Tatar, Maria. *The Hard Facts of the Grimms' Fairy Tales*. Princeton, NJ: Princeton University Press, 1987.

———. *Off with Their Heads! Fairy Tales and the Culture of Childhood*. Princeton, NJ: Princeton University Press, 1992.

Thomas, Joyce. *Inside the Wolf's Belly: Aspects of the Fairy Tale*. Sheffield, England: Sheffield Academic Press, 1989.

Thompson, Stith. *The Types of the Folktale: A Classification and Bibliography. A Translation and Enlargement of Antti Aarne's Verzeichnis de Märchentypen*. 2d revision. Helsinki: Academia Scientiarum Fennica, 1964. (FF Communications, no. 184).

Vandergrift, Kay E. "Journey or Destination: Female Voices in Youth Literature." In *Mosaics of Meaning: Enhancing the Intellectual Life of Young Adults Through Story*, edited by Kay E. Vandergrift. Lanham, MD: Scarecrow, 1996, 17–46.

Walter, Virginia A. "Hansel and Gretel as Abandoned Children: Timeless Images for a Postmodern Age." *Children's Literature in Education* 23: 4 (1992), 203–14.

Warner, Marina. *From the Beast to the Blonde: On Fairy Tales and Their Tellers.* London: Chatto & Windus, 1994.

Zipes, Jack. *Breaking the Magic Spell: Radical Theories of Folk and Fairy Tales.* Austin, TX: University of Texas Press, 1979.

———. "Recent Trends in the Contemporary American Fairy Tale." *Journal of the Fantastic in the Arts* 5 (1992), 13–41.

———. *Happily Ever After: Fairy Tales, Children, and the Culture Industry.* New York: Routledge, 1997.

CHAPTER 5

LITTLE RED RIDING HOOD

While the tale of the little girl and her sometimes-fatal encounter with the wolf in the forest has undergone many transformations during its printed history, the basic elements have remained constant. *A little girl is sent by her mother on a journey to her grandmother's house. She has a meeting with a wolf who discovers where she is going and, using a short cut, gets to the grandmother's house before the girl. Poor granny is sick in bed and cannot protect herself from the wolf, who gobbles her up. The wolf then dresses in the grandmother's discarded garments and climbs into bed to await the arrival of the little girl. The girl is suspicious of the physical appearance of the wolf and questions him about his eyes, ears, and teeth. The wolf's responses to her questions are satisfactory until the very last: "The better to eat you with, my dear."* If the tale is that of Perrault, the story ends with Little Red being eaten up. If it is of the Brothers Grimm, Little Red and Granny are both saved by a woodcutter who, alerted by their cries, stuns the wolf and frees the two from the stomach of the wolf. The empty cavity in the wolf's stomach is filled with rocks and sewn shut. When the wolf awakes he takes himself to the river for a drink, is unbalanced by the rocks, and falls into the water to drown.

Tale Type: AT 333

The Glutton (Red Riding Hood): The wolf or other monster devours human beings until all of them are rescued alive from his belly.

I. *The Wolf's Feast.* (a) By masking as mother or grandmother the wolf deceives and devours (b) a little girl (Red Riding Hood) whom he meets on his way to her grandmother's.

II. *Rescue.* (a) The wolf is cut open and his victims rescued alive; (b) his belly is sewed full of stones and he drowns; (c) he jumps to his death (Thompson, 125).

Motifs:

K 2011. Wolf poses as grandmother and kills child

Z 18.1. What makes your ears so big?

F 911.3. Animal swallows man (not fatally)

F 913. Victims rescued from swallower's belly

O 426. Wolf cut open and filled with stones as punishment

This type is also related to: AT Type 123, *The Wolf and the Kids*: The wolf comes in the absence of the mother and eats up the kids; the old goat cuts the wolf open and rescues them; AT Type 2027, *The Fat Cat*; and AT Type 2028, *The Troll (Wolf) Who Was Cut Open*.

A History of Little Red Riding Hood

Perrault's "Little Red Riding Hood," adapted from a tale from the oral tradition in France, thrived from its inception among both adult and child audiences and is one of the few literary tales that was reabsorbed by the oral folk tradition. It was this widespread acceptance and retelling of this tale in print as well as in storytelling that eventually led to the creation of the even more popular tale penned by the Brothers Grimm (Zipes 1993, 31).

Little Red Riding Hood in Oral Tradition

As an initiatory tale in the oral tradition, "Red Riding Hood" did more than symbolize the child's ability to defeat danger and evil by resorting to cunning: it also demonstrated the importance of women's knowledge to survival. In most general terms, the oral message focuses on the girl's relation to her (grand) mother (Bacchilega, 56).

According to Jack Zipes in *The Trials and Tribulations of Little Red Riding Hood*, this story was not an ancient tale. His research demonstrates that the tale appeared during the Middle Ages in France, Tyrol, and northern Italy as a cautionary tale for children warning against hostile forces surrounding them; these forces were portrayed as ogres, maneaters, wolves or werewolves (1993, 18). Zipes quotes Marianne Rumpf's research, where she theorized that the original villain in this story was a werewolf, a type of villain that, along with witches, was considered plentiful and dangerous by the peasant population of rural France during this time. Zipes concurs, stating that in the sixteenth and seventeenth centuries there was a virtual epidemic of trials of men accused of being werewolves and of eating children and other sinful acts (1993, 19). The correlation between the strong belief in werewolves, the high incidence of werewolf trials, and the story of "Little Red Riding Hood" in oral tradition is presented as evidence for this theory (Zipes 1993, 20).

An interesting element in the oral stories was the distinct lack of the motif of the red riding hood, or indeed the color of red at all (Zipes 1993, 23). Elements that were present in the oral tradition but modified by Perrault include:

a) motif of cruelty that may be a reflection of a "primitive structure"

b) motif of unintentional cannibalism when the blood and flesh of the grandmother were offered to her grandchild by the wolf

c) motif of the "familiar," the helpful animal who informed the child of the nature of the offered food

d) episode of the "ritual undressing" or a striptease by the child, who infuriates the wolf by her "ritual" question with each item of clothing removed

e) the happy ending, built on a scatological overtone, where the girl escapes through her own cunning (Zipes 1993, 20).

The tale was told for various reasons besides the obvious one of enjoyment: as a warning tale for children against the very real dangers in their environment; as a tale of celebration of a girl's coming of age; and as a tale celebrating cunning and self-sufficiency (Zipes 1993, 24).

Little Red Riding Hood in Print

Of all the tales in this study, "Little Red Riding Hood" is the one that surprises most people, who are not aware of the final ending provided by Perrault. For whatever reason, the more sanitized versions have captured the modern market.

Perrault

Christina Bacchilega reminds her reader of the literary importance of Charles Perrault's version of "Little Red Riding Hood." It was the very first printed version and, as such, shaped the ensuing literary tradition and powerfully affected subsequent oral retellings as well (54). The tale began to circulate in Great Britain only after Robert Samber translated Perrault's collection in 1729. It reached the Grimm Brothers from a teller who was familiar with the French version. Pre-Perrault versions of the tale collected primarily in the nineteenth century and in a specific area (the basin of the Loire in France, Tyrol, and northern Italy, where "Red Riding Hood" possibly originated and certainly was popular), and reconstructed by folklorists, demonstrate how Perrault presumably modified the story to suit his own narrative and ideological purposes when constructing a fairly atypical but authoritative text (Bacchilega, 54).

As with the oral versions, Perrault's tale also has an initiatory function, but now the focus is strictly heterosexual. "He foregrounds the dynamics between the wolf and the girl, and justifies the tale's violent outcome by pointing to the devil-associated red garment as evidence of the victim's complicity" (Bacchilega, 57). Perrault modified the oral tale dramatically, omitting the "crude episodes such as the cannibalistic eating of grandmother's flesh, the ritualistic striptease, and the ploy of going outside to defecate to escape the wolf's clutches"; changing the ending; and adding cautionary and satirical commentary for the pleasure of his intended audience (Dundes 1988, 21). Perrault transformed this courageous unnamed peasant girl into a spoiled bourgeois girl who deserved to be punished for her naive behavior. Instead of a celebration of the young girl's victory, the tale now served as a warning for women to follow the prescribed "path" of proper social behavior (Zipes 1995, 28). Zipes argued that "Perrault transformed a hopeful oral tale about the initiation of a young girl into a tragic one of violence in which a girl is blamed for her own violation" (1993, 7).

According to Zipes, the changes made by Perrault reflected his "low opinion of women and the superstitious customs of the peasantry" (1993, 25). The ironic tone of his retelling illustrated that his intended audience was adults who would appreciate the erotic and seductive themes inherent in his version. These themes and irony would not be noticed by a younger audience, who would appreciate the play between the wolf and the child and recognize the implicit warning of the tale (1993, 25). Perrault directed his collection to both of these divergent audiences at a time when literary salons were becoming the rage for adults at court and when the socialization of children and recognition of their independent culture were being developed and promoted. "Perrault's great artistic achievement consisted in his appropriating folk motifs, imbuing them with a different ideological content and stylizing the elements of the plot so that they would be more acceptable for upper-class audiences of children and adults" (1993, 26).

Marina Warner likens the traditional wolf to the "indigenous inhabitants of the countryside, hairy, wild, unkempt, untrammeled by imported acculturation, eating raw foods and meat, a native beast in the native landscape, where a specific age-old corpus of home grown literature flourishes and is passed on" (182). Perrault's urbane seducer is no longer a rustic villain but represents the "deceptions of the city and the men who wield authority in it" (183).

The Brothers Grimm

Marie Hassenpflug, a French Huguenot informant for Jacob and Wilhelm Grimm, related the story to them between 1811 and 1812. The story they heard was still too cruel, too sexual, and too tragic for them, and they made "suitable" alterations. Their adaptations responded to the changing social conditions and child-rearing ideology that had emerged in the century since Perrault first penned his tale. Their most significant change involved the ending, which was still moralistic but now ended on a happy note when they grafted on the ending from the tale of "The Wolf and the Seven Kids" (Zipes 1993, 32). Another major element added by the Grimm Brothers was the mother's warning at the beginning of their tale. Little Red Cap is instructed to behave and not to stray from the straight path to grandmother's house. When she disobeys, tempted by the delights of the forest, the "contract" is broken, and subsequently she must be punished and taught a lesson. This lesson is further emphasized by the anticlimactic moral appended to the story in which the girl meets a second wolf but knows to run to grandmother for help. Thankfully, grandmother is no longer infirm and capably dispatches the danger! The Grimms' version was much more prudish in that there is no striptease sequence; Little Red is simply swallowed by the wolf (Zipes 1993, 355).

"What had formerly been a frank oral tale about sexuality and actual dangers in the woods became, by the time the Grimms finished civilizing and refining, a coded message about rationalizing bodies and sex" (Zipes 1993, 34). There is also an undercurrent of anti-French and anti-Enlightenment sentiment in the conflict between freedom/nature/wilderness and order/school/straight path inherent in this version of the tale (Zipes 1993, 35). Zipes feels that another agenda was at play as well because this tale was recorded during the French occupation of Germany, and the invaders had been identified with wolves in the German literature of the time (1993, 35).

Table 5.1
Alterations Made by Perrault and the Brothers Grimm

Oral Tradition	Perrault	Brothers Grimm
Nameless child who is brave, forthright and shrewd, knows how to use her wits.	Little Red Riding Hood who is pretty, spoiled, gullible and helpless. (Zipes 1993, 26)	Little Red Riding Hood who is even more helpless and naive and must be punished for her disobedience.
Referred directly to actual conditions in the rural environment.	Referred to vanity, power and seduction and a girl who subconsciously contributed to her own rape. (Zipes 1993, 27)	Referred to obedience of parents, sensual experiences; wolf sent to teach her and the audience a lesson. (The Grimms' elaborated the scene in the woods to demonstrate the girl's desire "to break from the moral restraints from her society to enjoy her own sensuality (inner nature) and nature's pleasures (outer nature)." (Zipes 1993, 79)
No mention of a red hood or head covering of any color.	Red cap (*chaperon*) which was a small velvet (for aristocrats) or cloth (for middle class) cap worn during the 16th and 17th centuries.	Red cap given by her grandmother.
A warning against danger but has nothing to do with obedience or the curbing of sexual drives.	No warning from her mother about straying from the path.	Warning from her mother not to stray from the path and to behave properly while visiting with her grandmother.
Wolf a werewolf. "The firm Christian belief in werewolves in the 16th and 17th centuries derived from a strident campaign by the Church to exploit folk superstition in order to keep all social groups under its control." (Zipes 1993, 79)	Wolf an urbane seducer. During Perrault's time, the wolf was no longer thought of as a serious threat although his intended audience still identified the much maligned canine with the devil, insatiable lust and chaos. (Zipes 1993, 75)	Wolf an "old sinner."
	Speaks to the wolf in the woods; accepting a type of wager with him.	Wolf invites girl to appreciate nature rather than follow her mother's explicit instructions; mother has a much enlarged role.
Happy ending with girl escaping from hanger using her own talents.	Tragic ending with wolf swallowing (raping) grandmother and Little Red Riding Hood.	Happy ending with hunter saving both grandmother and Little Red Riding Hood; male hero.
Celebration of a girl's coming of age.	Cautionary tale warning little girls to beware of strangers.	Cautionary tale to follow mother's advice and not to indulge in sensual pleasures.
No explicit moral; reflected the sexual frankness of the peasantry during the Middle Ages.	Explicit moral(s) attached to tale.	Added an anti-climactic moral to demonstrate that the girl did indeed learn her lesson.

A Contemporary History of
Little Red Riding Hood in Print

The alterations of "Little Red Riding Hood" continued in the nineteenth and twentieth centuries. Both Perrault's and the Grimms' versions were deemed too cruel and violent with sexual undertones upsetting to children (Zipes 1993, 37). The story continued being sanitized, with references to touching and swallowing deleted and obedience stressed. "Many bowdlerized versions indicated a Victorian-minded censorship which feared that 'Little Red Riding Hood' might someday break out, become a Bohemian, and live in the woods with the wolf" (Zipes 1993, 37). In his study of the tale, Zipes charts the myriad of changes that it underwent in corresponding to social and cultural conditions. The years between the two world wars generated many retellings that were not all aimed at a young audience. The adaptations reflected changes in the labor and women's movements concerning sexual roles and child-rearing practices. After World War II, Little Red was much freer than before in her literary history: She did not need to curb her imagination and wait resigned for a strong male figure to rescue her (Zipes 1993, 58).

The civil rights movement as well as further development in child-rearing, the women's movement, and sexual freedom and education contributed to these literary changes. Three major thrusts are evident in the body of retellings of "Little Red Riding Hood" since that time. Many of the stories reflect the portrayal of the independent girl in oral tradition: She is feisty, courageous, and capable of handing danger on her own. The second thrust of retellings seek to rehabilitate the wolf in the world view, and the third focuses on "unusual aesthetic experiments, debunking traditional narrative forms and seeking to free readers and listeners so that they can question the conventional cultural patterns" (Zipes 1993, 59).

Overview of Critical Interpretations
of Little Red Riding Hood

"By the arrival of the 1980s, the body of criticism on Red Riding Hood had grown large enough that attention now centered on reviewing and evaluating such commentary, including the many parodies and adaptations of the tale done over the years" (McGlathery 1993, 69). McGlathery examines this large body of research with reference to the trends in critical analysis of literature and folklore pointing out that the majority of the interpretations of this tale have been based on the literary versions of the Grimms or Perrault (1993, 67). These submissions included a book by Hans Ritz (1981), which was addressed to a general readership and underwent its tenth printing in 1992. "The value of Ritz's little book lay especially in its critical survey of commentary on the story by others" (McGlathery 1993, 69). Ritz's book was followed in 1983 by Jack Zipes's *The Trial's and Tribulations of Little Red Riding Hood*, revised and reprinted in 1993, and Alan Dundes's *Little Red Riding Hood: A Casebook* (1989).

1865: Edward B. Taylor suggests that the tale might have solar significance: Little Red Riding Hood represents the sun, which is swallowed by night, and the subsequent release from the stomach signifies the dawn (Dundes 1988, 26).

1870: George W. Cox compares the wolf to night or darkness and the heroine in her red cloak to twilight (Dundes 1988, 26).

1874: Hyacinthe Husson suggests that Little Red Riding Hood symbolized the dawn (Dundes 1988, 27).

1894: Axel Olrik interprets the swallowing monster as death and the story as representing rebirth (Dundes 1988, 27).

1908: Sigmund Freud explains the tale in regards to children's ignorance of the birth process: "[T]he belly is slit and the child taken out, as happens to the wolf" (Dundes 1988, 30). Freud directs his attention to possible symbolic sexual content with the wolf in bed, the age of the child being near puberty, and her red clothing and seductive behavior (Thomas, 114).

1912: Otto Rank, agreeing with Freud, judges this tale to be "the best-known illustration of the infantile notion of either opening or cutting the stomach to induce birth" (Dundes 1988, 31).

1923: Pierre Saintyves argues that the tale reflects a seasonal battle in which spring (Little Red Riding Hood) conquers winter (the wolf) (Dundes 1988, 27).

1947: N. Glas interprets the tale as a spiritual parable: The grandmother is a weak old woman who needs succor, the heroine is the rescuer, and the huntsman is wisdom (not "mere intellectual cleverness"). Glas writes that this tale "describes thus in a most wonderful way the victory of the human soul over the wild and tempting forces of the wolf which wants to prevent it from treading the true path into the future" (Dundes 1988, 29).

1950–

1951: Paul Delarue asserts that Perrault's source for the tale was from the oral tradition, adapted to accord with the sensibilities of his audience and eliminating the cruder elements of cannibalism and defecation (McGlathery 1993, 67).

1951: Erich Fromm reads the "little cap of velvet" as a symbol of menstruation and Little Red Riding Hood as a young maturing woman confronting her sexuality and the seduction by the wolf (Dundes 1988, 31). Hate and prejudice against men are at the heart of the story, and the wolf (male) is made to appear ridiculous by "showing that he attempted to play the role of a pregnant woman, having living things in his belly." He is then killed by a symbol of sterility, the stones, which are put in his stomach (Dundes 1988, 32). He delineates the story's concerns with "parental intercourse and fantasized incest" by interpreting the bedroom scene of devourment as symbolic of the young child's conception of the sexual act as violent devouring behavior (Thomas, 114).

1951: Marianne Rumpf maintains that the tale was simply a cautionary tale told to keep young girls from straying into danger (Dundes 1988, 28). She proposes that the wolf was originally a werewolf. In her search in sixteenth- and seventeenth-century court records, she found many references to criminal proceedings against presumed werewolves who were "considered male counterparts of witches as ogresses, [and who] appear to have been attracted by the color red" (McGlathery 1993, 67). The tale warns against the dangers of the forest, of the wild animals, and of the sinister people who wait and prey on children (Rohrich, 114).

1963: Felix Freudmann judges the moral appended by Perrault as incongruous compared with the action of the story itself: "[T]he lessons Perrault appended were expressions of his realism in the face of all the magic found in the folktale" (McGlathery 1993, 68).

1968: Marc Soriano considers Perrault's literary version in view of the oral versions collected since Delarue's interpretation and concludes that the red hood or cap, "including its significance as a gift from grandmother, is not an essential feature of the story as a type" (McGlathery 1993, 68).

1972: Lee Burns looks at reception theory in regards to literature and compared the heroine's "innocent eroticism" (wanting to cuddle up with grandmother) with the wolf's interest in seduction. The child reader responds to the element of erotically charged fear, while the adult reader fully recognizes the erotic element (McGlathery 1993, 68).

1974: Julius Heuscher compares the tale with that of "Hansel and Gretel" (pre-Oedipal) and "Snow White" (latency period), placing it directly between them as an example of an Oedipal tale. Similarities between the tales include: "(a) a home; (b) a need for a path through the woods; (c) a period of getting away from the path; (d) the children finding a little house in the woods" (128). The little house arouses expectations of safety, but in both stories actually camouflages danger, whereas in the story of "Snow White," which has a similar structure, the house of the dwarfs is indeed a haven. Heuscher presents several reasons for regarding "Little Red Riding Hood" as an Oedipal tale: The girl is not frightened by the sensory world around her (in fact, she is quite attracted by it), and the girl is still fairly young, as she is given explicit directions to remain on the path and to behave at her destination. "While she is trusted to walk alone the half-hour-long, familiar path to her grandmother's home, she is still too young to help with household tasks such as the baking of the cake (unlike Snow White who has passed her seventh birthday when she becomes a good helper at the home of the seven dwarfs)" (129). She ultimately reestablishes communication with her mother against whom she rebelled—there is wisdom in what her mother says, and although she needed to deviate from the path to learn this lesson, she need not do it again (132). Heuscher perceives threatening aspects of sexual activity and Little Red Riding Hood's Oedipal conflict with her mother, which was extended to include her grandmother (Thomas, 114).

1975: Victor Laruccia analyzes Perrault's version of the tale according to semiotics and communication theory.

1976: Bruno Bettelheim discounts Perrault's version as one of little appeal because the wolf so obviously is a metaphor and is victorious. The story is "devoid of escape, recovery, and consolation" because it was never intended by Perrault to be a fairy tale but rather a cautionary tale "which deliberately threatens the child with its anxiety-producing ending" (1976, 167). The central themes are the child's fear of being devoured, the wrongness of disobedience of a parental request, and defiance in response to the child following her own path. The girl needs to temporarily deviate from the straight path to gain "a higher state of personality organization," reborn through her experience no longer a child but an adolescent (1976, 183). The tale speaks of human passions, oral greediness, aggression, and pubertal sexual desires (1976, 182). McGlathery states that not only was this study one of the widely heard critical voices in the 1970s, but Bettelheim's Freudian focus on the grandmother's gift of the red cap or hood was "especially intriguing" (1993, 69).

1978: Carole Hanks and D. T. Hanks find a philosophical cautionary message in the story. They note that Perrault's version, in contrast to the "double happy ending" of the Grimms', "points out that maturity is risky; there *are* dangers in the forest—if the maturing person makes a misstep (not necessarily through any personal fault), then he or she may perish" (McGlathery 1993, 69).

1979: Nancy Mavrogenes and Joan Cummins assert that "it is clear that the story of Red Riding Hood has never circulated widely where folk tales are learned orally; practically all versions are based upon Perrault's tale or on that of the brothers Grimm" (345). They maintain the tales found in other cultures were based on translations of Perrault.

1980: Anselmo Calvetti sees Little Red Riding Hood's journey from home as a rite of separation, her time in the forest as a "marginal or liminal period," the period in grandmother's house as her initiation test, and her rescue from the wolf's stomach as rebirth into adult society (Dundes 1988, 28).

1981: Jacques Barchilon and Peter Flinders consider Perrault's version of the story as an allegory of the seduction of a young child or woman. They credit the erotic innuendoes and the popularity of the story with the widespread use of the term "wolf" for seducer (71). They discuss the tale in great detail, including the finishing touches applied by Perrault. In the manuscript text, the child is described as unaware "that it is not good to stop and listen to a wolf," but the final version had "[S]he did not know that it is dangerous to stop and listen to a wolf." The addition of the word "dangerous" more effectively restated the warning and contributed to the suspense (103).

1981: Bruno Bettelheim claims that Perrault, like authors of invented fairy tales, deprived the story of the happy ending, "which requires equally that the evil wolf is destroyed and that Red Riding Hood is rescued" (1981, 19).

1981: Nicholas Tucker balances the psychoanalytic speculations of Erich Fromm and Bruno Bettelheim, concluding that "most readers prefer to hate and condemn the wolf and to excuse Red Riding Hood from any responsibility for what happens, even going to the extent of idealizing her" (90). He reminds us that Charles Dickens's first love was Little Red Riding Hood, as Dickens declared "I felt that if I could have married Little Red Riding Hood, I should have known perfect bliss" (90). "The wolf in the bed," Tucker confirms, "whatever else he may mean, also provides listeners with the delicious suspenses that go with any nursery rhyme or fairy story that ends on a sudden note of shout and grab, producing its usual chorus of terrified squeals and requests for more of the same" (92).

1982: Wolfgang Mieder explores the tale as a basis for ironic and satirical comments about modern society. "Usually it is the wolf who is portrayed as a successful seducer or rapist, taking advantage of the beautiful female. . . . The more sexual interpretations usually center around the questions that Little Red Riding Hood poses, to her grandmother, bringing to mind immediately the original fairytale scene" (27).

1983: Zohar Shavit concludes, in her examination of the concept of childhood reflected in folktales and their authors, that Perrault's "Little Red Riding Hood" is a satire about the urban gentleman who takes advantage of the poor peasant girl. It is clear, through the moral, that the wolf is not a real wolf but a metaphor for all sorts of dangerous people (143). Eroticism is a major factor in this retelling, reflected by the description of the girl's beauty, the color red, and the erotic bed scene (144). This last factor makes it quite clear that the tale is not about a real wolf gobbling up a child. She accounts for the differences between Perrault's version and that of the Grimms by their different perceptions of the concept of childhood. The child is no longer considered a source of amusement (as in Perrault's time) but as a "delicate creature who must be protected, educated and molded in accordance with the current educational beliefs and goals" (135). There is a marked difference in tone: It is no longer an ironic game played by the girl and wolf but a "realistic" portrayal of a young naive girl who follows her own inclinations rather than abides by her mother's wishes. The significance of the new ending is attributed to the educational views of that time: The child should derive a moral lesson from every experience and event (148). The tale was transformed from a satire to a story about learning a lesson, even to the items she carries in her basket, which vary from one adaptation to another depending on the adapter's views of what is best for a child.

1983: Jack Zipes demonstrates in *The Trials and Tribulations of Little Red Riding Hood* how the adaptations of the tale reflect the values and goals of the societies and groups in which they arise. "[I]n the folktale the little girl displays a natural, relaxed attitude toward her body and sex and meets the challenge of the would-be seducer." In Perrault, she "is chastised because she is innocently disposed toward nature in the form of the wolf and the woods, and she is *raped* or punished because she is guilty of not controlling her natural inclinations" (McGlathery 1993, 69). His premise is "that literary fairy tales were consciously cultivated and employed in seventeenth century France to reinforce the regulation of sexuality in modern Europe" (Zipes 1993, xi).

1984: Robert Darnton condemns Fromm's interpretation, which, he maintains, is based on details that were not part of the traditional oral tale. "Thus [Fromm] makes a great deal of the (nonexistent) red riding hood as a symbol of menstruation and of the (nonexistent) admonition not to stray from the path into wild terrain where she might break it. The wolf is the ravishing male. And the two (nonexistent) stones that are placed in the wolf's belly after the (nonexistent) hunter extricates the girl and her grandmother, stand for sterility, the punishment for breaking a sexual taboo" (11). Darnton states that more than half of the 35 recorded versions of the traditional tale end with the death of the child. She has done nothing to deserve such a fate, for in these tales, unlike the later retellings by Perrault and Grimms, there were no injunctions within the text for her to break. "It is the inscrutable, inexorable character of calamity that makes the tales so moving, not the happy endings that they frequently acquired after the eighteenth century" (54).

1984: Carl-Heinz Mallet analyzes four of the Grimms' tales, concluding that innocent Little Red Riding Hood "arouses erotic desires" that set this tale apart from all others in the canon (101). The catalyst in the tale is the grandmother, who in actuality has an extremely passive role and is quite different from a grandmother-figure. She lives alone, isolated in the midst of the forest, and is sent wine and cake to help with her illness. Mallet asserts that she is in reality an aspect of the mother, embodying certain secret and taboo wishes that are in direct opposition to the warning given to the daughter as she sets out on her journey (103). The daughter then reacts, as children have throughout time, by agreeing with her mother, paying lip service to her warnings, and following her own initiative when presented with a choice.

1985: Jeanne Morgan claims this tale is the most well-known of the stories in Perrault's collection. She analyzed Perrault's literary techniques in his construction of the tale and finds it notable for its sustained humor, which is apparent only from the viewpoint of the knowledgeable reader who is more aware of the situation than the characters. "The wolf's presumably innocent conversation and the heroine's supposition that her grandmother is merely *enrhumee* (to have a cold) are amusing to the reader/observer who knows the true situation" (115). Deadpan understatement incorporated sexual innuendo, made mockery of the girl's innocent stupidity, and contrasted in the reader's mind the body of the wolf and that of the elderly grandmother (115). "He enlarges the distance between the text and the reader, veiling his allusions to contemporary society until the final explicit *moralité.*" But, at the same time, Perrault was also careful to preserve the integrity of the original message to beware of wolves (118).

1985: Thomas Vessely investigates Bettelheim's findings in regard to Perrault's versions of the tales. "In folk tales, however, the wolf represented the real material dangers of the forest, and for Perrault's contemporaries this radical resetting may well have been a humorous betrayal of the adventures of the innocent girl" (226). Bettelheim's interpretation, therefore, may be based on the appeal that Perrault knew the story would hold for his adult audience.

1986: D. L. Ashliman notes that every element in the story, as penned by the Grimms, contributes to a sex-education interpretation (194). The red cap represents menstruation and, like adolescents of both sexes, Little Red revels in her newly achieved sexual maturity and flaunts it (195). The wolf "starts the seduction by tempting her with flowers and music (wild flowers and bird song). And he ends the process in bed, with naive Little Red Cap growing uneasy only as she discovers the unexpected size of his various body parts" (195). It is also a tale of fantastic justice: Red Cap is restored to life by a hunter who just happens along and cuts the wolf open. "The first stage of justice—restoring to the victim what she has lost—is thus quickly achieved; and the second stage—appropriate punishment, follows immediately" (195). She does not worry about an unwanted pregnancy for herself but, instead, impregnates the wolf with the stones she sews into his stomach. The wolf, discovering himself burdened with an unexpected and unwanted "pregnancy," goes into convulsions and dies (195). The tales was primarily told by women and provided a vehicle for the expression of forbidden desires and sexual freedom (196).

1986:   Gerhard Mueller discusses aspects of legal lore in the Grimms' fairy tales, focusing on the cannibalism and the image of the criminal as wolf. Quoting Jacob Grimm's work on German legal antiquities and professor Wilhelm Wilda, among others, Mueller points to the recognized practice of banishing criminals to the forest, making them equal to the wild beasts in all aspects. These outlaws were called *wargus* or *vargus*, "but a vargus is also the name of the wolf, so that both concepts truly merged: that of the unprotected animal pursued by all, and that of the human who finds himself in the same position" (225). Outlaws were also referred to as *lupus* (Latin for wolf) in the laws of early Norman kings (225).

1988:   Alan Dundes expounds on research on this tale, including studies on oral variants from China, Japan, and Korea and the similarities in the Oriental variants to the French oral versions discussed by Robert Darnton. They "could not possibly have been transmitted by the Perrault literary version since these elements are *not* found in that version" (Dundes 1988, 23). He discusses the varied approaches to analysis of the tale of "Little Red Riding Hood" and finds the research wanting. "Most of the interpretations cited failed to make use of the full panoply of oral texts of LRRH available" (1988, 41). His interpretation is based on antagonism between the heroine and the other female characters. The mother sends the child away from home, leading the child to seek revenge by eating her grandmother's flesh. He concludes that the tale is full of infantile fantasy: "The oral cannibalistic eating of the mother's body, the reference to defecating in bed, the toddler's rope (which is a direct allusion to LRRH being a *very* young child), and for that matter the very insistence upon Red Riding Hood's being called *little*" (1988, 43). In regards to reworkings of this tale in popular culture, Dundes states, "To the extent that some of the poetic and cartoon derivatives of the tale are sexually explicit, I would argue that the moralizing effects of Perrault's cautionary tale version and the Grimm brothers' recension have not been successful in stifling the underlying content of the oral tale" (1988, 44).

1988: Jack Zipes considers the role school boards and teachers have in the determination of which fairy tales are to be used or abused. Tales such as "Little Red Riding Hood" "have always been deemed acceptable because they instruct children through explicit warnings and lessons—even though some of the implicit messages may be harmful to children" (1988, 16). Zipes compares the retelling of the tales by Henri Pourrat in his 13-volume set published between 1948 and 1962 with those of Perrault and the Grimms. He finds Pourrat's to be more poetic, more literary, and more grounded in reality. Pourrat "describes realistically and succinctly the dilemma of an eight-year-old peasant girl who does not heed the warning of her grandmother. His description does not belabor her 'guilt' or naiveté but rather retains an ironic, comic tone that is keeping with her rescue at the end of the tale" (1988, 108).

1989: Alan Dundes's *Little Red Riding Hood: A Casebook* encompasses a critical bibliography of interpretations and commentary on the tale, including his 1988 study of the tale.

1989: Joyce Thomas considers this tale one of the few in the canon of fairy tales that actually had a child protagonist. The story illustrates the dire consequences of a child who had not learned how to survive in an adult world (42). Looking to Perrault's ending, Thomas states that Perrault communicated a basic human fear symbolized by cannibalism and the return to the quasiwomb: the loss of identity, the loss of one's self. Thomas feels that the young girl and the old woman, being on the polar regions of the womb-tomb, were more acceptable victims than adolescents (Thomas, 50). The Grimms' ending, the death of the wolf that echoes the stony deception of the Greek Cronus, suggests the "absurd posture of a male assuming any role approximating that of woman's pregnancy." This ending is logical in that the wolf dies in a manner reflecting his own oral actions (Thomas, 109). Thomas reflects on the classic dialogue between the girl and her "grandmother" that refers to the four senses of hearing, seeing, feeling, and tasting, commenting that it is ironic that the sense of smell escapes the child's notice in view of the wolf's natural physiognomy and reliance on that organ. "Her failure to perceive his large snout is logical . . . for that would best reveal the wolf as himself, whereas in Red Riding Hood's mind, she is perceiving the altered yet human features of her grandmother" (113). Thomas identifies the wolf as a werewolf in regards to the specific physical features believed in the Middle Ages to indicate a person being a werewolf: hairy palms (the better to hold you with), pointed ears (the better to hear you with), and eyebrows that grew together over the bridge of the nose. The werewolf was often tried for crimes such as murder, cannibalism, and dismemberment (115).

1991:   James McGlathery asserts this is a story about childhood; the beast the heroine confronts is not a man transformed into an animal, but simply a wolf who had the gift of speech accorded by fairy-tale convention. The danger is not loss of virginity but of being eaten alive (1991, 55). Although the possible erotic elements are recognized, this story is not considered a "Beauty and the Beast" type: "[T]he wolf is not a prospective suitor, nor even clearly a seducer of maidens as one usually thinks of the matter. His lust for Red Riding Hood's body is portrayed as gluttony, pure and simple. He is truly a wolf, not a man merely appearing in beastly form as a result of the casting of a magic spell" (1991, 58).

1991:   Lutz Rohrich classifies this tale in a special category: warning or scare tale that has no happy ending and is linked to legend rather than folktale. He determines the original tale must have had a tragic ending, as it was told primarily as a warning. The tragic ending was necessary to achieve the desired effect. It was only the Grimms' artful reworking that made this tale conform to the typical folktale structure. Rohrich asserts that the traditional tale was not composed merely as a cautionary tale; however, the wolf "probably originated as a werewolf or some other people-eating demonic figure which developed into an ordinary animal over time" (48). In the French and Italian oral versions, the wolf does not eat the grandmother all at once (leaving her intact) but has leftovers in the cupboard and a bowl of blood on the table. "Since a slaughtered grandmother whose flesh and blood the child has eaten cannot be retrieved alive from the wolf's stomach, the tale ends tragically with the death of both" (113). Rohrich refers to an experiment that was conducted in a girl's school consisting of children of German and French civil servants and military officers. The Grimms' version of this tale was read to a class of 10-year-olds; the tale was discussed; and the children were asked to draw pictures of the story. The German girls all drew Little Red Riding Hood with blond pigtails with a naive and fearful expression on her face and in her body language. The wolf was portrayed as a figure of demonic power. The French girls, on the other hand, drew the wolf as a domestic dog with no demonic traits, and Little Red Riding Hood, with her black hair tucked under her red cap, was a self-confident young woman showing no fear of the wolf at all (169).

1992: Maria Tatar, in reference to the history of this "ribald" tale, states that "it is not difficult to imagine what a skilled raconteur could do with this story . . . but in the hands of those who turned traditional tales into literary texts, the story of Red Riding Hood came to be orientated toward a new audience and transformed into a solemn cautionary tale warning children about the perils of disobeying mother's instructions" (3). The prohibition and the heroine's immediate violation of it play directly into the hands of people who wished to moralize and provide lessons in the tales. This is a true horror story because it now makes an example of the heroine, the figure of identification for the child audience, rather than the adult villain (8). The oral versions were less concerned with lessons and morals than with entertaining their audience with a "sequence of racy episodes and sensational events" (37).

> The shift from violence in the service of slapstick to violence in the service of the didactic added a moral backbone to folktales, but it rarely curbed their uninhibited display of cruelty. The Grimms' Little Red Riding Hood may be rescued (when the hunter slits open the wolf's belly!) but not before we are treated to two scenes in which both girl and grandmother are attacked and devoured—those are, significantly, the scenes to which illustrators habitually call attention (39).

1992:   Jan Ziolkowski argues that a medieval Latin tale can be considered the ancestor of this story. In the ancient tale, a five-year-old girl, wearing a red wool tunic given by her godfather at her baptism, is abducted by a wolf to be fed to her cubs. The baptism prevents the cubs from harming her, and the wolves instead lavish attention on her red tunic (McGlathery 1993, 70).

1993:   James McGlathery comments that this tale has attracted the most critical commentary of all the folktales. He briefly summarizes some of the major works.

1993:   Judith Rovenger, in her examination on variants of folktales, declares, "[T]he views on female autonomy and sexuality underlying each version are very much a part of the culture, time and personal value system of each teller" (134).

1993:   Jack Zipes, in his revised edition of *The Trials and Tribulations of Little Red Riding Hood*, declares that because rape and violence are at the core of this tale, it is the most notorious fairy tale in the Western world (1993, xi). It is not by chance, therefore, that most of the modern reworkings of the tale have been written by women as "the confrontations and situations that women experience in our society have compelled them to reflect upon the initial encounter between wolf and girl that they may have heard, read or seen as children"(1993, xii). Zipes reprints and provides commentary on numerous reworkings of the tale in prose, poetry, and picture-book formats. He clarifies:

> All this is not to say that the tale is outmoded and totally negative, that it should be censored by the women's movement and local school boards, or that it should be replaced by non-sexist versions. The problem is not in the literature, nor can it be solved through censorship. Given the conditions in Western society where women have been prey for men, there is a positive feature to the tale: its warning about the possibility of sexual molestation continues to serve a social purpose. . . . Until men learn that they need not be wolves or gamekeepers to fulfill their lives, the tale offers a valuable lesson for young girls and women—albeit a lesson based on the perversion of sexuality (1993, 81).

1994: Norma Livo refers to "Little Red Riding Hood" in her examination of sanitized tales and children's fears. She states that some of the warning tales such as "Little Red Riding Hood" have been re-written so often and so sanitized "that their serious messages have been lost in cuteness" (xxvi). Livo admonishes her audience that "many a timid child had been terrorized by an intimidating adult who says, "I could eat you up" as they pinch the child's cheeks" (xxvii).

1994: Marina Warner considers the aspect of the heroine's confusing the wolf with her grandmother: the crucial collapse of roles in the story. The wolf is kin to the crone or witch who dwells in the forest. In the witch-hunting fantasies of early modern Europe, both the werewolf and the crone/witch were associated with marginal knowledge; they possessed pagan secrets and in turn were possessed by them. Both granny (the crone) and the wolf are similar—they dwell in the forest and need food desperately—and the little girl could not tell them apart (180). The narrative concentrates on Little Red Riding Hood's act of disobedience as it "admonishes the protagonist for stopping to pick flowers in the woods and laying herself open to the wolf's wickedness: the wolf knows no better, but [Little Red] should have been better brought up" (243).

1995: Mary Douglas draws her interpretation from feminist anthropologist Yvonne Verdier's version of the tale, which is rustic, peasant, and independent of Perrault and Grimms. Douglas looks first at "our" version, questioning its appropriateness for small children. "Does this present an antique parallel to modern media violence?" (1). "Although our versions focus on the wolf as a child-eating monster, according to Yvonne Verdier's interpretation based on an analysis of all the available French versions, his role is quite incidental and unimportant. The brothers Grimm did something drastic to the story; it was gentrified almost out of recognition" (4). Verdier's study suggests that the heroine is approaching puberty: *Ma petite fille* translates to both "my little girl" and "my granddaughter." Verdier also discusses the relevance of the path of needles and that of pins: "pins are easy to use but only make temporary fastenings; needles are employed with skill and perseverance, they make permanent ties. Pins have no opening; putting a thread through the eye of a needle has a simple sexual connotation. The pin can be a symbol of the virgin intacta; the needle is the adult woman. Courting girls receive pretty pins as gifts from admirers, or throw pins into the wishing well" (4). The version by Perrault and the Grimms omitted the wolf's question about pins or needles, losing the framing cue for setting the story in the ritualized passage of the female generations (Douglas, 5).

1995: Jack Zipes proposes five reasons "Little Red Riding Hood" should be used with older students:

1. It is a mixed genre as it contains elements of the warning tale, the initiation tale, the fairy tale, and the fable.

2. It is a metaphorically erotic tale focusing on relations between the sexes and gender roles.

3. As an erotic tale, it poses the question of violence and sexism in the versions by Perrault and the Grimms.

4. It is a finely sculptured tale demonstrating key functions of narrative strategy (the necessary departure form home, the encounter with the "friendly" villain in the woods, the arrival at a supposedly safe destination, the comic interlude in bed, the sudden fall of the protagonist and, in the Grimms' version, the happy ending).

5. It is a shocking tale, particularly Perrault's version, as every child expects the girl to be saved from the wolf.

Zipes claims that Perrault's tale is the more honest as it reveals a great deal of how men blame the girl for her own violation, a victim of her own failings (1995, 28). This last point is considered again when Zipes states that the tales are filled with signals to children that they, not the adults, are the ones responsible if children are harmed or violated (1995, 221).

1996: John Goldthwaite considers Perrault's collection of tales "history's first real children's book" and "Little Red Riding Hood" the first story ever published that is a children's story in the modern sense. He maintains that it "is not properly part of the fairy-tale tradition of growing up to take one's inheritance of the world; only later was it straightjacketed into the role. Rather . . . a cross between the beast fable and the cautionary tale. . . . [The] point of this genre is that the story must end badly for the sake of some perhaps earnest, perhaps comical moral" (50). The subsequent retellings of this tale by the Grimms and others have often, in their attempt to make the ending come out right, created an ending that is more grisly than the original (51). Goldthwaite derides Bettelheim for dismissing Perrault's version because Bettelheim only wanted stories to be good. The story, instead, can be compared to Hilaire Belloc's *Cautionary Tales* in which children are burned up, gobbled up, and stamped flat (Goldthwaite, 51).

> This was the precedent set by "Little Red Riding Hood," then, the idea that, while it is predominantly an encouragement to growing up in the imagination and in the world, make-believe is also a literature of games, parody and burlesque and can renew itself by eating its own pieties, as the wolf had eaten little Red (52).

1996: Philip Lewis analyzes Perrault's treatment of this tale, the shortest in Perrault's collection. The stark ending is a narrative device to add drama to the oral telling of his tale. The marginal notation in Perrault's 1695 manuscript copy stated, "[T]hese words are pronounced in a stern voice in order to provoke fright, as if the wolf was going to eat the child" (Lewis, 167). Lewis examines the notations, moralities, and functions of "Little Red Riding Hood" for French society at the time. He maintains that the story is filled with suggestions that it be read aloud: "[T]he dramatizing effects with a cleverly onomatopoetic touch" are demonstrated at the door of grandmother's house and the disguising of the wolf's voice in imitating both Little Red Riding Hood and her grandmother (181). Until the girl climbs in bed with the wolf, her relationship with him is purely vocal. "In responding to the pretender's softened voice with her unfailing gullibility, she is doubtless giving herself over to the ambiguous voice she associated with a storyteller worthy of her confidence" (181). Lewis considers the episodic vocal tricks of the wolf in great detail as well as the connection between the chattering child and her storytelling grandmother. He takes the mother to task for not properly educating her daughter about possible dangers. "Thus the wolf, in usurping the mother's role and conveying to Little Red Riding Hood knowledge that she lacks, also assumes the grandmother's storytelling role and becomes the consummate speaker in the tale, the skilled user off a discourse of power in the service of desire" (184).

> The surprise . . . lies in the characterization of Little Red Riding Hood herself, notably in the resoluteness with which the narrative threads preserve her status as a child—not even an adolescent—whose unpreparedness eventually leaves her at a loss, unresponsive to the advances of a *coureur* or womanizer (193).

1997: Christina Bacchilega revisits the established history of the traditional tale and Angela Carter's reworkings in both short-story format and the movie *Company of Wolves*.

1997: Margery Hourihan reminds her reader that modern readers of "Little Red Riding Hood" will not be concerned with the oral and literary heritage of the tale but will only construct meanings from the version of the story presented to them. In fact, because the most common version of the story includes the hunter, the tale is considered a version of the hero myth (5). At the same time, the powerful appeal of this tale is due to its dramatic use of ancient motifs (25). Hourihan discusses the image of the wolf in the Middle Ages and the relationship with folkloric beliefs and folktales such as "Little Red Riding Hood." The wolf is considered "a malicious beast" in the Grimms' version and "wicked" and a sexual predator in Perrault's tale. Hourihan makes mention of Bettelheim's reading of the tale, which ignores the fact that the child cannot distinguish the wolf from her grandmother:

> This confusion, which is essential to the impact of the story, suggests a link with the werewolf hysteria of the fifteenth and sixteenth centuries, but also suggests that the tale is perhaps as much about sexual abuse within the family as about the dangers of wolves, the wilderness and male predation. It is the complex interplay of latent meanings which accounts for this story's continuing appeal (120).

Hourihan dives deeply into the history of the werewolf, including the case of Stubbe Peter, who confessed that it was one of his habits to roam the countryside, in wolf form, for female victims, whom he then raped and murdered and ate their hearts. This case may have influenced Perrault's retelling (122). This aspect of the telling helped the Grimms' version, with its hunter hero, to become the established version.

> At one level of significance the wolf represents male predatoriness; his dangerous presence in the world "proves" it is unwise for women to walk alone, to attempt to act independently. But, if the story ends, as Perrault's version does, with the eating up of Red Riding Hood, it leaves male power in a bad light, appearing as naked and ruthless dominance rather than as something natural, benevolent and essential. . . . Men's sexual predation is shown as 'wild,' a basic instinct which they cannot be expected to control; yet at the same time men are depicted as strong, resourceful and benevolent, the natural protectors of female virtue. Both these attitudes are adolescent fantasies, but the story presents them as valid images of adult masculinity, images which are internalized by young readers (198–99).

A Reworking of Little Red Riding Hood in Novel Form

Only one novel is discussed in this section. However, Gillian Cross's *Wolf* is so complex and intriguing that it can stand well alone!

Wolf

1990: Cross, Gillian. **Wolf**. London: Puffin.

"Aimed at young adult readers, this work transposes 'Little Red Riding Hood' from the forest to the urban wilderness of modern London, and canvasses a member of contemporary social issues including IRA terrorism. It investigates human behavior as well as the legendary behavior of wolves" (223). This 1991 winner of the Carnegie Medal for outstanding children's book in the United Kingdom addresses the gap between actual wolves and their mythical images. In her review of *Wolf* for *School Librarian*, Margaret Meek claims: "It explores mind and nature, mind in society, and approaches modern urban terrorism. It also makes a nonsense of the fact/fiction divide in narrative" (29).

Thirteen-year-old Cassy is sent by her grandmother, with whom she resides, to find her mother and stay with her. Instead of a basket of "goodies" she is given a bag of groceries that she is instructed not to give to her mother but to keep in a safe place. Nan sends Cassy out the door with money and a stack of postcards to send back to her twice a week. Cassy finally locates her mother, Goldie, who is living with her boyfriend Lyall and his son Robert. The journey, which takes only two pages in the novel, carries Cassy out of the organized urban life that she has known to the wilderness of London squats. Along with her mother, Cassy becomes involved with researching and creating a school presentation on wolves of both mythological and natural understanding. At the same time, there is a mysterious and sinister undercurrent in Cassy's relationships with her father, Mick; her mother; and her paternal grandmother.

Although Cross has had little to say about this novel, there has been a great deal of analysis from educators, all of whom recognize the strong connections to the traditional tale of Little Red Riding Hood. Cross's story uses the fairy-tale framework to explore the themes dramatized by the original story of "Little Red Riding Hood": aggression and the danger it represents for women, and the deceptiveness of surface appearances, especially the seeming safety of home compared with the uncertainties of the wider world. The adaptation of the story to a contemporary political and social context encourages young readers to look beyond conventional dualistic analyses of current issues (Hourihan, 224).

> *Wolf* is a book of many kinds of discourse. The fairy tales flicker and gleam throughout the pages. Details like Cassy's mac, the hooded raincoat which she wears outside as a coat and inside as a dressing gown, raise echoes of Red Riding Hood every time she puts it on; and this image is echoed in the hooded sweatsuits worn by both Mick and Lyall. The mere mention of a heavily coded word like hood or basket resonates throughout otherwise plain text. Similarly the motif of moongazing raises many kinds of echoes. Lyall is a moongazer; so is a wolf. Mick, in the picture, is always looking over Cassy's eyes and it

doesn't take much extrapolation to picture him gazing at the moon. The moon features in all the werewolf stories, but Goldie uses it as a shield when she lies to Lyall about why she is out in the night. Nan objects to mooning around (Mackey, 120).

Hourihan maintains that Cassy's father has the qualities tradition-ally attributed to wolves: He is cunning, predatory, ruthless, and irra-tional in his obsessiveness. Cassy, like Little Red Riding Hood, is innocent, well-meaning, and unaware of the dangers that surround her (Hourihan, 223). Kertzer, on the other hand, reports that

At first the two adult males, Mick Phelan and Lyall, ap-pear most wolflike with their padding feet and loping gait. In addition, Lyall, like Mick before him, is obsessed with wolves, their behavior, and the mythology that sur-rounds them. . . . But why has Cassy's mother left one wolf to live with another? . . . Granny Phelan has taught her granddaughter not to pay attention to her mother's voice, and Cassy, ever the obedient granddaughter, has learned her lesson well. . . . Even though Cassy then hears her mother announce her intention to take the wolf mask out of the room and observes her do it, Cassy is unable to understand what Goldie has done, unable to recognize her mother as an active participant in the narrative. For too long, she has read Goldie as a vulnerable Red Riding Hood (23).

Kertzer reminds us that Cassy, like many of the readers of *Wolf*, was raised on fairy tales and is familiar with the traditional roles of the key players. Nowhere in the traditional tales does the mother have a heroic role, and therefore it is difficult to assign one to Goldie either. "We come to the narrative expecting the wolf to be conventionally dangerous and masculine. Initially our expectations are met, at least partially. . . . Our certainty that he [Mick] is the wolf is destabilized, however, as character roles and narrative functions start to blur" (22–23). However, as Marga-ret Mackey states, "The correlation between the mythological wolf, the real wolf, the territorial lost cause and Mick the bomber seems very clear" (121). Mackey, in her doctoral thesis, examines the reading re-sponses of young-adult readers by using *Wolf* as the "control" novel. She thoroughly examines the formation of the novel, paying attention to Cross's use of the folktale:

> The Red Riding Hood story appears at the end of every second chapter, in a more or less continuous sequence, disguised as Cassy's dreams. The dreams are typographically marked with asterisks, indentations and italics; the language used is also radically different from that of the main story. In addition we have been warned from the very first page of the book, in a note before the beginning of Chapter 1, that it is very unusual for Cassy to dream (115).

"The dream sequences, powerful and portentous, inhabit the world of Red Riding Hood and emphasize the real terror which lurks in that story" (Mackey, 120). Interestingly, the comments of many of Mackey's informants demonstrate that although the traditional tale permeates the novel, they were not immediately aware of any connection to "Little Red Riding Hood" or any of the other wolf tales, such as "Three Little Pigs" and "The Boy Who Cried Wolf," that provide key images in the novel. This lack of recognition may be the result of the various inversions that Cross has embedded into her reworking: Cassy (Little Red) is sent away from the safety of grandmother's house to the unknown "wilderness" of her mother's living arrangements; the shopping bag (basket) is given to Cassy by her grandmother, but Cassy is told explicitly not to give it to her mother; and the postcard sent to grandmother carries the crucial line, "What should I do with the yellow stuff that was in the food bag?" Mackey pays homage to the long and varied history of this tale in the Western canon of tales and asserts that, regardless of the reader's individual knowledge of this history,

> the story of Little Red Riding Hood comes with a variety of implications and echoes added and subtracted over centuries. The story is simple, but its hinterland involves generations of evocation, enhancement, bowdlerization, speculation. . . . *Wolf* is the richer for being able to make use of the many contradictions in how Red Riding Hood is perceived; the story provides Cross with an opportunity to include levels of paradox that would be impossible to incorporate in the book without this kind of already-developed evocativeness (Mackey, 198).

Short Stories

> Little Red Riding Hood is a fairy tale that has been embraced by pop culture—from Sam the Sham's rendition in song to the brilliant Neil Jordan film *The Company of Wolves*, which combined several Angela Carter stories from *The Bloody Chamber*. Generally, the wolf is seen as predator, and Little Red Riding Hood and Grannie are viewed as helpless victims dependent on the woodcutter for rescue—or justice, depending on which version you read (Datlow and Windling 1993, 130).

In the following short stories, the characters of Little Red Riding Hood, the Wolf, and Granny undergo transformations and are interwoven in a myriad of new patterns.

1940: Thurber, James. **"The Little Girl and the Wolf."** *Fables for Our Times*. New York: Harper & Row, 5. Also in *Spells of Enchantment: The Wondrous Fairy Tales of Western Culture*, edited by Jack Zipes. New York: Viking, 1991. 618–19.

This parody uses many of the elements from the oral tradition: The nameless girl is courageous and cunning and constructs her own escape from danger. "In obvious disdain of Perrault's *moralité*, Thurber writes a blunter, more contemporary moral: It is not so easy to fool little girls nowadays as it used to be" (Zipes 1993, 56).

1979: Carter, Angela. **"The Company of Wolves."** *The Bloody Chamber and Other Stories*. London: Penguin, 110–18.

Highly evocative prose sets the scene for the reader, focusing on the danger of the wolf and its supernatural counterpart, the werewolf. It is Christmas Eve, and the young girl prepares for her journey through the woods to grandmother's house. She meets a young stranger on the way who befriends her and then offers her a challenge: a race to grandmother's house, she following the path and he, his remarkable compass. The prize of the wager is a kiss, a prize the girl hopes the young man will indeed win. Carter follows Perrault's story line, but the young girl, not necessarily the victor, is triumphant and ultimately tames the wolf. This gothic reworking recalls the superstitious past in order to reclaim it (Zipes 1993, 64). Margaret Atwood says of this story, "As in the original story, girl and wolf make a bet about which one can get to granny's house first, and also as in the original, wolf eats Granny. But the girl cannot be rescued by the hunter, because the wolf *is* the hunter. So she has to rescue herself" (130). Following the older oral versions, Carter has her young girl, when faced with the knowledge that she is about to become a victim, overthrow her fear, perform a striptease, and climb willingly into the bed with the wolf. She offers herself, not as meat, but as flesh (Bacchilega, 63).

1979: Carter, Angela. "The Werewolf." *The Bloody Chamber and Other Stories*. London: Penguin, 108–10.

In this chilling tale, the protagonist protects herself from the werewolf by slashing at it with her knife and cutting off its right forepaw. She carries this trophy to her grandmother but finds her ill from a fever and a missing right hand. The girl calls for help, and because the neighbors recognize the wart on the now-human severed hand, they take the old woman out into the snow and stone her to death. The winter setting and Carter's foregrounding of the historical and ideological distance that separates her and her reader from the fictional world constructs a cold and violent replication of the French peasant world of the seventeenth century that historian Robert Darnton discussed in his analysis of the tale (Bacchilega, 60). "While the mother's warning and the happy ending for the girl with help from the woodsmen indicate that the Grimms' version is in the background, the shape-shifting devils, witches, and werewolves of the folkloric tradition have not only repopulated the tale but also unmade the girl, wolf and granny as we know them from the Grimms or Perrault" (Bacchilega, 61).

1980: Baker, Russell. "Little Red Riding Hood Revisited." *New York Times Magazine*, 13 January.

Russell Baker satirizes jargon in his retelling of the tale. Because of his flagrant use of dull and pretentious phrasing, this short essay is often reprinted in journalism and writing textbooks.

1983: Lee, Tanith. "Wolfland." *Red as Blood (Or Tales from the Sisters Grimmer)*. New York: DAW, 91–118.

In Scandinavia in the nineteenth century lives a young girl named Lisel. She has heard stories about her famed maternal grandmother,

Anna the Matriarch, but has never met her, so Lisel is nonplused to find that she has been summoned to travel through the woods to visit her at her "great wild chateau in the great wild forest" (91). She has also been given a gift of a "swirling cloak of scarlet velvet." Lisel has only heard rumors about her deceased grandfather as well. These rumors mention his handsome appearance and his lust and savage demeanor. He was allegedly mysteriously killed one night.

A sled, horse and driver, and three outriders are arranged to take Lisel into the woods. She hears the howling of wolves, but the men around her reassure her that they will keep her safe. But their plans are soon derailed as their way is blocked by a carriage sent by Anna. Lisel transfers carriages and continues on alone, accompanied by wolves running alongside the carriage. Things get even stranger once she arrives at grandmother's house. One of her grandmother's companions is a dwarf who allows a huge wolf access to the house. When she tries to leave, her grandmother tells her the story of her grandfather, his death, and his wife's revenge. Lisel drinks the wine made out of a yellow flower that grows in the winter. (It is not identified in Lee's story but must be wolfsbane, also known as aconite. See Gillian Cross's *Wolf* for additional references to this poisonous plant.) Lisel discovers she now shares more than a secret with her grandmother!

1985: Lanigan, Carol. "**All the Better to See You**." In *Rapunzel's Revenge: Fairy Tales for Feminists*. Women in Community Publishing Course 1984/85. Dublin: Attic Press, 27–29.

Granny is quite dismayed at the turn of events when her 15-year-old granddaughter Rosa Hood drops in unexpectedly. Granny had just offered Billy Wolf a hiding place from the police when Rosa drops in and decides to save her old granny. Rosa is the hero, Billy goes to jail, and Granny is, as usual, ignored.

1985: Sharpe, Anne. "**Not So Little Red Riding Hood**." In *Rapunzel's Revenge: Fairy Tales for Feminists*. Women in Community Publishing Course 1984/85. Dublin: Attic Press, 47–49.

Scarlet encounters the man in gray on her walk through the forest to her grandmother's house. Deep in thought, she hardly notices him, even when he extends an invitation for a date. His anger at being ignored turns him into a beast, but when he attacks her at her grandmother's gate, he is the unhappy recipient of her martial arts training. Evocative language.

1989: Yolen, Jane. "**Happy Dens; or, A Day in the Old Wolves' Home**." In *The Faery Flag: Stories and Poems of Fantasy and the Supernatural*. New York: Orchard Books, 103–19.

Young Nurse Lamb begins her new job at the Old Wolves' Home with trepidation but is soon regaled with stories from three old (and obviously misunderstood) wolves: the architect Oliver, the Lone Wolf and his adventures with Peter, and Wolfgang the poet. It is Wolfgang who meets the young lass in the woods while contemplating the perfect rhyme. She becomes lost while delivering a basket to her grandmother's house, a basket containing carrot cake—Wolfgang's favorite food. In an attempt to save the cake from her grandmother's habit of making mush out of all food, the little girl suggests they play "Let's Pretend." She directs Wolfgang through the game, coaching him with the "proper" questions and answers, followed by a picnic. It is now too late for the little girl to continue on her journey, so Wolfgang helps her find her way home. The child, Elisabet Grimm, assures him that she will find something to tell her mother about the missing cake: " 'Oh, I'm a storyteller . . . I'll think of something.' And she did." (19)

1993: Koja, Kathe. "**I Shall Do Thee Mischief in the Wood**." In *Snow White, Blood Red*, edited by Ellen Datlow and Terri Windling. New York: William Morrow, 147–60.

Told from the predator's point of view, the story takes place during the Middle Ages on successive market days. The young girl arrives, noticeable in her formerly fine red cape that barely covers her rags. Jude, who is bored with waiting in the small community, watches her carefully. He offers her money and she hurries away "toward the wood, the wood where she could lose him in instants, the wood her home and he an interloper with nothing but lust and money to recommend him. . . ." (155) When she later asks for help against the beast in the woods, he accompanies her, toying with her as he believes it all a game until . . . he meets . . . the "only one beast in the woods." (160)

1993: Wheeler, Wendy. "**Little Red**." In *Snow White, Blood Red*, edited by Ellen Datlow and Terri Windling. New York: William Morrow, 130–46.

This tale is for more mature readers, as it delves into the contemporary wooing of the mother Helen and the seduction of the 14-year-old stepdaughter, Regina, by the narrator, an urbane and hirsute man. Wheeler's storyline follows the traditional pattern of Perrault's tale with a few exceptions: Grandmother is no longer living, making it possible for Helen to meet her lover in secrecy at her house; and the "wolf," Josef

Volker, becomes infatuated with a photograph of Regina long before he meets her. A chilling tale.

1994: Brooke, William J. "**Little Well-Read Riding Hood**." *Teller of Tales*. New York: HarperCollins, 103–18.

"My stories are not disrespectful! They're different, it's true, but they're meant to illuminate the originals, not to corrupt them" (109). The teller is aghast when he is told his reader misunderstands his purpose in retelling the tales in this interrelated collection of reworked folktales. When the girl, in her scarlet hood, meets the wolf on her way through the woods, she is not frightened, as she knows exactly why the wolf has such big eyes, ears, and teeth. She has read a book about wildlife in the forest. But grandmother, not sure the wolf knows what is written in the book, has the woodcutter chop the wolf in half.

1994: Garner, James Finn. "**Little Red Riding Hood**." In *Politically Correct Bedtime Stories: Modern Tales for Our Life and Times*. New York: Macmillan, 1–4.

In this politically correct parody of the Grimms' tale, the woodchopper-person's actions unite the three main characters, and they decide "to set up an alternative household based on mutual respect and cooperation. . ." (4).

1994: Monfredo, Miriam Grace. "**The Apprentice**." In *The Year's Best Fantasy and Horror, 7th Annual Collection*, edited by Ellen Datlow and Terri Windling. New York: St. Martin's Press, 446–54.

"Little Red Riding Hood" is just one of the tales Kelsey hears from "the sorcerer" who lives across the street. Other characters she meets are Huck Finn, Aladdin, Oliver Twist, and the White Rabbit from *Alice in Wonderland*. However, it is her travels with Little Red to grandmother's house that help Kelsey confront the cause of her terror. Monfredo effectively uses the series of participatory reading expeditions to explore sexual abuse in a child. A absorbing mingling of mystery, fantasy, and childlike conjecture to resolve the problem.

1995: Velde, Vivian Vande. "**The Granddaughter**." In *Tales from the Brothers Grimm and the Sisters Weird*. New York: Harcourt Brace, 37–50. Also in *The Year's Best Fantasy and Horror, 9th Annual Collection*, edited by Ellen Datlow and Terri Windling. New York: St. Martin's Griffin, 1996, 362–66.

In this parody, Lucinda, a spoiled, demanding, and opinionated granddaughter, is put in her place by grandmother and her close friend, the wolf. At first the wolf could not believe the tales his friend told him about Lucinda, but soon after meeting the young girl, the wolf realized that no exaggeration had been advanced . . . the child was truly dreadful. "After a few minutes that felt like an hour or two, the wolf was thinking that he was in serious danger of being bored to death" (42). When he hurries to grandmother's house to warn his friend of her granddaughter's visit, he finds grandmother ill in bed; she cannot flee the scene. Something else must be done! Wolf pretends to be granny (who is hiding in the closet in desperation), and when he jumps out of the bed a slapstick routine follows: Little Red screams loudly and continuously, and the wolf becomes entangled in the bedsheets and throws a chair against the closet door, entrapping granny, who cannot be heard because of the commotion. The noise fetches a woodcutter, who fires at the wolf but misses because he steps into the basket of goodies . . . and so on. All is put to rights, and the three friends celebrate on a picnic, leaving Little Red locked in the closet. Appropriate for upper elementary and junior high readers.

1995: Galloway, Priscilla. "The Good Mother." In *Truly Grim Tales*. Toronto: Lester, 74–96.

A science fiction tale reflecting postnuclear disaster for a mature reading audience. Galloway follows the Grimms' structure for the tale but with acute differences: The type of beast is never clarified, other than she is the "good mother" of the title. The story celebrates three generations of strong females cooperating for survival of not only the human race but of others as well in the aftermath of nuclear destruction. Grandmother, living on an island, spills her medicine and cannot replenish it herself. Ruby is sent to deliver the basket of medication by her mother, who cannot leave her radio position at the time. She warns her daughter of danger, but Ruby is quite unprepared to meet the talking beast. The beast arrives at grandmother's house before the young girl, removes the grandmother but keeps her alive for later, and crawls into bed with an oxygen mask after receiving an electrical shock. When Ruby recognizes the form in the bed, she flees in terror to a cave where she encounters the beast's cubs. Taking one as hostage, Ruby returns to her grandmother's house and discovers the meaning behind cooperation.

1996: Walker, Barbara. "Little White Riding Hood." In *Feminist Fairy Tales*. San Francisco, CA: HarperSanFrancisco, 165–70.

Barbara Walker attempts to correct the misconceptions in this tale by pointing out, "[W]olves are not known to eat living people. Thus, the old tale's version of wolfish appetite for human flesh is another canard, probably created to make children fear and loathe the dogs of the forest because of their possible impact on pastoral economics" (Walker, 165).

White Riding Hood welcomes a visit to her grandmother's house. Her grandmother, a witch, has taught her to appreciate the gifts of nature, particularly the friendship of the maligned wolves. Anger at two trappers carrying a dead female wolf puts White Riding Hood into danger from the two men. It is only the threat of retaliation from her grandmother that controls the two men and causes them to leave her alone. Later, with her grandmother, White Riding Hood finds the newly orphaned wolf cubs and springs all the traps on the hunter's trap line. They leave one intact and place it in grandmother's cottage. Grandmother puts on a wolf mask, and when the trap catches its prey, she disposes of it by chopping it in pieces and feeding it to the wolves.

1996: Yolen, Jane. "**Wonder Land**." In *Sisters in Fantasy II*, edited by Susan Shwartz and Martin H. Greenberg. New York: ROC, 17–19.

As Allison runs through the forest towards her best friend Marcie, she thinks of all the great things she wants to tell her about—the animals she saw, but mostly about Billy and where he tried to touch her. Absorbed in her thoughts, she has a meeting with a wolf who stares at her, grins, licks its mouth (she does as well), and then leaves her in the forest . . . with her hoping for another meeting with young Billy and his "big hands." Yolen uses the meeting of the girl and the wolf in the forest to explore the blossoming of sexual awareness.

1997: Hopkinson, Nalo. "**Riding the Red**." In *Black Swan, White Raven*, edited by Ellen Datlow and Terri Windling. New York: Avon, 56–60.

The narrator of this tale is the grandmother, who would like to relate her own experiences as a young girl and her first encounters with the "wolf" to her granddaughter. The grandmother is bemoaning the fact that the girl's mother has never been told the story and now wishes to keep it from her own daughter, whom she deems too young to hear it. "But it's the old wives who best tell those tales, oh yes. It's the old wives who remember. We've been there, and we lived to tell them" (58).

Feature Films

Film adaptations of fairy tales, other than the animated versions of Disney, are often compared to *Company of Wolves*, with its harking back to the oldest possible interpretation of the tale.

1984: Carter, Angela, and Neil Jordan. **Company of Wolves**. Starring Angela Lansbury and Sarah Patterson. Directed by Neil Jordan. Produced by Chris Brown and Stephan Woolley. Incorporated Television Company (ITC), 95 minutes.

The movie has been discontinued for sale but is widely available in library collections and video stores. It features state-of-the-art special effects to aid the grandmother (Angela Lansbury) as she tells the tales of wolves and little girls who stray from the path to her granddaughter. The movie, reworking the three "women-in-company-of-wolves" stories in Carter's *The Bloody Chamber,* also employs several of the shorter narratives within these stories as dreams. "Carter's adaptations depend upon the viewer's familiarity with her work—the literary text is thus both prerequisite for and superior to the film" (Cartmell et al., 6). "Its concentric narrative structure, lurid colors and general lack of realist devices announce it as a defamiliarizing film, and it combines storytelling with an exploration of the stories' implicit meanings . . . [which] enables the film to envision numerous transformations between wolves and humans" (Neale, 103–4). In this movie Carter reflects on the internal fantasies of a young girl as the moment of her adolescence and in the face of her first intimations of sexuality (Mulvey, 237).

> The film reproduces the story of the folk tale itself. . . . These different layers of story-telling and belief are excavated through the power of the cinema, moving through a young girl's contemporary appropriation of the story for her own interior psychic needs to the social setting of oral culture, and then to the exteriorization of the irrational in the ancient belief in monsters (Mulvey, 239).

Christina Bacchilega considers the movie a prime example of metanarrative as she discusses how the traditional tale of "Little Red Riding Hood" is invoked on at least three significant levels. These are:

1. As narrators and characters succeed each other in the framing and embedded narratives, *Company of Wolves* represents the social history of the fairy tale as genre. Class interests compete over time, as the medieval folktale is appropriated by the upper classes in the eighteenth and nineteenth centuries, and then by the family-centered interpretations of twentieth-century psychoanalysis (67).

2. By telling and retelling stories within stories, and in different situations to differing effects, the movie reproduces the process of storytelling itself.

3. The girl actively and critically participates not only in the process of (primarily women's) storytelling, but in the related determination of choices (68).

Bacchilega believes the movie's violent ending undermines much of the women-centered initiatory storytelling of the stories within the dream. "After all, the young girl appears again as a victim of her own sexuality and of deadly appetites. Re-enter Perrault unfortunately, since that final image would seem to confine any transformation of sexual politics to the dream world and punish the girl" (69). "In a personal communication Jack Zipes also confirmed that Angela Carter was angry about the last scene, which had not been part of her screen play" (Bacchilega, 164).

Poetry

The story of the girl and her encounter in the woods has formed the basis for a wide variety of poems.

1971: Sexton, Anne. "**Little Red Riding Hood**." In *Transformations*. Boston: Houghton Mifflin, 73–79. Also in *Disenchantments: An Anthology of Modern Fairy Tale Poetry*, edited by Wolfgang Mieder. Hanover, NH: University Press of New England, 1985, 103–7.

In her retelling of the Grimms' story, Sexton focuses on the theme of deception, not only within the tale but also in modern society: respectability cloaking adultery, con artists defrauding citizens, suicides committed on the eve of media success, and relocation from the nuclear family. "Her poems depict how women are used as sex objects and how their lives become little more than commodities or hollow existences when they follow the social paths designed for them. She . . . cynically concludes the tale with the 'saved' grandmother and Red Riding Hood in a state of social amnesia" (Zipes 1993, 64). "Sexton's 'transformation' takes place in the language and the framing of the tale, both of which bring it into the middle of the twentieth century as if to underscore the story's continued power" (Walker, 56). Walker points to the "pregnant" state of the wolf after he consumes both women and they are freed finally with "a kind of Caesarean section." "The wolf is thus both predator and mother, and the final horror of Sexton's poem is that the two women retain no memory of being swallowed and set free, so that by implication it could all happen again, just as the tale is told over and over" (Walker, 56).

1977: Broumas, Olga. "**Little Red Riding Hood**." In *Beginning with O*. New Haven, CT: Yale University Press, 67–68. Also in *Disenchantments: An Anthology of Modern Fairy Tale Poetry*, edited by Wolfgang Mieder. Hanover, NH: University Press of New England, 1985, 111–12.

Broumas uses the voice of the female narrator and the story of Little Red Riding Hood to lament the lack of continuity in her female line. She followed her mother's directions all her life: not to stray from the path and to beware of wolves. She was obedient, but her final reward seems to be loneliness. "As the speaker recreates in images her difficult birth, Broumas addresses her real subject—patriarchy's subjugation of women. The mother cramps her baby with a patriarchal legacy of rules" (Hoogland, 14). The imagery of this tale is used to talk about alienation, fear, and subjugation in a female context (Hoogland, 15).

1982: Hay, Sara Henderson. "**The Grandmother**." In *Story Hour* by Sara Henderson Hay. Fayetteville, AR: University of Arkansas Press, 3.

This is a cry for companionship from a lonely woman living on her own in the woods. While her granddaughter sometimes visits her, it is not enough. In this introspective monologue, grandmother considers opening her home to the "poor mongrel stray" that lurks around her cottage for company.

1983: Dahl, Roald. "**Little Red Riding Hood and the Wolf**." In *Revolting Rhymes* by Roald Dahl. New York: Alfred A. Knopf, 30–34. Also in *Disenchantments: An Anthology of Modern Fairy Tale Poetry*, edited by Wolfgang Mieder. Hanover, NH: University Press of New England, 1985, 113–14.

In keeping with this collection of poetic reworkings, Dahl uses parody and perhaps a little inspiration from the short story by James Thurber to entertain his reading audience. Told in third person and from the wolf's point of view (for the most part), the poem concentrates on his wolfish appetites. Appropriate for upper elementary readers. There is no sexual tension although the poem does involve violence.

1985: Carryl, Guy Wetmore. "**Red Riding Hood**." In *Disenchantments: An Anthology of Modern Fairy Tale Poetry*, edited by Wolfgang Mieder. Hanover, NH: University Press of New England, 100–101.

Carryl plays on the virtuousness of a little girl who always obeys her parents until she reaches puberty and has a fateful visit to her grandmother's house. His satirical commentary follows a list of the child's accomplishments over the years before it considers the positive aspect of Little Red Riding Hood's demise: "[J]ust think what she might have become!" (101) As in Perrault, the poem concludes with a moral, but unlike the original, this moral is a clever pun on a proverb.

1985: Hope, A. D. "**Coup de Grace**." In *Disenchantments: An Anthology of Modern Fairy Tale Poetry*, edited by Wolfgang Mieder. Hanover, NH: University Press of New England, 102.

A short, colorful account of the wolf's attempt to swallow Little Red Riding Hood. However, she is an accomplished miss with a very wide mouth indeed. Great fun.

1985: Riley, James Whitcomb. "**Maymie's Story of Red Riding Hood**." In *Disenchantments: An Anthology of Modern Fairy Tale Poetry*, edited by Wolfgang Mieder. Hanover, NH: University Press of New England, 95–99.

A retelling of the entire Grimms' version of the tale in dialect, as told by an astute storyteller. Originally published in 1916.

1985: Sklarew, Myra. "**Red Riding Hood at the Acropolis**." In *Disenchantments: An Anthology of Modern Fairy Tale Poetry*, edited by Wolfgang Mieder. Hanover, NH: University Press of New England, 109–10.

The images from Red Riding Hood are intermingled with those of classical mythology in this poetic rendering of the Grimms' version of the tale.

1985: Zupan, Vitomil. "**A Fairy Tale**." In *Disenchantments: An Anthology of Modern Fairy Tale Poetry*, edited by Wolfgang Mieder. Hanover, NH: University Press of New England, 108.

This short poem, about a "very strange fairy tale," interweaves the image of Little Red Riding Hood's grandmother being eaten and spilled milk.

1990: Strauss, Gwen. "**The Waiting Wolf**." In *Trail of Stones*. New York: Alfred A. Knopf, 14–17.

This poem is told as a first-person narrative by the wolf while he is waiting in grandmother's bed for the little girl he had met previously in the wood. His thoughts focus on her youth and his anticipated meeting with her in the bed, but at he same time he wonders if she had envisioned the exchange all along.

1994: Steiber, Ellen. "**Silver and Gold**." In *Black Thorn, White Rose*, edited by Ellen Datlow and Terri Windling. New York: William Morrow, 307–09.

Little Red Riding Hood muses while at the doctor after she and her grandmother were rescued from the wolf. She had been warned and warned by her mother, but the temptation to follow the wolf proved so irresistible that she would not hesitate to do it again.

Picture Books

"Little Red Riding Hood" seems to be a favorite tale to be tackled by illustrators. In this section, however, we will concentrate on only a few titles that, in our minds at least, are outstanding reworkings or new visions of the tale appropriate for the young-adult audience.

1983: Perrault, Charles. **Little Red Riding Hood**. Illustrated by Sarah Moon. Mankato, MN: Creative Education.

Winning the 1984 Premio Grafico in Bologna for this title awarded Sarah Moon more interest than she could possibly imagine. She was pilloried by many, and the book has been banned in many libraries in the United States. Using stark black-and-white photographs, Moon translated Perrault's version of the tale into a modern urban context. This achieved a disturbing documentary effect that offers "no escape . . . for the reader, no way to dispatch what we see and read to a remote fairy-tale world where children are 'gobbled up' but just as quickly come back to life with the aid of a passing woodsman. *This* violence is immediate. It is also final" (*Bookbird*, 8).

> [T]he theme of violence, the violation of a child's will, is treated in a more somber way in Sarah Moon's remarkable *Little Red Riding Hood*. Using Charles Perrault's 1697 text with her own stark, contemporary photographs of a young girl on her way to grandmother's house at night in an urban setting, Moon addresses the topic of violence in our society and shifts the blame for the girl's rape and/or death to the predators or to social conditions. This revised version . . . is a haunting photographic essay about the dangers girls face in our streets. Not only do the photos demand that we reexamine Perrault's text carefully, they also make us aware of the insidious threatening climate in which young girls grow up in dread" (Zipes 1994, 148).

The *Bookbird* tribute to this book reminds the reader that this book is still in print and the message just as important or even more so in the 1990s as the early 1980s, when Moon published the tale and insisted that child abuse should not be surrounded by silence. The review, first published in the *Minneapolis/St. Paul Magazine* and quoted here, states: "The greatest virtue of these photographs is that they enrich the tale with very contemporary psychological ambiguity, and they will certainly provoke discussion, especially with teenagers" (*Bookbird*, 9). This certainly has been the case in our experiences with this title. Many of our colleagues at the university would like to see this book disappear, as they feel it is too graphic and frightening for young children. These people have forgotten who the original and primary audience for this tale should be. And in the words of a 15-year-old female when she first read the book: "Cool. It is so cool!"

1988: Grimm, William. Dear Mili. Illustrated by Maurice Sendak. New York: Farrar, Straus & Giroux.

Sendak's *Dear Mili* unconsciously or consciously reillustrates the history of "Little Red Riding Hood" in a fascinating way (Zipes 1994, 145). The girl, who is about eight years old, wears a red dress and Sendak uses this color, in a variety of hues, to play upon the theme of courage and sin (Zipes 1994, 146).

1991: Bang, Molly. Picture This: Perception and Composition. Illustrated by the author. Boston: Little, Brown.

Molly Bang published this study of visual perception and design as a result of a course that she taught to eighth and ninth graders. She uses the tale of "Little Red Riding Hood" as her model to demonstrate principles of illustration. She discusses, among other things, the features of wolves that most frighten the reader (the teeth); red as a color that evokes a range of disparate, even conflicting feelings; and the use of space in telling a story.

Internet Resources

The Little Red Riding Hood Project can be found at http://www-dept.usm.edu/~engdept/lrrh/lrrhhome.htm. This site, maintained by the University of Southern Mississippi, is a text and image archive of English versions of the tale from the eighteenth, nineteenth, and early twentieth centuries. Complete instructions for comparison of the 16 tales and the various illustrations are given in the prologue of the site.

Classroom Extensions

As in all the suggested exercises in this book, many of the following can be easily adapted for use with any of the fairy tales.

Deconstruction: Gaps in the Text of *Wolf*

> The object of deconstructing the text is to examine the *process of its production*—not the private experience of the individual author, but the mode of production, the materials and their arrangement in the work. The aim is to locate the point of contradiction within the text, the point at which it transgresses the limits within which it is constructed, breaks free of the constraints imposed by its own realist form. Composed of contradictions, the text is no longer restricted to a single, harmonious and authoritative reading. Instead it becomes *plural*, open to re-reading, no longer an object for passive consumption, but an object of work by the reader to produce meaning (Belsey, 104).

Margaret Mackey states that a beginner's text to deconstructive reading may suggest starting with class (or politics), race, and gender (123). Discussion of these three elements are virtually absent in the novel. Do you agree with the following "gaps" as presented by Mackey? Why or why not? Do these gaps interfere with the reading of the novel for young adults outside of Great Britain?

Politics

There is no description of the Irish case against the British, no voice for Mick. By the unanimous vote of the schoolchildren (whose own nationalities are not explored), Mick is reduced to werewolf, monster, horror story. Nothing is too bad to be true in this book, and nothing is important enough to justify bombing innocent children. It is cut and dried and relatively simple; all you have to do is decide which side you are going to be on (Cross, 95). But the story of British colonialism in Ireland in not simple, and the fact that Lyall and Robert (who come as close as anyone does to speaking for the Irish when they talk about wolves defending their territory) are also presumably colonials of one sort or another, by virtue of their blackness, does nothing to justify the singular "English" voice, which is all that is on offer. Cassy's decision is purely a moral one, never a political one (Mackey, 123).

Race

Cross herself raises the issue of race. Lyall and Robert are Black. Does this matter? Many of the readers with whom I have discussed this book have either failed to notice this fact or forgotten it as an insignificant detail. Cassy sees Lyall as the werewolf, but Lyall is able to pull off the mask. "It was only for a moment." It is hard to imagine how the text could be more explicit. Is it just accidental that Lyall is Black, that he can therefore be read as representing another perceived threat in English society in the twentieth century (Mackey, 125)?

Gender

> [T]he story of Cassy and her parents would alter very little if Cassy were a boy. The dynamics of this particular family do not revolve around the gender of the child. However, it is a different matter when we come to the infiltration of the story of Red Riding Hood. The gender of Red Riding Hood is not accidental or neutral. Furthermore, in the dreams, the sexual threat is extremely clear (Mackey, 125).

Development of Childhood Revealed Through the Story of Little Red Riding Hood

The result of childhood being considered a perceptibly different phase of life was the lavishing of attention on materials directed for children such as books, toys, and clothes and on theories of education and proper behavior. Perrault's tales provided models of behavior for children that reinforced the prestige and superiority of upper-class society. The heroines of all his tales are "pretty, loyal, dedicated to their household chores, modest and docile and sometimes a little stupid insofar as it is true that stupidity is almost a quality in women for Perrault" (Zipes 1993, 31). If, as Zipes announces, this tale is studied in light of the male-dominated French society and Perrault's personal prejudices towards women, "the *underlying* history of the tale and its reception, as it spread throughout western Europe and America in its changing literary form, assumes greater significance than the history of the original oral tale" (Zipes 1993, 31). Do you agree with Zipes's position?

Illustrations: A Comparison

Zipes (1990, 355) identifies three major scenes that are almost always illustrated:

1. The warning given by the mother, exemplified by the raising of her finger when speaking to the little girl. "In the minds of illustrators the girl is already guilty before a crime is committed; she is made responsible for whatever might happen."

2. The first meeting with the wolf, which is portrayed "as a type of pact or seduction scene," and the girl does not appear to be afraid of the beast.

3. If the version illustrated is Perrault's, the wolf is illustrated as violating the girl, representing the consequence of her illicit desires and designs; if the Grimms' version, the hunter becomes the focus of the illustration.

Choose several picture-book renditions of "Little Red Riding Hood" and look for these images in each of the books. Discuss how each illustrator has made these images unique (if indeed they are). Why do these three images or elements receive such a focus when illustrating a tale? Which images or elements are almost never included in the picture-book versions of this folktale?

Illustrations: Trina Schart Hyman's Tale

Hyman's illustrations have been criticized by school officials in the United States for portraying a red-nosed, wine-imbibing grandmother who is too unconventional for these officials, and they have pulled the book off the shelves of their schools. What does Hyman say about these illustrations? In the article "Cut It Down, and You Will Find Something at the Roots," Hyman speaks of her fascination with this tale from early childhood on. "I so strongly identified with that less-than-clever trusting little twit of a heroine, and was so fascinated by her encounter with the wolf and her adventures in the forest and at Grandmother's house, that I became literally enchanted by the tale. I was so obsessed with it that the fine and wavering line between story and real life became invisible to me" (293).

Hyman drew her images for this tale from her own life: "Little Red was, of course, myself at age four. Her mother was my mom, and her grandmother my own Rhode Island grandmother. . . . I knew a man across the river in Vermont who had timber wolves for pets, so I used real wolves as models for that wicked old trickster" (299).

Hyman has acknowledged the critics' response to the bottle of wine in Little Red's basket and the charge of alcoholism leveled at granny but has not made further comment. How would you feel if your own family was not only challenged but banned in school libraries?

Wolves: Reality and Folklore

"The tidiness of the school show in assimilating all the disparate fragments of information about wolves . . . is a feature of the surface text and can be cited with page references; readers may react differently to this aspect of the book but it takes no reading against the grain to observe it" (Mackey, 128). Cross offers a great deal of information about the role of wolves in both folklore and nature. What is Cross trying to say with this information? Would a school project such as that portrayed in the novel be an effective way to inform people about the "real" nature of wolves? Conduct your own research for a display on wolves.

Bibliography

Ashliman, D. L. "Symbolic Sex-Role Reversals in the Grimms' Fairy Tales." In *Forms of the Fantastic: Selected Essays from the Third International Conference on the Fantastic in Literature and Film*, edited by Jan Hokenson and Howard Pearce. New York: Greenwood Press, 1986, 193–98. (Contributions to the Study of Science Fiction and Fantasy, no. 20).

Atwood, Margaret. "Running with the Tigers." In *Flesh and the Mirror: Essays on the Art of Angela Carter*, edited by Lorna Sage. London: Virago, 1994, 117–35.

Bacchilega, Christina. *Postmodern Fairy Tales: Gender and Narrative Strategies*. Philadelphia: University of Pennsylvania Press, 1997.

Barchilon, Jacques, and Peter Flinders. *Charles Perrault*. Boston: Twayne, 1981.

Belsey, Catherine. *Critical Practice*. New Accents. London: Methuen, 1980.

Bettelheim, Bruno. *The Uses of Enchantment: The Meaning and Importance of Fairy Tales*. New York: Vintage Books, 1976.

———. "Fairy Tales as Ways of Knowing." In *Fairy Tales as Ways of Knowing: Essays on Marchen in Psychology, Society and Literature*, edited by Michael M. Metzger and Katherina Mommsen. Bern: Peter Lang, 1981, 11–21. (Germanic Studies in America, No. 41).

Cartmell, Deborah, et al. *Pulping Fictions: Consuming Culture Across the Literature/Media Divide*. London, Pluto, 1996.

Darnton, Robert. *The Great Cat Massacre and Other Episodes in French Cultural History*. New York: Basic Books, 1984.

Douglas, Mary. "Red Riding Hood: An Interpretation from Anthropology." The Thirteenth Katherine Briggs Memorial Lecture, November 1994. *Folklore* 106 (1995), 1–7.

Dundes, Alan. "Interpreting Little Red Riding Hood Psychoanalytically." In *The Brothers Grimm and Folktale*, edited by James M. McGlathery. Urbana-Champaign, IL: University of Illinois Press, 1988, 16–51.

————, ed. *Little Red Riding Hood: A Casebook*. Madison, WI: University of Wisconsin Press, 1989.

Goldthwaite, John. *The Natural History of Make-Believe: A Guide to the Principal Works of Britain, Europe, and America*. New York: Oxford University Press, 1996.

Haase, Donald, ed. *The Reception of Grimms' Fairy Tales: Responses, Reactions, Revisions*. Detroit: Wayne State University Press, 1993.

Heuscher, Julius E. *A Psychiatric Study of Myths and Fairy Tales: Their Origin, Meaning, and Usefulness*. 2d ed. Springfield, IL: Charles C. Thomas, 1974.

Hoogland, Cornelia. 1994. "Real 'wolves in those bushes:' readers take dangerous journeys with 'Little Red Riding Hood.' " *CCL* 73 (1994), 7–21.

Hourihan, Margery. *Deconstructing the Hero: Literary Theory and Children's Literature*. London: Routledge, 1997.

Hyman, Trina Schart. "Cut It Down, and You Will Find Something at the Roots." In *The Reception of Grimms' Fairy Tales: Responses, Reactions, Revisions*, edited by Donald Haase. Detroit: Wayne State University Press, 1993, 293–300.

Kertzer, Adrienne. "Reclaiming Her Maternal Pre-Text: Little Red Riding Hood's Mother and Three Young Adult Novels." *Children's Literature Association Quarterly* 21:1 (1996), 20–27.

Laruccia, Victor. "Little Red Riding Hood's Metacommentary: Paradoxical Injunction, Semiotics & Behavior." *Modern Language Notes* 90 (1975), 517–34.

Lewis, Philip. *Seeing Through the Mother Goose Tales: Visual Turns in the Writings of Charles Perrault*. Stanford, CA: Stanford University Press, 1996.

Livo, Norma. *Who's Afraid . . . ?Facing Children's Fears with Folktales.* Englewood, CO: Teacher Ideas Press, 1994.

Mackey, Margaret. *Imagining with Words: The Temporal Processes of Reading Fiction.* Ph.D. thesis, University of Alberta Press, 1995.

Mallet, Carl-Heinz. *Fairy Tales and Children: The Psychology of Children Revealed Through Four of Grimm's Fairy Tales.* Translated by Joachim Neugroschel. New York: Schocken Books,1984.

Mavrogenes, Nancy A., and Joan S. Cummins. "What Ever Happened to Little Red Riding Hood? A Study of a Nursery Tale." *Horn Book* (June 1979), 344–49.

McGlathery, James M. *Fairy Tale Romance: The Grimms, Basile, and Perrault.* Urbana-Champaign, IL: University of Illinois Press, 1991.

———. *Grimms' Fairy Tales: A History of Criticism on a Popular Classic.* Columbia, SC: Camden House, 1993.

Meek, Margaret. Review of *Wolf. School Librarian* 39: 1 (1991), 29.

Mieder, Wolfgang. "Survival Forms of 'Little Red Riding Hood' in Modern Society." *International Folklore Review* 2 (1982), 23–40.

Morgan, Jeanne. *Perrault's Morals for Moderns.* New York: Peter Lang, 1985.

Mueller, Gerhard O. "The Criminological Significance of the Grimms' Fairy Tales." In *Fairy Tales and Society: Illusion, Allusion, and Paradigm*, edited by Ruth B. Bottigheimer. Philadelphia: University of Pennsylvania Press, 1986, 217–27.

Mulvey, Laura. " Cinema Magic and the Old Monsters: Angela Carter's Cinema." In *Flesh and the Mirror: Essays on the Art of Angela Carter*, edited by Lorna Sage. London: Virago, 1994, 230–42.

Neale, Catherine. "Pleasure and Interpretation: Film Adaptations of Angela Carter's Fiction." In *Pulping Fictions: Consuming Culture Across the Literature/Media Divide*, edited by Deborah Cartmell et al. London: Pluto, 1996, 99–109.

Rohrich, Lutz. *Folktales and Reality.* Translated by Peter Tokofsky. Bloomington: Indiana University Press, 1991.

Rovenger, Judith. "The Better to Hear You With: Making Sense of Folktales." *School Library Journal* (March 1993), 134–35.

Shavit, Zohar. "The Concept of Childhood and Children's Folktales: Test Case—"Little Red Riding Hood." In *Little Red Riding Hood: A Casebook*. Edited by Alan Dundes. Madison, WI: University of Wisconsin Press, 1989, 129–58.

Tatar, Maria. *Off with Their Heads! Fairy Tales and the Culture of Childhood.* Princeton, NJ: Princeton University Press, 1992.

Thomas, Joyce. *Inside the Wolf's Belly: Aspects of the Fairy Tale*. Sheffield, England: Sheffield Academic Press, 1989.

Tucker, Nicholas. *The Child and the Book: A Psychological and Literary Exploration*. Cambridge, MA: Cambridge University Press, 1981.

Vessely, Thomas R. "In Defense of Useless Enchantment: Bettelheim's Appraisal of the Fairy Tales of Perrault." In *The Scope of the Fantastic—Culture, Biography, Themes, Children's Literature: Selected Essays from the First International Conference on the Fantastic in Literature and Film*, edited by Robert A. Collins and Howard D. Pearce. Westport, CN: Greenwood Press, 1985, 221–30. (Contributions to the Study of Science Fiction and Fantasy, no. 11).

Walker, Nancy A. *The Disobedient Writer: Women and Narrative Tradition*. Austin, TX: University of Texas Press, 1995.

Warner, Marina. *From the Beast to the Blonde: On Fairy Tales and Their Tellers*. London: Chatto & Windus, 1994.

Zipes, Jack. "A Second Gaze at Little Red Riding Hood's Trials and Tribulations." *The Lion and the Unicorn* 7/8 (1983/84), 78–109.

———. *The Brothers Grimm: From Enchanted Forests to the Modern World*. New York: Routledge, 1988.

———. *The Trials and Tribulations of Little Red Riding Hood*. 2d ed. New York: Routledge, 1993.

———. *Fairy Tale As Myth, Myth As Fairy Tale*. Lexington, KY: University of Kentucky Press, 1994. (Thomas D. Clark Lectures, 1993.)

———. *Creative Storytelling: Building Community, Changing Lives*. New York: Routledge, 1995.

CHAPTER 6

RAPUNZEL

The winner of the 1998 Caldecott award, given by the American Library Association for best illustrations in a children's book, was Paul Zelinsky's *Rapunzel*. The story, although popular, has not been as frequently retold or reworked as "Snow White" or "Cinderella" or "Little Red Riding Hood." It does not, perhaps, offer as much scope for reworking as the other popular tales do because it contains fewer symbolic elements and plot incidents. But the image of the golden-haired maiden locked in a high tower and the line "Rapunzel, Rapunzel, let down your hair" are part of our core folktale vocabulary. John Goldthwaite speculates that perhaps the story began in the Middle Ages "as the complaint of some Romeo against the convent system that had cloistered his Juliet" (58). Goldthwaite suggests that he could have taken the tower from the legend of Saint Barbara, whose cult was very popular in the late Middle Ages. Barbara was shut up in a tower by her father so that no man might see her. Princes came to court her anyway, but while her father was away on a trip she became a Christian and shut herself up in his bathhouse to live as a hermit (Farmer, 31). This tale "became the stuff of a troubadour's romance and later, perhaps overheard by the servants, it entered oral tradition" (Goldthwaite, 58). Goldthwaite is only using "Rapunzel" and its hypothetical history as an example in his discussion of the medieval origins of some of the tales collected by the Brothers Grimm. But his conjecture makes a charming introduction to the story itself.

A woman and her husband have long wished for a child, and she becomes pregnant. From a window she can see into the garden of a witch who lives next door, and she develops an overwhelming craving for a type of lettuce called rapunzel, or rampion in English, which she can see growing there. She longs for it so much that she becomes ill. Her husband steals some lettuce for her and she eats it ravenously, but soon she wants more. The husband climbs over the wall into the witch's garden again, and this time he is caught in the act of taking the rapunzel. The witch, whose name is Frau Gothel, demands the child, once it is born, in compensation for his trespass and theft, and the terrified man agrees. A daughter is born to the couple, and the witch names her Rapunzel and takes her away. Rapunzel grows up beautiful, and when she is 12 years old, the witch shuts her up in a high tower that has neither door nor stairs but only a small window at the top. When the witch wants to get into the tower, she calls out: "Rapunzel, Rapunzel, let down your hair." Rapunzel takes down her magnificent hair, as fine as spun gold, and lets it fall from the high window to the ground so that the witch may climb up it. One day a prince passes by the tower in the forest and sees Rapunzel singing at her window. There is no way for him to reach her, but he keeps coming back until one day he hears the witch tell Rapunzel to let down her hair and sees her climb up the tower. The next day he comes again, calls out "Rapunzel, Rapunzel, let down your hair," and climbs up. Rapunzel is frightened at first because she has never seen a man before, but he reassures her gently, and soon she agrees to marry him. The prince comes to see her at night because the witch comes during the day. One day, Rapunzel lets slip a comment about the prince's visits. In a rage, the witch cuts off Rapunzel's long braids and takes her to a desert to live in poverty and misery. When the prince comes that night, the witch lets down Rapunzel's braids for him and confronts him in the tower room. In despair at having lost Rapunzel, he jumps out the window and lands in a thorn bush that scratches his eyes out. He wanders blindly for several years, searching for Rapunzel, until he comes to the desert place where she has been living with the twins she has borne. He recognizes her by her singing, and when Rapunzel sees him she embraces him and weeps. Her tears fall on his eyes and restore his sight. The prince takes her and the twins to his country where they are welcomed with rejoicing.

Tale Type: AT 310

"Rapunzel" is identified as *The Maiden in the Tower*. It falls within the larger category 300–99, *Supernatural Adversaries*, and the subcategory 300–59, *The Ogre (Giant, Dragon, Cobold, etc.) Is Defeated*. The description is short: "Rapunzel. The hair ladder for the witch. The prince is blinded" (Thompson, 101).

I. *Promise of Child.* To appease a witch whom he has offended, a man promises her his child when it is born.

II. *The Hair Ladder.* (a) The girl is imprisoned in a windowless tower that the witch enters by climbing her hair as a ladder. (b) The king's son watches and does likewise.

III. *Abandonment and blinding.* (a) When the witch discovers the deceit, she cuts off the girl's hair and abandons her in a desert. (b) When the prince comes, he saves himself by jumping from the tower and is blinded.

IV. *Blindness cured.* Finally his wife's tears falling on his eyes heal them.

Motifs:

S222: Man promises (sells) child in order to save himself from danger or death

G204: Girl in service of witch

R41.2: Captivity in tower

T381: Imprisoned virgin to prevent knowledge of men (marriage, impregnation)

F848.1: Girl's long hair as ladder into tower

L162: Lowly heroine marries prince (king)

S144: Abandonment in desert

S165: Mutilation: putting out eyes

F952.1: Blindness cured by tears

A History of Rapunzel

The entry for tale type 310 lists 91 different variants of "Rapunzel," including Lithuanian, Irish, French, Catalan, Flemish, German, Italian, Sicilian, Serbo-Croatian, Polish, Russian, Greek, Turkish, Franco-American, Spanish-American, and West Indian (Black) tales. The first printed version appeared in Giambattista Basile's *Pentamerone*, published in Italy in 1634, but the form of the story that is the basis for most literary versions comes from the collection of the Brothers Grimm, the first volume of which was published in 1812.

Rapunzel in Oral Tradition

According to Max Lüthi, "Rapunzel" is originally a Mediterranean folktale. The basic outline that underlies the tale is the following: A woman who is greedy for some kind of lettuce or herb steals it from the garden of a witch. Caught in the act, she must promise to give her unborn child to the witch. The witch comes for the girl when she is 10, 12, or 14 years old; bites her on the arm or bites off a finger and earlobe; drags her off; and shuts her up in a tower. While she is imprisoned in the tower, the girl learns magic from the witch. Eventually, a handsome young man uses the girl's long hair to climb up to her. The two decide to flee together. The witch pursues them, but the girl uses magic to confuse their trail or to render the witch harmless, or even kill her. The girl is often named Parsley or Fennel.

Lüthi notes that the Mediterranean variants have a great deal of humor in them. For example, the witch hides herself in the ground to catch the parsley thief, and the woman thinks the witch's ear is a mushroom and tries to pick it. Or, more commonly, Rapunzel fools the witch about the prince's visits in the tower by using clever tricks. In a Maltese variant, Rapunzel takes balls of magic yarn with her when she runs away with the prince. The first one she throws behind her is a green one that turns into a large garden. The witch asks the gardener if he has seen the young runaways, but the gardener either is or pretends to be deaf, and the conversation frustrates the witch dreadfully while it amuses the audience. The tone of the Mediterranean variants is generally much lighter than that of the Grimms, and the ending very different.

Rapunzel in Print

The summary of Rapunzel at the beginning of this chapter reflects the Grimm version of the tale, number 12 in the Grimms' collection, which is the basis of most retellings and reworkings in English.

Basile

There are substantial differences between Basile's seventeenth-century Italian version and the Grimms' nineteenth-century German version. Basile's "Petrosinella" (the name derives from parsley) follows the Mediterranean outline. The pregnant woman herself steals the parsley and promises away her child. The ghula, or ogress, comes for the child when she is old enough to go to school. She meets the child on the way to school daily and tells her to remind her mother of her promise, until finally the mother responds to the repeated messages by telling her daughter that the next time she meets the old woman she is to say "take it." Petrosinella, "who was not possessed of too much wit" (Basile, 117), does as she has been told, and the ghula carries her to a dark forest and shuts her up in the tower. The prince sees her and climbs up to her, and there is nothing said of Petrosinella being frightened of him. Petrosinella gives the ghula something to make her sleep when the prince comes at night, but the young couple is betrayed by an acquaintance of the ghula. Fortunately, Petrosinella overhears the betrayal conversation. She and the prince escape by means of a rope ladder she makes, taking with them the three magic acorns the witch hid in the rafter to charm the girl. The ghula chases after them, but the first acorn that Petrosinella throws behind them becomes a ferocious dog, the second a lion, and the third a wolf, who finally eats the ghula up. The young couple reach the prince's kingdom, where he marries Petrosinella with his father's permission.

The women are much stronger characters in Basile's story than in the Grimm one. The mother herself steals the parsley and gives away her child not once but twice. Her actions are wrong, but they are her own. Petrosinella deliberately deceives the witch rather than innocently (or stupidly) betraying herself and the prince, and, rather than being left to pine in a desert, she saves herself and the prince from the ghula. Basile makes it plain that Petrosinella and the prince become lovers: "Jumping in from the window into the room, he sated his desire, and ate of that sweet parsley sauce of love" (Basile, 118). The Grimms say only that the prince asked Rapunzel "if she would have him for her husband" (Grimm, 48) and leave the birth of the twins to make clear the implications of that request. Basile's Petrosinella enjoys the prince's attentions, while the Grimms' Rapunzel "saw that he was young and handsome [and] she thought: 'He will love me better than my old godmother' " (48), a thought that suggests childish self-interest rather than reciprocation of passion.

While the Grimms' tale is tragic, Basile's is much lighter in mood. The irritation of Petrosinella's mother when she instructs the daughter to tell the ghula "Take it," Petrosinella's drugging of the ghula, and the episodes with the dog, the lion, and the wolf all have an element of humor. The death of the ghula ends the danger to Petrosinella and her prince in typical folktale fashion. In the Grimm version, Rapunzel's lonely exile in the desert, the birth of the twins, the blinding of the prince, and Rapunzel's tears that restore his sight give the story pathos.

The Brothers Grimm

The Grimms took their version of the story from a work by an eighteenth-century German novelist named Friedrich Schulz. They thought he had heard the story as a German folktale that he had elaborated and expanded, and that they could excavate the folktale by removing his inventions. But their German source was actually a translation of a long French story, based on a French folktale, written by Charlotte-Rose Caumont de la Force and published in her collection *Les Contes des Contes* in 1697, the same year in which Perrault published his *Histoires, ou contes du temps passé*. Both de la Force and Schulz wrote for an adult readership. The ending of the Grimm tale, twins and all, is de la Force's invention. In her story the girl's name is Persinette; the name Rapunzel comes from Schultz (Lüthi).

Wilhelm Grimm made a number of changes to "Rapunzel" in later editions of the Grimms' collection of tales. In the first edition, the owner of the garden in which the rapunzel grows is called a fairy (*Fee*), but in the second edition she is a "*Zauberin*," sorceress (Lüthi 1976, 81). A sorceress is a much more frightening figure than a fairy, and Manheim translates *Zauberin* freely as witch. In the first edition, Rapunzel gives the prince's visits away to the fairy by saying to her, "Tell me, Godmother, why my clothes are so tight and they don't fit me any longer." In the second edition, she asks "Tell me, Godmother, why is it that you are much harder to pull up than the young prince?" Tatar points out that this revision was probably made to take an audience of children into account because it removes "any hint of a causal relationship between the prince's visits and Rapunzel's pregnancy" (1987, 45); and that the revised passage is "a good deal less colorful" than the original (18). To this comment I would add that it also changes the character of Rapunzel. A young woman who has been shut up in a tower since childhood might well not know the facts of life and could sensibly ask the question in the first edition. But Rapunzel's question in the second edition could only be a sign of stupidity; either she hasn't realized that the prince's visits would be forbidden if the witch knew about them, or she hasn't the wit to conceal them effectively. Thus, probably unintentionally in this case, Wilhelm Grimm weakened the character of Rapunzel further. Ruth Bottigheimer notes that in preparing the second edition of their collection, Wilhelm Grimm changed much of the direct speech to indirect speech or description by the narrator. Rapunzel, like other "good" female characters in the Grimms' tales, is a victim of what Bottigheimer calls textual silencing; in the 1857 edition, Rapunzel speaks twice, her mother once, and the witch six times, while the father and the prince speak twice each (181).

Overview of Critical Interpretations of Rapunzel

This tale has not provoked the same amount of scholarship as "Cinderella" or "Snow White." There is no one major source to go to, like Hearne's book on "Beauty and the Beast." However, there is no shortage of discussions and interpretations of the tale.

1962: Max Lüthi reads "Rapunzel" as a story of maturation. The theme of psychological development comes through much more clearly in the Mediterranean variants than it does in the Grimms' story. In the Greek, Maltese, Italian, and French tales he considers, the stages of development stand out, and each is connected with danger and fear. Both danger and fear are overcome at each stage, and the tale ends happily. Lüthi interprets the mother's longing for the herb or lettuce as a human longing for a mysterious higher good, because the plant grows in a sorceress's garden and it is dangerous to get it. Promising the unborn child to a frightening stranger is an example of human weakness on the part of parents, who are not yet aware of their responsibility for their child. When the child is torn away from its home, the painful bite emphasizes the frightening nature of the experience. Psychologists have noted that life transitions like the beginning of school, puberty, marriage, or the birth of one's first child are often marked by anxiety dreams in which the dreamer is abducted by some demonic figure. Human beings tend to cling to the familiar, and to sense that moving forward to a new stage of life means a kind of death of the old. Every transition takes courage. But when the transition has been made successfully, the strange and new become familiar and new strengths and abilities develop. In this tale, the witch or sorceress comes to love Rapunzel, and the girl lives happily in the tower for several years, forgetting all about her mother. When the prince first appears, Rapunzel is frightened of him but grows to love him and willingly goes away with him. To leave behind her life in the tower, Rapunzel has to elude or conquer the witch in order to detach herself successfully from the previous stage of her life. In some variants, the witch even becomes reconciled to Rapunzel's marriage to the prince, a maturing development on the part of the witch that allows healthy integration of the past with the present.

1974: Heuscher considers the significance of the golden hair of the hero in folktales. It occurs, he says, both in tales from cultures where blond hair is common and in tales from cultures where blond hair is rare or even unknown. Golden hair is not simply a poetic synonym for blond hair; golden hair is something special. It represents more than the physical riches of metallic gold because hair is alive, delicate threads radiating from the human head, and so is connected with thought and meaning. In folktales, gold is often given spiritual value. Rapunzel's extraordinary golden hair is a link to the world outside her tower. By letting the prince climb up it she is rejecting "an atavistic insight into spiritual matters which inhibited her further human evolution" (219). The atavistic insight is represented by the witch. When she is banished to the desert, her hair is cut off: She is completely isolated. But, Heuscher reminds us, it undoubtedly grew back before her prince found her.

1976: Bruno Bettelheim has no complete chapter on "Rapunzel" but does comment on the tale in several places in *The Uses of Enchantment*. "Rapunzel" is the story of a jealous mother (the witch) who tries to keep her maturing daughter from becoming independent of her. The witch can also be read as a substitute mother successfully keeping her child safe from all dangers. When the child comes to find the security oppressive, her own body gives her the means to escape it (Rapunzel's long hair); that is, she is capable in herself of freeing herself (16–17). Her body also completes the happy ending in that her tears restore the prince's sight. According to Bettelheim, the tale also expresses the Oedipal problem of girls who resent their mother for coming between them and their father but also want the mother's love and care. Rapunzel is taken away from her father and kept away from all male lovers by the witch, who embodies the selfish mother, while her real mother and father are helpless (112–13). As happens in all folktales, according to Bettelheim, the Oedipal difficulty is successfully resolved as part of the developmental process, and Rapunzel finds great happiness at the end (198–99).

Bettelheim reads Rapunzel's question about the witch being heavier to pull up than the prince as "one of the rare 'Freudian slips' to be found in fairy tales: Rapunzel, obviously guilty about her clandestine meetings with the prince, spills her secret . . ." (148). He explains the fact that the witch is not punished at the end of the story as follows. A child can understand loving someone so much that one wants that person entirely to oneself. The witch clearly loves Rapunzel, and while her love is selfish and therefore wrong, it is not evil. So she loses Rapunzel but is not otherwise harmed (149). Rapunzel's years in the desert and the prince's years of wandering blindly, in which nothing of interest apparently happens, are a period of inward growth and recovery from the trauma of the escape, a period of "inner, silent development" necessary for maturation. At the end, "they are ready not only to rescue each other, but to make a good life, one for the other" (150). The Mediterranean variants of the folktale obviously do not support these last two interpretations.

1988:   Of the various approaches to psychoanalysis, the Jungian one has made the most systematic use of folktale and myth in psychotherapy. According to Jungian Sibylle Birkhauser-Oeri, the mother figure in its broadest sense means the unconscious. In "Rapunzel," the witch is the active mother figure and, like the unconscious, can be both negative and positive. The witch both nurtures and imprisons Rapunzel. The pregnant woman's craving for rapunzel suggests she needs it for the proper growth of the child in her womb. Rapunzel is a plant with long, thick roots that go deep into the earth, and therefore a symbol for inner values rooted deep in existence. It grows in the witch's garden, which is also the unconscious. "Translating this into psychological terms, we could say that something benevolent and nourishing has grown deep in the unconscious" (86). Rapunzel's imprisonment in the tower is actually a positive thing: The tower protects her during a necessary period of incubation and, when this stage of development is finished, within the magic circle of the tower two opposites (Rapunzel and the prince) meet and germinate. The prince may represent something in Rapunzel's psyche, a spiritual impulse of some kind, and her pregnancy then represents her capacity for renewal. Rapunzel gives herself away to the witch because she must, in order to be released from the tower. The cutting off of her hair means she is being cut off from fantasies and idealism; she is sent to the desert (a destructive rather than nourishing place) to encounter her own destructive feminine side. By giving birth she wins out against the sterile desert, and the twins signify both the emergence of life out of her relationship with the prince and the union of opposites. For the prince, Rapunzel in the tower represents an idealistic anima whose dark side he does not recognize. His blinding means he must face the darkness in himself. He wanders in the forest, at the mercy of the unconscious, until he finds Rapunzel again. She can heal his sight because she has experienced herself in her own darkness. Rapunzel represents eros, love which is necessary to heal the psyche. The prince represents logos, and together eros and logos make a whole.

1989: Joyce Thomas considers the meaning of towers in folktales. In "Rapunzel" the fact that the tower stands alone in the forest, not part of a castle as towers normally are, emphasizes both its position at the center of the story and its "unnatural purpose" (180). Without a door and stairs, it is like a clock without hands, denying change and time passing, or like a coffin rather than a cocoon. The witch wants to make time stand still and keep Rapunzel as her little girl. But because Rapunzel is alive inside it, she finds her own way out.

Thomas also points out the pattern of repetitive variation in the Grimm version of the story. The story has three sets of action, of which the first two mirror each other with the name "Rapunzel" as the connector. Rapunzel vegetable and Rapunzel as young woman are both forbidden to others and defended by a wall; both are desired by someone (mother and prince) and both trespassers are heavily punished (loss of child and blindness). The third set of actions, the reunion of Rapunzel, the children, and the prince, "sees a happy return to narrative equilibrium and provides a harmony that had not previously existed in the tale," a complete and stable family (258).

1989: William Thompson analyses "Rapunzel" to show "how a fairy tale can express a lost cosmology" (10). At the structural level, he notes several patterns. The little window at the back of the house is echoed by the little window high up in the tower; the garden is surrounded by a wall and the tower by thorn bushes; the father and the prince must climb up, but when they come down they get into trouble; the pattern repeats itself in twos, right down to the twins at the end (19). At the anthropological level, Thompson looks at sets of pairs and finds that one of the themes of the story is "the achievement of a stable couple" (20). The father and mother at the beginning of the story represent "a weak and unstable patrilocal society." Next door is "the Neolithic garden of the ancient matriarchy:" Rapunzel and Mother Gothel, the only two characters who are named, are the archaic, prehistoric coupling of the old woman and the maiden, Demeter and Persephone, and this pair remains stable much longer than the mother and father or Rapunzel and the prince in the tower. When Rapunzel and her prince reach his kingdom and are married, the story ends "with the achievement of a stable patriarchy in the realm of the king" (21). The complications, contradictions, and tensions of sexuality destabilize couples, but at the end of the story the "dangerous power of sexuality has been sublimated into a higher form" (22). One of the sets of pairs that Thompson identifies is the prince's sperm that makes her pregnant and Rapunzel's tears that cure her blindness. The tears, coming from the head, are a higher fluid and Rapunzel is a figure of the Sophia archetype, women's knowledge flowing from the love and compassion of the heart. When this higher fluid is added to the lower (from the testicles) generative fluid of the male, "then a truly stable couple is achieved" (23). The opening line of the story, "Once upon a time there were a man and his wife," indicates that Rapunzel "is not simply a story about sexuality, but *the story* of sexuality" (23).

For his interpretation on the cosmological level, Thompson investigates the plant rapunzel. It is a biennial herb that can be planted in fall and used in winter for salads. It is autogamous, or hermaphroditic, and therefore can fertilize itself. The flower has a tall central column, like a tower. If the plant is not fertilized by insects, "the column will split in two (the one becomes two again) and the halves will curl like braids or coils on a maiden's head, and this will bring the female stigmatic tissue into contact with the male pollen on the exterior surface of the column" (31). Ergo, the story of Rapunzel in brief. Thompson concludes that the story must have grown in a culture with a deep knowledge of the life of plants. Considering the variants of the tale that have parsley rather than rapunzel in them, he points out that a pregnant woman could well have a craving for parsley because it is a herb recommended for kidney and urinary problems. Thompson goes further and looks at the fivefold flower of rapunzel. Fivefold flowers are associated with the planet Venus. Then perhaps Rapunzel is Venus, and the prince could be the planet Mars, the lover of Venus. Frau Gothel's name means "Bright God," and she must be the moon, the heavenly orb of goddesses. The mother could be Mother Earth, and since the father is simply a messenger between the mother and Frau Gothel, he is the planet Mercury, the messenger of the gods. The prince's father, the king, is the sun. Thompson sees in the tale the cosmology of Neolithic Europe (around 4000 BCE).

1991: McGlathery understands "Rapunzel" as a tale "about a magical older woman's effort to prevent the fulfillment of young desire" (120). But, he points out, the older woman does not actually work any magic. She may magically have given Rapunzel her amazing hair, but after that it is Rapunzel's to use, not the witch's. McGlathery suggests that the witch may have made Rapunzel's hair grow so that the witch could call out "Rapunzel, Rapunzel, let down your hair," as a lover asks his beloved to let down her hair. The sexual pleasure she takes from this command to Rapunzel is probably the only such pleasure she has ever known. While in the Grimm tale Mother Gothel's love for Rapunzel is that of a jealous lover, in Basile's "Petrosinella" the ghula is simply possessive about the girl; she doesn't fly into a rage when she hears about the prince's visits because she is certain the girl can't escape. McGlathery points out that the witch sets up her own defeat in that she inadvertently teaches Rapunzel how to bring a lover up into her bedroom. Rather than seeing Rapunzel as a passive victim, he puts her in the category of "fetching maidens" who are themselves "the prime movers in overcoming the obstacles to their desire's fulfillment" (152). Certainly Basile's Petrosinella is a good deal more active than the Grimms' Rapunzel, but even the latter attracts the prince with her song and lets down her hair to bring him up to her.

1993: Trina Schart Hyman made a beautiful and feeling-ful picture book version of "Rapunzel." She later wrote about her reading of the story:

> To me, the key figure in the story is Mother Gothel, the witch. She cares for the girl-child like a mother and then, at the onset of puberty, locks her up in a tower. What strange things love makes us do! As a model for the witch, I used my dear friend and neighbor, who at seventy-six was one of the most attractive and enchanting women I have ever known; she could indeed be terrifying as well as kind (298).

The Grimm text does not mention the witch again after the Rapunzel is exiled and the blind prince begins his wandering. But Hyman keeps her in the story. The last picture in the book shows the witch watching Rapunzel, the prince, and the twins walking away to his kingdom and their new life together. She is only watching, not pursuing. Apparently she has not simply abandoned Rapunzel; she is letting her go.

1993: McGlathery quotes Kay Stone's feminist interpretation of the fact that Rapunzel, like Snow White and Sleeping Beauty, is removed from the world at puberty. She sees this repeated treatment of girls who are about to become women "as a reaction of men to the threat of female sexuality" (quoted in McGlathery 1993, 65). As a short comment on this reading, McGlathery quotes himself from his 1991 book: "My view was that the story [of Rapunzel] is about an older woman's efforts 'to prevent the fulfillment of young desire' out of jealous attachment to the girl" (65).

1997: Margery Hourihan points out that in folktales brides are never allowed to refuse a prince. The prince enters Rapunzel's tower uninvited. "His forcible entry into her secluded tower could be read as a story of violation, of a powerful, free agent taking advantage of an utterly powerless and completely inexperienced woman," but the happy ending persuades us that his coming was necessarily a good thing (198). When he asks her to take him as a husband, she has a choice only between her restricted life as it is and the first man she has ever seen. "The hero story naturalizes the powerlessness of women and their domination by men, and presents this as a desirable state of affairs for women as well as for men!" (198).

Reworkings of Rapunzel in Novel Form

There are only two novels that use "Rapunzel" as their framework. Both were published as books for young adults, but there the similarity between them ends. Adèle Geras's *The Tower Room* is realistic fiction set in our contemporary world, with never a trace of magic, and the narrator is Rapunzel (Megan in the book) herself. The focus, therefore, is on the adolescent protagonist. Donna Jo Napoli's *Zel* is fantasy, and the character who dominates the novel is Rapunzel's foster mother, the witch. While both novels are intended to be taken seriously, Napoli's is by far the more profound of the two.

The Tower Room

1990: Geras, Adèle. **The Tower Room**. London: HarperCollins. (Republished in 1992 by Lions [London]).

This novel is the first in Geras's "Egerton Hall" trilogy. It is set in England and begins in 1955. Rapunzel is Megan, who is orphaned at the age of 11 when her parents are killed in an accident in Africa. She has been living at Egerton Hall, a girl's boarding school, where a friend of her mother's is headmistress. There she forms a close friendship with two other girls, Alice (Sleeping Beauty in the second novel) and Bella (Snow White in the third novel). The three of them share a bedroom in the tower that forms part of the school building. Dorothy, the headmistress, and sorceress, or witch, of the folktale, adopts her.

When Megan is 17 and studying for A-levels, she falls in love with Simon, a young science instructor at the school. The tower is surrounded by scaffolding because it needs repairs, and Simon climbs up it to assignations with Megan in her room. Intensified by the secrecy of their meetings, the relationship becomes sexual before the two really get to know each other. Unfortunately and absurdly, Dorothy is also in love with Simon. When she discovers that he and Megan love each other, there is a confrontation in the tower room. Dorothy is beside herself with pain and rage. In her fury she stamps on Simon's glasses and orders both of them to leave Egerton Hall that very night. The two go to London, where Simon finds a job in a lab and Megan works in a coffee bar to make ends meet.

Megan finds herself feeling trapped in this new life. She misses her friends and is too exhausted by the day's work to read or study as she had intended when she brought her texts and notes with her to London. She gets letters from her friends and teachers at the school asking her to come back. Although she loves Simon, she decides to return to Egerton Hall. In the farewell letter she leaves for Simon, she writes:

> I can't think what my future will be if I stay, Simon, and that's the truth. If I go back, we can write to one another, see each other in the holidays. . . .
>
> I hope you read this, my dear love, by the time I return. I have an appointment with Armand, Bella's hairdresser. He is going to cut my hair. I know you will be angry with me. I know how much you love it. . . . But whenever it's

done up in a plait, which is most of the time, I think of it as
a rope that's hung down my back for years, tying me
down, tying me together, tying me to Dorothy and my
childhood. . . . Bella will think me fashionable at last, but I
will know that what I am is free. (143)

The book ends with this passage.

Geras makes significant changes to the Grimms' "Rapunzel," but
the story is recognizable. The tower and Megan's long, golden hair are
the obvious connection. Megan is in effect given away by her parents to
the witch when they choose to go to Africa and leave her behind, and
Simon climbs up the outside of the tower to Megan. Simon's broken
glasses parallel the blinding of the prince, and their unsatisfactory life in
London is a sort of desert for both Megan and Simon. The differences that
give the story a new meaning are Dorothy's love for Simon and Rapunzel's return to the school. The witch does not want to keep Rapunzel for
herself. Megan is shut away from life in the tower, but only as any girl in
a boarding school is—as a protection from sexual and emotional involve-
ments that may come too early, and to enforce concentration on the academic work that is an important part of her development. The witch
wants the prince for herself. And although Rapunzel also wants the
prince, leaving the tower is exile for her rather than freedom. She is not
finished yet with that necessary stage of her life, and the prince has come
too early. But she has learned something from her time with Simon in
London that frees her to decide what is necessary for herself. So Rapunzel/
Megan chooses to go back, but she also chooses to cut off her hair. Although she needs to return to the school, she is no longer the schoolgirl
she was before.

Zel

1996: Napoli, Donna Jo. **Zel**. New York: Dutton.

Napoli sets her version of "Rapunzel" in a place that might well be
Switzerland and in a time that might well be the late Middle Ages. The
story begins with Mother and Zel, who live all alone in an alpine
meadow far from the nearest village. Their life together is a contented
one, full of simple pleasures, and they love each other dearly. Zel will be
13 years old in a few days, and the two of them make the long walk to
town, as they do twice a year, to buy the things they can't grow or make
themselves and some special treats for Zel's birthday. Because Mother
wants to keep the presents as a surprise, she lets Zel wait for her at the

smithy. Zel loves animals and helps the smith control a horse who is being shod. The young man who owns the horse admires Zel and wants to give her a gift. But before he can return with it, Mother snatches Zel away and hurries back to the alpine meadow. The young man is Count Konrad, and his father is arranging a marriage for him. But Konrad has become obsessed with Zel and refuses the marriage. He rides out every day to scour the countryside for the girl he cannot get out of his mind.

Meanwhile, Mother realizes that Zel has formed an interest in this young man and that if he comes looking for her and finds her, she may come to love him. To keep this from happening, Mother tells Zel that they must go far away because Zel has a secret enemy who will kill her if he can. Mother will find a way to destroy this enemy, but meanwhile Zel must be shut up in a high tower to keep her safe. Zel believes Mother completely, but she grows to hate the loneliness and boredom of the tower and her own heavy hair, which is growing unnaturally quickly.

At this point the reader gets the story of how this situation came about. A barren woman longs for a child "with every drop of blood, every bit of flesh, every hair, every breath of her body" (127). She sells her soul for the promise of a daughter, and is given a single gift, a magic way with plants. The price is twofold. When her daughter comes of age, the woman must explain everything to her and try to persuade her also to sell her soul for a gift from the devils; and the girl must be a virgin and unattached to anyone but the woman herself. The other part of the price is the woman's eternal damnation. The woman, called only Mother (always with a capital M) or the barren woman throughout the book, grows a marvelous garden of vegetable and flowers. The pregnant woman living in the next house asks the barren woman to sell her some of the lettuce called rapunzel, but Mother refuses. When the woman sends her husband a second time to steal some rapunzel, the barren woman makes a hedge of thistle grow around him and demands the child when it is born in return for freeing him. The thistles scratch him so terribly that when they grow high enough to reach his eyes he gives in. When the man tells his wife that he will decry the barren woman as a witch and rally the village to burn or hang her, the barren woman makes grapevines grow to block the doors and windows of his house until he promises not to mention the witch to anyone. When the child is born, the barren woman takes her far away. "They became Zel and Mother" (138).

We understand now that Mother has shut Zel up in the tower because she must keep her free from attachments to anyone but Mother until Zel is old enough to make her choice. If Zel chooses the gift of the devils, Mother will have her with her forever. But by shutting her up in the tower she has already lost Zel:

> I hold that child in a tower. The only one I love, the one I
> love more than life itself; for two years I have held that
> one in a stone room.
>
> And I live alone. I live the life I would have lived if I had
> never had Zel in the first place. Only it is far worse—for I
> know what I have lost. (142)

Mother comes to loathe herself, and Zel has gone mad in the isolation of the tower.

Konrad finds Rapunzel in the tower and woos her. The day after the two become lovers, Zel demands her freedom from Mother, and Mother finally tells Zel her story and gives her the choice. Zel is horrified at what Mother has done to her. She tells Mother about Konrad, and Mother makes the trees grow into the tower room and carry Zel far away into a desert. Then Konrad arrives with a dagger to protect Zel from the mysterious enemy and a rope ladder so that they can leave the tower together. Mother lets down the braids she bit from Zel's head, and he climbs up. But he sees through the window that Zel is gone, and when he realizes his loss he reaches in with the dagger to kill Mother. Mother lets go of the braids to ward him off, and he falls. Knowing that she is using her very last strength, Mother forces the brambles at the foot of the tower to grow higher so that they will break his fall. Konrad is badly injured and blinded, but he lives. Mother dies in the tower. Zel, far away, makes her own way out of the desert with much hardship. She is taken in by kindly folk, becomes a painter and potter, goes faithfully to church, and gives birth to girl twins. Konrad finds her there, and her transforming tears restore his sight. And in that last chapter we hear Mother's voice again. She sees through the eyes of the bird that searches with Konrad for Zel. She hears through Konrad's ears, she feels with a lover's heart, and she is part of Zel's and Konrad's happiness. We are left to explain that to ourselves—perhaps Mother's self-sacrifice in the tower was her salvation.

Napoli's version of "Rapunzel" follows the Grimms' tale closely. Her fleshing out of the bones of the tale has a great deal of depth and complexity, and it is a very strong book. But it is, in a sense, monotonous. We get the story from three different perspectives because the point of view shifts around among Mother, Zel, and Konrad. But only Mother's story is told in first person narrative, and her rigid intensity and obsession with Zel set the mood for the entire story. Even the domestic detail is fraught with an inner tension, and nothing relieves the tragedy of the story.

Short Stories

The seven short stories collected here represent a wide range of reworkings of "Rapunzel." "Rapunzel's Revenge" (1985) and "The Princess in the Tower" (1993) are funny. "The Root of the Matter" (1993) and Anne Bishop's "Rapunzel" (1997) both have three characters telling the story in turn from their perspectives. In "The Root of the Matter" the narrators are the witch, Rapunzel, and the prince. Bishop lets us hear Rapunzel's birth-mother, the witch, and Rapunzel. "A Bed of Peas" (1995) is unusual in being entirely the birth-mother's story. Of the seven, Bishop's and Donoghue's stories stand out for both their interpretation and their writing.

1985: Fleet Street Fairies. "**Rapunzel's Revenge.**" In *Rapunzel's Revenge: Fairy Tales for Feminists*. Dublin: Attic Press, 36–41.

As the title and the group name of the authors suggest, this story is a spoof. Rapunzel Murphy, unemployed and looking for a job in Dublin, is offered 50 pounds to be a test subject for a new shampoo. Her hair is beautiful already, but after three washings with the shampoo it begins to grow ridiculously quickly. The fine print of her contract with the shady cosmetic company specifies that she can't leave the company's premises until they are ready to let her go, so she is locked in a comfortable suite of rooms on the top floor of the building while they figure out what to do about this disaster. Shortly she's sitting on a pile of her own hair five feet high, being served tea from a stepladder, while a barber continuously hacks off feet of her hair and a steady stream of employees carries full garbage bags of cut hair out the back door. Just as the company's executive board decides they'll have to kill her to cover up the fiasco, Rapunzel's ecologically conscious friend, Pauline, arrives to rescue her. Pauline tells Rapunzel to put her advanced weaving course to good use and weave a big web out of the heaps of cut hair. Pauline rapidly sets up a press conference. Rapunzel, Pauline, and a helpful office boy carry the golden web to the boardroom and capture the scheming executives with it just as the reporters and television cameras arrive. The ecologically unsound testing practices of the cosmetics company are exposed, and the two friends head off for a quiet weekend in the country, where Pauline will find a herbal remedy for Rapunzel's runaway tresses.

1993: Frost, Gregory. "**The Root of the Matter**." In *Snow White, Blood Red*, edited by Ellen Datlow and Terri Windling. New York: Avon, 161–95.

The introduction to this story states that "Frost walks the line between fantasy and horror and emerges with a memorable tale" (161). The horror consists of Gothel's demented hatred of men because she was repeatedly raped by her father when she was a young child. She runs away from home, and, filthy and starving, is cared for by luminous beings living in a forest. This is the fantasy part. Gothel learns how to use her magic powers from the fairies and goes back to the city. She becomes the star attraction in a brothel, where she never lets men touch her but makes them grovel and abase themselves like beasts. She makes one of her clients buy her a piece of land in the fairy forest, and she builds a house with a wall around it, safe from men forever. But one day she realizes she is now surrounded by a suburban subdivision. Before she moves on, she works magic on the bossy pregnant woman next door who bullies her children. Using the standard rapunzel lure, she gets the newborn child and leaves. At Rapunzel's first menses, Gothel removes both of them to the top of a disused lighthouse and builds a maze of hawthorn bushes around it.

Here the point of view shifts to Rapunzel. She is a resentful teenager who spends her time lying around listening to tapes of baroque music, the only kind Gothel will bring her. Gothel's way in and out of the lighthouse is Rapunzel's long braids. Over the years Gothel has continually ranted on about the evil of men, the violence they do women, and the painful horror of sexual intercourse. The only one who is going to touch Rapunzel is Gothel herself. (As she does, for her pleasure and Rapunzel's, every time she washes Rapunzel in her bath.) One day, a wandering seaman finds his way through the maze and, after a visit or two, Rapunzel seduces him. She learns that Gothel was wrong about sex and thinks that the seaman's promises of love and marriage are true. When Rapunzel starts getting morning sickness and tells Gothel her clothes are too tight, all is revealed. Gothel makes a horrible scene, magically whisks Rapunzel off to a desert, and confronts the seaman, who falls off the top of the lighthouse and is blinded by the hawthorns.

Now the point of view shifts to the seaman. It turns out Gothel was quite right. He really was only after Rapunzel's body. But, blind and wounded, he realizes the shamefulness of his behavior and sets out to find Rapunzel so that he can atone and love her truly. He wanders for years, telling his sad story for tips, until he finds her, sunburned and weather-wrinkled, eking out a miserable existence with the twins in a desert. Her tears heal his blindness, and they form a happy family. When they go back to visit the lighthouse, they find it has fallen down.

All of the elements of the Grimms' "Rapunzel" have been faithfully worked into the story. Frost's reading of the tale is an interesting possibility, and his interpretation of Mother Gothel could have been chilling or pitiful or both. But the writing is so flat and the characterization so banal that the result is not horror but sleaze.

1993: Lynne, Elizabeth A. "**The Princess in the Tower**." In *Snow White, Blood Red*, edited by Ellen Datlow and Terri Windling. New York: Avon, 197–213.

The story is set in an idyllic village somewhere in Italy, some time like the present. In this village, good food, especially sausages, is the most important thing in life; the girls are commonly named after various types of pasta; and no woman is considered beautiful until she weighs 250 pounds. Poor little Margheritina is different from the rest. She never wants more than one helping of any dish and can't be fattened up. In shame and sorrow, her mother takes her out of school when she is 13 years old and makes her stay at home. There she dances around the villa to Beatles songs and makes herself outlandish clothes. One day, a young hiker of good family comes by and sees her on the balcony singing "I Want to Hold Your Hand." He falls in love at once. He climbs up to her balcony. Margheritina serves him a big breakfast, and after the family drives off to the market, she cuts off her long hair so that she looks like a boy, and the two run away together. They get married on the run and settle down in another town far away. It turns out that Margheritina is a fabulous cook, and they run a successful restaurant. She sends family pictures to her mother and talks to her on the telephone, but she refuses ever to go back. And she does put on a respectable amount of weight.

1995: Galloway, Priscilla. "**A Bed of Peas**." In *Truly Grim Tales*. Toronto: Lester, 36–59.

Although the title suggests Andersen's "The Princess and the Pea," this is a reworking of "Rapunzel." In all of the stories in her collection, Galloway takes the point of view of a character other than the protagonist, as if going around the story and looking at it from the back. "A Bed of Peas" is told by Rapunzel's birth mother, and because she has a place only in the beginning of the traditional tale, this story is more extension than interpretation. It begins with a young princess in an unnamed Arab kingdom who runs away with the gardener. (In her rejection of all the royal suitors her father parades before her, we get a quick echo of the Grimms' "King Thrushbeard.") She and her young man, who is a Bedouin chieftain's son taken as a slave, end up in a mountain village rather than in his father's camps as they had planned. Her pampered princess body isn't fit for that much riding (hence the title—she reflects that a princess should be tough enough to sleep on a whole bed of peas, for her own sake).

Their daughter is taken from them by the witch and named Letitia in reference to the lettuce that bought her. The father promised the unborn child to the witch only to save her life and that of her mother, not out of fear for himself. The mother goes mad with grief for a while and begins to recover only when her husband and she begin the long search for their child. In the following years she becomes physically hardened and strong. When the two finally locate Letitia's tower, their daughter has just fled with her prince. They have escaped before the witch could discover them, so Letitia spends no time in the desert and the prince is not blinded. Again the parents search, and when they find her they take service as gardeners for the prince's father to be close to her. At the end, Letitia is pregnant and the mother is about to reveal herself as the unborn child's grandmother; she wants to make sure "any new little princess learns to ride as she learns to walk. No soft princess body for her. She can learn to sleep on a bed of peas" (59). It is Letitia's mother who has learned from suffering in the desert.

1997: Bishop, Anne. "**Rapunzel**." In *Black Swan, White Raven*, edited by Ellen Datlow and Terri Windling. New York: Avon, 122–41.

Three of the characters tell this interesting story in turn. Rapunzel's birth-mother speaks first. She is a selfish manipulator who craves whatever she cannot have. Her husband, who is a good man, promises their unborn child to the witch because he truly believes his wife will die without the lettuce. After the child is born, he leaves his wife. The second speaker is Gothel, the witch. She thinks all men are thieves: "You put your heart and magic into something to make it beautiful, you build walls to keep it untainted by the world, you nurture it for the pleasure it will bring you, and they'll sniff it out, no matter how high the walls, and taint the pleasure, sully the beauty" (131–32). Her words apply to both her garden and Rapunzel, and they betray *her* selfishness. Her care is never for the life she nurtures in and of itself, but for the pleasure it gives her.

The third voice is Rapunzel's. She lives now as the wise woman, or witch, of a kindly village, successor to the woman who took her in and healed her after she found her way out of the desert. Her husband is a good, hard-working man whom she married because he loved her instead of merely desiring her. She grows enough rapunzel for the whole village in her garden and gives it away to any pregnant woman, always making very clear that she expects nothing in return. She and her husband will teach their daughters that they need not crave what belongs to someone else because they "can have what they want most if they'll give it their hearts and their hands" (140). And they will teach their sons "not to be so blinded by passion that they cannot see the other textures of love" (140).

1997: Donoghue, Emma. "**The Tale of the Hair**." In *Kissing the Witch: Old Tales in New Skins*. New York: Joanna Cotler Books/ HarperCollins, 81–99.

In the "Tale of the Hair" Rapunzel tells her story. She does not know how she came to live in the forest with the woman who cares for her. She begins with the tower that she asked the woman to build for her so that she may live above the shadows of the trees and feel the warmth and light of the sun on her face. Rapunzel is blind. When she begins to have nightmares about a hunt in which men are the hunters, the stags, and the dogs, she asks the woman to wall up the tower so that she may feel safe. This is the first of several reversals. Rapunzel deliberately lures the prince to her with her song. But there is no prince; it was the woman deepening her voice to speak like a man. Rapunzel, furious at the deception, cuts off her own hair for a rope to climb out of the tower. When the woman climbs to the top of the tower and finds Rapunzel gone, she throws herself off the tower. Rapunzel edges forward to find her and discovers her with blood on her face from the thorns that had pierced her eyelids. To clean the wounds Rapunzel weeps salt tears over her eyes. The story ends there: "I didn't know whether they would heal, or whether she would have to learn the world from me now. We lay there, waiting to see what we would see" (99).

1997: Spar, Lisa Russ. "**Rapunzel's Exile**." In *The Year's Best Fantasy and Horror, 10th Annual Collection*, edited by Ellen Datlow and Terri Windling. New York: St. Martin's Griffin, 315–16.

This extremely short story tells about Rapunzel's being walled up in the tower. It is so tightly written that it is difficult to summarize. The voice is Rapunzel's. The onset of her menses brings about a greater change in the witch than in her. There is no magic in the story to make the journey to the tower easy; the suffering of both women is physical as well as emotional.

Feature Films

1978: **Rapunzel, Rapunzel**. Directed by Tom Davenport. Delaplane, VA: Davenport Films.

Only one film of "Rapunzel" has been made. In 1978, Tom and Mimi Davenport produced *Rapunzel, Rapunzel* as the second film in the series that was to become *From the Brothers Grimm*. Like all of the Davenport films, it was made in a realistic, live-action style and set against an American background. The time is the end of the nineteenth century, and the place is the Appalachians. The film goes against the tradition by giving Rapunzel black hair, but other than that all the elements of the Grimms' tale are there. Davenport uses a voice-over narrator to move the action along.

From the promise of the unborn child to the witch in her garden, the film moves directly to Rapunzel as an adolescent in the tower. In the first scene in the tower, Rapunzel, her long black hair trailing on the floor, is singing to a doll, and the witch feeds her a cookie. Rapunzel is shown as far too childish for her age and passively dependent on the woman who holds her so closely. Anthony Manna describes the film as "a sullen, turn-of-the-century drama about the nature of love, the conflict between repression and autonomy, and the human need for independence" (143).

Poetry

Seven of these nine poems are conveniently brought together in Wolfgang Mieder's anthology, but the original source of each is also given in case it proves more convenient to locate. Sexton (1971) and Broumas (1977) tell "Rapunzel" as a love affair between an older and a younger woman.

1920: Untermeyer, Louis. "**Rapunzel**." In *The New Adam*. New York: Harcourt, Brace and Howe, 57. Also in *Disenchantments: An Anthology of Modern Fairy Tale Poetry*, edited by Wolfgang Mieder. Hanover, NH: University Press of New England, 45.

Either Mother Gothel or the prince could be speaking these two verses of seven short lines each. Rapunzel's hair is both trap and security, the cause of joy and unhappiness for the speaker. Rapunzel is asked to let her hair down, not in tight braids but loose and free. The ambivalence of the love described in the first verse is carried into the second when the speaker asks to be buried there (in the tower? in her hair?) and that Rapunzel be buried with him or her.

1938: Davidman, Joy. **"The Princess in the Ivory Tower."** In *Letter to a Comrade*. New Haven, CT: Yale University Press, 24. Also in *Disenchantments: An Anthology of Modern Fairy Tale Poetry*, edited by Wolfgang Mieder. Hanover, NH: University Press of New England, 46.

An ambiguous poem that may be read as expressing the hopes the prince has of Rapunzel or, just possibly, the hopes Rapunzel has of the prince. Or could it be the witch? There is a suggestion that the witch is dead and that the speaker has murdered her and is deeply troubled by that death.

1964: Mandel, Eli. **"Rapunzel (Girl in a Tower)."** In *Black and Secret Man*. Toronto: Ryerson Press, 29. Also in *Disenchantments: An Anthology of Modern Fairy Tale Poetry*, edited by Wolfgang Mieder. Hanover, NH: University Press of New England, 48.

Rapunzel herself is the tower, a difficult puzzle for the man who wants her. Farm and garden imagery makes vivid metaphors for Rapunzel's inaccessibility.

1970: Meyer, Gerard Previn. **"Rapunzel Song."** In *The New York Times Book of Verse*, edited by Thomas Lask. New York: Macmillan, 93. Also in *Disenchantments: An Anthology of Modern Fairy Tale Poetry*, edited by Wolfgang Mieder. Hanover, NH: University Press of New England, 49.

A reflection on the nature of folktale. The poem considers the prince and how little is known about him. He, and that night, are remembered only because he climbed Rapunzel's hair "and mounted swiftly into time."

1971: Sexton, Anne. **"Rapunzel."** In *Transformations*. Boston: Houghton Mifflin, 35–42. Also in *Disenchantments: An Anthology of Modern Fairy Tale Poetry*, edited by Wolfgang Mieder. Hanover, NH: University Press of New England, 50–54.

The poem begins with sexual love between an unnamed older woman and a young one. The older woman's voice is heard at first until an unidentified narrator takes over. The mother-daughter aspect of such a relationship is captured in the phrase "They play mother-me-do." Then Sexton retells the story of "Rapunzel." Her version faithfully follows that of the Brothers Grimm in its outline. Mother Gothel and Rapunzel also play mother-me-do, but the prince comes by and their happily-ever-after proves "that mother-me-do can be outgrown." Mother Gothel is left alone, never to love again. Sexton's tone has flashes of the sardonic when she writes about "the cure-all" of Rapunzel's tears and that lesbian love can be outgrown "just as the fish on Friday / just as a tricycle."

1977: Broumas, Olga. "**Rapunzel**." In *Beginning with O*. New Haven, CT: Yale University Press, 59–60. Also in *Disenchantments: An Anthology of Modern Fairy Tale Poetry*, edited by Wolfgang Mieder. Hanover, NH: University Press of New England, 55–56.

Broumas uses a quotation from Sexton's "Rapunzel" as an epigraph for her poem: "A woman / who loves a woman / is forever young." In Broumas's poem the young woman speaks to the older woman who is her lover, comparing their love and desire to that of unfulfilled women who are trapped into settling for men. The young woman is able to speak out and to be angry at those who insult their relationship because she has grown up in a more liberal time.

1982: Hay, Sara Henderson. "**Rapunzel**." In *Story Hour*. Fayetteville, AR: University of Arkansas Press, 18. Also in *Disenchantments: An Anthology of Modern Fairy Tale Poetry*, edited by Wolfgang Mieder. Hanover, NH: University Press of New England, 47. Also in *Don't Bet on the Prince*, edited by Jack Zipes. New York: Methuen, 121.

The prince has proved faithless to Rapunzel, and she struggles against memories and the pain of betrayal.

1989: Yolen, Jane. "**The Golden Stair**." In *The Faery Flag: Stories and Poems of Fantasy and the Supernatural*. New York: Orchard, 85–86.

Replacing the universal once-upon-a-time with modern reality, Yolen looks into the life of Rapunzel some years after she married the prince. Rapunzel tells us that she has just had her long, golden hair cut to a short bob. The passion has gone out of their marriage, worn down or swamped by endless royal duties like visits to factories and day care centers.

1990: Strauss, Gwen. "**The Prince**." In *Trail of Stones*. New York: Alfred A. Knopf, 11–12. Also in *The Year's Best Fantasy and Horror, 4th Annual Collection*, edited by Ellen Datlow and Terri Windling. New York: St. Martin's Press, 1991, 494–95.

The prince is an old man speaking to Rapunzel. Their love and passion for each other are still very much alive. He recalls that when he first saw her he knew nothing about love and had only desire to offer. He learned to love in the years of blind wandering. Now they cultivate together the garden she made in the desert.

Classroom Extensions

Films

Walt Disney Studios has not made a film version of "Rapunzel," although Tom Davenport has. What does "Rapunzel" have, or not have, that might discourage Disney from making a film of the story? Could Rapunzel sing a song about her dream prince?

An Illustrated Version of Rapunzel

In the picture book *Rapunzel*, written by Barbara Rogasky and illustrated by Trina Schart Hyman, the illustrator gives her interpretation of "Rapunzel" in pictures rather than in the text. Look closely at Hyman's illustrations and put her interpretation of the story into words. How do these illustrations compare with other interpretations by other illustrators of this traditional tale?

Initiation

The first chapter of this book argues that folktales are tales of initiation. How does "Rapunzel" work out the initiatory scenario? Compare "Rapunzel" with one of the other tales in this book. Is one more meaningful to you than the other? Why?

Poetic Interpretations

Louis Untermeyer's poem "Rapunzel" is spoken by a lover who could be Mother Gothel or the prince. The speaker could also be someone who is using the picture language of "Rapunzel" as a metaphor for his or her love for the beloved. How does the poem change depending on whether Mother Gothel or the Prince is the speaker? If some other lover is speaking of his or her beloved, what images and understanding might the writer be expecting readers to bring to the poem from the story of "Rapunzel" as told by the Brothers Grimm? How would the poem work if a reader knew only the story called "Rapunzel's Revenge"?

Joy Davidman's poem, "The Princess in the Ivory Tower," is full of ambiguity. If Rapunzel is the speaker for the entire poem, what meaning does it make? What if the witch is speaking? What happens to the meaning if the witch is the speaker in only the first and last verse, and the prince speaks the other verses?

Anne Bishop's 1997 "Rapunzel" says a great deal about different kinds of love and how they bring about the events of the story. How well do the various interpretations of "Rapunzel" summarized in the "Overview of Critical Interpretations" section of this chapter apply to Bishop's version of "Rapunzel"?

Rapunzel's Hair

In Emma Donoghue's "The Tale of the Hair" (1997), Rapunzel cuts off her own hair and uses it as a rope to climb down from the tower. She could have done this in any of the other versions of the tale, including that of the Grimms. Why does this Rapunzel use her own hair as a way out, while that possibility does not exist for either the prince or Rapunzel in any of the other versions, including the Grimm one?

The Tower

A tower is often read as a phallic symbol. Rapunzel is shut up in a tower standing in a forest. Is there anything in the story that would allow this tower to be a phallic symbol?

The Witch

The woman who shuts Rapunzel in the tower was first called a fairy in the Grimms' tale, and then a *Zauberin*, a sorceress or enchantress. Reworkings of the story variously call her enchantress or sorceress or witch. The word "witch" seems automatically to call up "wicked," although it need not and should not do so. Is the woman sometimes called a witch in the story of Rapunzel necessarily wicked or evil?

Bibliography

Basile, Giambattista. "Petrosinella." In *The Pentameron*, translated by Sir Richard Burton. London: Spring Books, 1952, 116–19.

Bettelheim, Bruno. *The Uses of Enchantment: The Meaning and Importance of Fairy Tales*. New York: Vintage Books, 1976.

Birkhauser-Oeri, Sybille. *The Mother: Archetypal Image in Fairy Tales*. Toronto: Inner City Books, 1988.

Bottigheimer, Ruth. *Grimms' Bad Girls and Bold Boys: The Moral and Social Vision of the Tales*. New Haven, CT: Yale University Press, 1987.

Farmer, David Hugh. *The Oxford Dictionary of Saints*. Oxford: Oxford University Press, 1987.

Goldthwaite, John. *The Natural History of Make-Believe: A Guide to the Principal Works of Britain, Europe, and America*. New York: Oxford University Press, 1996.

Grimm, Jakob, and Wilhelm Grimm. "Rapunzel." In *Grimms' Tales for Young and Old: The Complete Stories*, translated by Ralph Manheim. Garden City, NY: Anchor Press, 1977, 46–49. [Based on the 1819 ed. of *Kinder- und Hausmärchen*].

Heuscher, Julius E. *A Psychiatric Study of Myths and Fairy Tales: Their Origin, Meaning, and Usefulness*. 2d ed. Springfield, IL: Charles C. Thomas, 1974.

Hourihan, Margery. *Deconstructing the Hero: Literary Theory and Children's Literature*. London: Routledge, 1997.

Hyman, Trina Schart. "Cut It Down and You Will Find Something at the Roots." In *The Reception of Grimms' Fairy Tales: Responses, Reactions, Revisions*, edited by Donald Haase. Detroit: Wayne State University Press, 1993, 293–300.

Lüthi, Max. *Once Upon a Time: On the Nature of Fairy Tales*. Bloomington, IN: University of Indiana Press, 1976.

Manna, Anthony L. "The Americanization of the Brothers Grimm, or Tom Davenport's Film *Adaptation of German Folktales*." *Children's Literature Association Quarterly* 13: 3 (1988) 142–45.

McGlathery, James M. *Fairy Tale Romance: The Grimms, Basile, and Perrault*. Urbana-Champaign, IL: University of Illinois Press, 1991.

———. *Grimms' Fairy Tales: A History of Criticism on a Popular Classic*. Columbia, SC: Camden House, 1993.

Rogasky, Barbara. *Rapunzel*. Retold by Barbara Rogasky and illustrated by Trina Schart Hyman. New York: Holiday House, 1982.

Tatar, Maria. *The Hard Facts of the Grimms' Fairy Tales*. Princeton, NJ: Princeton University Press, 1987.

Thomas, Joyce. *Inside the Wolf's Belly: Aspects of the Fairy Tale*. Sheffield, England: Sheffield Academic Press, 1989.

Thompson, Stith. *The Types of the Folktale: A Classification and Bibliography. A Translation and Enlargement of Antti Aarne's Verzeichnis de Märchentypen*. 2d revision. Helsinki: Academia Scientiarum Fennica, 1964. (FF Communications, no. 184).

Thompson, William Irwin. *Imaginary Landscapes: Making Worlds of Myth and Science*. New York: St. Martin's Press, 1989.

CHAPTER 7

RUMPELSTILTSKIN

"But now, as adults, we find that pain can be transformed, like the fairy-tale maid who spins straw into gold. The coin I have minted from the straw of childhood is a daily, childhood sense of wonder that the world is so much brighter than the world I left behind" (Windling, 370).

While many people are familiar with the story of a miller's daughter who is propelled into danger through no fault of her own, the terrible price she is asked to pay, and the gamble she takes to save her child, they do not particularly like the tale, the maiden, or the little man. In fact, of all the tales we are looking at in this book, this is one that seems to have no redeeming characters at all!

Once upon a time, the miller boasted about his daughter's prowess in spinning straw into gold. When called on his words by the greedy neighborhood king, he left his daughter to her fate. Thrown into a room filled with straw, the young girl is told to spin the straw into gold during the night or she will not live to see another day. Thrown into despair by this threat, the girl retreats into tears but is saved by the appearance of a little man who, taking her ring in payment, proceeds to do the spinning for her. The king immediately rewards the young girl's efforts with a larger straw-filled room and renewed threats. The little man again comes to her rescue, this time in payment for the girl's necklace. She is not saved yet, as the greedy king throws her into an even larger room and offers her marriage as a reward for her efforts. The little man bargains with the young girl, who has no

233

other material goods to offer him. He initiates a promise of her firstborn child. All goes well for the new queen until the little man returns for his payment. She pleads with him, and he decides to give her a chance to keep her child. She must guess his name in three days or pay the price. The first two nights she exhausts all the names she knows. She sends a servant out to discover any unusual names, and as luck would have it, the servant comes across a strange little man boasting about his name and his bargain with the queen. Armed with this inside information, the queen teases the little man with several wrong guesses before she proudly proclaims the correct name. The little man is so angry and frustrated that he tears himself in two, disappears into the ground, and is never seen or heard from again.

As for the queen, the story never mentions if she ever has to spin again!

Tale Type: AT 500

The Name of the Helper [the maiden learns the name of her supernatural helper]

I.   *Impossible task*: (a) a girl wedded to prince is compelled (to fulfil her mother's false boasting) to spin an impossible amount of yarn OR (b) to spin gold.

II. *Bargain with helper*: (a) a supernatural being agrees to help the girl OR (b) reward the man; (c) but she must give him her child OR (d) herself; (e) if she cannot within a certain time guess his name OR (f) his age.

III. *The Helper overcome*: (a) by chance the name (age) is discovered; (b) the name is pronounced, and the helper vanishes.

Motifs:

H914. Tasks assigned because of mother's foolish boasting

H1092. Task: spinning impossible amount in one night

H1021.8. Task: spinning gold

D2183. Magic Spinning. Usually performed by a supernatural helper

S222. Man promises (sells) child in order to save himself from danger or death

S222.1. Woman promises her unborn child to appease offended witch

H512. Guessing with life as a wager

H521. Test: guessing unknown propounder's name

H521.1. Test: guessing unknown propounder's age

N475. Secret name overheard by eavesdropper

C432.1. Guessing name of supernatural creature gives power over him
(Thompson, 167–88)

A History of Rumpelstiltskin

"Rumpelstiltskin" is possibly the best-known example of Tale Type 500, but the tale was widely known in Europe before it was captured in print by the Brothers Grimm.

Rumpelstiltskin in Oral Tradition

The activity of spinning, as with other repetitious domestic tasks, is closely associated with the telling of tales, and what better subject matter than the task at hand? Spinning and the getting of husbands were a focus of many tales in various cultures. And, as Maria Tatar points out, if male protagonists must routinely submit to character tests and demonstrate compassion, the tests for their female counterparts would involve demonstrations of their competence in the domestic domain (1987, 116). The tale is well known throughout Europe under a variety of names. A quick search of *The Storyteller's Sourcebook* supplies the following examples: Rumpelstiltskin (Germany), Tom Tit Tot (England), Ripopet-Barabas (France), Peerifool (Scotland), Duffy and the Devil (Cornwall), the White Hen (Ireland), Trillevip (Denmark), and Whuppity Stoorie (Scotland) (MacDonald, 121). Other variants include Tittle-te-tot (England), Terrytop (England), Skane (Norway), Gilitrutt (Iceland), and in North America, Rompetailtailskin (Louisiana) and Tambutoe (Clarkson and Cross, 105).

Rumpelstiltskin in Print

While the Grimms' tale is the most prominent version in North America, several other literary versions proceeded the first edition of the Grimms' *Household Tales*.

Mademoiselle L'Heritier's *Ricdin-Ricdon*

In this first literary form of "Rumpelstiltskin"(1705), spinning was accorded great respect by the aristocratic population. Rosanie is employed by the queen to spin flax into yarn and thread and does so magnificently. She attains her royal marriage by her own virtues and royal birth rather than false pretenses. "Throughout the entire tale, spinning and female creativity remain the central concern and are upheld as societal values that need support, especially male support" (Zipes 1994, 67).

Basile

In "Saporita Tasty" (Tale IV: 4), the lazy protagonist manages, through the aid of her mother's and her own craftiness, to convince a wealthy merchant of her industriousness and marry her. He puts her to work immediately! While he is away for 20 days, she must spin 80 skeins of flax. She spends the first 19 of those days eating, and on the 20th, she panics. She assembles, and hangs from the terrace, an absurd contraption for preparing the flax. Some fairies who happen to be passing by laugh so hard at the contraption that, out of appreciation for the entertainment, they spin the flax, dye it, and make it into cloth.

The Brothers Grimm

The 1810 manuscript was based on an anonymous oral tale recorded by Jacob Grimm in 1808. "The 1857 *Rumpelstiltskin* is an amalgamation of literary and oral tales that the Grimms carefully reworked to represent the dilemma of a young peasant woman who cannot spin to save herself" (Zipes 1994, 55). The changes, maintains Zipes, were a "social-historical statement about the exploitation of women as spinners and the appropriation of the art/craft of spinning by men" (1994, 55).

> The tale, as we now know it, is an amalgamation of several oral traditions including that of "The Three Spinners" which reflects the beliefs of the Germanic peoples of the spinning and weaving capabilities of elves and dwarves. Another tradition is that of offering aid and/or wealth in return for either something young or the first thing that greets the returning hero. By the time Wilhelm Grimm collected the tale of "Rumpelstiltskin" from Dortchen Wild in 1811, the plot had evolved from one in which the elves offered aid freely to one in which the girl's father's boasting propels her into the hands of the greedy king and forces her to make a bargain with the supernatural helper (Bottigheimer 1982, 148).

Ruth Bottigheimer observes that the motivation for this tale was completely shifted by Wilhelm Grimm when, in 1812, he transformed the girl who could spin nothing but gold and bargained for release from this affliction to a girl who was forced to spin gold at the risk of her life (1982, 149). The evil or guilty are also treated with more cruelty by the Grimms. Notice that in the 1810 manuscript version, Rumpelstiltskin simply flies out the window on a spoon. As the story is revised, he becomes more and more angry and more and more violent, so much so that he eventually tears himself in two (Ellis, 79).

Table 7.1
Alterations Made by the Brothers Grimm

Oral Version	1810 Manuscript	1812 Manuscript	1857 Manuscript
No parental involvement: girl spins flax into gold.	Given task of spinning flax, but can only spin gold.	Girl in distress because she must spin gold into flax or die.	Miller boasts his daughter can spin flax into gold; she cannot.
Maiden's predicament: failure to do her job properly.			Daughter's predicament: lie told by her father makes it seem she can do an extraordinary feat.
Maiden willingly agrees to little man's terms.	The dwarf will see to it that she marries a prince, in exchange for her first child. "Here the girl's problem is that she is ripe for marriage and dreams of wedding a prince, as symbolized by her inability to spin anything but gold. The dwarf does not do anything about the spinning problem itself" (McGlathery, 1991, 184).		Daughter threatened by the king; accepts the bargain with little man under duress.
Female servant sent out by queen to discover name of little man.	Faithful maid discovers the name of the helper.	Girl discovers name only by accident through her husband.	Male messenger sent out by queen to discover name of little man.
Little man flies out the window on a cooking ladle.	No changes.	Little man becomes angry, runs off, and is never seen again.	Little man, in rage, tears himself in two.
Spoof with no need of blackmail on the part of the master spinner.			Undermines the value of spinning and the autonomy of the spinner.

Overview of Critical Interpretations of Rumpelstiltskin

While the number of contemporary reworkings of "Rumpelstilt-skin" is not as high as some of the other tales in this book, it is easy to see that the story has fascinated psychologists, folklorists, and other inter-preters of tales. Since the first full-length study of "Tom Tit Tot" to the present, researchers have focused on the power of names, the identity (or purpose) of the supernatural helper, the cautionary aspects of the tale, and the role of spinning in the lives of women and society. Others have focused on connections between this story and ancient beliefs and leg-ends and the functions of riddling. I have to admit to a particular fascina-tion with the varied scope of interpretations offered in this section. What is it about a tale that has been told with little variation over the years, has no heroic characters, and has an ambivalent ending?

1898: In his primary study *Tom Tit Tot: An Essay on Savage Philosophy in Folk-Tale*, folklorist Edward Clodd examines variants of the tale and expounds on the basic similarities. He states that in all the variants "the plot centers round the discovery of the name of the maleficent actor" (17), and that there are three main incidental features of all the stories: the superstitions about iron, spinning, and the element of outwitting the malevolent agent (32–33). In his discussion on spinning, he traces the importance of women in agricultural development and the image of spinning and distaffs in classical mythology and recent superstitions. Clodd also ex-pounds on the "gullible devil" and the importance of outwitting him in a bargain for both body and soul in folklore and story. He then examines more ancient motifs evident in the tale, such as "barbaric ideas about names" (53) as well as essays on other ele-ments in folklore such as the power of words, taboos, and magic.

1913: Freud interpreted a dream about Rumpelstiltskin as being about a penis (Miller, 74).

1951: J. L. Rowley connected the aspect of the power of naming (identi-fying) as a therapeutic value (Miller, 74).

1961: According to Edmund Bergler, "Rumpelstiltskin" has one basic theme: "the child's jealousy of woman's unique ability to pro-duce children" (65). The story also includes, along with various mentions of negative descriptions of males, five indictments of the male gender:

1. The father's self-aggrandizement

2. The king's greed and his marriage to a peasant because of her ability to appease his greed

3. The little man, who is described as absurd and, like the king, is also propelled by greed

4. The little man again, who symbolically represents the male sex organ and is made to appear ridiculous because he must depend on the girl, not his magic, to produce a child (65).

5. The second part of Rumpelstiltskin's name, "*Stilzchen*," which is a diminutive of the German word for stilts. "Thus man is again defined as one who puts on airs, elevates and elongates himself artificially . . . and is therefore to be ridiculed and regarded with contempt" (66). There is no acknowledgment within this article of the variants of this tale or folkloric elements such as the power of the name.

1964: Gonthier-Louis Fink maintains that the symbolism of the "gifts" the miller's daughter gives to the little man represents the desire he has for her body. Fink considers this an addition made by the Brothers Grimm but points to erotic elements in French variants of the tale (McGlathery 1991, 184). Fink sees the story as originally belonging to the type of foolish devil stories, particularly in the exorcising of the devil by calling him by name (McGlathery 1991, 185). "Fink judged that Rumpelstiltskin's demand that the girl give him her first born child was a later development, belonging to the tale's evolution from one based on superstition to dramatic, realistic farce, with concurrent deepening of the psychological element" (McGlathery 1993, 78).

1965: Hornyansky concludes that the tale of Rumpelstiltskin concerns an adult world filled with characters who are not above using other people to achieve their desires. "Daddy is a social-climbing miller," the king is purely greedy, and the little man, who is the only character who shows the least bit of decency, is "cheated . . . by modifying the bargain with his special name-guessing clause" (130). The evidence of the little man's identity is displayed throughout the tale: He is superhuman, he demands a steep price in exchange for bargains, and he disappears into the earth below when he flies into a rage. "There are only two beings in the universe who have secret names, unknown to all but the adept: one of them is God, whose holy Name must not be spoken; the other, over whom mortal man may gain power by pronouncing his mysterious proper name, is the devil" (130). This is why the little funny man is not funny and why the listener feels relieved at his defeat, however unjust (131).

1965: Wittgenstein's thesis states that in "naming Rumpelstilzchen (a term once used as a synonym for a penis), [the queen] destroys her former image of man as being merely a productive and exploitive genital, and is able to turn to her husband in a genuine intersubjective relationship that alone can safeguard the healthy growth of the child" (Heuscher, 268).

1966: Otto Kahn argued that this was an ancient tale and that the central figure was originally a member of a prehistoric European indigenous population. His goal "was to marry the girl in order to improve his social and legal status, in view of his membership in that repressed group; and that the girl is not bound by her promise if she finds out his name because she would then recognize that she had no legal or moral obligation to him since he is of that shunned indigenous population" (McGlathery 1991, 185).

1972: Lutz Rohrich attempts to reveal the prehistoric origins of the tale through a philosophical approach. Focusing on related narrative traditions in legends and folktales, Rohrich concludes that the demand for the child parallels that of the dwarfs in legends "who foist their own ugly children on people as changelings and steal human children for themselves" (McGlathery 1993, 78). Rohrich also reports that the allowance of a way out of an agreement was typical about stories about pacts with the devil, but that this enhancement was a later development in the evolution of the tale (McGlathery 1993, 79). "[O]ne associates the name 'Rumpelstilzchen' first of all with the notion of a *Rumpelgeist*, a poltergeist, a goblin, that is, of a dwarf-like creature. Yet wherever a Martin Luther or Johannes Fischart [i.e., German authors of the sixteenth century] speak of a 'Rumpelgeist' they always already mean the devil" (McGlathery 1991, 185).

1973: Marshall briefly compares "Tom Tit Tot" with six variants: "Whuppity Stoorie" (Scotland), "The Lazy Wife" (Isle of Man), "King Olav, Master Builder of Seljord Church" (Norway), "Purzinigle" (Germany), and "Straw into Gold" (North Carolina). He accords the secondary function of the tales as a didactic lesson on the "perils of indolence or false boasting." (52). Other similarities include the typical household activity of woman—spinning—with the exception of the Norse legend, which centers on a national hero; the ridicule of the devil-figure, who is proven not to be as clever as humans after all; and the motif of name guessing.

1974: Heuscher identifies Rumpelstiltskin, a force of tremendous power, as the keen intellect (266). It is "a system or a spiritual being which has given us knowledge and self-awareness, but which will lead not only to our physical but to our spiritual destruction, if we are not able to recognize it and find his name in time" (267).

He reassures his reader that this theory no way conflicts with "a more one-sided psychoanalytic interpretation" of the story representing the maturation of the heroine as discussed by Wittgenstein (267).

1974: Iona and Peter Opie feel that it is a moral tale demonstrating the perils of boasting. It is a fairy tale because of the supernatural helper and magic; a dramatic tale focusing on the most terrifying of all sacrifices, that of the firstborn child; and a primitive tale because of the belief in the power of the name. The story has folk appeal because of the motif of outwitting the devil (253).

1977: Natov declares Rumpelstiltskin to be the most interesting character in the tale. He is the one with all the power but at the same time is an extension of the miller's daughter. He is powerful only when she is not; when she guesses his name he ceases to exist (72). The story, therefore, is a tale about the power of creative energy and what happens when it is not recognized. Rumpelstiltskin represents the artist, the one who makes connections between the ordinary and the extraordinary; the heroine also learns to use her creative powers when she enters into the guessing of the name and claims his creative powers for her own. "The manner in which he does so reveals the dual nature of potentially creative energy and why we are afraid of our own creative impulses" (72). The story demonstrates that when people do not recognize or use these creative impulses, the impulses turn on them, "becoming a terrorizing demon" that is either repressed or unleashed in some destructive way (75).

1978: Roger Sale discusses the relations between parents and children in the eighteenth and nineteenth centuries as demonstrated in the folktales. The parents in "Hansel and Gretel" abandon their children in the forest; the father in "The Frog Prince" forces his daughter to bed with a frog; and the father in" Rumpelstiltskin" sells his daughter because of a boast (27). Sale deduces that the tale has a hateful power because "it is not the miller who boastingly vaults his daughter into peril, or the avaricious, cruel king who marries her, but the little man who helps her and wants only a child for himself who is singled out for punishment" (44). Along with the tale of "Sleeping Beauty," in which the king rapes the sleeping princess, the story of "Rumpelstiltskin" is one Sale would be hard-pressed to include in a collection of acceptable tales were he "interested in shielding the young from the darker and more malicious aspects of human nature and history" (Sale, 51). His sympathy for Rumpelstiltskin makes this tale morally unacceptable to Sale, as the heroine must be cruel to the only character who has shown her any kindness at all.

1979: Zipes cites this tale as an example of a story that "demonstrated how we must seek the power to name the forces acting upon us if we want to be free and autonomous" (1979, 177). To demonstrate two different approaches of retelling the tale, Zipes translated Grimms' version followed by reworkings by Rosemarie Kunzler and Irmela Brender, originally published in German in 1976 and summarized below in the section on short stories.

1982: Bottigheimer explores the two voices that are evident in all of the "spinning" tales in the Grimms collection. The first voice is that of Wilhelm Grimm, who purports to present the material faithfully as it was collected. The second voice is the one that must be teased out from under Wilhelm's editing and refining throughout the various editions (1982, 142). These two voices contradict each other; the first affirms spinning as a worthwhile enterprise, while the other is dissatisfied with this archetypal female employment and identity (1982, 143). She assesses the "spinning" tales using three tools: vocabulary, plot analysis, and motifs and themes. Vocabulary analysis opens a window into the mindset of the nineteenth century, particularly that of Wilhelm Grimm; exploring motifs opens another window into the oral tradition that provided the raw materials for the written collection; and plot analysis reveals four subgroups. (1982, 145). The four subplots are:

- Spinning as the subject of the tale. These tales feature female protagonists who detest spinning and resort to any means to avoid it ("The Three Spinners") and focus on the female's point of view, whether it be a mother who wishes her lazy daughter to spin, a queen who is looking for an industrious daughter-in-law, or a daughter who makes an advantageous bargain with three spinners. "Trickery and deception are women's weapons in a generally unyielding environment which is ultimately controlled by men because only they can promise the security which marriage offers, security which nowhere appears attainable outside of marriage" (1982, 146).

- Spinning as an indicator of the character of the female protagonists. Among the tales (e.g., "King Thrushbeard," "Frau Holle") in this category, there are four diligent and capable females and three who are lazy or incompetent.

- Spinning as an action that advances the plot but is peripheral to the central theme. It is a common occupation for females and features in tales about women (e.g., "Briar Rose," "Rumpelstiltskin") . Bottigheimer refers to the traditional telling of the Rumpelstiltskin tale in which the help with the spinning is freely given by the supernatural helper (1982, 149).

- Spinning as it symbolizes the female gender. Spinning is work that is appropriate to the female and/or onerous toil of the captive or poverty-stricken female. There are no well-known tales in this group (1982, 149).

1983:   Rinsley and Bergmann stresses the sexual aspects of the relationships of all the characters. Miller states that Rinsley and Bergmann "ultimately viewed Rumpelstiltskin as a maternal figure from whom the queen must separate through having and keeping a baby of her own" (74).

1984:   Robert Darnton discusses eighteenth-century French society and the use of child labor as a survival tool for the peasant folk. Numerous French folktales involve an indignant parent's attempt to get rid of a gluttonous and lazy child by bragging of the child's skill in spinning. Darnton refers to the French version of Rumpelstiltskin in which a mother beats her child for not working. When a passing king asks the mother to explain her behavior, the mother seizes the chance to unload an unproductive family member. In reality, marriage would not be a help for the young girl; spinning would just be another task added to her already long day (35).

1985: Miller discusses the various ways this tale is used in psychoanalysis because it easily lends itself to transference of feelings with women patients. Miller himself has been identified "as the miller, a braggart who makes them take all the risks and do all the work, or as Rumpelstiltskin who can do magic but who will ultimately try to take away their most treasured possession" (74).

After looking briefly at previous interpretations of this tale, Miller concludes that "when one thinks that poor Rumpelstiltskin represents an older child who has experienced the birth of a younger sibling, a sympathetic view of him emerges, a view that can be useful in our attempts to understand our patients" (76).

1987: Maria Tatar discusses several themes in this tale. She points out the ambiguous status of spinning in the lives of women, because while spinning is an indication of industry and achievement, it also represents physical oppression and enslavement. The story of Rumpelstiltskin is ironic as the girl "works her way up the ladder of social success through her alleged accomplishments as a spinner, yet also manages to avoid sitting down at a spinning wheel" (1987, 123). A second theme is the economic and crass motivations for marriage inherent in the tale. Regardless of the variant, the heroine is always a woman of humble origins who must, through trickery and deceit, free herself through promises from a perilous situation. The tale therefore rests on the premise that a girl who can make a good marriage is one who produces wealth either through labor or magical means (1987, 126). Spinning ultimately has little value as the heroine is elevated to a higher social rank through magical means rather than skill (1987, 133). Tatar also addresses the fact that it is the males in the miller's daughter's world that put her in peril. The father in his attempt to impress the king puts her life in the hands of the greedy king, who threatens her with death. In order to save herself from the king, the girl must enter into a bargain with the supernatural helper who eventually demands her child. She is thrust into a succession of crises by the very figures who liberated her from the previous crisis and, in nearly every case, deceit propels her into the situation and deceit rescues her (1987, 128).

1988: In his essay on the quest of meaning, Lutz Rohrich refers to psychoanalytic interpretations when he states that for some psychoanalysts, Rumpelstiltskin, represents a penis. "Thus, according to the Grimm version, Rumpelstiltskin is a stiff being, rummaging a lumber room, hoping about on one foot, a being that bakes and brews and demands the queen's child" (9).

1989: According to Jane Schneider, taking a close look at spinning and early cloth production as portrayed in the canon of "spinning" tales, the stories depict spinning as a form of punishment or subjugation for women and "suggest that malevolent spirits can heighten the perils of spinning." Just look to "Briar Rose" and "Sleeping Beauty," she admonishes, to determine how spinning tools or the raw materials are the instruments of a curse: "A mere scratch puts whole kingdoms to sleep for a hundred years" (177). Achieving status through marriage carries a negative connotation in the "Rumpelstiltskin" tales. The status is achieved through a willingness to risk their lives with a devilish pact rather than through their own industriousness. Rather than traditional folkloric benign supernatural helpers, Rumpelstiltskin represents danger. "Fear of such danger found daily expression in spinning communities, where it was the custom to place carded flax under a weight and remove the belt from the spinning wheel before retiring for the night, to discourage unsolicited spirit help" (178). Schneider shows correlation to the evolving spinning tales and the intensification of linen manufacture in the seventeenth and eighteenth centuries. "If the Rumpelstiltskin tale mirrored the experience of linen producers in Early Modern Europe, it did so as a sociological and moral reflection on the ambivalence of spinners and flax growers, as they weighted in the contradictory implications of a new mode of production" (179) She also discusses spinning bees and their role in telling tales and imparting information to young females and their courting partners. Because men hung around the spinning circles not only to flirt but to evaluate the skills of their potential brides, the spinning tales "warned of risk to the daughters of the poor who overcommitted their labor to marry up, or had it overcommitted by their parents" (196). She concludes that "the demonized spirits of the spinning tales did not seek to eliminate linen manufacture," and in fact "Rumpelstiltskin and the witch-like crones contributed to its development, magically producing yarn and facilitating the status mobility through marriage that the linen schemes promised as the reward for diligent spinning" (207). There was a heavy price to pay for this mobility, however, as the tales continually pointed out.

1989:   While Thomas does not analyze the meaning of this story, she brings interesting insight into two aspect of the tale: the possible identity of Rumpelstiltskin as a dwarf (i.e., a fairy-tale dwarf, not merely a short person) and the importance of language and words as an intricate part of this tale. In her general discussion on fairy-tale dwarfs, Thomas addresses the fact that although Rumpelstiltskin is never identified as a dwarf, he shares similar characteristics: skill in both metal and magic (when spinning straw into gold) and greed for material goods (including a child). The third similarity is his connection to the demonic when he is thwarted by the queen's "guessing" of his name. "His frenzied action returns him to earth, the dwarf's element, at the same time that it demonstrates the destructive capability of what must be a supernatural fury" (90).

Thomas also asserts that this story is a perfect example of the use of language because it has:

- A symmetrical two-part structure of the two riddles facing the miller's daughter. The first riddle is physical, involving the process of spinning straw into gold, while the second, the guessing of the name, is verbal, a test of knowledge. The first riddle is also a test of accomplishment for the young girl in her role in society.

- The two riddles advancing in a three-part sequence of action and building tension.

- Dialogue between the two central characters as a major element in both riddle sequences, with the narrator offering only background information and occasional descriptions.

- The second riddle embodying "the story's overall concern with language and the inherent power of words. This true riddle shows the tale to be a primitive one in that it revolves around a decidedly primitive belief: the belief in the interdependence of one's name and identity, even one's life" (229).

- A verbal play on words that is the reason why the young girl, regardless of the variant, becomes the pawn in her transfer from parent to king to little man. "The opening scene . . . serves to create a tension between the exaggerated or unthinking use of words and their appropriate, literal use" (230). Thomas demonstrates how the unthinking use of words propels the action for all the characters involved: The parents are insecure braggarts; the kings are literalists and mercenary; and the young girl, in desperation perhaps, unthinkingly bargains the life of her future child. Rumpelstiltskin himself falls prey to the same fault; he unthinkingly makes a second bargain with the queen for the child, confident in his ability to win the contest. "In the confrontation between that little man and his name, one sees the proper use of language as the single word is turned against Rumpelstiltskin and is used, at last, in a truly literal fashion" (232).

1991: Samuel Denis Fohr provides a different nuance to this tale. This tale and its variants feature evil people and the well-known motif of selling one's soul for material gain. "Naming these little devils represents recognizing their true nature and hence recognizing the pitfalls of greed and other cravings" (88).

1991: McGlathery finds the character of Rumpelstiltskin very puzzling because it is unclear what his motivation is for wanting the child. Perhaps, the author states, Rumpelstiltskin wishes for a child to raise for himself as his "approach to the miller's daughter somewhat resembles that of a suitor, albeit one of the childish, regressive type" (1991, 177). This is exemplified by the three gifts (bribes) that he obtains from the girl. These presents are symbolic representations of love and marriage. The necklace is "an intimate part of a woman's attire"; the ring, an engagement token, and the child, an indirect symbol of the offering of herself, her body (1991, 177). Rumpelstiltskin, however, is not a lecherous soul; he wishes instead to be a father without having to be a lover. Equally as puzzling is Rumpelstiltskin's second bargain with the mother—to allow her a chance to retain the child he so desperately desires. "His challenge to her . . . is childish and is . . . one that under other circumstances might be posed by a lover, as part of the mating game . . ." (1991, 178). His childish rage over the loss of the game is "partly that of a little boy who has been bested by a little girl and partly that of a jealous lover who, though he did not covet a maiden's body, greedily yearned to possess the fruit of her womb" (1991, 178).

1991: Lutz Rohrich discusses the need for knowledge of the folktale's historical development before any form of reliable analysis can be considered. In regards to the story of "Rumpelstiltskin," which he declares an ancient legend, Rohrich claims that while the interpretations usually cite the tale as a model example of the power of name magic, it actually has nothing to do with that at all. "[T]he demon's downfall actually results when Rumpelstiltskin bursts into excessive rage because she guessed his name and he loses the reward" (1991, 70). It is therefore not a story of name power but that of a riddle-bet.

> An archaic feature of "Rumpelstiltskin" and other riddling contests is that the prize is existential: Life itself is at stake. One either guesses or perishes. When the riddle is solved, the Sphinx plunges into the abyss; the Eddic dwarf Alwis turns to stone when struck by sunlight. But the wager itself, not name magic, determines the contestant's fate (1991, 70).

Rohrich asserts that it is a mistake to claim the story is from the sixteenth century because of the spinning wheel as "the spinning wheel is not a vital element in the folktale's reality and therefore does not provide a criterion for dating, particularly as older versions mention the spindle" (1991, 92).

1992: Maria Tatar looks at the equation between gluttony and idleness as demonstrated in the many variants of "Rumpelstiltskin." Marriage is the reward when the misinterpretation of an expression of astonishment at her greed is taken as praise for her industry. "The heroines of 'Rumpelstiltskin' become attractive marriage partners as soon as they are perceived to be hard workers rather than big eaters" (1992, 116).

1993: Jones includes "Rumpelstiltskin" in his canon of persecuted heroine tales. The generic plot paradigm include three acts or locations. Act One: The heroine is persecuted or threatened in her family home. Act Two: The heroine is attacked, interfered with, or otherwise abused in her attempt to be married. Act Three: The heroine is displaced, slandered, or calumniated after she has given birth to children (Jones, 17). According to Jones, "Rumpelstiltskin" conforms to this pattern in the following way: The girl is put into danger by her father's boasting (Act One); she marries the king after much trial and tribulation and a promise to give away her firstborn child (Act Two); and she desperately fights to save the life of her child by discovering the name of her supernatural helper (Act Three) (18).

1994:   Zipes ponders the fact that folklorists, psychoanalysts, and literary critics have all focused on Rumpelstiltskin's name and his role in the story rather than on the miller's daughter and her persecution and spinning as symbolic of female creativity. He acknowledges that the guessing of the name performs five important functions within the tale: It adds tension and humor to the story; it demonstrates the cleverness, cunning, and luck of the spinner when she guesses the correct name; the power of names is an important folk belief and, in this tale, demonstrates internal power as well; the significance of the naming can be "a designation of the oppressor, a separation from the devil, a capitulation to male authority, or a completion of the initiation as spinner"; and the act of naming is about the spinner rather than the figure being named (1994, 51). The story is not only about the persecution of a young woman at the hands of her parent, her sovereign, and her helper, but also about the capitalistic intensification of linen manufacturing and the appropriation of the womanly skill that would historically aid a young woman in securing a husband. "She must depend on a man, who has miraculous powers of spinning (almost like a machine), and her only quality lies within her capacity to reproduce the species" (1994, 68). Like Schneider a few years previously, Zipes connects the role of spinning, spinning bees, and spinning tales with the Industrial Revolution and the gradual replacement of women with factories run by men. Spinning was destroyed as a craft, which created great hardships for peasant women who could no longer identify with the spinning arts. Indeed, as Zipes points out, the changing attitude towards spinning is aptly demonstrated by the shift in the meaning of the word *spinster*. Originally it referred to the occupation of a spinner but gradually shifted to denote an unmarried female, an old maid (1994, 66).

1996:   Martin Hallett and Barbara Karasek mention that this tale is distinguished by the fact that the villain is actually the central character. He has a "human side" but at the same time is "of nether-worldly (and thus wicked) origin. . . . His generosity must be seen in the light of its deceitful and exploitive motive; his 'guess-my-name' offer to the Queen is based on the conviction that he is setting her an impossible task" (113). The authors speak to the ambivalent feeling of the reader or listener to this tale: "[W]e can identify with the Queen's acceptance of the bargain offered to her by Rumpelstiltskin, since she is left with no alternative—but when the time comes to face the consequences, we again assume the voyeuristic role, torn as we are (an appropriate turn of phrase, considering the story's ending!) between the natural desire of the Queen to keep her baby and Rumpelstiltskin's apparent benevolence in offering her another chance" (114).

1996: Jack Zipes, in his exploration of storytelling, devotes a chapter to the story of "Rumpelstiltskin" because of the questions raised within the tale: parental abuse, the craft of spinning compared to the art of spinning tales, and the nature of helpers who can be both benign and malignant (1996, 58). For Zipes, it is a tale of threefold functions: boasting and its consequences, demonstrating "how the craft of spinning was taken from the hands of women and turned against them," and exploring the fallout of the Industrial Revolution on the cottage industries (1996, 58–59).

A Reworking of Rumpelstiltskin in Novel Form

Sleeping in Flame

1988: Carroll, Jonathan. **Sleeping in Flame**. New York: Doubleday; repr. New York: Vintage Books/Random House,1990.

It is somewhat unfortunate that I must advise that this novel is suitable for mature readers only because the author spends a great deal of time exploring both the history of "Rumpelstiltskin" and the changes made by the Grimms. The contemporary novel revolves around Walker, his relationships with his lover Maris, and his quest for his father. As the story unfolds, Walker (and the reader) is given increasingly pointed clues to the identity of his father. While in Austria, Walker feels that he is being followed and sees a man on a bicycle with "a long Rumpelstiltskin beard" (60). This figure calls Walker "Rednaxela" (61). Later, Walker has a strange dream: He is a baby in a crib and a woman looks down on him. She is in despair. "I've done everything, but I never knew there were so many names. . . . People coming from everywhere, everywhere with new names. . ."(71). Walker is greeted by two old women on the street. They know him as Rednaxela and tell him he is doing well but will give no other information to him. A passing couple point out that the entire conversation with the two women was conducted in an unknown language—unknown to Walker, at any rate (85–87).

Walker's encounters with his supposed heritage rapidly become more and more conflicting and confusing. He is shown a vision of a midget who claims he was his father in a past life (121); and he has a dream in which he is a Russian, Alexander Kroll, called Rednaxela as a child by his father (125). Walker continues to unearth past memories, and the suspense builds at the same time as the allusions to the traditional tale become stronger and stronger. Walker finally realizes that his father is a midget who keeps returning in successive generations to raise a son whose mother has died in childbirth. In a dream, Walker discovers more of the story through a discussion with his father. He remembers his mother crying because there were too many names (198). He is told that one of her worse faults was that she did not keep promises and "thought she would be beautiful enough to make the king forget about gold when he saw her. And he thought she *was* beautiful, but he loved gold more" (198). Walker's father rants that once she became queen, he was no longer needed and that she did not even know his name although he gave her a final chance. "She thought my name was Rumpelstiltskin. What desperation! I can't even say that name. You know what the funniest part is? All she had to do was ask. All she had to say was 'Please tell me what your name is.' And I would have done it immediately" (201).

With threats to his future child and happiness, Walker is now desperate for help and looks into the history of the story for guidance. He questions both the traditional tale and the motivation behind the changes made to it. "Although it is a famous story, I didn't realize how short it was. Before reading, I did a quick line count and saw it was no more than 1500 words" (218). Then. . .

> comes the first intriguing part of the story. When the girl has nothing left to give but still must spin gold for the king, the little man demands her first child when she becomes queen. She agrees! Until that point we're obviously supposed to not only be on her side, but feel great pity for both her poverty and helplessness. But if she is so virtuous, why would she accede so quickly to such a terrible and inhuman demand? (219)

Walker "started thinking about motivation. The little man falls in love with the girl and does her spinning. He thinks she'll love him for it, even though he's not a 'real' man because he's incapable of taking her to bed. But that makes him fight all the harder for her because he hopes that by doing all these magical things, she'll love him anyway" (220).

Walker finally realizes that in order to stop the destructive life and death cycle, he needs to remember (find) his father's name. And he does. In a climactic and magical moment, Walker arranges a meeting between his father and the Wild sisters, Dortchen and Lisette, who were the main informants for Jacob and Wilhelm Grimm. They tell him how they had made up the story, and . . .

> how the Grimms had laughed at the name Rumpelstilt-skin. They wanted to record the girls' story, but felt it was much too sad and wrong in its original form. Little magical men shouldn't be able to get away with stealing human children. It was simply too strange and immoral. No their story would end with the good and virtuous queen guessing the little man's name because she was so worried about losing her child. Of course his name had to be Rumpelstiltskin because it was the craziest, funniest name either of them had every heard (268).

By telling the "actual" story to Walker's father, the sisters break the cycle and the little man disappears forever, allowing Walker to settle down to be a normal man with his lover and expected child. The book ends when this normal life is interrupted by a knock on the door by a young girl wearing a red cape and hood! And his father's real name . . . well, I'll let you read the story.

Ellen Datlow, in her summation of the best of horror 1988, states that *Sleeping in Flame* "is about magic and the darkness just around the corner—and is the 'true' story of 'Rumpelstiltskin'; a brilliant and satisfying build-up leads to a disappointing last page. But this time [Carroll] almost makes it all work. Highly recommended" (xxv–xxvi).

Short Stories

It is interesting to note that until 1979, when Jack Zipes translated the two German reworkings in short-story form, it was not common to find reworkings of this tale in English. It was not until 1994 that a "bumper crop" of new short stories appeared, all based on some aspect of "Rumpelstiltskin." This trend has not abated in the years since.

1976: Brender, Irmela. "**Rumpelstiltskin.**" Translated by Jack Zipes. In *Breaking the Magic Spell: Radical Theories of Folk and Fairy Tales*, edited by Jack Zipes. Austin, TX: University of Texas Press, 1979, 181–82.

Brender, sympathetic to Rumpelstiltskin's point of view, expounds on the unfairness inherent in the Grimms' story. All the queen needed to do, she states, is invite the little man to live with them in the castle and be companion with the child. "Through critical reflection her narrative shifts the goal of the Grimms' story from gold and power to justice and more humane relations based on mutual consideration and cooperation" (Zipes 1983, 66).

1976: Kunzler, Rosemarie. "**Rumpelstiltskin.**" Translated by Jack Zipes. In *Breaking the Magic Spell: Radical Theories of Folk and Fairy Tales*, edited by Jack Zipes. Austin, TX: University of Texas Press, 1979, 180. Also in *Spells of Enchantment: The Wondrous Fairy Tales of Western Culture*, edited by Jack Zipes. New York: Viking, 1991, 716–17.

The story begins with the king locking the miller's daughter into the room of straw for the first time. It follows the traditional story structure until the third episode, when the little man asks for the miller's daughter's unborn child when she becomes queen. This jolts her and opens her eyes to her situation—not only will she not make that promise, but she also has no intention of marrying the king. The little man destroys himself in his rage, accidentally opening the door, and the girl escapes.

Maria Tatar refers to this tale as an effective example of "abrupt plot reversals as devices for inducing reflection on cultural stories that have become ossified in printed form" (1992, 237). Kunzler's version is a "succinct critique of male exploitation and domination of women" (Zipes 1983, 66).

1994: Brooke, William J. "**Rumpelstiltskin by Any Other Name.**" In *Teller of Tales*. New York: HarperCollins, 47–72.

A retelling of the traditional tale precedes the actual story about a little girl and the teller of tales in this multifaceted story. After hearing it for the first time, the teller asks reasonable questions about the tale: "Why would anyone make such a foolish boast?" "And why would the King marry her?" "And why would the little man want a human child?" "And why would he admit that she had guessed his name?" (55) The ending of the story is retold by the teller in order to answer his own questions. The little man in the new story refuses to acknowledge the name Rumpelstiltskin, and the queen must discover another means of saving her child. She does so, but years later the disgruntled child runs away from her family and turns up at the home of Rumpelstiltskin, where he gives her the power of a secret name (and a sympathetic ear).

1994: Garner, James Finn. **"Rumpelstiltskin."** In *Politically Correct Bedtime Stories: Modern Tales for Our Life and Times*. New York: Macmillan, 13–16.

In this spoof, the miller starts a rumor about his daughter in order to attract a financially sound suitor. When Esmeralda is locked into a dungeon filled with straw, she meets a "differently statured man" who offers his help. When the straw is used to thatch a farmer's roof, the farmer becomes more productive. Eventually the children of the kingdom are educated, the kingdom becomes a utopia, and the greedy king is done away with. Esmeralda is rewarded for her gift of straw with numerous chests of gold. When demanding his price of her firstborn child, the "diminutive" man offers Esmeralda a chance to guess his name. This is quite an easy task because he is wearing his name badge from the "Little People's Empowerment Seminar." Esmeralda moves to California and establishes a birth control clinic to protect women's reproductive rights.

1994: Kress, Nancy. **"Words Like Pale Stones."** In *Black Thorn, White Rose*, edited by Ellen Datlow and Terri Windling. New York: William Morrow, 8–29.

The author uses images from the Rumpelstiltskin tale to explore the power of words and creative energy. This evocative horror story, told from the female protagonist's point of view, is faithful to the traditional telling but is embellished with creative aspects such as the introduction of the spinning wheel to the community, the magic embedded in the wheel so gold can be continually spun, and the devaluation of gold when it becomes so plentiful. When her child is born, Ludie knows she must save him from his father and his own dark powers. Following a dream, she binds the child to her supernatural helper with the magic words and name: *rampel* (the real) *stillskin* (with quiet skin).

1994: Yolen, Jane. **"Granny Rumple."** In *Black Thorn, White Rose*, edited by Ellen Datlow and Terri Windling. New York: William Morrow, 204–16.

Presented as a personal oral story by the narrator, with all the elements of digression, explanation, and inflection found in conversation, Yolen's story blends the traditional tale with European Jewish history documenting aspects of the "blood libel." The protagonist is the wife of an ugly little moneylender who, out of compassion, twice lends money to a poor, non-Jewish miller's daughter to help her fulfill her father's boastful bargain. When the young girl marries well and has a child, the young Jewish wife of the moneylender goes to collect the loan. She is accused by the ungrateful borrower of being a "Demon! Witch! Child stealer!" (213) and unfortunately incites a pogrom in the ghetto during Passover preparations. The miller's daughter explains her terror by telling her husband a "fairy tale . . . complete with a little, ugly black imp with an unpronounceable name who had sworn to take her child for unspeakable rites" (214).

Yolen successfully reworks the traditional tale into a lesson of history. As she admonishes her audience, it is as true as a man distributing food to multitudes using only a few loaves of bread and several fish or a man parting the sea to grant freedom to a people. She also points out that the only moral character in the traditional tale is the one who makes a promise and keeps it. Ironic in tone, the author's voice, her explanations of Yiddish words and culture and the blood libel, and her understanding of the traditional story make this a powerful tale.

1995: Galloway, Priscilla. "**The Name.**" In *Truly Grim Tales*. Toronto: Lester, 1–15.

This first-person narrative describes a man's lonely but privileged childhood, his disability as result of polio, and his meeting with the young woman who steals his heart and becomes pregnant with his child. When his father refuses to let him marry her, she becomes the wife of the miller's son. When the man's father dies 20 years later, the narrator returns to his childhood home and discovers that his lover had been abused by her husband and eventually died. The miller and "his" daughter were on their way to the king when the narrator decides to step in and help. Following the traditional story structure, the girl is forced to spin straw into gold as result of her father's boasting. The narrator changes the straw into gold coins with the help of the guards all three times and then attends the wedding. When he returns for his grandchild he is faced with a dilemma—to take the child to ease his loneliness or to cause his own child unhappiness. He offers her a chance to redeem the child by guessing his name. He does this, in actuality, to buy time to solve the dilemma. Should he take the child or arrange for his manservant to accidentally reveal his elvish name?

Galloway meshes all the elements of the traditional tale with her interpretation of the nature and aspirations of the title character. There is no magic involved in this tale set in the Middle Ages; instead, it revolves around humane considerations and logical and rational explanations. A somber and thought-provoking reworking.

1995: Kilworth, Garry. "**Masterpiece**." In *Ruby Slippers, Golden Tears*, edited by Ellen Datlow and Terri Windling. New York: William Morrow, 33–53.

The contemporary female narrator meets a strange man while walking and she is immediately apprehensive: He knows her by name and has met with her expressly to offer her a proposition. The man also knows of her relationship with her father and her father's expectations for her, and he offers to help her satisfy both her father's need for financial security and hers for artistic expression. The proposition involves aiding her in becoming a famous painter. The price: "Think of that which you possess and would not part with for the world—*that* is my price—for it is the world I'm offering you, and the world doesn't come cheap" (39). She agrees easily and becomes absorbed in her paintings, acquires an agent, and falls in love. Eventually, when she paints a masterpiece, a female version of the man knocks on her door demanding payment. The narrator now has to make a choice. What is her most precious possession: her masterpiece, her child, or her lover? A chilling tale about ambition and choice that is for mature readers.

Editorial comment identifies an inherent problem in the traditional tale as that of unfairness to the title character and proposes that the tale is "obviously a variation on the deal with the devil story, as is Shakespeare's play *The Merchant of Venice*." In the play, "Shylock never wins but he *does* get his day in court, and in some productions he has been portrayed as more noble that those around him, who make deals they have no intention of honoring" (Datlow and Windling 1995, 34).

1995: Vande Velde, Vivian. "**Straw into Gold**." In *Tales from the Brothers Grimm and the Sisters Weird*. San Diego, CA: Harcourt Brace, 1–26.

In this parody for younger readers, Della is put into the position of having to spin straw into gold, not because of her father's boasting but because of his bad planning. She is rescued by a young elf named Rumpelstiltzkin who, while unable to spin straw into gold, can transmute gold from his world to fill the room and does so three times. When her daughter is born a year later, Della is incensed with the king's disinterest in a female child. Along with Rumpelstiltskin, she devises a plan to gather the king's interest in his daughter. Alas, she is not much better as a planner than her father, but the plan does produce a happy ever after—for Della, her daughter and Rumpelstiltzkin himself.

1997: Donoghue, Emma. "**The Tale of the Spinster**." In *Kissing the Witch: Old Tales in New Skins*. New York: HarperCollins, 117–29.

In this reworking all of the characters are female and there is no magic involved. The narrator is the daughter of a weaver and "cursed" by her dying mother to become the most successful spinster ever. When the work becomes too much, the young woman advertises for an assistant whom she calls "Little Sister." As her reputation and wealth grows, the young woman makes rash promises to keep Little Sister with her and finally promises her unborn child. When the child is conceived and born, the narrator keeps her word, proclaiming the child as belonging to her assistant. When the narrator's rashness and greed undermine the household, Little Sister leaves, taking the baby with her. During all the time she was part of the household, the assistant was never asked her name . . . nor the baby's either.

A rather strident retelling of the tale with no one character being particularly positive. The tales in this collection are interwoven, a character from the previous tale telling the next to answer the question "Who were you before . . .?"

Feature Films

As with the novel form, this story has not been adapted into many films. The two mentioned below are not exceptional reworkings at all and are only mentioned in passing.

1987: **Rumpelstiltskin.** Directed by David Irving and featuring Amy Irving. Distributed by Media Home Entertainment/Heron Communication. Action/Adventure. Rating G. Time 84 minutes.

Summary (from E! Online Fact Sheet [http://www.eonline.com/Facts/Movies/0,60,14753,00.html]): "The Irving clan shines in this lavish production of the classic fairy tale about a magical elf who helps a miller's daughter turn straw into gold for a royal fee. Amy Irving stars, brother David directs, and mother Priscilla Pointer plays Queen Grizelda."

1996: **Rumpelstiltskin.** Directed by Mark Jones and featuring Kim Johnston Ulrich and Max Grodenchik. Distributed by Republic Pictures Home Video (Malofilm Video). Horror. Rating R. Time: 91 minutes.

Summary (from E! Online Fact Sheet [http://www.eonline.com/Facts/Movies/0,60,44233,00.html]): "In this chiller from the director of 'Leprechaun,' the horrible demon Rumpelstiltskin runs rampant through the streets of Los Angeles after a young mother finds a 'wishing stone' in a thrift shop." While I haven't watched this movie myself, my 17-year-old daughter reported that it was a "wicked movie!"

Short Films

The only short version of "Rumpelstiltskin" suitable for young-adult audiences is part of the acclaimed series by Faerie Tale Theatre.

1982: **Faerie Tale Theatre: Rumpelstiltskin**. Directed by Emile Ardolino and featuring Ned Beatty, Shelley Duvall, and Herve Villechaize. Distributed by 20th Century Fox Home Entertainment. Rating: Family. Time: 40 minutes.

Summary (from eonline fact sheet [http://www.eonline.com/Facts/Movies/10,60,5742,00.html]): In the tradition of the Faerie Tale Theatre productions, the film is filled with puns, slapstick, and tongue-in-cheek dialogue as it follows the traditional structure of the fairy tale.

Poetry

In comparison to other poetic retellings of traditional folk tales, "Rumpelstiltskin" has not appeared often. Those who use images from this tale seem to focus on the inherent darkness in the tale rather than any humor in the plot, the characters, or the situation. Of the five poems included in this section, the first three are recommended for mature readers.

1971: Sexton, Anne. "**Rumpelstiltskin**." In *Transformations*. Boston: Houghton Mifflin, 35–42. Also in *Disenchantments: An Anthology of Modern Fairy Tale Poetry*, edited by Wolfgang Mieder. Hanover, NH: University Press of New England, 1985, 170–74.

For Anne Sexton, "Rumpelstiltskin" represents the old, small, and malformed essence residing within all of us, a metaphor for internal darkness. She introduces this image at the beginning of the lengthy poem and follows it with her faithful retelling of the traditional tale. Sexton adds commentary and asides to her retelling, introducing the image of a grape for the miller's daughter and reinforcing the little man's inability to father a child by having him repeat, "no child will ever call me Papa." It is his joy of "becoming" a father that is transmitted to the reader, "and the dwarf took pity," allowing the queen to fight for her child. His disappointment and anger at the end results in his splitting into two: "one part soft as a woman, one part a barbed hook, one part papa, and one part Doppelganger" (22).

1975: Hathaway, William. "**Rumpelstiltskin Poems.**" In *Disenchantments: An Anthology of Modern Fairy Tale Poetry*, edited by Wolfgang Mieder. Hanover, NH: University Press of New England, 1985, 175–79.

In the first of a series of five poems, the image of the dwarf's temper and demise are explored. The second poem investigates the state of loneliness and sexual coupling, while in the third poem, the reader is introduced to the nasty nature of the little man in the contemporary world. Images of a tennis match are the focus of the fourth poem, and the fifth poem discusses Rumpelstiltskin as an example of one of the few honest men.

1977: Broumas, Olga. "**Rumpelstiltskin.**" In *Beginning with O.* New Haven, CT: Yale University Press, 63–66.

An exploration of certain elements of a lesbian relationship, the poem's only reference to the tale is its title.

1982: Hay, Sara Henderson. "**The Name.**" In *Story Hour*. Fayetteville, AR: University of Arkansas Press, 14. Also in *Disenchantments: An Anthology of Modern Fairy Tale Poetry*, edited by Wolfgang Mieder. Hanover, NH: University Press of New England, 1985, 169.

Sara Hay focuses on people's misguided beliefs in the power of names and magic. This poem is a rather sardonic first-person musing by a man who has many names, one of which is Rumpelstiltskin. It is a short poem (14 lines) that could result in a myriad of interpretations and much discussion.

1990: Strauss, Gwen. "**Her Shadow.**" In *Trail of Stones*. New York: Alfred A. Knopf, 28–29.

This poem is a first-person introspection from a heartsick mother and young woman. Although she saves her child, the price she has to pay is much too high. After all, the shadow was her welcome companion through dire circumstances. It is her misguided pride that drives her and causes the death of someone special. The poem has an interesting viewpoint that is accessible to young-adult readers.

Picture Books

While there are many picture-book versions of "Rumpelstiltskin" in print, the majority basically tell the same tale: the daughter finds herself in a predicament because of the father's boasting, the triad of spinning challenges and helpful responses from the strange little man, and the winning of the day (for the female protagonist) by accidentally finding out the answer to the riddle. The major difference is in the illustrators' interpretation of the little man. "Illustrators of Rumpelstiltskin have never been kind," declares Maria Tatar. Rumpelstiltskin is "burdened with a physiognomy that displays devilish features to the world; his physical appearance, in tandem with his harsh contractual terms, colors the story with somber overtones" (1987, 129). This is true of versions as varied as Paul Zelinsky's character, who "is positively repulsive with his bug-eyes, elongated misshapen hands, and spindly legs" (Hearn, Clark, and Clark, 177), and the Zemachs' *Duffy and the Devil*, based on a popular nineteenth-century Christmas play performed in Cornwall, England. But two recent, and very different reworkings of "Rumpelstiltskin," are the focus of this section.

1994: Moser, Barry. **Tucker Pfeffercorn: An Old Story Retold**. Boston: Little, Brown.

Moser offers a distinct perspective on the tale by setting his version in the contemporary American Southern states. Bessie Grace Kinzalow, a young widow and mother of baby Claretta, is put into the untenable position of having to spin cotton into gold through the agency of the company gossips telling each other tall tales. The stories are overheard by Hezekiah Sweatt, the meanest and richest man in the area and the owner of the mines, the cotton fields, and the company store and housing. His greed colors the denials of the storyteller and Bessie Grace. Claretta is taken as hostage, and strong-willed Bessie Grace is at the mercy of a peculiar little man who comes to her aid. The peculiar little man never asks for anything in payment until one day when he returns and demands the child. Bessie Grace walks through the dark in search of inspiration and, in a cemetery, overhears the answer she is seeking. The peculiar little man, in a state of temper, tears himself in two, and Bessie Grace and Claretta leave the community to take up residence under happier skies.

Moser's text and full-page realistic watercolor paintings complement each other. These are people we can see in any small community, and we can only empathize with Bessie Grace in her troubles. The foreshadowing on the front cover is evocative of the evil that one may encounter inside the story. The thoughtful adaptations made to the tale are conceivable and faithful to the spirit of the traditional Grimms' tale. For example, the bragging of the parent is creatively and realistically represented by the old men in front of the company store. There is no issue of a "marriage reward," however, as the child is in the picture at the beginning of the telling. The commanding text, filled with the cadence of the

American South, begs to be read aloud. I have used this book extensively
with a wide range of young adults and highly recommend it.

1997: Stanley, Diane. *Rumpelstiltskin's Daughter*. New York: William Morrow.

Diane Stanley's reworking of the traditional tale visits the next generation. Stanley's miller's daughter does not marry the king but the little
man who has come to her rescue in exchange for her "necklace, which
was made of gold-tone metal and wasn't worth ten cents," "her cigar-
band pinkie ring," and a chance to adopt her firstborn child when she
marries the king. Instead of the third bargain, which the miller's daughter will not even consider (she would rather marry the little man) so he
spins a ladder from gold and the two escape down into married bliss.
The action begins again when their daughter is 16 and is captured by the
king's tax collector when she redeems some of her father's gold at the
goldsmith. The tyrant king (the same greedy man) recognizes her as her
father's daughter and commands her to spin gold out of straw. However,
Rumpelstiltskin's daughter has grown up with tales of this man's gluttony and decides it is up to her to modify the situation. She explains to
the king that she cannot spin gold but remembers how her grandfather
grew it. The king immediately, but not entirely with grace, follows her
instructions to disburse some of his gold to the farmers for planting. In
the fall, he is astounded by the plentiful harvest but, although his people
now regard him as a hero, it is not gold. Rumpelstiltskin's daughter
moves forward into phases two and three of her plan. The king eventually decides to reward the girl by making her his queen, but she would
rather be prime minister, and so it is. And they all live much happier than
they had before. " Oh, and I forgot to tell you—Rumpelstiltskin's daughter had a name, too. It was Hope."

Aimed at a younger audience than Moser's retelling of the tale, this
book is still pertinent for young adults. The full-page, cartoonlike illustrations are filled with comic allusions to classic and modern art, the
French court, and the color gold as well as a playful perspective. The text
is filled with humor and reads well.

Internet Resources

"The Name of the Helper," translated and edited by D. L. Ashliman
(1997), can be found at http://pitt.edu/~dash/type0500.html. This information is found under the broader title Folklore and Mythology Electronic Texts and includes the complete texts of six versions of type 500

translated into English. (As Internet resources are very fluid, there may be alterations on this site in the intervening years. When I first found the site, there were only three versions presented.) The texts (from the December 27, 1997, revision of the site) are:

1. "Rumpelstiltskin" from the first edition of the Grimms' *Kinder- und Hausmärchen*, published between 1812 and 1815. The translated text is accompanied by a note stating: "[T]he Grimms dressed this tale up considerably in succeeding editions. The most notable change is the introduction of the spinning wheel as a device for turning straw into gold. Further, in later editions the queen discovers the dwarf's name through a messenger whom she herself sends forth to collect strange names, not through her husband's chance meeting with the little man." There are also links to the German-language version of 1857 (the Grimms' last version) as well as an English translation of the 1857 version.

2. "Dwarf Holzruhrlein Bonnefurlein," published in 1854 in Germany.

3. "Purzinigele, " from Austria and translated from a source first published in 1852.

4. "Tom Tit Tot," from Joseph Jacob's *English Fairy Tales*.

5. "Penelop," from Wales from a source published in 1901.

6. "Kinkach Martinko" (a Slav folktale), translated from a source first published in 1896.

There are also various sites written by children exploring various viewpoints on the tale and parodies. They may be useful as samples of extended writing exercises and can be found by searching for "Rumpelstiltskin" with any search engine.

Classroom Extensions

The following suggestions may be adapted for use with other fairy tales as well.

The Hobbit and *Rumpelstiltskin*

Clarkson and Cross draw a parallel from this tale to the riddles in *The Hobbit*:

> When the reluctant hero . . . encounters the dragon Smaug, he is not so unskilled in dragon lore as to let Smaug know his name. Bilbo knows that dragons have to be talked to in riddling talk . . . it "is the way to talk to dragons, if you don't want to reveal your proper name (which is wise), and don't want to infuriate them by a flat refusal (which is also very wise)" (Tolkien, chapter 12/ Clarkson and Cross, 107).

Is the role of the riddle the focus of the variants in tale type 500?

Interpretations Through Illustrations

Compare the physical interpretations of the characters as portrayed in picture books. Is the little man always misshapen? Although the tale is often titled "Rumpelstiltskin," it is more often set in other countries than in Germany. Which ones and why?

Variants of Rumpelstiltskin

Clarkson and Cross offer a sample comparison paper of tale type 500 in the appendix of *World Folktales*. They also offer a tabular analysis of the four major variants ("Rumpelstiltskin," "Duffy and the Devil," "Whuppie Stoorie," and "Ramstampelsam" from South Carolina) (406–7). Using their template, add to the table by examining other variants as well.

Make a similar table for the short stories included in this chapter. What are their basic themes? Genres? Who are telling the tales and why?

Bibliography

Ammon, Bette D., and Gale W. Sherman. *Worth a Thousand Words: An Annotated Guide to Picture Books for Older Readers*. Englewood, CO: Libraries Unlimited, 1996.

Bergler, Edmund. "The Clinical Importance of 'Rumpelstiltskin' As Anti-Male Manifesto." *American Imago* 18: 1 (Spring 1961), 65–70.

Bottigheimer, Ruth B. "Tale Spinners: Submerged Voices in Grimms' Fairy Tales." *New German Critique* 27 (Fall 1982), 141–50.

———. *Grimms' Bad Girls and Bold Boys: The Moral and Social Vision of the Tales*. New Haven, CT: Yale University Press, 1987.

Clarkson, Atelia, and Gilbert B. Cross. *World Folktales: A Scribner Resource Collection*. New York: Scribner's, 1980.

Clodd, Edward. *Tom Tit Tot: An Essay on Savage Philosophy in Folk-Tale*. London: Duckworth, 1898; repr. Detroit, MI: Singing Tree Press, 1968.

Clute, John, and John Grant. *The Encyclopedia of Fantasy*. London: Orbit, 1997.

Darnton, Robert. *The Great Cat Massacre and Other Episodes in French Cultural History*. New York: Basic Books, 1984.

Datlow, Ellen. "Summation 1988: Horror." In *The Year's Best Fantasy: Second Annual Collection*. Edited by Ellen Datlow and Terry Windling. New York: St. Martin's Press, 1989.

Ellis, John M. *One Fairy Story Too Many: The Brothers Grimm and Their Tales*. Chicago: University of Chicago Press, 1983.

Fohr, Samuel Denis. *Cinderella's Gold Slipper: Spiritual Symbolism in the Grimms' Tales*. Wheaton, IL: Quest Books, 1991.

Hallett, Martin, and Barbara Karasek, eds. *Folk and Fairy Tales*. 2d ed. Peterborough, ON: Broadview Press, 1996.

Hearn, Michael Patrick, Trinkett Clark, and H. Nichols Clark. *Myth, Magic, and Mystery: One Hundred Years of American Children's Book Illustrations*. Boulder, CO: Roberts Rinehart, 1996.

Heuscher, Julius E. *A Psychiatric Study of Myths and Fairy Tales: Their Origin, Meaning, and Usefulness*. 2d ed. Springfield, IL: Charles C. Thomas, 1974.

Hornyansky, Michael. "The Truth of Fables." In *Only Connect: Readings on Children's Literature*. 2d ed. Edited by Sheila Egoff, et al. Toronto: Oxford University Press, 1965. 121–32.

Jones, Steven Swann. "The Innocent Persecuted Heroine Genre: An Analysis of Its Structure and Themes." *Western Folklore* 52 (January 1993), 13–41.

MacDonald, Margaret Read. *The Storyteller's Sourcebook: A Subject, Title, and Motif Index to Folklore Collections for Children*. Detroit: Gale, 1982.

Marshall, Howard Wight. "Tom Tit Tot: A Comparative Essay on Aarne-Thompson Type 500—The Name of the Helper." *Folklore* 84 (1973), 51–57.

McGlathery, James M. *Fairy Tale Romance: The Grimms, Basile, and Perrault*. Urbana-Champaign, IL: University of Illinois Press, 1991.

———. *Grimms' Fairy Tales: A History of Criticism on a Popular Classic*. Columbia, SC: Camden House, 1993. (Studies in German Literature, Linguistics, and Culture).

Miller, Martin. "Poor Rumpelstiltskin." *Psychoanalytic Quarterly* 54:1 (1985), 73–76.

Natov, Roni. "The Dwarf Inside Us: A Reading of 'Rumpelstiltskin.' " *The Lion and the Unicorn* 1: 2 (1977), 71–76.

Opie, Iona, and Peter Opie. *The Classic Fairy Tales*. New York: Oxford University Press, 1974.

Rohrich, Lutz. "The Quest of Meaning in Folk Narrative Research." In *The Brothers Grimm and Folktale*, edited by James M. McGlathery et al. Urbana-Champaign, IL: University of Illinois Press, 1988, 1–15.

———. *Folktales and Reality*. Translated by Peter Tokofsky. Bloomington, IN: Indiana University Press, 1991.

Sale, Roger. *Fairy Tales and After: From Snow White to E. B. White*. Cambridge, MA: Harvard University Press, 1978.

Schneider, Jane. "Rumpelstiltskin's Bargain: Folklore and the Merchant Capitalist Intensification of Linen Manufacture in Early Modern Europe." In *Cloth and Human Experience*, edited by Annette B. Weiner and Jane Schneider. Washington, DC: Smithsonian Institution Press, 1989, 177–213.

Tatar, Maria. *The Hard Facts of the Grimms' Fairy Tales*. Princeton, NJ: Princeton University Press, 1987.

———. *Off with Their Heads! Fairy Tales and the Culture of Childhood*. Princeton, NJ: Princeton University Press, 1992.

Thomas, Joyce. *Inside the Wolf's Belly: Aspects of the Fairy Tale*. Sheffield, England: Sheffield Academic Press, 1989.

Thompson, Stith. *The Types of the Folktale: A Classification and Bibliography. A Translation and Enlargement of Antti Aarne's Verzeichnis de Märchentypen*. 2d revision. Helsinki: Academia Scientiarum Fennica, 1964. (FF Communications, no. 184).

Windling, Terri. "Afterword: Surviving Childhood. In *The Armless Maiden and Other Tales for Childhood's Survivors*. New York: TOR, 1995, 354–72.

Zipes, Jack. *Breaking the Magic Spell: Radical Theories of Folk and Fairy Tales*. Austin, TX: University of Texas Press, 1979.

———. *Fairy Tales and the Art of Subversion: The Classical Genre for Children and the Process of Civilization*. New York: Methuen, 1983.

———. *Fairy Tale as Myth, Myth as Fairy Tale*. Lexington, KY: University of Kentucky Press, 1994. (Thomas D. Clark Lectures, 1993).

———, ed. *Spells of Enchantment: The Wondrous Fairy Tales of Western Culture*. New York: Viking, 1996, 48–84.

CHAPTER 8

SLEEPING BEAUTY

"The most famous curse in all of romantic folktales is surely that placed on the newborn princess in the Sleeping Beauty story." (McGlathery 1991, 117)

Everyone knows the story of the beautiful princess who, cursed by a vengeful fairy, falls asleep for 100 years and is awakened by the kiss of a prince who, unlike a multitude of princes before him, conquers the rose hedge. They marry and live happily ever after. An interesting aspect of this story is that in the Perrault's version of the tale, which is the foundation for most of the retellings, there is no awakening kiss and the happily-ever-after ending comes much later, after many more trials and tribulations for the poor princess. The Opies state, in their collection of *Classic Fairy Tales*, that Perrault's version is "a tale so finely told it is no surprise that the retellings which folklorists have subsequently found have been flat or foolish in comparison" (102). This, then, is Perrault's "The Sleeping Beauty in the Woods."

✍ ——————————————————————————————————————

    There was once a king and queen who tried everything but could not conceive a child. One day, long after they had given up hope, the queen found herself pregnant and soon gave birth to a daughter. The king invited all the fairies that could be found (seven) to the christening so they could give her a gift. He had made for each fairy a magnificent place setting. But on the day of the christening an old fairy whom they had not invited arrived. (She had not been seen for more than 50 years and was assumed dead.) She felt slighted because there was no place setting for her and responded with a curse rather than a gift. "The Princess should have her hand pierced with a spindle and die of the wound" (Opie, 109). Fortunately for the child, a young fairy who had been sitting near the older one had overheard her discontent and hid herself away until the old fairy was finished with the child. The young fairy amended the curse, saying "[T]he Princess shall indeed pierce her hand with a spindle; but instead of dying, she shall only fall into a profound sleep which shall last a hundred years, at the expiration of which a King's son shall come and awake her." (Opie, 109). The king immediately proclaimed the exile of spindles. "About fifteen or sixteen years after, the King and Queen being gone to one of their houses of pleasure, the young princess happen'd one day to divert herself in running up and down the palace, when going from one apartment to another, she came into a little room at the top of a great tower, where a good woman was spinning with her spindle" (Opie, 109). The princess touched the spindle and immediately fell down in a swoon. The good woman "not knowing very well what to do in this affair, cried out for help" (Opie, 109). The king and his court laid the sleeping princess in a very fine bed. The young fairy, hearing of this from a dwarf, arrived in a fiery chariot drawn by dragons. She touched everything in the castle (except the king and queen) and they all fell asleep on the spot. The king issued a proclamation that no one should disturb the sleeping castle, but this was not necessary because a bramble hedge grew up quickly, surrounding the castle and protecting it from outsiders.

    At the end of 100 years, a King's son asked about the towers hidden by the great wood. "Everyone answered according as they had heard. Some said, that it was an old castle haunted by spirits; others, that all the sorcerers and witches of the country kept there their Sabbath, or weekly meeting. The most common opinion was, that an Ogre liv'd there, and theat he carry'd thither all the little children he could catch hold of, that he might eat them up at his leisure, without any body's being able to follow him, as having himself only the power to pass through the wood (Opie, 111). The prince, however, met a man who heard his father speak of what his grandfather knew: that there was a sleeping princess who lay in the castle awaiting a King's son to awaken her after her 100 years' sleep. The Prince made his way to the wood, which immediately made way for him but would not allow anyone else through. He found the most beautiful princess sleeping on a magnificent bed and fell down on his knees before her. The enchantment was at an end, the Princess awakened and said to the prince, " 'Is it you, my prince, I have waited a great while. . . .' Their discourse was not well connected, they wept more than they spoke, little eloquence, a great deal of love. He was more at a loss than she, and we need not wonder at it; she had time to think on what to say to him; for it is very probable, (tho' history mentions nothing of it) that the good fairy, during so long a sleep, had given her very agreeable dreams" (Opie, 114). *The rest of the castle awoke, and overcome with hunger, had supper served before any wedding plans were made.* "*They slept very little, the Princess had no occasion*" (Opie, 114). *The prince left the next day to return home, telling his parents that he had lost his way while hunting. He kept up this story for two years (by which time he was the father of twins, Morning and Day).*

When his father died, the Prince felt it time to bring his wife and family home to meet his mother, who just happened to be an ogre. The mother-in-law waited until her son was away at war and put forth a plan to have her grandchildren and daughter-in-law served roasted with Sauce Robert (Opie, 115). *The clerk of the kitchen substituted lambs for the children but could not think of an animal that would do for the young queen, who "was past twenty, not reckoning the hundred years that she had slept: her skin was somewhat hard, though fair and white"* (Opie, 116). *He turned to her and she bid he take her because her children had already been killed. He assured the queen that this was not so and that he would substitute a hind for her. All was well until the day the ogre overheard the children and realized that she had been deceived. She commanded that the next morning a large tub be brought into the court yard and be filled with toads and all kinds of serpents. Into this vat were to be thrown the young queen, her two children, and the clerk of the kitchen and his wife (who had housed the children). As they were brought to the courtyard with their hands tied behind them, the King arrived unexpectedly.* "*The Ogresse, all enraged to see what had happen'd, threw her self head foremost into the tub and was devoured in an instant*" (Opie, 118). *The King was a little dismayed at the loss of his mother but soon comforted himself with his beautiful wife and his pretty children.*

Tale Type: AT 410

It is interesting to look at the tale type entry for this tale, as there is no mention of the second part of the tale, and the frog prophesy, added by the Brothers Grimm, has become part of the recognized type, as has the famous kiss!

Sleeping Beauty. The king's daughter falls into a magic sleep. A prince breaks through the hedge surrounding the castle and disenchants the maiden.

I. *The Wished-for Child*: A frog announces the birth of the much-desired daughter of the king.

II. *The Fairies' Gifts*: (a) A fairy who has not been invited to the celebration (christening) makes a wish that the princess shall die of a wound from a spindle. (b) Another fairy changes the death into a 100-year sleep.

III. *The Enchanted Princess*: (a) The prophesy is fulfilled: with the maiden all the dwellers in the castle sink into a magic sleep and all about grows a hedge of thorn.

IV. *The Disenchantment*: After 100 years a prince breaks through the hedge, awakes the princess with a kiss, and has a happy marriage.

Motifs:

B211.7.1: Speaking frog

B493.1: Helpful frog

F312: Fairy presides at child's birth

F361.1.1: Fairy takes revenge for not being invited to feast

G269.4: Curse by disappointed witch

M412.1: Curse given at birth of child

F316: Fairy lays curse on child

M341.2.13: Prophesy: death through spindle wound

F316.1: Fairy's curse partially overcome by another fairy's amendment

M370: Vain attempts to escape fulfillment of prophesy

D1962.1: Magic sleep through curse

D1364.17: Spindle causes magic sleep

D6: Enchanted castle

D1960.3: Sleeping Beauty. Magic sleep for definite period (e.g., 100 years)

D1967.1: Person in magic sleep surrounded by protecting hedge

F771.4.4: Castle in which everyone is asleep

F771.4.7: Castle inhabited by enchanted princess

N711.2: Hero finds maiden in (magic) castle

D1978.5: Waking from magic sleep by kiss

D735: Disenchantment by kiss (Thompson, 138)

A History of Sleeping Beauty in Print

While we know the tale had its origin in the oral tradition, there has not been a great deal of scholarly discussion of the tale in that format. The major thrust of the discussion has been on the major changes made to the tale from the Italian to the French and German versions with which we are most familiar. The harbinger of all the "Sleeping Beauty" tales seems to have been a fourteenth-century prose romance, *Perceforest*, which sought to link the legends of Alexander the Greek with those of King Arthur (Opie, 104). In this tale, Themis, a disgruntled goddess, casts the spell.

Basile

Basile's " Sun, Moon and Talia" (Day 5, tale 5 of the *Pentamerone)* tells the story of a young girl who, in fulfillment of a curse, falls down as if dead. Her grieving father locks up her body in the castle in which they had been living and leaves her, and his home, forever. It is her father—the mother is never mentioned—who gave her the name Talia (i.e., Thalia, Greek *Thaleia* 'the blossoming one'), but once she is sleeping he plays no further part in the story (McGlathery 1991, 98). Another man, a king, finds her and "plucks the fruits of love" while she is in her sleeplike state. When he returns he finds that she is now awake after giving birth to twins while still asleep. He promises to return yet again and rejoins his wife at home. However he constantly mumbles Talia's name and the names of the twins, Sun and Moon, in his sleep, and his wife discovers his infidelity. His wife eventually perishes in the fire she had prepared for Talia, and the twins and the king marries his beloved "sleeping beauty." The story tells of adultery, a harsh tale in which "the first wife, in her infertility, commits a crime against the family" (Warner, 221).

Perrault

The Opies comment that it is evident from the Basile version that Perrault's retelling is not the entire story, and is, in fact, "in part defective" (Opie, 102). In Marina Warner's opinion, Perrault's adaptation of Basile's tale speaks of a more palatable crime: "cannibalism seemed then much less scandalous that rape, adultery, and bigamy, and more suited to the childish fantasy of the involved audience" (222). Perrault begins the story of the wicked mother-in-law at the precise point of the story where most successive versions of the story end (Tatar 1987, 138). However, his modified but still gruesome coda to the tale no longer appeared after the eighteenth century in children's editions. These edited versions followed the Grimms' more romantic and innocuous account that ends with the famous kiss that awakens the beauty and leads to their wedding (Warner, 222). Few people today are even aware of the secondary sub-plot of Sleeping Beauty's troubles with her mother-in-law and the near-fatal ending of herself and her children at the hands (and mouth) of this ogre.

The final version of Perrault's tale had two morals. The first stressed, with a touch of erotic humor, the unlikelihood of such a long sleep; the second expanded on the same message, highlighting the "female sex's ardor in seeking marriage" (Barchilon and Flinders, 70). Morgan states that Perrault relaxes his strict observance of propriety in adapting Basile's tale only once, and that is when he gives a logical reason for their lack of sleep after the wedding. "By implying one reason and stating another, Perrault maintains a surface decorum while exploiting the adult humor of the situation" (Morgan, 85). "Basile's villain was a jealous wife, Perrault's a jealous mother-in-law; in our times, bad women come in the form of (step)mothers" (Warner, 222).

The Brothers Grimm

Jacob Grimm's preoccupation with discovering a connection between Germanic mythology and German folktale are reflected in his notes for Dornroschen. He associated the wall of thorns surrounding the castle of the sleeping princess "with the slumbering Brunnhilde who is encircled with a wall of flames" (McGlathery 1993, 37). He also noted not only the connection to German mythology but also a correlation to Perrault's version and Basile's tale "The Face" (McGlathery 1993, 38). But less and less attention is paid to these notes as the Grimms repackage the tale for their growing audience. In their first recorded version of the story, Briar Rose sleeps for 100 years while the hedge grows peacefully around the castle. However, in successive editions the successful prince who penetrates the thorny barrier discovers the grisly fate of the numerous unsuccessful suitors who died a painful death (Tatar 1987, 6). Wilhelm Schoof discussed the changes made in the subsequent editions of Sleeping Beauty and "praised Wilhelm's [Grimm's] gift for making the stories appealing for children while at the same time providing an artistic imitation of the style of folk narrative" (McGlathery 1993, 45). Ellis, on the other hand, maintains that not only was the original "voice" or style destroyed by these "elaborations," but also motivational factors were added that changed the characters and the logic of the tale. For example, the addition of the bravery of the prince and the information that all the would-be rescuers were princes, meant that the successful prince did not succeed because he was a prince and therefore adequate for the task, but for no logical reason at all. "[W]hile the Grimms' intent may well have been to fill out the story, the result is an inherently less well-motivated plot, and a corresponding greater reliance on fairy tale clichés which substitute on occasion for the original motivation" (Ellis, 59).

Table 8.1
Adaptations Made by the Brothers Grimm in Sleeping Beauty

1810 manuscript	First edition	Second edition	Sixth edition
Crab delivers prophesy.	No change.	No change.	Frog delivers prophesy. (This change in motif is not explained by the Grimms. Ellis maintains the change is the result of a deliberate analogy with the "Frog King" story that opens the collection, and that many scholars do not look closely at this change and instead discuss in detail the importance of the frog motif, which did not exist in the earlier editions) (Ellis, 83).
12 fairies invited because of number of available plates.	No change.	Wise women rather than fairies.	No change.
13th fairy, uninvited, appears and prophesies that daughter will prick her finger with a spindle and die at age 15.	Just as the 11th fairy had said her gift, the uninvited fairy arrives and cries that the daughter, at age 15, will prick her finger on spindle and die.	No change.	No change.
Other fairies decreed sleep for 100 years rather than death.	12th fairy still had a wish and changes the death threat to 100 years' sleep instead.	No change.	After the shock wears off, the 12th fairy alters the curse.

1810 manuscript	First edition	Second edition	Sixth edition
King ordered all spindles destroyed. Parents left for the day when she was 15.	Basically no change except for the acknowledgment of the girl's beauty.	"But all the gifts of the wise women were fulfilled in the girl, for she was so beautiful, well-behaved, friendly and intelligent, that everyone who saw her had to like her."	No change.
Climbs tower, finds a door with a yellow key which she turns; inside is an old woman spinning flax.	No change.	No change.	"In the lock was a rusty key, and when it turned, the door sprang open."
Girl asks to spin, pricks her finger, and falls immediately into a deep sleep.	No change.	Girl asks the old woman what she is doing, and when the woman answers "Spinning," the girl takes the spindle in her hand; "curse of the witch was fulfilled," and she pricks herself with it.	"Spell [not curse of the witch] was fulfilled."
Everyone else falls asleep as well, including the return-ing parents. A thorn hedge grows around the castle.	Everyone falls asleep as well. Here the Grimm brothers list all the members of the household and how and where they fall asleep. This is a large elaboration on earlier statement: "Because in that moment the king and his court had returned, everything in the castle began to sleep, even the flies on the walls." Thorn hedge begins to grow around the castle.	No change.	No change.

1810 manuscript	First edition	Second edition	Sixth edition
King's son, who had heard the story from an old man who heard it from his grandfather, attempts to gain access through the thorn hedge where other men died trying.	"Princes, who had heard of the beautiful Thorn-Rose, came and wanted to free her, but could not penetrate through the hedge. . . . They remained hanging in them, and died pitifully." Then one year, a king's son hears the tale of the princess and the deaths of the other princes.	No change.	No change.
Thorns part in front of him, produce roses, and allow him access.	Undaunted, the prince vows to try, and the thorns are replaced by flowers until he passes by, when they become thorns once again.	"Now, on exactly the day on which the king's son came, the 100 years were up. And when he went up to the thorn-hedge, they were nothing but large beautiful flowers."	No change.
Kisses the sleeping princess; she and the castle inhabitants awake; the two marry.	Great detail about the sleeping court and the beauty of the princess whom he kisses. Every one wakes up and resumes their activities, and the princess and the prince are married.	The inhabitants of the castle do not stir until Thorn-Rose and the prince descend the staircase. "And then the marriage of the king's son with Thorn-Rose was celebrated in magnificent style."	No change.

A Comparison of the Four Early Versions of Sleeping Beauty

Several scholars have paid attention to the antecedents of this extremely popular (and changed) tale. Some of these changes reflect the country of origin of the tale, the time in which it was told, and the usual audience for the tellings. For example, Basile "has the father and daughter in a more intimate relationship, living together in a secluded sylvan palace, while Perrault and the Grimms have her living with both parents in the father's royal residence" (McGlathery 1991, 108). Lüthi points out that the kiss that awakens the princess in the Grimms' version has no obvious connection with the enchantment, while in Basile's variant the flax fiber that puts Talia to sleep also plays a role in her awakening (1976, 31).

In the second part of the tale, both Basile and Perrault "relate how these children and the heroine herself have to suffer persecution at the hands of the evil queen, how they are to be killed and how they are saved through the compassion of the hired assassin" (Lüthi 1976, 33). Basile's version demonstrates power and vitality; Perrault's, elegance and incisiveness; and the Grimms', sensitivity and refinement. And while all three are characterized by humor, "Basile's often indelicate jokes are not intended for children; but the other two other tales have the power to charm and exhilarate both children and adults" (Lüthi 1976, 34).

Table 8.2
A Comparison of *Perceforest*, Basile, Perrault,
and the Brothers Grimm

Perceforest	Basile	Perrault	Grimms
1528 (translated into French); 1531 (translated into Italian)	1636 (published in Italy)	1697 (published in France)	1810-1856 (published in Germany)
	"Sun, Moon, and Talia"	"The Sleeping Beauty in the Wood"	"Briar Rose"
Three goddesses invited to celebrate the child's birth. Themis, angry because there is no knife beside her place, utters the curse that a thread will pull off the distaff while she is spinning and she will have to sleep until it is pulled out of her finger. Venus, the third goddess, promises to arrange for rescue.	Astrologers foretold the fate of the child upon request by her father. Daughter is named Talia by her father; the mother is never mentioned. (Talia is from the Greek Thaleia, "the blossoming one" (McGlathery 1991, 98).	Seven invited fairies and one uninvited fairy who utters the curse. She was not invited because she had not come out of her tower for 50 years and was presumed to be dead or under a spell.	Twelve wise women and one malevolent one. The 13th women uttered the curse because of the slight in not being invited to the feast.
		Age not specified for spell.	Age of 15 specified.

Perceforest	Basile	Perrault	Grimms
	Does not specify that she will die or fall into a deep sleep; rather vague presence of danger.	Will fall into a deep 100-year sleep and will be awakened by a young prince. Allows for the "pleasure of pleasant dreams." That these dreams were about a handsome prince arriving to court her is made clear by the princess's greeting to him on awakening: "Is it you, my prince? You've certainly kept me waiting a long time" (McGlathery 1991, 118).	
	Splinter of flax.	Spindle.	Spindle.
	Girl dies, father closes up castle and leaves.		Parents and court all fall asleep at the same time as Briar Rose.
	A married king accidentally finds her, cannot rouse her, and "cohabited with her; then he left and forgot the whole affair" (Bettelheim, 227). McGlathery translates it as "plucked the fruits of love" (1991, 98).	A prince arrives after 100 years. The princess awakens when he approaches her (no kissing here), and they are married the same day.	Prince kisses the princess to wake her up.
	Illegitimate twins (Sole and Luna) begotten; they nurse from her breast, but one child sucks on the splinter in her finger and draws it out. Talia awakes.	Two legitimate children begotten in the two years of secret visits by the Prince.	Story ends with Beauty waking up.

Perceforest	Basile	Perrault	Grimms
	King remembers her suddenly and is delighted to find her and her two children. He tries to keep them secret from his wife but mumbles their names in his sleep.	Prince has cannibalistic ogress mother. Keeps his marriage a secret for two years until his father dies. Departs for battle and leaves his family in the care of his mother.	No mention of Prince's family.
	Wife finds out and orders the children to be cooked and served to her husband. Cook hides the children and serves goat kids instead.	She wishes to eat the children.	
	Queen plans to throw Talia in fire but is thwarted by the husband who, instead, throws the queen in the fire.	Plans to throw Sleeping Beauty into a vat of vipers; is thrown in instead.	
	He marries Talia, and they are reunited with the children.		

Overview of Critical Interpretations of Sleeping Beauty

1896: Friedrich Vogt considers the versions by Basile, Perrault, and the Grimms to have originated in the myths of the seasons. Spring is represented by the girl's awakening from her long deep sleep (McGlathery 1993, 73).

1915: Franz Kampers states that the origin of the basic motifs was found in the backdrop of myths of the birth of the sun god from the womb of an earth goddess (McGlathery 1993, 73).

1917: Robert Petsch discusses Jacob Grimms' notation that this tale may have originated in connection with Nordic tales about Brynhild's awakening by Sigurd. He concludes that while there were "certain connections" between the two tales, there was no evidence of direct descent. Petsch points out that there were many richly developed versions of "Sleeping Beauty" outside the Germanic language area. He maintains that the persecution suffered by the heroine after her awakening derives from the Greek myth of Thaleia, but that not all versions contained this motif. His "intent was to counter the claim that the Grimms' version represents a shortening of Perrault's tale and other Romance versions through omission of the story's second half, which Petsch considered to be unmotivated by the events of the first half" (McGlathery 1993, 73).

1933: Steff Bornstein interprets the tale as sexual awakening. The pricking by the spindle symbolizes menstruation and defloration, and the thorn hedge represents the girl's anxiety about men (McGlathery 1991, 129). He construes the role of the wise women and the woman with the spinning wheel as projections of the girl's feelings about her mother. His interpretation is based "largely on the assumption that the tale was invented by an adolescent girl," and he supports his findings by referring to puberty rites among primitive peoples, especially as regarding menstruation, defloration, and female circumcision (McGlathery 1993, 74).

1933: Alfred Romain compares Perrault's version with that of the Grimms to demonstrate that the Grimms, in the course of their editions, borrowed from Perrault where it suited them, but at the same time adapted the tale according to the "German Biedermeirer culture of their time." He considers the tale to be literary rather than from the oral tradition. He states that the Grimms "used Perrault's version where it was more concrete, dramatic, poetic, or the like, yet cast the family as that of a patriarchal German lord of the manor instead of a ruler of the Baroque period, and replaced erotic elements with an emphasis on the girl's spiritual virtue as a source of her appeal" (McGlathery 1993, 73).

1939: Bruno Jockel assumes the spindle to be "a decidedly male symbol that points directly to sexual intercourse." He also connects the giddiness of climbing the tower's long winding staircase to sensations experienced by "a young person at the onset of physical maturity" (McGlathery 1991, 129). The father has a romantic attachment to his daughter, and "the girl is hindered by her own father in the development which would lead to another man [i.e., to a husband]" (McGlathery 1993, 75).

1958: Jan de Vries compares the versions by Basile, Perrault, and the Grimms with the earliest recorded example of the tale, *Perceforest*, focusing on the origins of the story rather than interpretation (McGlathery 1993, 74).

1962: Max Lüthi interprets the tale spiritually as little more than a stylized love story of a woman who retreats into herself until the spell is broken by a youth in love. "The tale depicts the endowing, threatening, paralyzing, and redeeming of not only some girl or other but of mankind in general" (McGlathery 1991, 129).

1974: Heuscher dedicates the early part of his discussion to the role of the role and symbolism of the frog, the 12 golden plates that grace the table for the wise fairies, and the loss of the golden age with the deathlike sleep. This tale, he writes, focuses upon the growth of a young girl. "The phase of the loss of early spirituality, which coincides with the onset of adolescence, is just as inescapable as the menarche which, from a psychoanalytic angle, is seen symbolized by the blood brought forth by the sting of the distaff" (Heuscher, 164). The perishing of the young men on the thorns is a sign that neither they or the sleeping beauty are mature; the parting of the thorns represents this moment of readiness. Heuscher contrasts the "polished, delightfully witty, delicately sophisticated style" (168) of Perrault with the "plainer, simpler, frank style" of the Grimms. (169). But while Perrault's retelling is more sophisticated, it loses depth by concentrating on an "everyday" setting rather than basic human development (169). This tale explores the critical period of the child's awakening into adulthood, the time of adolescence, the time of the reawakening of a spiritual conception of the world (169). Sleeping Beauty "awakens from the sleep into which the intensified instincts and the spinning of the intellectual threads have plunged her by separating her from the live, paradisiacal world of earlier childhood, from a world which she had experienced in a carefree way but without much self-awareness" (170).

1975: Barbara Bucknall compares various interpretations of Perrault's version to argue that while many explanations can be made, none of them are exhaustive, and therefore no single interpretative view can be deemed correct (McGlathery 1993, 75).

1975: P. L. Travers discusses the sleeping motif, the idea "of somebody hidden from mortal eye, waiting until the time shall ripen" within this tale and the similarities to many other folklore characters such as Snow White in her glass coffin, Brynhild behind her wall of fire, Charlemagne in France, King Arthur in the Isle of Avalon, Muchukunda the Hindu king, and Oisin of Ireland (51). In her analysis of the tale type she points to the often familiar introduction of the tale—the wish for a child. This lack of the child demonstrates to the audience the need for what the child represents—"the new order, the renewed conditions, the throwing forward of events, the revivifying of life" (54).

The antagonist role of the unwanted guest is examined, not just to avenge an insult but to thrust the drama forward and the main character over the threshold of character development. This role, she maintains, is played frequently by wicked stepmothers. "The true mother, by her very nature, is bound to preserve, protect, and comfort; this is why she is so often disposed of before the story begins" (57). The wicked fairy is the essential character; without her there would be no story! She is responsible for all the events that subsequently take place. She places the curse; she is responsible for the absence of the protective parents on the fateful day; she is responsible for the inner prompting that propels Beauty up the staircase; and she is present in that tower room. Though it is never explicitly stated in any of the versions dealing with the spinning motif, it is evident that the wicked fairy and the old woman with the spindle are one and the same (57). The prince is the one hero in all the tales who has no hero's task to perform; he is merely in the right place at the right time (59). The heroine has very little action to perform. She has all the gifts and none of the travails of other folktale heroines. Her one role is to follow her fate, prick her finger, and fall asleep (59). Travers asserts that it is these two elements, the beauty of the heroine and the long sleep, that set the listener questioning; "she is not merely a pretty girl waiting, after an eon of dreams, to be awakened by a lover" (59).

1976: For Bettelheim, this tale is directed at adolescents, emphasizing "the long, quiet concentration on oneself. . . . During the months before the first menstruation, and often also for some time immediately following it, girls are passive, seem sleepy, and withdraw into themselves" (225). This tale allows the young adult not to worry about this passivity as they will not permanently be in this inactive state (225). Bettelheim reassures his readers that ancient as this tale is, it has a more important message for our modern youth than many of the other tales: "Presently many of our young people—and their parents—are fearful of quiet growth, when nothing seems to happen, because of the common belief that only doing what can be seen achieves goals" (226). Contemplation and concentration on the self is often necessary for sexual maturity. He accuses Perrault of not taking his fairy tales seriously, being "most intent on the cute or moralistic verse ending he appended to each. With two such incongruous parts to this story, it is understandable that in oral telling—and often also in printed form— the story ends with the happy union of the prince and Sleeping Beauty" (230). Bettelheim reminds his audience that, regardless of the history and variations in this tale, there is one central motif: the inability of parents to prevent the sexual awakening of their child. Both Perrault and Grimms affirm, by their similar beginning of the tale, that "one might have to wait a long time to find sexual fulfillment, as indicated by having a child" (231). There is no need to hurry towards sex, as it loses none of its rewards if one needs to wait, and parents cannot stop the natural maturation of their children. He also points to several Freudian symbols in the tale: circular staircase (sexual experiences), locked room (female sexual organs), and turning the key in the lock (intercourse). He concludes that this tale illustrates that "full self-fulfillment of the female does not come with menstruation. Female completeness is not achieved when falling in love, not even in intercourse, nor childbirth . . . it comes only with having given life, and with nurturing the one whom one had brought into being" (235). Bettelheim states that the death of the unsuccessful in the fairy tales, such as the hordes of men attempting to penetrate the thorn hedge, symbolizes the unreadiness and immaturity of the characters who attempt a task beyond their abilities at that point in time (180).

1976: Lüthi interprets this tale as one of death and resurrection in which the flowering of the hedge and the awakening of the princess "suggests the earth in lifeless repose which, touched by spring, begins to live anew and blossom as young and beautiful as ever" (1976, 24). The tale represents puberty and the time of sexual awakening for both genders; the male is self-conscious, the female retiring. A growing hedge of thorns surrounds them, seemingly to protect them, but it is this seclusion that allows them the time to mature (1976, 24). However, the tale is more than an imaginatively styled love story; it portrays the endowment, peril, paralysis, and redemption of all mankind (1976, 24). It is a story of contrasts of mercy and threat. The fairies are both a blessing and a curse; the royal palace is both paradise and a prison for the child; and the deathlike sleep is both a spell and a refuge (1976, 25).

1978: Sale does not consider "Sleeping Beauty" a fairy tale because of the rape, conception, and birth of the two children before the princess eventually comes back to life. Horrible events such as rape, he states, do not take place in fairy tales (23).

1978: William Wood interprets the tale, and the Grimms' version in particular, as "a story of self-meeting, and its eternal promise is that of self-realization, the blossoming thorn, the curse turned to joy" (McGlathery 1993, 75).

1980: Derek Brewer's concern is about the ancient essential motif of this tale. "The heroine is put into an apparently unending sleep by a parent-figure (the ill-tempered Fairy at the christening) and surrounded by an apparently impenetrable barrier" (34). The hero does arrive, however. This is a metaphor for the maturation of the adolescent or the awakening into adulthood. Brewer maintains that one of the earliest and most powerful versions of this story is that of Brunhilde in the *Volsunga Saga* made so popular through Richard Wagner's opera. Brewer briefly comments on the well-known subsequent retellings of this tale: "[I]t is plain that the goddess, or old woman, or disgruntled Fairy, is a symbol for a hostile mother-figure" (35). The long sleep represents the parent's desire to stop the maturation process of their daughter. He also considers the sexuality and rape scene of some of the earlier variants. He is reluctant to agree with the Opies that "rape" is indeed a correct term to use, as "that would imply a violence on his part, and a reluctance on hers, for neither of which there seems to be any evidence" (35). The scene implies the inadequacy of Sleeping Beauty to respond positively to sexuality; she is, in fact, emotionally passive. The unusual feature in these tales is the birth of the twins, but they perhaps represent "aspects of the heroine's vulnerability, extensions of her, whereby a hostile mother- or father-figure can further persecute her" (36). Brewer then delves into traditional relationships between mothers- and daughters-in-law and their battle for power and control in the household. But, as Perrault's ending demonstrates, evil destroys itself!

1981: Barchilon and Flinders discuss the realistic elements that Perrault incorporated in all his retellings. The resemblance between Sleeping Beauty's castle and that of Louis XIV is not superficial or unconscious; both had courtyards paved with marble, huge halls of mirrors, menageries of animals, and violin and oboe concerts (97-98). These details were provided to correspond to the social environment of Perrault's intended audience. A brief history of the sleep motif is discussed, including the 57-year sleep of the Greek Epimenides, the 200-year sleep of the Seven Sleepers of Epheus, Surya Bai from Indian mythology, and Brunhilde's sleep in the *Volsunga Saga* (93). The authors also discuss the "censoring, editing and pen" of Perrault himself that is so evident in the collection (93). The violent rape in Basile's tale had to be modified and softened so as not to offend his courtly audience or a group of children. The most amusing modification was the inclusion of the recipe of Sauce Robert in the instructions for the cooking of the two children (113). According to the authors, Perrault "articulated the idea of sleep as a symbol for the passive, introspective period of puberty" (122). Several remarks included in Perrault's version emphasize the value of sleep as a period of learning. These remarks have been disliked and dismissed as extraneous interpolation by subsequent retellers and critics alike (122). The first translation into English was a faithful rendition of Perrault's tale; however, "what happened afterward in England and in the United States is a story of constant change and adaptation, including bowdlerized versions—theater performances and film adaptations at all levels—adult or 'childish' " (113). They remind their readers the most famous adaptation of all time, that of Disney, does not acknowledge Perrault's authorship at all (113).

1981: Eugen Weber explores several aspects in discussing realities expressed in the folktales and two in particular in reference to "Sleeping Beauty": eating meat and the status conferred by clothing styles. "Until the later nineteenth century the typical carnivores lived either in cities or in *chateaux* and palaces. That may be why we have a lot of legends about highborn ladies eating little children" (100). The reference here is to the second segment of Perrault's version of the tale where, with the enhancement of Sauce Robert, the mother-in-law presumes to eat her grandchildren. The Grimms' prince is unaware of the changes in clothing styles as he notices no differences in the garments of the sleeping princess, but Perrault's prince is much more observant; she dresses like his great-grandmother. Bettelheim's dissatisfaction with Perrault's frivolity is cited, but "awareness of chronological time is peculiar to certain types of society, and Perrault (who was a magistrate and a courtesan) must have been well aware that his seventeenth-century readers would not fail to think of the changes time had wrought precisely because they lived in a society that took change for granted, whereas the contemporary peasant population did not" (105). A reference is made to a much later tale, Washington Irving's "Rip Van Winkle," where the changes occurring in time are the entire point of the tale (106).

1981: Ester Zago says that Basile "deemphasized the theme of incest and illicit desire, compared with his possible sources, out of personal reserve and discretion regarding sex that contrasted with his predilection for the scatological" (McGlathery 1993, 75).

1983: Jack Zipes discusses Perrault's method of weaving notions of *civilité* into the fabric of his tales, exemplified by the gifts the infant Sleeping Beauty receives: "beauty, the temper of an angel, grace, the ability to dance perfectly, the voice of a nightingale, and musicality" (1983, 24). It is her *manner* of speech that charms the prince. She is bred to be the ideal aristocratic lady, practicing patience in sleeping for 100 years waiting for rescue, in waiting for two years hidden from her husband's family, and while her children are taken from her by her mother-in-law. The moral "sings a hymn of praise to patience" (1983, 24).

1984: Robert Darnton comments that the oral version of "Sleeping Beauty" has the same nightmare quality as the other French peasant tales as it includes the ravishing of the princess in her unconscious state (14).

1984: Max Lüthi contrasts the Perrault and Grimm versions of "Sleeping Beauty" as part of his exploration of *The Fairytale as Art Form and Portrait of Man*. The Grimms' versions are less-ornamented derivations of Perrault's tale. Four flaw elements play a role in the Grimms' tale. The flaw is an imperfection in the midst of the perfect fairy tale world as is well embedded in the style of European fairy tales (1984, 64). These flaws are:

1. Only 12 golden plates—the king could not invite the 13th fairy; in Perrault's version, the eighth fairy is unknown to the king, it is not a conscious slight.

2. The hostile nature of the 13th fairy.

3. The weakening of the curse from death to a 100-year sleep.

4. The only remaining spindle in the entire kingdom being located in the royal castle (1984, 61).

1985: Jeanne Morgan explores the similarities between Basile's tale and that of Perrault and the allusions in Perrault's tale to his social environment for his listeners. The latter include the details of the splendor of Versailles, the hall of mirrors, the hierarchy of the castle inhabitants, and passages that satirize or describe aspects of court life and language (81). Recognition by the modern reader of these humorous associations depends upon the knowledge of that time and place. "We are still amused by la sauce Robert—not only because of the incongruity between the gruesome dish and the elegant 'queenly' sauce, but because 'Sauce Robert' is still used in modern cooking" (84).

1986: Karen Rowe includes "Sleeping Beauty" in her discussion on classic English folktales of romance that focus on the crucial period of adolescence. This tale, along with "Cinderella," "Snow Drop," "Beauty and the Beast," and "The Frog Prince" dramatize the archetypal female dilemmas and socially acceptable resolutions (212). Marriage is still offered as a woman's *only* option, perpetuating the patriarchal *status quo* (221).

1988: Betsy Hearne analyzes six picture-book versions of Sleeping Beauty in her examination of publishing market shifts and the further reshaping of the Grimms' tales for market considerations. Three are typical of expensive, lavish, single-edition picture-book retellings created by well-known fairy-tale illustrators: Trina Schart Hyman, Warwick Hutton, and Mercer Mayer. The other three are mass market books: *Sleeping Beauty with Benjy and Bubbles*, *How to Wake a Sleeping Beauty*, and *Sleeping Beauty*. Hearne discusses the types of illustrations and the faithfulness of the books to the traditional tales, concluding that "at least three, perhaps four, of the six versions have so altered the basic elements and tone of the tale that the motivation for their publication must have been marketing potential rather than aesthetic or psychological appreciation of the story's value" (233).

1988: Kolbenschlag begins by outlining nine common elements of most Sleeping Beauty versions. These elements create a parable about the onset of puberty and the resulting confrontation with sexuality, introducing the superego as a check to the libido (5). Sleeping Beauty therefore is a symbol of passivity and by extension is a metaphor for the spiritual condition of women. Kolbenschlag draws attention to Wagner's opera *Ring of the Nibelung* as a variant of the "Sleeping Beauty" motif. "Brunhilde, the warrior-maiden, is punished for attempting to aid the hero, Siegmund. Wotan— the patriarch of the gods—casts a spell of "sleep" over his daughter, and surrounds her with a wall of fire until the destined hero penetrates it and awakens her with a kiss" (5).

1988: Jack Zipes states that it is the Grimms' more economical and circumspect version that became frozen into "a bourgeois myth about the proper way that males save . . . comatose women" (1988, 152). Zipes explores the "seemingly innocent" messages that the Disney film conveyed through this film: Women are all naturally curious and this curiosity can be dangerous; men are daring, persistent, and "able to bestow life on passive, or dead women whose lives cannot be fulfilled until rescued by a prince"; women are helpless, almost comatose, without a man; and "male energy and will power can restore anything to life, even an immense realm in a coma. We just need the right man for the job" (1988, 152). He also examines several modern retellings of this tale including poetry by Anne Sexton and Olga Broumas and the early chapter-book parody *Sleeping Ugly* by Jane Yolen.

1989: Thomas examines the symbolism of the prophesy of the frog and the role of the spindle in the Grimms' version of the tale. The frog's birth prophesy lays the foundation for all future actions in the tale, anticipating all the subsequent prophesies and establishing the narrative pattern (139). The symbolism of the spindle is not often appreciated by modern audiences. "While we unfortunately lost this recognition of the Wise Women, the tale's previous audiences had not, and would have doubly appreciated the spindle's presence in this tale, for the spindle or distaff was the typical implement of the Fates, often portrayed as being used by them to 'spin' and measure out the span of one's life, used as the medium by which the tapestry of one's fate was woven" (Thomas, 210). Thomas charts the three principal actions of the tale that each center around a different character: the opening in which the queen is the central character and incorporates the birth prophesy and the actual birth of her daughter; the feast, declared by the king, the revenge and prophesy by the wise women, and the king's proclamation against spindles; and the third and final act where Sleeping Beauty matures and becomes an active agent, thereby initiating the fulfillment of the prophesy. The role of the prince is incidental; his kiss does not awaken the sleeping princess; the predetermined end of the spell does (Thomas, 33).

1990: Jacques Barchilon points to the presence of erotic desire in Basile's likely source, *Perceforest*, in which the Prince Charming figure, Troylus, violates the sleeping Zellandine, his fiancee, at the urging of the goddess Venus, "who speaks with the voice of the lover's own erotic desire" (McGlathery 1993, 75).

1991: McGlathery asserts that "Sleeping Beauty" explores a crisis in the relationship of father and daughter. The father yearns for a daughter and then, when the finally is granted his wish, is loath to let her mature naturally. Because of his banning of spinning in his attempt to best the curse, his daughter is "prevented from indulging in the traditionally concomitant pastime of building romantic castles in the air (cf. German *spinnen* in the sense of 'fantasizing')" (1991, 98). Sitting at the spinning wheel "is associated with building castles in the air and a woman's pricking herself with a spindle, needle, or the like usually occurs, in folktales, in association with dreams about becoming pregnant" (1991, 117). "I commented, too," reports McGlathery on his later summary of his critique of the tale, "on the feelings of the fairies toward the baby daughter in the Grimm and Perrault versions, seeing them as identifying with the girl as an eventual object of erotic desire" (1993, 76).

1991: Nelson explores the symbolism of waiting, which is illustrated by the long period of time until the birth of the child, a sign of the ultimate importance of this child, and the waiting that is repeated by the long sleep. She also examines the role of the father who tries to protect his beloved daughter from "the wound of lost childhood" and the role of the tower. "As a protective holding area for the sleeping princess, it offers the masculine rules of convention and society, of patriarchal values and opinions, of rules and education" (Nelson, 258).

1991: Lutz Rohrich compares the treatment of heroes and heroines by Perrault and the Grimms, stating that Perrault's heroes are realistic and human rather than models of virtue. Perrault's Sleeping Beauty "pricks herself with the spindle because she is thoughtless, flighty and clumsy" (164). Perrault is always rational, demonstrated by his mention of the passing of time when the princess awakens. The Grimms do not calculate the effect of the magical sleep while Perrault's princess has hard skin; the musicians play outdated music; she is wearing an old-fashioned dress; and she is already quite rested for the wedding night (164). Rohrich credits Perrault with creating the psychological folktale, using subtle connections to reality, often bordering on parody, in moving the tale from an unconscious to a conscious level. Sleeping Beauty's first words reveal that she knows that she has slept for a very long time (165). The fairy, too, is important for reality in Perrault's version as she personally touches each person with her magic wand. In the Grimms' tale, the simple prick of the spindle sends everyone to sleep. The fairy is not needed at all (165). "[W]ith such psychological realism and individualism, it is understandable that Walt Disney's folktale films more commonly rely on Perrault's texts for a model than the Grimms" (166).

1992: Jacoby, a Jungian analyst, discusses this tale in regards to a teenage patient suffering from anorexia. The symbolism of the king, queen, bathing, frogs, and fairies from the Grimms' tale are interpreted as well as the repression of sexual maturation of the child, represented by the banning of spindles. Fifteen is the age of sexual maturation, and this awakening can strike as a poison if the young girl is not prepared. The old woman in the tower is interpreted as "a version of the evil fairy who uttered the curse and is now seeing to its realization" (188). The resulting sleeping state is connected to the unawakened state and feelings of loneliness. Jacoby points out the fluctuating meaning of time: "[E]ach person's hundred years can be of a different length, depending on the problem involved and his or her personal rhythm. Attempts at speeding things up run afoul of the briar hedge" (Jacoby, 193). Also, Jacoby reminds the reader that this tale is not dramatic; the heroine is passive and the hero does nothing heroic—he only must be in the right location at the right time. "[T]he prince is only able to redeem her because the time of the evil fairy and her curse is over and a new period is beginning" (194).

1993: Jones includes "Sleeping Beauty" as one of the tales in the sub-genre "Innocent Persecuted Heroines" (along with Rapunzel, Snow White, and Cinderella). These tales share individual episodes such as the heroine being persecuted or threatened in her family home, the abuse of the heroine in her attempt to be married, and the displacement or accelerated abuse after the heroine gives birth to children (17). While Jones demonstrates that "Sleeping Beauty" shares the first two of these episodes, he does not point out that the third episode is also evident in regards to the secondary plot in Perrault's original version.

1993: McGlathery states that the amount of critical commentary on the tale of "Sleeping Beauty" is second only to that of "Little Red Riding Hood" (McGlathery 1993, 72).

1994: Marina Warner compares the various classical versions of the tale, pointing out the resemblance of Perrault's tale to Basile's and both to the fourteenth-century prose romance *Perceforest*.

1996: John Goldthwaite discusses the important precedents of Charles Perrault to the world of fantasy. The third, and most important, is the advent of the fairy godmother. But who is this character? "She did not enter twinkling. The seven fairies summoned . . . [to the Christening] are authorities in the kingdom to whom even the king must defer. They come to sponsor the princess's baptism, and it is their power to bless or to damn her that drives the plot" (52). With the advent of the fairy godmother, the threshold of the church has been crossed, and the seven fairies seem to be a composite of Christian and pagan elements. Their gifts to the princess are the same gifts as traditionally given by the three Graces of Greek mythology and the muses (53). In the later version published by the Brothers Grimm "we can see the tale reverting to such a pagan ancestry. The fairy godmothers have vanished, and in their place appear thirteen "Wise Women" (53). Goldthwaite, after declaring the baptism as a Christian sacrament not to be presided over by pagan deities, introduces an earlier version of this story as presented in the Gospels in Luke 8: 52–55. Luke's maid is 12 years old, Perrault's 15: they have both reached puberty. Neither this maid or Perrault's princess are awakened by a kiss; the famous kiss comes later in the history of the tale.

What Perrault found could easily have been the corruption of a popular miracle story disseminated across Europe by Christians over the intervening years. The Gospels make that same, saving allowance for worldly appetites that pagan and children's lores require. In Perrault the guests awakening in the disenchanted castle "presently began to feel mortally hungry" and are shortly bidding the lovers come down to the feast. In Luke, Jesus "commanded to give her meat" (53).

1996:   Philip Lewis states that of all of the eight tales in Perrault's collection, "Sleeping Beauty" is the only one that seems to conform to the five-stage model of traditional fairy tale as established by folklorist Bengt Holbek. It is also the only tale in the collection with an ending that involves the acceptance of a newlywed by in-laws and an adult role in society. Lewis concentrates on the final episode of Perrault's version, asserting that it is crucial in setting the tone and establishing a context for the collection as a whole (131). "Instead of reverting to the ogre's natural, animalistic inclination to eat raw flesh, the cannibalistic queen mother holds onto the rituals of culture: she places an order for human meat disguised with a pungent sauce, and whether she is fed with meat from domestic animals or with game, she is well satisfied by the cook's fine cuisine" (133). Lewis also points to the fact that the beasts that consume the ogress are not carnivores but earth-crawling reptilian creatures. This opening tale, then, offers an interpretative enigma that centers on the mother-in-law ogress, her relation to food prepared for humans, and her transformation into food for lowly beasts (133). Lewis also considers the repetition between the story segments. The beautiful young queen is threatened with death once again. Rather than sleeping for 100 years, she goes into hiding, is foiled by a renewal of the death threat, and is saved just in time, again by her husband (150).

1997:   Margery Hourihan maintains that the heroine in this tale is not a character at all but a symbol: a trophy bride. As such, she represents the subordination of women: "[T]hough both royal and beautiful they exist only in order to be bestowed upon the hero"

(52). Hourihan states that this model has influenced women's perceptions of themselves and their appearances, attitudes, and behaviors. "It has also helped create a lingering belief that it is natural for women to be submissive and self-denying, sacrificing their interests to the needs of the men in their lives" (193). The slenderness of these beauties is an indication of their extreme youth and the actual age that women were once married. Sleeping Beauty is 15 or 16 in Perrault's version and 15 in the Grimms' tale (195). She is also the perfect example of female passivity. Life does not exist for her until her prince arrives. "Her relationships with her parents and everyone else who has surrounded her in her childhood, her interests, her very awareness of being—all are suspended until his coming" (197). She gives herself freely to the prince when he first appears and does so without hesitation. Hourihan's response to the "rape scene" in Basile is caustic. "The dressing up of the extremes of masculine dominance and female passivity as something glamorous and romantic has made 'Sleeping Beauty' one of the most important of all fairy tales; clearly it appeals to some widely held fantasies" (200). But whose?

1998:   Francine Prose revisits this tale from an adult feminist perspective. She considers the deceptive layers under this seemingly simple and romantic tale. Do men really prefer their women to be asleep rather than active partners in their lives? Prose looks first at contemporary fiction depicting this image to modern generations of women and men: Edgar Allan Poe ("Annabel Lee"), E. T. A. Hoffman ("The Sandman"), Heinrich von Kliest ("The Marquise of O"), Tommaso Landolfi ("Gogol's Wife"), Thomas Hardy (*Tess of the D'Urbervilles*), Felisberto Hernandez ("The Daisy Dolls"), Yasunari Kawabata (*The House of Sleeping Beauties*), and Alfred Hitchcock (the movie *Vertigo*). Prose then returns to Charles Perrault's tale asking if one moral of his tale is "that the long sleep of girlhood is a brief, welcome interval of peace between the battles (with other women!) that deform childhood and adult life?" (293). To answer this question, Prose reaches further back in time to Basile's story of Talia and her twins, which were begotten while she lay unconscious. "The insensate, slumbering woman is not only the ideal lover and mate, but also—as it turns out—the perfect mother" (294).

Reworkings of Sleeping Beauty in Novel Form

The story of "Sleeping Beauty" has attracted the interest of several powerful authors. In a way, this is rather ironic because the tale features one of the most passive of princesses in the fairy-tale world. Geras retells the traditional tale in her novel, updating specific aspects of it for the story to operate in our contemporary world. In Margaret Mahy's novel, the tale is used as a guide and an allegory, while both Sheri Tepper and Jane Yolen embrace the tale to provide a commentary on both the negative and positive aspects of our contemporary Western society. Robert Coover has his "Sleeping Beauty" (and the prince) explore the demands romance places on our lives.

The Changeover: A Supernatural Romance

1984: Mahy, Margaret. **The Changeover: A Supernatural Romance**. London: Magnet.

Mahy uses the framework of the "Sleeping Beauty" story to present her own powerful tale. In this contemporary tale Laura, her young brother Jacko, and her mother are in flux. Laura is warned about approaching danger but does not know either the nature of the threat or how to avoid it. There is a new man in the mother's life and a new "interest" in Laura's. But for Laura, this flux is more than a natural progression of things; it is supernatural. When Jacko is threatened, Laura must undergo a metamorphosis from her human self into a witch in order to save him. The Sleeping Beauty pattern is offered to Laura as a mystical marriage, "uniting her two halves in an androgynous whole" as well as an initiation ritual (Gose, 8).

> The changeover begins with the pricking of her finger. Do you suppose the Sleeping Beauty had a moment to suck her finger after she pricked it? And what dreams did she have because of it? She'd never pricked her finger before, so perhaps that was the first time she'd tasted her own blood. As for you, you must travel back into yourself, Laura (Mahy, 137).

The Carlisle women who are aiding this change help Laura marry herself to some sleeping aspect of herself in order to wake it (139). Sorry Carlisle, himself a witch, is her guide to her past memories. When he asks for a kiss, not part of the ritual but an aspect he thought would be nice, Laura replies that she will only kiss him because she wants to and not for any other reason. Sorry easily accepts that—and the kiss before she goes through the gate into a "forest that was all forests, the forest at the heart of fairy tales, the looking-glass forest where names disappeared, the forests of the night . . . and Laura's own forest, the forest without trees, the subdivision, the city" (144).

> She saw dwarfs, lost princes, beautiful girls who had committed themselves to silence in order to save brothers turned into swans or ravens, young men who thrived on sunshine and dwindled with darkness, mutilated maidens who wept over their own silver arms, and then simpler people, three bears, the girl in the red cloak, the lost children who found their way home, the lost children who didn't and were covered with leaves by the robins. Once the road divided, but the true path was always marked by her own drop of blood and she followed it faithfully. . . . Briars crept over the road and she pushed through them, scratching herself so that she dripped blood once more. . . . The briars thickened and Laura at last drew the sword and began to cut her way through them, but though this lessened her troubles in one way, it increased them in another (145–46).

Once Laura has successfully gained her powers, she sets out with Sorry to rescue Jacko from the spell that has been draining the life out of the little boy.

Betsy Hearne declares that "far from being sexist, the fairy tale here becomes a paradigm for a woman's inner voyage" (1989, 142). Adam Berkin states that Mahy "encourages the reader to question the use and meaning of the mythic images of 'Sleeping Beauty' through her dialogue, and she poses alternatives through her symbolism" (245). Sleep is only important in this novel because it heralds awakening. Highly recommended!

Watching the Roses

1991: Geras, Adèle. **Watching the Roses**. New York: HarperCollins.

The second book in the Egerton Hall School series concerns the tale of Alice who, after being raped at her 18th birthday party, stops speaking to people and retreats into herself and her own limited world. Her only communication is with her journal, which is interspersed with botanical notes and drawings about roses. These flowers have assumed great importance for Alice, who has always been surrounded by them as her father is an expert on roses.

The journal entries offer much material about Alice's family and her many and varied aunts. At her christening all of the aunts but one gave her wonderful gifts. "[A]ll the real presents symbolized the gift that each aunt wanted to pass on to me. . . . Aunt May wanted me to have intelligence, so she gave me a book . . ." (84). The "odd" aunt, Violette, gave Alice an ill-wishing. "That's what I wish for Alice: never to grow old. Just one last, magnificent final fling and then out like a candle. At 18, perhaps? Yes, like a candle. Extinguished" (92). This ill wish was accompanied by a jet mourning broach. Aunt Marguerite, having arrived late and missed the gift-giving to this point, amended her gift to soften Violette's one. She wishes the child a long life. "There may be an accident or an illness, or something of that kind, but Alice will live to a ripe old age" (94).

Through the therapy provided by writing in her journal and the quiet persistence and care of her boyfriend Jean-Luc and friends Megan (Rapunzel) and Bella (Snow White), the sleeping spell is broken. "He thinks I am someone worth climbing gates and creeping through windows for, someone for whom he is prepared to tear roses from the sills, someone worth searching for. He kissed me then" (137). The novel is suggested for grades 8–12 but will appeal to young teens.

Beauty

1991: Tepper, Sheri. S. **Beauty**. New York: Bantam.

This multilayered time travel fantasy novel begins in the Middle Ages with the birth of the daughter of the Duke of Westfaire. She receives numerous pleasant gifts at her christening, but no one gave her the gift of intelligence as that grace is not highly valued in the world of Faery. The first section of the book is a reworking of the "Sleeping Beauty" story. The uninvited aunt utters a curse, and the father of the child hides all the spindles, but one is found by his daughter from another liaison who was born the same day as Beauty. The curse had been modified by stating:

"When Duke Phillip's beautiful daughter reaches her 16th year, she shall prick her finger . . . ," but as Carabosse, the keeper of the secrets of time explains, "the bit about the 100 years and the prince is pure invention. I never said the child would die" (32). And of course, it is not Beauty who falls into the deep sleep but her half sister, Beloved. Beauty, who has Faery blood in her veins from her mother, is protected from the sleeping curse and leaves the castle. She takes her mother's box, the cloak of invisibility, and seven-league boots that she has made with the contents. She immediately meets a group of people from the future who are documenting the "vanishment of magic from England and from the world." Beauty is transported back with them to the twenty-first century, where she is appalled by the ugliness and lack of magic. Soon, with several members of the documentary crew, Beauty steals aboard a time machine and travels back to July 1991.

Beauty's story continues in the United States between 1991 and 1993. Beauty comments on the number of homeless as refugees from the bleak future. "It was odd that the authorities of the 1980s never caught on to the fact that the homeless sprouted rather suddenly. [Time travel was perfected in 2080 with a hundred year limit.] . . . many of them with limited communication skills, covering up by pretending to be crazy" (94). Beauty is then transported back into the Middle Ages, arriving three years after she had originally left and pregnant as the result of a rape in the twentieth century. The hedge of roses around her home is now 60 to 80 feet high. It is the time of the Black Death, and there is much destruction and havoc. She seduces and marries Ned, the son of the householder where she resides, to gain a father for her child. The child is born and enjoyed until it reminds Beauty too much of its birth father. Beauty leaves to find a way to the land of Faery to find her mother. Here she discovers that she is to be used as a teind to Hell and aids the mortal Janet in saving her Faery lover, Tam Lin.

Traveling between the land of Faery, the Middle Ages, and the 1990s costs Beauty because time passes differently in each "time zone." She ages rapidly. Back in the Middle Ages as a mature woman, she meets her daughter Elly and her daughter's stepmother and stepsisters. "Knowing that Elly was at the root of a fairy tale made me have some hope for her future, at least" (261). Beauty acts as Elly's fairy godmother and marries her off to Prince Charme (Charming as it is said in the twentieth century!) Elly becomes pregnant but does not want a child as pretty as she is. This baby will have her mother's dark hair and her father's pale skin and red lips. Beauty is worried, for Elly has a great deal of her father in her, and he was not known for his kindness and understanding. However, when the baby is born, Elly dies. The child is named after a spring flower that blooms through the snow. Fifty years pass before Beauty, now 86, comes back to the Middle Ages; seventy years since the curse activated. It is now the time of witch burnings and the spread of Christianity in the vernacular. Elly's husband is married to Irene, a witch who has made a pact with the Dark Lord. Her beauty will only be hers as long as there is no one else in the kingdom as beautiful as she, so she causes Beauty's beautiful granddaughter Galantha (Snowdrop) to vanish. "Hadn't one fairy tale been enough? Of course, that bit with the mirror had been a dead giveaway. . . . Irene tried but couldn't kill Snowdrop. . . . Snowdrop is one-eighth fairy, after all. Witches can't be allowed to go around killing off fairies, even part ones" (348). Beauty eventually finds her granddaughter. "She was dressed very simply, in a full white shift with puffy sleeves and a kind of laced bodice over it. Disney got that part right" (353). She and the dwarfs (who are Basques in this book) attempt to break the spell. "In the story it was a prince's kiss, wasn't it? Or was that only my story? Or was it Disney? I simply couldn't remember" (356). When Snowdrop coughs up the piece of apple, Beauty discovers that her granddaughter takes after Prince Charming, who was never long in the brains department! Snowdrop is soon pregnant and has a son. Beauty leaves the baby her inheritance and returns to the land of Faery and her battle with the Dark Lord. She is treacherously used as the teind, which breaks the covenant between the Dark Lord and Faery, and is sent to Hell. However, she manages to escape and returns to the Middle Ages, extremely old. Unable to sew a Cap of Wisdom because of her feebleness, she drops the last hank of magic thread into the well and sobs in frustration. A bewitched frog retrieves it and tells Beauty his story: While looking for his missing foster father he chanced upon an old fairy insisting that the maiden Rapunzel let down her hair from a tall tower. He was immediately transformed into a frog and will remain in his frog state until he is kissed by a princess. Beauty recognizes him as her great grandson and realizes that she is now 116 years old. The 100 years' enchantment is at an end. She kisses the frog and tells him to go to Westfaire where he will kiss the beautiful princess who is sleeping and waiting for him.

> No matter what Joyeause said about a hundred years, this spell was laid forever . . . all will sleep until the conditions of this enchantment are fulfilled and someone or something wondrous arrives to kiss beauty awake once more. Not a prince. Or not merely a prince. More than a prince. A rebirth of some kind. And not soon. And beauty sleeps! (462).

This novel is a serious commentary on today's society and our rush towards a future that may be as bleak as that portrayed in the novel. Tepper looks at our "affinity" for horror, our numbing toward horrific news and events, and loss of innocence and beauty in this involved and sometimes funny novel that, at the same time, explores romance, love, and magic.

> Most things done in Faery have no meaning in the world. However ... words written here are really written. When I go out of this place, they will come with me into the other world. Promises made here are transferable. Songs sung here can be sung out there. Meaning is meaning, whether in the world or in Faery. Only our outward seeming does not go from one place to the other (378).

Briar Rose

1992: Yolen, Jane. **Briar Rose**. New York: TOR. (Fairy Tale Series).

Named by the American Library Association as a "Best Book for Young Adults" and nominated for the Nebula Award, Jane Yolen's reworking of "Sleeping Beauty" is a powerful examination of a Holocaust survivor. Jack Zipes stated that Jane Yolen's *Briar Rose* is by far the most experimental of the series of fairy-tale novels edited by Terri Windling.

> It moves through memory, flashbacks, and a retelling of "Sleeping Beauty" from the present to the horrors of the Holocaust. In her haunting narrative that reads somewhat like a mystery novel, Yolen demonstrates that fairy tales can be used to address the most atrocious crimes of the Nazi period in a manner that generates hope in readers who, Yolen believes, must come to terms with Auschwitz and its consequences (1994, 152).

Gemma, grandmother to three sisters, tells them stories, but the most requested tale of the youngest, Rebecca, is that of "Sleeping Beauty." This contemporary novel begins with the three girls, already grown, visiting Gemma in the nursing home. She keeps trying to tell them the story again and again, but only Becca is willing to listen. It is through the telling of this story and the memories that are brought forth that Gemma passes on her personal story to the next generation, and Rebecca discovers her own self as well. The fairy tale is separated from the rest of the story by italics, and the girls (and the reader) are fed only tantalizing pieces of the story bit by bit. In the midst of these pieces, slivers of the past are found. "Not the bad fairy. Not the one in black with big black boots and silver eagles on her hat" (Yolen, 22). When Gemma dies, Becca, a journalist, goes on a journey through the past and to Europe to find the beginning of Gemma's story and the castle that is part of Gemma's dying wish. Part 2 of the book is Gemma's early story told by an old acquaintance in Poland.

> How does one become a man of honor (he asked); how does one redeem a life? Think of Oskar Schindler. He was a gambler, a womanizer, a drunk, a profiteer, a Nazi. His life was spelled out in one dishonor after another. Yet he saved 1,200 people. The Jews he saved said, "Among the unjust, we do not forget the just" (165).

Gemma was found, after being thrown in a pit of corpses, by several members of the Underground. She is barely alive; in fact, she dies in their arms and it is only through their perseverance that she breathes on her own once again. She has no memory other than one of a fairy tale: "I do not know its name. But in it I am a princess in a castle and a great mist comes over us. Only I am kissed awake. . . . I only remember the fairy tale and it seems, somehow that it is my story as well" (177). Gemma joins the group, falls in love, and is married only to scarcely miss being slaughtered once again. Once Gemma and her unborn child escape to America, her own story recedes until again only the fairy tale is remembered. "I honestly don't think she remembered. Not you, not my grandfather, not any of it consciously. It had *all* become a fairy tale for her. She must have told us the story of Briar Rose a million times. But it was all there, buried" (194).

This is a difficult book to summarize, as the myriad of layers and stories are interwoven so well that the individual threads are often too complicated to unravel, particularly for the mere satisfaction of analysis. This is a novel that never fails to run chills up my spine while I marvel at the intricate pattern established. It also makes an interesting companion to an earlier reworking of another fairy tale referring to the Holocaust (see the entry on *Kindergarten* in the "Hansel and Gretel" chapter).

Recommended for grades 6 and up.

Briar Rose

1996: Coover, Robert. **Briar Rose**. New York: Grove Press.

> The good fairy's boon to this child, newborn, was to ar-
> range for her to expire before suffering the misery of the
> ever-after part of the human span, the wicked fairy in her,
> for the sake of her own entertainment, transforming that
> well-meant gift to death in life and life in death without
> surcease (80).

Robert Coover loosely bases his poetic novel on Basile's version of
this tale. The story is told again and again by the different voices of the
sleeping princess, the prince in the thorns, and the good/bad fairy who
orchestrates the entire event. This allegorical parody focuses on the demands that romance places on our lives: the role love plays in our dreams
and desires. Impossible to paraphrase, Coover's novel is ultimately readable but may not be accessible for younger readers.

Short Stories

This tale is also extremely popular with writers of short stories.
Tanith Lee turns to the tale to explore two very different aspects, while
Jane Yolen, who wove the tale into her discussion of the Holocaust,
played with the story in a much different frame of mind. (Jane Yolen's
attraction to this story is further evidenced by the early chapter book parody discussed in the picture-book section below.) Time, sleep, dreams,
and a variety of points of view offered ironically, sardonically, and
romantically grace the reworkings of "Sleeping Beauty" in short-story
form.

1975: Travers, P. L. "**The Sleeping Beauty**." In *About the Sleeping
Beauty*. New York: McGraw-Hill, 3–45.

This retelling of the story is set in the Middle East. Travers has
amended all aspects of the traditional tale to reflect the mores and values
of that culture. She has added a great deal of description along with
authorial comment and asides for the reader, but essentially the story is
the same as the abridged Perrault tale.

1983: Lee, Tanith. "**Thorns.**" In *Red as Blood (or Tales from the Sisters Grimmer)*. New York: DAW, 29–38.

An 18-year-old prince in exile, and in disguise, meets an old woman on his travels. She warns him of traveling in a certain direction, but that just makes him curious, so he continues on towards the ruined city. He breaks his stay in a strange village—strange because it does not have any sharp implements or tools or any spinning wheels or spun goods. When he attempts to cut through the wall of thorns surrounding the ruined castle, he is stopped by an old man. This man was born at the exact hour that the curse took hold and knows that the spell will last a few more hours yet. The prince listens to the old man and when he is given the signal, easily enters the castle to find everything transfixed in time. He applies the "kiss of life" on the sleeping girl and resuscitates her and everyone else in the castle. However, he cannot stay because the passage of time, the 100 years, stands between them. The old woman, the 13th Lady, has the last laugh.

1985: Swift, Carolyn. "**The Sleeping Beauty Wakes Up to the Facts of Life.**" In *Rapunzel's Revenge: Fairytales for Feminists*. Dublin: Attic Press, 42–46.

This sleeping beauty wears the same name as the cinematic beauty in Disney's film and the dancing beauty of the ballet: Aurora. She is filled with discontent for her husband and her idle way of life as a princess. She hopes that her fairy godmothers do not waste their gifts on her unborn child as they did with her. "They'd do a whole lot better to give her strength and dexterity and a good head for figures" (46).

1985: Yolen, Jane. "**The Thirteenth Fey.**" In *Faery!* edited by Terri Windling. New York: Ace Fantasy, 13–24.

This work is narrated in first person by the 13th child in the fairy family, who relates the background of her family, their binding to the locality through the royal family, the negative characteristics of the barren queen and the greedy king, and the birth of the child from the prophesy of the frog through the celebration of the birth of Talia. The king insists all fey folk attend the christening and bring a gift, but the narrator is ill that fateful day and is left behind. When she awakens she decides to follow them and, in her feverish state, takes with her the only gift she can find: "an old linden spindle, knotted about with the thread of long life, in the family trunk" (15). In presenting the spindle to the child, she stumbles and the thread breaks, leaving a very short piece. Her gift now represents an early death, at age 15, rather than a long life. The thread is quickly knotted again and the 'gift' is adjusted by the narrator's mother:

At age 15 Talia shall fall into a deep sleep until the knot is unraveled. Time quickly passes, and all is well until Talia's 15th birthday party, a "Sleep-Over Ball." As is expected, the spell comes to pass. The narrator, who has studied Logic, activates a plan to unravel the knot by creating a similar knot around the palace and readjusting the length of time for this to come to pass. She has some knowledge of the future, and it is quite likely that before the 100 years are over, democracy will arise and this royal family will no longer have the power to hold the fey folk to the land. "Sometimes freedom is won by long patience, something that works far better than any magical spell" (24). Yolen is obviously well acquainted with the folkloric history of the tale and demonstrates this knowledge with her tongue-in-cheek tale told from a different point of view. Jack Zipes proclaimed Yolen's tale "an amusing parody of the decadent monarchy" (1994, 156).

1991: Lafferty, R.A. "The Story of Little Briar Rose, A Scholarly Study." In *The Year's Best Fantasy and Horror*, 4th Annual Collection, edited by Ellen Datlow and Terri Windling. New York: St. Martin's Press, 463–68.

A parody of the serious rhetoric of folklorists, the narrative caricatures an oral presentation of an academic paper that "traces" the historical development of "Sleeping Beauty." A trio of excerpts from this offering demonstrate the language and tone Lafferty affected. "Using the technique of diffusion and parallelism, the tireless Brothers Grimm, sometimes employing as many as one hundred oral versions of a story from all Europe and the Near East, were able to reconstruct and to date approximately (or so they believed) the original stories" (466). "In the Perrault version there are eight fairies (seven good ones and one bad one). In the Grimm version there are no fairies at all. The two brothers, the crown princes of the fairy-tale industry, seldom used fairies. Instead of fairies, there were 13 wise women, 12 good ones and one bad one" (466). "Little Briar Rose was an incomparably intricate and spacious and wise person. Since she had no speaking parts in any of the versions of her own story, it is something of a mystery how we know that she was so intricate and wise and spacious, but it's always been known about her" (467).

1992: Brooke, William J. "A Fate in the Door." In *Untold Tales*. New York: HarperCollins, 101–22.

A brash young (well, if you are 146 years old, almost anyone would be considered young) man visits a widow in her cottage, insisting that he must kiss her awake. But she is already awake, having been married and widowed since the spell ended. The prince is distraught. The woman is his last chance. Twenty-five years ago, on his way to kiss her awake, he had been distracted by a young girl in a glass coffin. The prince thought it would be a good place to practice his kissing. "How was I supposed to know she'd wake up and all the birds and animals and everything would come pouring out, congratulating us and making plans for the wedding?" (108). Eventually, Snow White's "proper" prince arrives (he had been distracted by a girl in a high tower) and this marriage ended, so the first prince decided to continue on his former quest. The woman decides to let him kiss her and immediately falls asleep! "I have almost no house-cleaning skills, but I do have a terrific sense of humor" (121).

1994: Downer, Ann. **"Somnus's Fair Maid."** In *Black Thorn, White Rose*, edited by Ellen Datlow and Terri Windling. New York: William Morrow, 58–85.

Downer's story begins with the unexpected arrival of Great-Aunt Olympia Winceley to the christening of Persephone Aurora Pemberly. Her gift to the child is the pronouncement that when the child is six, she would reside with her great-aunt. This comes to pass through the unfortunate death of her mother and father. She lives in isolation and solitude for 10 years until she is dressed and put on display to be married to an elderly gentleman. Meanwhile, the young swains of the area are bemused by her beauty and seek her out. One young "prince" is enchanted by her but, alas, has not the finances to make an offer. Blackmail, intrigue, and regency romance feature in this gentle tale where sleeping sickness can indeed be cured by a kiss. Will appeal to female rather than male adolescents.

1994: Le Guin, Ursula K. **"The Poacher."** In *The Year's Best Fantasy and Horror, 7th Annual Collection*, edited by Ellen Datlow and Terri Windling. New York: St. Martin's Press, 1–11. (First published in *Xanadu*, edited by Jane Yolen. New York: TOR, 1993.)

This story is narrated in first person by a poor and abused peasant adolescent who, living at the edge of the wood, is drawn by the thorn hedge and what it protects. He needs to discover the interior and spends several years breaking a path. "As the first year came round, I had hacked and sawn and chopped a passage about my height and twice my length into the hedge" (5). He eventually penetrates the hedge and explores the castle and the luxuries that were part of it. Inviting the reader into his thoughts, the young poacher explains his lack of fear and his reasons for staying in the sleepy enclosure. Food appears and he eats it; he satisfies other appetites with a young lover, who fell asleep disheveled and satiated with her own lover; but eventually he becomes lonely. He discovers the princess's collection of fairy tales that are kept in the tower room along with the sleeping princess herself. During the many long years that he resides in the castle grounds, he does not look at her, knowing full well that it is not in his power to wake her. "When the prince comes riding, and strikes his way clear through the hedge of thorns—my two years' toil—with one blow of his privileged, bright sword, when he strides up the winding stair to the tower room, when he stoops to kiss her, and the spindle falls from her hand, and the drop of blood wells like a tiny ruby on the white skin, when she opens her eyes slowly and yawns, she will look up at him" (11). But by that time, the elderly poacher will be dead! Le Guin's character is credible and, if not exactly admirable, understandable and memorable.

1994: Wrede, Patricia. "**Stronger Than Time.**" In *Black Thorn, White Rose*, edited by Ellen Datlow and Terri Windling. New York: William Morrow, 30–57. Also in Patricia C. Wrede's *Book of Enchantments*. San Diego, CA: Harcourt Brace, 153–83.

The old woodcutter has lived in the shadow of the keep and the thick thorns and bleached bones surrounding it for many years until the young prince comes to him for help. He needs to hear the story of the keep and its curse; the woodcutter is the only one left who will tell it. But it is the prince who tells the story of the witch, her curse, and its alteration by the girl's mother. The witch's death spell is turned "outward, protecting the girl for one hundred years by killing anyone who sought to enter her resting place" (38). Unfortunately, the mother was too specific in the wording, and she named a precise date and particular man, who, impatient, came a day too soon and died in the attempt. The spell must be broken by other means, and the young man hopes the woodcutter will help him. Appealing characters, a strong sense of place, and skillful use of foreshadowing enrich this tale of supernatural romance and destiny.

1995: Garner, James Finn. "**Sleeping Persun of Better-Than-Average Attractiveness.**" In *Once Upon a More Enlightened Time: More Politically Correct Bedtime Stories*. New York: Macmillan, 65–75.

When the "magick" person is snubbed in this parody of the tale, she curses: "May you grow up thinking you can't be complete without a man, put unrealistic hopes of perfect and total happiness on your marriage, and become a bored, dissatisfied and unfulfilled housewife!" (68). This curse is modified to incorporate a 100-year sleep, for perhaps by that time, "men will be more evolved and your pain in finding a progressive, affirming lifemate will not be so great" (69). But does this come to pass?

1995: Koja, Kathe. **"Waking the Prince."** In *Ruby Slippers, Golden Tears*, edited by Ellen Datlow and Terri Windling. New York: William Morrow, 272–84.

Koja "mirrors historical and contemporary perspectives adding a nod to changing gender roles and a dollop of sexual politics" (272). This story is actually two intertwined but separate stories of two young men. One is the sleeping prince and the devastation his sleep causes his father, the king; his mother, the now-demented queen; and the kingdom itself as the royal home is moved elsewhere and the prince is left alone, still sleeping, in his chamber. The second story is told through the contemporary eyes of Cissy about her new "perfect" boyfriend who is not reliable about keeping promises or ever remembering them . . . almost in a dreamlike state. Koja uses the image of the sleeping beauty and the curse in her exploration of relationships.

1995: Kress, Nancy. **"Summer Wind."** In *Ruby Slippers, Golden Tears*, edited by Ellen Datlow and Terri Windling. New York: William Morrow, 54–67.

The editors state that "generally, the 'sleeping beauty' is powerless, and the story is told from the point of view of the young, ambitious prince. In Kress's version, beauty is not utterly passive and the reader is taken into the world inside those briars to experience the price one pays for wisdom and power" (55). The medieval castle and its inhabitants slumber peacefully behind the destructive thorn hedge. All the inhabitants but one, that is. Young Beauty is awake and aware of her situation and the painful demise of her numerous unsuccessful suitors. She is also aware of the passing of time and of the aging process. In her attempts to regain and maintain her sanity through the many years, she sews magnificent clothing for the other inhabitants and dresses them in the finery that causes no end of bewilderment when a prince actually does successfully break through the hedge. She leaves it all behind, however, to join the other seven elderly women who are waiting for her. Kress's character is appealing in this tale of loneliness and pain.

1995: Lee, Tanith. **"She Sleeps in a Tower."** In *The Armless Maiden and Other Tales for Childhood's Survivors*, edited by Terry Windling. New York: TOR, 42–45.

A dark reworking of the tale, drawing on the rape scene in Basile's version, this story is told by a childhood survivor of abuse and incest. She now has three young daughters who earn their living by catering to the general fantasy of the men in the area: awakening the "sleeping beauty" in the tower.

1995: Oates, Joyce Carol. "**The Crossing**." In *Ruby Slippers, Golden Tears*, edited by Ellen Datlow and Terri Windling. New York: William Morrow, 72–96.

Martha has been in an accident, and her husband Roger sits at her hospital bedside throughout her long, deathlike sleep. Readers are invited into his thoughts, pain, and love for his wife at the same time as they are introduced into Martha's experiences visiting an old aunt. Subconsciously aware of the confining hospital, Martha revisits the home haunts of her youth, slipping further and further away from reality (and life) as she realizes that "time keeps its own hours" (82). Her one salvation is her "flirtation" with the red-headed train engineer who waves at her each morning at the railroad crossing. On the day she realizes the horror behind the sleepy little town, she hitches a ride with her engineer and, at the same time, stops breathing in the hospital bed. A chilling tale that uses some of the motifs from the traditional tale to evoke two distinct and brilliant settings.

1997: Blumlein, Michael. "**Snow in Dirt**." In *Black Swan, White Raven*, edited by Ellen Datlow and Terri Windling. New York: Avon, 20–55.

A beautiful woman is found buried and in a comalike state. She is eventually returned back to the earth where she was found once she awakens, becomes a famous model, and ingests experimental rejuvenation drugs when she becomes desperate to regain her beauty. This tale is more a borrowing of several of the motifs of "Sleeping Beauty" than an actual reworking of the tale.

1997: Donoghue, Emma. "**The Tale of the Needle**." In *Kissing the Witch: Old Tales in New Skins*. New York: HarperCollins, 167–82.

The narrator explains one of her childhood games: when she snapped her fingers, all the servants in her father's castle would immediately freeze in place until she snapped her fingers once more. It was a game she particularly enjoyed! She was cherished, and her every wish was a command and she was contented . . . or perhaps it was "more like sleep than joy" (170). This sleepy environment was surrounded by a bramble hedge. But as she ventured into adolescence, she became weary of the cocoon she was wrapped in by her parents and decided to explore the only part of her world she had never seen: the tower. In it she meets an old woman seated at a spinning wheel . . . and her life changes forever. Using most of the elements of the traditional tale, Donoghue writes an engaging rendition of this sheltered princess.

1997: Fowler, Karen Joy. "**The Black Fairy's Curse**." In *Black Swan, White Raven*, edited by Ellen Datlow and Terri Windling. New York: Avon, 14–19.

This story is presented as a series of dreams and uses elements from other familiar tales. The girl's abrupt awakening bothers her for two reasons. She is angry because it disturbs her lovely dream, and she is upset as to the manner of awakening: A stranger covered in scratches and blood kisses her.

1997: Westgard, Sten. "**The Dog Rose**." In *Black Swan, White Raven*, edited by Ellen Datlow and Terri Windling. New York: Avon, 179–97.

Edward is a young gardener who hears a story from a traveling merchant about Thorn Castle and the rumors of the roses that are to about to bloom. Although his father disregards the rumors, Edward is reminded of the stories his grandfather used to tell. "If the roses are in bloom . . . they'll part for the right man" (184). Edward's father tells him that it is the job for a prince, not a gardener, and derides his ambition to set out for the castle. Eventually, Edward cannot resist. But is it not for the sake of Beauty that he makes the journey; it is for the serving girl Cleome, the girl his grandfather was to marry before the Sleep. Edward gets caught in the thorns, but fortunately a prince travels through shortly after and Edward does not share the fate of all the others who attempted to get through the hedge. He manages to secure the job of a gardener . . . and the interest of the newly awakened serving maid.

Feature Films

1959: **Walt Disney's Sleeping Beauty**. Directed by Clyde Geronimi. Walt Disney Productions; distributed by Buena Vista Pictures. 75 minutes.

The 16th animated feature from the Walt Disney Studios cost approximately six million dollars to produce. In 1959 this was the highest cost ever for an animated film, and unheard of. It also took about six years to make. Never shy to adapt other people's efforts, the Disney Studio based the storyline on Perrault's version and the musical score on that of Tchaikovsky. The music was nominated for the 1959 Academy Award for Best Score for a Musical Picture. Although the video is marketed as a classic, the initial reaction from the moviegoing public was not very encouraging. It is not a children's story, an action film, or a comedy. It is simply an animated romance. Regardless, both Disneyland and Disneyland Paris (EuroDisney) include Sleeping Beauty's Castle.

The castle in California was originally going to be Snow White's abode, but because of the imminent release of the *Sleeping Beauty* film, Walt Disney felt it would be great publicity for the movie as the castle of the sleeping princess. The movie has undergone a massive transformation in popularity with the advent of videos. It was one of the first Disney movies offered for sale in 1986 when the VCR population was beginning to blossom. It sold more than one million copies in the two years that it was offered for sale. It had been more than a decade since the film was shown in theaters when the Disney Studio's marketing team released the Special Limited Edition Video in August 1997 for six months, after which it went "back to sleep."

The film version freely adapted Perrault's tale and Tchaikovsky's ballet. For example, the princess Aurora is raised by the three good-hearted and bumbling fairies Flora, Fauna, and Merryweather. The Prince, who actually has a name (Philip), battles the evil witch, Maleficent, and destroys her in her dragon-shape before he awakens the princess with a kiss. The artists were to create "a moving illustration" in which each frame of the film could exist independently as a picture. According to the website selling animated cells of the Disney film (http://www.ara-animation.com/Sleeping.htm), Disney enlisted the talents of studio background artist and color stylist Eyvind Earle to enhance the film's illustrated look. Earle did this by fusing Gothic French, Italian, and Renaissance influences with his own style of realism to create the formalized beauty and angular characters of the film. They also mention that the wicked witch (fairy) Maleficent is the character who leaves the greatest impression. "Like the evil Queen in *Snow White and the Seven Dwarfs*, Ursula in the *Little Mermaid* and Jafar in *Aladdin*, Maleficent transforms into something even more frightening than her wicked self: the dragon" (http://www.ara-animation.com/Sleeping.htm).

Ballet

Perrault's French tale of "Sleeping Beauty" also transcended cultural borders to be set as a Russian ballet by Tchaikovsky (op. 66) and choreographed by Pepita. Since its first performance in St. Petersburg in 1890, it has been one of the most popular ballets in the classical canon. Prima ballet Evelyn Hart, who danced as Aurora for the Royal Winnipeg Ballet production in 1997, stated "It's just the *Star Wars* of the 1800s. *The Sleeping Beauty* was made for spectacle—a good reason for lots of dancing and lots of jewels" (Anthony, C1).

The ballet begins with the christening scene where little Princess Aurora receives her graces from her six fairy godmothers. But before the Lilac Fairy is able to give her gift, the evil fairy Carabosse enters the room and curses the child to die on her 16th birthday. The Lilac Fairy alters the curse from death to sleep for 100 years and the breaking of the curse by a kiss from a handsome prince. This action is set in the prologue of the ballet; the three subsequent acts highlight the following scenes from the "Sleeping Beauty" story.

Act One: At Aurora's 16th birthday celebration, Aurora is presented to four princes interested in marrying her. They all present her with roses. Carabosse, disguised as an old woman, also attends the celebration and presents Aurora with a bouquet of flowers. Unfortunately for the diligent father who has protected his daughter faithfully from any sharp objects, there is a spindle hidden in these flowers. Naturally Aurora collapses, but the Lilac Fairy reassures the court (and the audience) that it is but a sleeping spell. The Lilac Fairy bespells the entire court once Aurora is made comfortable. A thick forest grows around the palace.

Act Two: It is now 100 years later. Prince Florimund is visited by the Lilac Fairy, who tells him of the enchanted palace and sleeping princess. She guides him through the forest. He discovers the princess and immediately kisses her, and the spell is destroyed. Carabosse is also destroyed, overpowered by virtue and goodness. The entire court awakens, and everyone welcomes the engaged couple.

Act Three: The wedding ceremony is completed with a large group of fairy-tale characters who dance in homage to the newlywed couple. These characters include Tom Thumb, Puss 'n Boots, the White Cat, the Bluebird, Red Riding Hood, and the Wolf.

Poetry

Wolfgang Mieder, in his preface to his collection of modern fairy-tale poetry, writes that "Sleeping Beauty is clearly the fairy tale that today's poets react to most frequently. . . . [T]his tale of love, beauty, and sleep is often reinterpreted along emancipatory and sexual lines" (xv). Terri Windling, in her article on fairy-tale retellings in poetic form, also affirms that Sleeping Beauty is the single tale that has inspired the greatest number of poetic retellings. She comments briefly on several poems including *The Sleeping Beauty*, the book-length sequence of poems by Hayden Carruth about war, communism, and other social issues (27–28). Jack Zipes exclaims that Sexton and Broumas seek to break the prison house of male discourse: Sexton by questioning whether the awakening is truly an awakening, opening our eyes to the situation of women whose "resurrected" lives may be as desperate as their deaths, and Broumas who is stridently optimistic and flaunts society's taboos (1988, 154).

1916: Riley, James Whitcomb. "**A Sleeping Beauty**." In *The Complete Works of James Whitcomb Riley, Vol. 2*. New York: Harper, 464–65. Also in *Disenchantments: An Anthology of Modern Fairy Tale Poetry*, edited by Wolfgang Mieder. Hanover, NH: University Press of New England, 1985, 119–21.

An evocative vision that recalls the age-old story of a princess and her "dead-ripe kiss of a hundred years" within the narrator's own world far from the woods and castles of earlier times.

1920: de la Mare, Walter. "**Sleeping Beauty**." In *Collected Poems 1901–1918, Vol. 2*. New York: Henry Holt, 72. Also in *Disenchantments: An Anthology of Modern Fairy Tale Poetry*, edited by Wolfgang Mieder. Hanover, NH: University Press of New England, 1985, 117.

The still and beautiful face of the sleeping princess amid the scent of bramble fascinates this poet. There is no retelling of the story in this poem, first published in 1901, beyond the underlying one that is held in the reader's unconsciousness.

1931: Watson, Evelyn M. "**A Sleeping Beauty**." In *Symbols of Immortality*. Boston: Christopher Publishing House, 50. Also in *Disenchantments: An Anthology of Modern Fairy Tale Poetry*, edited by Wolfgang Mieder. Hanover, NH: University Press of New England, 1985, 123.

A commentary on the state of dreams using the sleep scene of "Sleeping Beauty."

1934: Hillyer, Robert S. "**And When the Prince Came**." In *The Collected Verse of Robert S. Hillyer*. New York: Alfred A. Knopf, 27–28. Also in *Disenchantments: An Anthology of Modern Fairy Tale Poetry*, edited by Wolfgang Mieder. Hanover, NH: University Press of New England, 1985, 124.

The prince explains how, because of his overwhelming love for the sleeping princess, he did not kiss her awake but left her slumbering on. She would never know dissatisfaction or sorrow in her suspended state, and he could not promise that he could keep her safe from these things if he would resuscitate her.

1947: Wylie, Elinor. "**Sleeping Beauty**." In *Collected Poems of Elinor Wylie*. New York: Alfred A. Knopf, 246. Also in *Disenchantments: An Anthology of Modern Fairy Tale Poetry*, edited by Wolfgang Mieder. Hanover, NH: University Press of New England, 1985, 122.

Sleeping Beauty sleeps within the marble block awaiting for the narrator, a sculptor, to awaken her and bring her forth.

1951: Hutton, Mary. "**The Sleeping Beauty**." In *Disenchantments: An Anthology of Modern Fairy Tale Poetry*, edited by Wolfgang Mieder. Hanover, NH: University Press of New England, 1985, 127.

Using the image of the roses, the 100 years, and sleep, Mary Hutton examines relationships between the genders.

1958: Mayo, E. L. "**The Sleeping Beauty**." In *Summer Unbound and Other Poems*. Minneapolis: University of Minnesota Press, 20. Also in *Disenchantments: An Anthology of Modern Fairy Tale Poetry*, edited by Wolfgang Mieder. Hanover, NH: University Press of New England, 1985, 128.

The narrator reveals his thoughts as he breaks through the formerly impenetrable hedge to find the place where time has held still.

1962: Freeman, Arthur. "**Beauty, Sleeping**." In *Disenchantments: An Anthology of Modern Fairy Tale Poetry*, edited by Wolfgang Mieder. Hanover, NH: University Press of New England, 1985, 130.

Rather than a reworking of the tale, the poem makes use of the image of sleep as privacy and solitude.

1963: Owen, Wilfred. "**The Sleeping Beauty**." In *The Collected Poems of Wilfred Owen*, edited by C. Day Lewis. London: Chatto and Windus, 132. Also in *Disenchantments: An Anthology of Modern Fairy Tale Poetry*, edited by Wolfgang Mieder. Hanover, NH: University Press of New England, 1985, 118.

The metaphor of the awakening of the kiss is the focus here. The narrator realizes that the time has not yet arrived to "kiss her to the world of Consciousness" although, unlike the traditional sleeping princess, this Beauty is not asleep. Originally published in 1914.

1966: Cohen, Leonard. "**The Sleeping Beauty**." In *Canadian Anthology*, edited by Carl E. Klinck and Reginald E. Watters. Toronto: W. J. Gage, 486. Also in *Disenchantments: An Anthology of Modern Fairy Tale Poetry*, edited by Wolfgang Mieder. Hanover, NH: University Press of New England, 1985, 129.

A short tongue-in-cheek look at fairy-tale heroines and heroes." 'You don't understand what story I am from,' she said" (129).

1966: Swift, Joan. "**Vancouver Island**." In *Disenchantments: An Anthology of Modern Fairy Tale Poetry*, edited by Wolfgang Mieder. Hanover, NH: University Press of New England, 1985, 133.

Motifs from the tale are applied to the weather patterns of this island on the western coast of Canada. "Old Crone South Wind weaves her an evil weather" (133).

1968: Knight, Douglas. "**Sleeping Beauty, August**." In *Disenchantments: An Anthology of Modern Fairy Tale Poetry*, edited by Wolfgang Mieder. Hanover, NH: University Press of New England, 1985, 134.

The month of August with "her" release from academic endeavors is compared to the Sleeping Beauty of the traditional tale. But alas, for some, the sleep is much shorter than the original 100 years. "When young September breaks the magic spell" (134).

1969: de Ford, Sara. "**The Sleeping Beauty**." In *Disenchantments: An Anthology of Modern Fairy Tale Poetry*, edited by Wolfgang Mieder. Hanover, NH: University Press of New England, 1985, 135.

Filled with compassion for the child that did not receive the gift of graces but only sleep, the narrator looks at what the ravages of time and age have wrought.

1969: Jarrell, Randall. "**The Sleeping Beauty: Variation of the Prince**." In *The Complete Poems*. New York: Farrar, Straus & Giroux, 95–96. Also in *Disenchantments: An Anthology of Modern Fairy Tale Poetry*, edited by Wolfgang Mieder. Hanover, NH: University Press of New England, 1985, 125–26.

This poem contains the voice of the prince as he explains to the sleeping princess why, instead of awakening her, he will lay down beside her and wait patiently for the final sleep, death.

1970: Johnson, Charles. "**Sleeping Beauty.**" In *I Heard a Scream in the Street: Poems of Young People in the City*, edited by Nancy Larrick. New York: M. Evans, 104. Also in *Disenchantments: An Anthology of Modern Fairy Tale Poetry*, edited by Wolfgang Mieder. Hanover, NH: University Press of New England, 1985, 136.

The image of the sleeping beauty refers to a Black man who is sleeping on the streets.

1971: Sexton, Anne. "**Briar Rose (Sleeping Beauty).**" In *Transformations*. Boston: Houghton Mifflin, 107–12. Also in *The Armless Maiden and Other Tales for Childhood's Survivors*, edited by Terry Windling. New York: TOR, 1995, 46–49.

Sexton's poetic rendition opens and closes with accounts of incest between the father and his beloved daughter. Nancy Walker, in her analysis of the poem, states "the prefatory stanza recapitulates the process of a woman recapturing childhood memories through hypnosis, 'swimming further and further back,' until she is two years old sitting on her father's lap" (59). The tone of this preface is threatening and echoes the Grimms' tale, and the final lines suggest that this memory dooms the girl to forever remain in a state of childhood. Between these two passages, Sexton retells the tale with graphic details in a sardonic tone. The visual images are contemporary: "The king looked like Munch's *Scream*." There are allusions to Biblical figures such as Jesus and his crucifixion (princes held by the thorns) and Moses (parting the briars). Instead of living happily every after, or even being challenged by a monster of a mother-in-law, Sexton's Sleeping Beauty is eternally terrified of sleep.

1973: Nemerov, Howard. "**Sleeping Beauty.**" In *Disenchantments: An Anthology of Modern Fairy Tale Poetry*, edited by Wolfgang Mieder. Hanover, NH: University Press of New England, 1985, 137.

Listening to stories at bedtime when you are a child sometimes leads one to strange places—particularly in your sleep. The power of sleep and dreams is the subject of this poetic reworking.

1977: Broumas, Olga. "**Sleeping Beauty.**" In *Beginning with O*. New Haven, CT: Yale University Press, 61–62.

Rather than reworking the tale, Broumas uses only the singular motif of a kiss to wake the sleeping beauty when addressing the distaste of society confronted with a kiss between two women.

1978: Kumin, Maxine. "The Archeology of a Marriage." In *Disenchantments: An Anthology of Modern Fairy Tale Poetry*, edited by Wolfgang Mieder. Hanover, NH: University Press of New England, 1985, 138–39.

A sardonic look at a marriage with the "magic" ebbing. Their relationship began with a stolen weekend just before he was to ship out to fight in World War II and has never caught up to reality in the years between. They coexist. Neither of them are happy or content, but both maintain equilibrium.

1979: Caskey, Noelle. "Ripening." In *Disenchantments: An Anthology of Modern Fairy Tale Poetry*, edited by Wolfgang Mieder. Hanover, NH: University Press of New England, 1985, 142.

A deliberation on the use of the thorns to help define relationships.

1979: Ditsky, John. "Epithalamium." In *Disenchantments: An Anthology of Modern Fairy Tale Poetry*, edited by Wolfgang Mieder. Hanover, NH: University Press of New England, 1985, 140.

Both the princess and her prince are in a state of suspension waiting for someone to awaken them. They both eventually awaken, only to die.

1979: Sheck, Laurie. "Sleeping Beauty." In *Disenchantments: An Anthology of Modern Fairy Tale Poetry*, edited by Wolfgang Mieder. Hanover, NH: University Press of New England, 1985, 141.

This sleeping person does not wake up, not with the kiss of her visitor or with any of the other stimulation that can be found in the institution where she subsists.

1981: Shore, Jane. "Sleeping Beauty." In *Disenchantments: An Anthology of Modern Fairy Tale Poetry*, edited by Wolfgang Mieder. Hanover, NHCT: University Press of New England, 1985, 143–44.

A strong analogy between the sleeping princess's plight to marry the first face she sees with that of the new queen bee of the hive.

1982: Carruth, Hayden. "Dornroschen (The Sleeping Beauty)." In *The Sleeping Beauty*. New York: Harper & Row, 48. Also in *Disenchantments: An Anthology of Modern Fairy Tale Poetry*, edited by Wolfgang Mieder. Hanover, NH: University Press of New England, 1985, 145.

She lays there, dreaming what?

1982: Hay, Sara Henderson. "**The Sleeper.**" In *Story Hour*. Fayetteville, AR: University of Arkansas Press, 6–7. Also in *Disenchantments: An Anthology of Modern Fairy Tale Poetry*, edited by Wolfgang Mieder. Hanover, NH: University Press of New England, 1985, 131–32.

A poem in two voices: She is filled with discontent with the noisy world she now finds herself in and has no desire to open herself to the "clumsy trespasser"; he is equally as miserable with his princess in an awakened state.

1990: Strauss, Gwen. "**Sleeping.**" In *Trail of Stones*. New York: Alfred A. Knopf, 33–34.

This sleeping princess never dreams but hides herself from the world outside because they will not leave her be. She knows that one day, when the 100 years have passed, she will meet the man of her dreams.

1995: Shapiro, Farida S. T. "**This Century of Sleep or, Briar Rose Beneath the Sea**." In *Ruby Slippers, Golden Tears*, edited by Ellen Datlow and Terri Windling. New York: William Morrow, 68–71.

> Because in most traditional tellings Briar Rose is a passive young girl who doesn't do much but sleep and wait to be rescued, [Shapiro] didn't feel comfortable admitting her intrigue with the story until Jane Yolen's novel about the Holocaust, *Briar Rose* was published. Since then Shapiro has done almost obsessive research of both fairy tales and the Holocaust (68).

This poem is a variation on these blended images, rendering a horrific portrayal of a body that will never awaken.

Picture Books

Both titles in this section are not really picture books as the phrase is usually understood. *Sleeping Ugly* is an illustrated early chapter book told (in a "simple manner") tongue-in-cheek as only master storyteller Jane Yolen can tell it. Don't dismiss the appeal of this story to young adults because of the format. Just read it to them! *The Wedding Ghost* has the traditional format of a picture book, but it too is an illustrated text of a complex and fascinating story.

1981: Yolen, Jane. **Sleeping Ugly**. Illustrated by Diane Stanley. New York: Coward-McCann.

The adventures of Princess Miserella (beautiful on the outside but not on the inside), Plain Jane (who of course is the other way around), and the fairy (who gives three wishes but not without evaluative commentary) as they bespell each other into "one of those famous hundred-year-naps that need a prince and a kiss to end them" (Yolen, 44). Eventually (at the end of 100 years to be precise) Jojo, the youngest son of the youngest son, ventures into the woods and finds the three sleeping ladies. He knows his folktales, but because he never really had a chance to kiss anyone before, Jojo decides to practice his kisses first before attempting to kiss the beautiful girl. He kisses the fairy on the nose and then Plain Jane on the lips. Just as he moves to the princess, Jane wistfully utters, "I wish he loved me." "Good wish," agrees the fairy, and so Plain Jane and Jojo live happily ever after, with a most unusual but beautiful coat rack gracing their house.

Great fun! Jack Zipes, however, moans that "though provocative, Yolen's tale ends on a traditional, homespun note that subverts her questioning of the classical tale" (1988, 155).

1985: Garfield, Leon. **The Wedding Ghost**. Illustrated by Charles Keeping. New York: Oxford University Press.

The story begins with the rush of wedding preparations and the wedding announcement requesting "the pleasure of the world and his wife's company (with but one trifling exception)" (4) to the wedding of Jack and Gillian. Everyone responds to the invitation and are coming with the exception of Jack's old nurse, who had not been invited. "She'd long ago retired and lived so far away that it would have been an unkindness to have asked her and expected her to pay her fare and bring a gift besides" (5). Jack receives a mysterious map that has arrived as a wedding gift. It is addressed to Jack alone, and he soon becomes obsessed with following it. The streets are shrouded in fog, a river must be found and crossed, and the forest he treads carefully within is full of human bones. He eventually finds a castle, finds a sleeping beauty, and kisses her awake. His marriage to this beauty is superimposed on his wedding to the less glamorous Gillian; he is married to the homely real as well as the romantic ideal (Hearne 1989, 143). "Once he had awakened the Sleeping Beauty, she would always be with him, would always be haunting him, and filling his heart with restless uncertainty and desire" (Garfield, 64).

Keeping's illustrations are haunting, filled with sinister mystery and power. Garfield's writing is powerful, filled with images that are matched effortlessly by the black pen-and-wash drawings. Although the book is packaged as a picture book, the format is deceptive as to the content and intended audience. "Illusions of time, allusions to literature, and some terrifying graphic images make it a supernatural tour de force" (Hearne 1989, 143). Bette Ammon and Gale Sherman agree with Betsy Hearne's assessment of this title. "This classic ghost story will appeal to readers who devour books by R. L. Stine and Christopher Pike. Students can note how the evocative illustrations enhance the spine-tingling tale" (51).

Graphic Novels

The first entry in Linda Medley's series *Castle Waiting* is a graphic novel that quickly sold out its first printing and was revised and reprinted in 1999. The second edition includes activity section specifically geared towards reading/creative writing programs.

1996: Medley, Linda. **The Curse of Brambly Hedge**. Petaluma, CA: Olio.

The Curse of Brambly Hedge heralds a regular comic book series, *Castle Waiting*, that continues the story of the famous castle and its inhabitants left behind once the former sleeping princess moves out of the castle (and story) to her new kingdom home.

Characters in the graphic novel and series include both animals and humans interacting without concern. The graphic novel begins in a peaceful kingdom where there is unhappiness because the queen wishes for a child. The king seeks the help of the wise women but is overheard by the imp familiar of the wise women's sister Mald, the evil witch. When the female child is conceived and born, it is named after one of the wise women, who are all invited to the feast. The story follows the traditional pattern: The uninvited Maud gains entrance into the feast because of her knowledge of people's guilty secrets; the child is blessed with gifts; and Maud gives her a gift as well. There is a spell of protection around the baby to ward off any attempt by Maud, but she is very careful with her wording: "I predict she'll be an *irresistible* child—so beautiful, modest, and good-natured that everyone who *sees* her is bound to *love* her . . . Fully blessed with all my sisters' gifts . . . for *fifteen years*. And on her 15th birthday, Princess *Perfect* will prick her finger on a spindle and drop down *dead*."

However, Maud is caught by her own words because her oldest sister has not yet given her gift. The wise woman changes the spell from death to a century-long sleep that will end when the princess is awakened by the prince who is her one true love. All spindles and spinning wheels are destroyed and outlawed and a master spinner is appointed to come once a year to spin the clothing needs for the castle. His name: Rumpelstiltskin! At the end of this first chapter, the oldest sister discloses the gift that she was planning on giving the child: wisdom. She is not worried, however; the child is a princess, after all, and she will always have someone around to be wise for her!

Chapter 2 opens on the dawning of the princess's 15th birthday. Her parents have been delayed (by the witch's familiar) and are not at the castle. Maud arrives with a spindle, the princess falls into her deep sleep, and Maud, in her arrogance, is destroyed by her master, the devil. The castle members fall asleep, one by one; the brambly hedge grows high and wild and the townspeople flee. "Weeds claimed the town just as the woods had claimed the castle. Eventually there was nothing left of happy Putney but silence, and ruins, and the legend of the haunted castle."

Chapter 3 begins a century later. The right prince arrives, manages the hedge, and kisses the princess awake. She leaves the castle and the people without a word and the people just stand there open-mouthed (for four panels). The scene switches to some of the same faces, visibly aged, who are telling this tale to Mr. Adjunct, who has come to govern the castle. His name is Rackham and he is a stork. (This character is based on the illustrator Arthur Rackham, who often depicted himself as a stork.) Here the story ends!

When the story continues in the comic-book series, it is the story of some of the inhabitants of the castle, including Rackham and a visitor who is seeking refuge. Lady Jain's story is the focus of the first issue of *Castle Waiting*. Along her journey she meets some familiar characters: the three pigs who are the proprietors of the "Wolf's Head Inn," numerous musicians heading for the fair at Bremen, and the horse Falada. Comments on the series, drawing analogies to the movies *The Princess Bride* and *Time Bandits*, are included at the end of this issue The subsequent issues follow Princess Jain's adventures at the castle. Each of these issues contain articles about children's literature, including annotated bibliographies and information on the series and publishing comics. The illustrations are deceptively simple black-and-white line drawings that allow the reader to watch the gestures made by the characters while the story is being told. The dialogue is strong and natural with a lovely sense of irony and fun. Highly recommended by critics and the young adults in my workshops on graphic representations of familiar tales. Finalist for the coveted Eisner Award for "Best Graphic Novel—New."

Internet Resources

In comparison to many of the other tales we have discussed in this book, the tale of "Sleeping Beauty" has not garnered much in the way of interest on the Information Highway. The major sites that discuss this tale are strictly interested in the Walt Disney movie and the memorabilia from the world of the Disney film. One site, http://www.darkgoddess. com /fairy/sb.htm, briefly comments on the changes made to the tale by the Brothers Grimm. Marina Warner and her explorations of *Perceforest* and, as it is referred to here, Giambattista's "Sun, Moon and Talia," are mentioned along with a brief discussion of the changes Perrault made for his own version. Information can be found about Tchaikovsky's ballet. The words to Anne Sexton's poems can be found at http://www-eland. stanford.edu/%7Ejenkg/Sexton/briarrose.html. When searching the Internet using the phrase "sleeping beauty" you can find numerous sites selling mattresses and even more sites that are best left to the imagination!

Classroom Extensions

Many of these suggestions can be adjusted for use with other tales as well.

The Discord of the Apple: A Familiar Beginning

Eris, the goddess of strife, was enraged because she was not invited to the wedding celebrations of Thesis, the goddess of the sea, and her mortal husband, Peleus. Eris furiously crashed the wedding party, threw down a golden apple as a gift for the most beautiful person at the party, and vanished. Hera, Athena, and Aphrodite fought for the apple and the claim as most beautiful woman. What famous event did this "curse" precipitate?

The Importance of Food

Besides the famous recipe for Sauce Robert and the obvious delight the ogress mother-in-law has in consuming her relative meals, food plays a role in this story. Discuss the instances of food and its importance. How does this relate to the images of food in other tales such as "Hansel and Gretel" also discussed in this study?

Louis XIV's Palace

Several articles refer to the similarities between Perrault's description of Sleeping Beauty's home to that of the Sun King's palace at Versailles. Find a description and photographs or drawings of this palace and compare it to Perrault's descriptive text. Why would these details be so important to Perrault's intended audience? How different is this palace from that of the one in Italy (Basile) or Germany (Grimm)? How does it compare to the castle that is visualized in the Walt Disney film?

Sleeping Beauty: Illustrated

There are numerous commentaries regarding the traditional renderings of this tale. Betsy Hearne, in her article "Booking the Brothers Grimm: Art Adaptations and Economics," compares the illustrative styles and interpretation by Trina Schart Hyman ("romantic, but darkly so"), William Hutton ("more restrained") and Mercer Mayer ("illustrations are Celtic in motif, Gothic in tone, medieval in costume and setting") (231). Jack Zipes, in *The Brothers Grimm: From Enchanted Forests to the Modern World*, compares three illustrated editions of the story as well. He looks to Hyman, Mayer, and Ruth Sanderson's interpretation of Jane Yolen's text. Zipes claims that none of these books are intended for children; they yield no new content or substance about either Sleeping Beauty or the myth that surrounds her sleep (1988, 163). Find copies of these books (along with any other illustrated copies of the tale) and compare the illustrations for style, extension of the story, intent of the illustrator, and intended audience. What are the key scenes that are the focus of the illustrators in general? Why do you think these pieces of the story appeal to the illustrators over other elements?

Wagner's Brunhilde

Several critics compared the story of Sleeping Beauty with that of Brunhilde in Richard Wagner's opera *Ring of the Nibelung*. Contrast and compare these two "sleeping beauties" and the role their sleeping plays in their respective stories.

Bibliography

Ammon, Bette D., and Gale W. Sherman. *Worth a Thousand Words: An Annotated Guide to Picture Books for Older Readers*. Englewood, CO: Libraries Unlimited, 1996.

Anthony, Pamela. "The Sleeping Beauty: 'It's Just the Star Wars of the 1800s.' " *The Edmonton Journal*, 21 February 1997, C1.

Barchilon, Jacques, and Peter Flinders. *Charles Perrault*. Boston: Twayne, 1981.

Berkin, Adam. " 'I Woke Myself': *The Changeover* as a Modern Adaptation of Sleeping Beauty." *Children's Literature in Education* 21: 4 (1990), 245–51.

Bettelheim, Bruno. *The Uses of Enchantment: The Meaning and Importance of Fairy Tales*. New York: Vintage Books, 1976.

Brewer, Derek. *Symbolic Stories: Traditional Narratives of the Family Drama in English Literature*. Cambridge, England: D. S. Brewer, 1980.

Darnton, Robert. *The Great Cat Massacre and Other Episodes in French Cultural History*. New York: Basic Books, 1984.

Ellis, John M. *One Fairy Story Too Many: The Brothers Grimm and Their Tales*. Chicago: University of Chicago Press, 1983.

Goldthwaite, John. *The Natural History of Make-Believe: A Guide to the Principal Works of Britain, Europe, and America*. New York: Oxford University Press, 1996.

Gose, Elliott. "Fairy Tale and Myth in Mahy's *The Chageover* and *The Tricksters*." *Children's Literature Association* Quarterly 16: 1 (Spring) 1991, 6–11.

Hearne, Betsy. "Booking the Brothers Grimm: Art, Adaptions, and Economics." In *The Brothers Grimm and Folktale*, edited by James M. McGlathery et al. Urbana, IL: University of Illinois Press, 1988, 220–33. (Originally published in *Book Research Quarterly* 2: 4 [Winter 1986–87].)

———. *Beauty and the Beast: Visions and Revisions of an Old Tale*. Chicago: University of Chicago Press, 1989.

Heuscher, Julius E. *A Psychiatric Study of Myths and Fairy Tales: Their Origin, Meaning, and Usefulness*, 2d ed. Springfield, IL: Charles C. Thomas, 1974.

Hourihan, Margery. *Deconstructing the Hero: Literary Theory and Children's Literature*. London, England: Routledge, 1997.

Jacoby, Mario. "Sleeping Beauty and the Evil Fairy: On the Problem of Excluded Evil." In *Witches, Ogres and The Devil's Daughter: Encounters with Evil in Fairy Tales*, edited by Mario Jacoby, Verena Kast, and Ingrid Riedel. Boston: Shambhala, 1992, 177–96.

Jones, Steven Swan. "The Innocent Persecuted Heroine Genre: An Analysis of Its Structure and Themes." *Western Folklore* 52: 1 (January 1993), 13–41.

Kolbenschlag, Madonna. *Kiss Sleeping Beauty Good-Bye: Breaking the Spell of Feminine Myths and Models*. San Francisco: Harper & Row, 1988.

Lewis, Philip. *Seeing Through the Mother Goose Tales: Visual Turns in the Writings of Charles Perrault*. Stanford, CA: Stanford University Press, 1996.

Lüthi, Max. *Once Upon a Time: On the Nature of Fairy Tales*. Bloomington, IN: Indiana University Press, 1976.

———. *The Fairytale as Art Form and Portrait of Man*. Translated by Jon Erickson. Bloomington, IN: Indiana University Press, 1984.

McGlathery, James M. *Fairy Tale Romance: The Grimms, Basile, and Perrault*. Urbana-Champaign, IL: University of Illinois Press, 1991.

———. *Grimms' Fairy Tales: A History of Criticism on a Popular Classic*. Columbia, SC: Camden House, 1993.

Morgan, Jeanne. *Perrault's Morals for Moderns*. New York: Peter Lang, 1985.

Nelson, Gertrud Mueller. *Here All Dwell Free: Stories to Heal the Wounded Feminine*. New York: Fawcett Columbine, 1991.

Opie, Iona, and Peter Opie. *The Classic Fairy Tales*. New York: Oxford University Press, 1974.

Prose, Francine. "Sleeping Beauty." In *Mirror, Mirror on the Wall: Women Writers Explore Their Favorite Fairy Tales*, edited by Kate Bernheimer. New York: Anchor, 1998, 283–94.

Rohrich, Lutz. *Folktales and Reality*. Translated by Peter Tokofsky. Bloomington, IN: Indiana University Press, 1991.

Rowe, Karen E. "Feminism and Fairy Tales." In *Don't Bet on the Prince: Contemporary Feminist Fairy Tales in North America and England*, edited by Jack Zipes. New York: Methuen, 1986, 209–26. Originally published in *Women's Studies* 6 (1979), 237–57.

Sale, Roger. *Fairy Tales and After: From Snow White to E. B. White*. Cambridge, MA: Harvard University Press, 1978.

Tatar, Maria. *The Hard Facts of the Grimms' Fairy Tales*. Princeton, NJ: Princeton University Press, 1987.

Thomas, Joyce. *Inside the Wolf's Belly: Aspects of the Fairy Tale*. Sheffield, England: Sheffield Academic Press, 1989.

Thompson, Stith. *The Types of the Folktale: A Classification and Bibliography. A Translation and Enlargement of Antti Aarne's Verzeichnis de Märchentypen*. 2d revision. Helsinki: Academia Scientiarum Fennica, 1964. (FF Communications, no. 184).

Travers, P. L. *About the Sleeping Beauty*. New York: McGraw-Hill, 1975.

Warner, Marina. *From the Beast to the Blonde: On Fairy Tales and Their Tellers*. London: Chatto & Windus, 1994.

Weber, Eugen. "Fairies and Hard Facts: The Reality of Folktales" *Journal of the History of Ideas* 63:1 (Jan-Mar 1981), 93–113.

Windling, Terri. "Breadcrumbs, Beasts and Transformations: Fairy Tales Are Plentiful in Poetry." *Realms of Fantasy* (August 1996), 24–29, 75.

Zipes, Jack. *Fairy Tales and the Art of Subversion: The Classical Genre for Children and the Process of Civilization*. New York: Methuen, 1983.

———. *The Brothers Grimm: From Enchanted Forests to the Modern World*. New York: Routledge, 1988.

———. *Fairy Tales as Myth, Myth as Fairy Tale*. Lexington, KY: University of Kentucky Press, 1994. (Thomas D. Clark Lectures, 1993).

CHAPTER 9

SNOW WHITE

While "Little Red Riding Hood" and "Sleeping Beauty" have engaged the most critical commentary from scholars, the story of "Snow White" is perhaps the most beloved tale in North America. One of the reasons for this may be because Walt Disney chose it for his first feature-length, animated film (McGlathery 1993, 76). Because of this, a large majority of people today only knows this tale through the interpretive medium of Walt Disney studios.

> The story of Snow White and the Seven Dwarfs is one of the most disturbing in the fairy tale canon. In spite of Walt Disney's best attempts to turn the earthy dwarfs into benignly comic, almost genderless creatures, and the amoral stepmother into a one-dimensional caricature of evil, the story remains chilling in its evocation of a mother's hatred toward her child and an aging beauty's obsession with a younger rival in a world where beauty is the basis of power (Datlow and Windling, 105).

While we will delve with some detail into the Disney version of the tale, this chapter will be focusing on the tale as first written down by Basile and reshaped by the Brothers Grimm.

The queen wishes for a child "as red as blood, as white as snow and as black as ebony wood." She dies in childbirth and the king remarries a vain woman who consults a magic mirror to ensure that she is the most beautiful in all the land. The stepmother discovers through the agency of her magic mirror that Snow White, now aged seven, has become more beautiful than herself. The jealous stepmother orders her huntsman to take Snow White into the forest, kill her, and bring back her lung and liver as a token of her death. The huntsman allows Snow White to escape, kills a boar, and brings the substitute lung and liver to his queen, who subsequently eats them. After fleeing fearfully through the forest, Snow White discovers a haven, a cottage for seven dwarfs. She eats and falls asleep. When the dwarfs return from the mine, they discover her and invite her to stay with them as housekeeper. The queen consults her magic mirror for the third time and discovers that she has been deceived. She disguises herself as an old peddler woman and approaches Snow White at the cottage. Snow White invites her inside and allows her to tightly tie a lace bodice that takes Snow White's breath away. Snow White falls as if dead but the dwarfs find her, revive her, and warn her of further danger. The queen questions the mirror for the fourth time, discovers her failure, and in a second disguise approaches Snow White with a poisoned comb. The dwarfs revive Snow White a second time and warn her again. When the queen questions the mirror for the fifth time, she is incensed that the girl is still alive and prepares a poisoned apple. She tricks Snow White into taking a bite and Snow White dies. Upon questioning the mirror again, the queen is satisfied that she is once again the fairest in the land.

The dwarfs cannot revive Snow White this time. They mourn her for three days and place her in a glass coffin. An owl, raven, and dove weep over the coffin. The body of Snow White remains preserved, and she lays as if sleeping for a long period of time until a prince arrives and wishes to purchase the coffin and its contents. The dwarfs will not sell the girl in her coffin, but they give them to the young man because of his good nature and unselfish love. While transporting the coffin down from the mountain, the apple is dislodged accidentally and Snow White is revived. The prince proclaims his love and the wedding is arranged. The queen, upon receiving an invitation to the wedding, questions the mirror for the final time and discovers her failure. She nevertheless attends the wedding, where she is forced to dance to her death in red-hot iron shoes.

Tale Type: AT 709

The story of "Snow White" is summarized as: "The wicked stepmother seeks to kill the maiden. At the dwarfs' (robbers') house, where the prince finds the maiden and marries her" (Thompson, 245). The story is often referred to as Grimms Number 53 as it was the 53rd tale in their collection.

I.   *Snow White and her stepmother.* (a) Snow White has skin like snow and lips like blood. (b) A magic mirror tells her stepmother that Snow White is more beautiful than she is.

II. *Snow White's rescue.* (a) The stepmother orders a hunter to kill her, but he substitutes an animal's heart and saves her, or (b) she sends Snow White to the house of the dwarfs (or robbers) expecting her to be killed. The dwarfs adopt her as sister.

III. *The Poisoning.* (a) The stepmother now seeks to kill her by means of poisoned lace, (b) a poisoned comb, and (c) a poisoned apple.

IV. *Help of the Dwarfs.* (a) The dwarfs succeed in reviving her from the first two poisonings but fail with the third. (b) They lay the maiden in a glass coffin.

V.   *Her Revival.* A prince sees her and resuscitates her. The stepmother is made to dance herself to death in red-hot shoes.

Motifs:

Z65.1: Red as blood, white as snow

L55: Stepdaughter heroine

M312.4: Prophesy: superb beauty for girl

D1311.2: Mirror answers questions

D1323.1: Magic clairvoyant mirror

S31: Cruel stepmother

S322.2: Jealous mother casts daughter forth

K512.2: Compassionate executioner: substituted heart

F451.5.1.2: Dwarfs adopt girl as sister

N812: Giant or ogre as helper

N831.1: Mysterious housekeeper. Men find their house mysteriously put in order. Discover that it is done by a girl (frequently an animal transformed into a girl)

K950: Various kinds of treacherous murder

S111: Murder by poisoning

D1364.16: Hairpin causes magic sleep

D1364.9: Comb causes magic sleep

D1364.4.1: Apple causes magic sleep

S111.2: Murder with poisoned lace

S111.3: Murder with poisoned comb

S111.4: Murder with poisoned apple

F852.1: Glass coffin

F852.2: Golden coffin

F852.3: Silver coffin

N711: King (prince) accidentally finds maiden in woods (tree) and marries her

E21.1: Resuscitation by removal of poisoned apple. By shaking loose the apple from the throat of the poisoned girl the prince brings her to life

E21.3: Resuscitation by removal of poisoned comb

Q414.4: Punishment: dancing to death in red-hot shoes (Thompson, 245–46)

A History of Snow White

"Snow White," long considered an appropriate tale for young children by many people, is one of several tales classified as "a persecuted heroine cycle" where the heroine repeatedly faces hostilities directed at her in one environment after another. The pattern of the hostilities repeats itself as well. The heroine receives a threat, she is attacked, and she either escapes on her own or is expelled from the environment and ultimately is rescued from persecution (Jones 1990, 28). Other stories that could be considered as part of this cycle include "Cinderella," "Cap O'Rushes," and "The Maiden in the Tower." "Snow White" has been a popular tale in many oral traditions before it was first set down in print by Giambattista Basile. This story has had a long tradition of being reworked and retold by various "storytellers" throughout the ages, including the Brothers Grimm and their modern counterpart, Walt Disney.

Snow White in Oral Tradition

More than 400 variants have been collected across Europe and in the Middle East, Africa, and North America. Steven Swann Jones found that the tale was actually more popular outside of Germany, with 70 versions found in Italy and Greece, 100 in Scandinavia, 50 in Ireland, and 30 in the "New World" (1990, 14). Within this broad array of oral variants there are numerous fluctuations in these key elements of the story: methods of murder; the companions in the woods; ingenious ways of expelling the heroine from her childhood home; and in the treatment of her corpse after her death.

Snow White in Print

"Snow White became progressively sweeter and tidier as her story was translated into print and made its way from Germany to the United States" (Tatar 1987, xix). The Brothers Grimm reported that their version of the tale was collected from two sisters in Cassel. The Opies, in their consideration of the history of the tale, felt that while it contained anti-quated folk elements, it might not be an ancient story at all but one that had probably been influenced by the story of Lisa written by Basile and published in 1634 (Opie, 227).

Basile

After reading the German 1749 translation of Basile's *Pentamerone*, the Grimms realized that two-thirds of these tales were being told in Germany. In the notes to their 1822 edition of tales, they offered a general account of Basile's collection, together with a precis of each of the tales and a table of analogs between these tales and their own. These precis were omitted in later editions of the Grimms' tales, but they retained both the general account and the table of analogs (Penzer, 279).

The specific similarities between the Grimms' tale of "Snow White" (53) and three of Basile's tales are shown in the following adapted table.

Table 9.1
Comparison of Basile and Brothers Grimm

Basile	Grimms	Points of Resemblance
Day/Tale	Tale	[either story types as a whole, or separate motifs]
II. 8	53	Comb causes apparent death, but on removal life is restored. Girl placed in seven crystal chests/a glass coffin.
IV. 9	53	King/mother wants wife/child as red as blood, as white as marble/snow, with hair as black as a raven/window frame.
V. 9	53	Prince/mother wants wife/child as red as blood and as white as curds/snow.

(Penzer, 279-285)

The most striking resemblance to the tale of "Snow White" is that of Basile's "The Young Slave" [Day II, Tale 8]:

When Lisa was born her mother took her to the fairies to have her blessed and all did so, except for one who twisted her ankle in trying to see the child. This fairy cursed her for the pain, "saying that when she should reach her seventh year, her mother in combing her hair would forget the comb sticking in the hair on her head, and this would cause her to die" (Burton, 160). Regardless of the warning, the curse comes to pass and the girl dies. The distraught mother has seven crystal chests built, one inside the other, and placed her daughter's body within, locking it away in a chamber. When the mother's health deteriorates she gives the key to her brother and asks him not to open the door. He agrees, but when he takes a wife and asks her not to use the key, she takes the first chance she can to open the door. She sees the beautiful girl within the crystal chest "and she had grown as any other child of her age would, and the chests lengthened with her" (Burton, 161). Jealous, she storms the room and lifts the girl up by her hair, dislodging the comb. When she awakens the wife immediately cuts her hair and treats her as a slave. She eventually escapes this state and is found a handsome and worthy husband, and the wife is punished and exiled.

The Opies state that elements in this story help to explain an anomaly in the Grimms' version of this story: how can a girl of seven, who is not much older when she is murdered by her stepmother, be of marriageable age when awoken by the prince (Opie, 227)?

The Brothers Grimm

"Snow White" underwent several revisions in the various editions of this classic collection of tales.

Table 9.2
Changes Made by the Brothers Grimm

1810 manuscript	1812 text	1819 text
Queen is Snow White's natural mother.	No change.	Natural mother dies and Snow White's father remarries. "Replaced by one of the most infamous wicked stepmothers of all time" (Tatar 1987, 143).
Queen takes Snow White into the forest and leaves her there.	Queen orders the huntsman to murder Snow White.	No change.
When Snow White awakens at the home of the dwarfs, they "took pity on her and persuaded her to remain with them and do the cooking for when they went into the mines. However, she was to beware of the queen and not to let anyone into the house" (Zipes 1988, 13).	"The dwarfs took pity on her and said: "If you keep house for us and cook, sew, make the beds, wash and knit, and keep everything tidy and clean, you may stay with us, and you will have everything you want. In the evening, when we come home, dinner must be ready. During the day we are in the mines and dig for gold, so you will be alone. Beware of the queen and let no one into the house" (Zipes 1988, 13).	No change.
Snow White's father discovers her body and, with the help of royal physicians, revives her.	The prince discovers Snow White in the coffin, and two disgruntled servants revive her by dislodging the apple when they strike her in anger (Stone 1991, 57).	No change.

1810 manuscript	1812 text	1819 text
Father arranges a marriage for his daughter and punishes the queen. In the margin of their 1810 manuscript, the Grimms remarked: "This ending in not quite right and is lacking something." Their own finishing touches could only be topped by the prudish changes by that twentieth-century sanitation man, Walt Disney (Zipes 1983, 53).	Snow White marries the prince, and queen dances to her death at their wedding.	No change.

In each subsequent edition minor revisions were made until the text became frozen in print and time. The mother figure was by this time divided into two separate characters to demonstrate the two different aspects of maternal love and malicious envy. It is this "authoritative" 1857 edition that is the subject of the majority of research on this tale. Not everyone agrees that the changes were devastating. McGlathery cites an essay by Wilhelm Schoof, who, comparing the tales as found in 1808 letters from Jacob Grimm to Friedrich Karl von Savigny with the tales in the 1810 manuscript and 1812 first edition, cited the changes Wilhelm Grimm made in "Snow White" to be "striving, with rhetorical techniques of every sort—particularly through sticking in lines of rhyming verse, expanded depictions, intensifications of motifs, and much else—to go beyond folk art and sophisticated art to create a classical fairy-tale style, without thereby altering the actual content" (1993, 43). McGlathery, however, finds this latter claim dubious, to say the least.

Overview of Critical Interpretations of Snow White

Steven Swann Jones, in his recent study of "Snow White," comments that the tale had been interpreted "alternatively as literary history, as psychological allegory, as religious dogma and as sexist propaganda" (1990, 83). One of his major concerns in his study is the fact that only rarely had previous research been consulted for subsequent discussions on related issues in regards to this tale. Our survey of the research begins in 1864, a mere few years after Grimms published their final edition of their tales. During the 1930s there was not a great deal of interest in the tale, but since 1974, when Bettelheim published his theories, the tale has been the focus of much debate and deliberation. Because of the major study conducted by Steven Swann Jones on "Snow White," we have included a healthy helping of his interpretation of this story.

1864: Karl Schenkl finds similarities between "Snow White" and William Shakespeare's play *Cymbeline.* He discusses the following five points of resemblance: an evil queen who attempts to poison her stepdaughter; a heroine who survives by her beauty and innocence; a cave or hut that provides safety; a heroine who keeps house for her rescuers; and a poisoning attempt resulting in the sleep of the heroine (Jones 1990, 83).

1892: Alfred Nutt determines that the story of "Snow White" influenced the telling of lai of Eliduc by Marie de France (Jones 1990, 84).

1910–
1915: Ernst Boklen provides a comparative catalogue of motifs in his geographical-historical study of the approximately 80 versions of " Snow White" he collected. His major "endeavor [was] to draw a comparison between the punishment given to the persecutor of the tale and the trials and tribulations endured by the heroine of the story" (Jones 1990, 87). He does not offer any interpretations of the material, however. (McGlathery 1993, 76).

1913–
1933: Bolte and Polivka, in their massive companion to the Brothers Grimm collection, devote 14 pages to a brief study of "Snow White" that include isolating common traits to most versions of the tale. They also note the similarities between *Cymbeline* and "Snow White" as well as similarities between "Snow White" and other folktales such as "Hansel and Gretel" and "Sleeping Beauty" (Jones 1990, 88).

1929: Kurt Heyman provides a lighthearted reading of the tale while examining it from the point of view of modern medicine (Jones 1990, 88).

1934: J. F. Grant Duff parallels the tribulations of "Snow White" with traditional tribal puberty rites, including the "learning and practicing of housekeeping by the girl and in the defloration of the girl as symbolized by the eating of the apple" (Jones 1990, 89).

1940: A. N. Foxe projects the character, Snow White, as a psychologically disturbed patient whose ultimate problem is "her consummate masochism" (Jones 1990, 89).

1942: A. S. Macquisten and R. W. Pickford read the story as symbolizing the developing relationship between a child and its parents (Jones 1990, 89).

1974: Julius Heuscher advances "an interesting and useful case for viewing [the story] as a primer for adolescent development, and his analysis presents a valuable perspective on the folktale" (Jones 1990, 92). Heuscher demonstrates how this tale provides precise demarcation between the three periods of childhood: the formative years, the latency period, and adolescence, while, at the same time, focusing on the middle period (Heuscher, 138). The formative years, represented by the first seven years of Snow White's life, is a time of relative tranquillity before her emerging beauty (and identity) compels a crisis. During her sojourn at the dwarfs' home, Snow White learns to share, and this ability to share "willingly and happily is a result of the harmonious completion of the seven formative years, during which the child learns to accept and respect the rights of others and the relationships between them" (Heuscher, 141). This accomplishment is severely put to the test during the latency period, the time when children are learning skills that enable them to be independent and self-sufficient (Heuscher, 141). The ordeals set by her stepmother are directly aimed at confining this development. "The comb referring to the head poisons the thinking, the narrow vest tied too strongly around the chest strangles the emotions, while the poisoned bite from the apple permanently strangles the actions or will-impulses, when it reaches the stomach" (Heuscher, 143). The latency period ends with Snow White's death and her subsequent awakening into adolescence and eventually adulthood.

1974: Bruno Bettelheim echoes the research of Macquisten and Pickford by focusing on the folktale as a projection of the fears and wishes of the child (Jones 1990, 92). The tale, according to Bettelheim, tells of the destruction of a parent who is jealous of her own child. This may be the result of something problematic in the parent's own childhood (Bettelheim, 195). One major theme is preparation for sexual bleeding in menstruation and, later, in initial intercourse. The story also warns of the evil consequences of narcissism through the stepmother and again through Snow White when she disregards the dwarfs' warnings and accepts beauty aids (Bettelheim, 203). According to Bettelheim, this attraction to the laces and combs expresses the passage of time, as Snow White is now an adolescent (211). This tale "teaches that just because one had reached physical maturity, one is by no means intellectually and emotionally ready for adulthood, as represented by marriage" (213).

1977: N. J. Girardot connects the story and the ritual and initiatory pattern underlying it by examining the three phases of a "typical" pattern of initiation and the corresponding elements from the 1857 Grimm version of "Snow White." He also establishes 25 key statements from the tale organized within these parameters. Jones praises the research for revealing "the philosophical premises, the religious implications, and the moral values present in 'Snow White'" (Jones 1990, 95). Girardot concludes that "Snow White" is "a moral tale, a cautionary fable concerning the destructiveness of pride and self-love; but this is only part of the message, since it can be read in a more intensive way . . . an amazingly rich portrayal of a particular vision of human life as a sacred round, a dance, that speaks of the necessity of sacrificing self-love in order to discover true love; also speaks of the terrors and ordeals of growing up, and suggests that the world is not simply a meaningless chaos but an enchanted realm where man is not alone and can expect a happy destiny if he will listen to his own soul, and the voices of tradition and the gods" (Girardot, 298).

1978: Roger Sale, in his examination of children's literary classics, claims "Snow White" to be one of the greatest tales because of the treatment it accords fears and wishes. (38). He repudiates much of what Bettelheim had to say about this tale because he feels Bettelheim was adamant that most fairy tales concerned relationships between parents and children. Because the tales were taken out of context, moved from one century to another to a time of strong family sentiments and practices, Bettelheim invented parents and relationships when they could not be found in the traditional tale. An example of this is the huntsman who, according to Bettelheim, represents Snow White's father (Sale, 39). Sale asserts that the theme of this tale is not one of narcissism because there is no evidence that the queen received any pleasure from her beauty; "what is stressed is the anger and fear that attend the queen's realization that as she and Snow White both get older, she must lose; this is why the major feeling involved is not jealousy but envy; to make beauty that important is to reduce the world to one in which only two people count" (Sale, 41). Sale also discusses the role and power of beauty for women in a world where people grew old quickly and men have the more permanent power—permanent because it does not erode with age and loss of "beauty." "For an older woman to fight against these facts and values made her frightening, and no fairy tale can imagine defeating such a woman without also destroying her" (Sale, 43).

1979: Sandra M. Gilbert and Susan Gubar analyze the tale in the context of the enclosure of women in patriarchal Western society. "[W]omen are trapped in our society just as the mother figure is framed by the ebony window at the start of "Snow White" and by the mirror later on" (Jones 1990, 96). The victory of female passivity is represented by the exhibition of the beautiful but inert Snow White as she is displayed in her glass coffin (Jones 1990, 96). All the themes are introduced in the first paragraph: sewing, snow, blood, and enclosure, and these are all associated with key themes in female lives (Gilbert and Gubar 1979, 37).

1980: Derek Brewer considers the story of "Snow White" in his examination on traditional narratives of family drama in English literature. He focuses on the first English version of the story published in 1823 as "Snow Drop," looking at the image of the home in the story and at the story as a metaphor for the maturation process.

> The protagonist is driven out or wants to leave home, for very good reason, and that is a fundamental *donnee*. It symbolizes the need to grow up and the play of forces around the need. But the protagonist . . . also has to stay at home, because there (though we do not believe it when young) is where the action is. In our end is our beginning, and we travel in order to find our starting place (32).

Brewer assesses the dwarves as a substitution for sibling solidarity towards a parent, and because of the obvious age differences between them and the young princess, they also serve as a father-figure. Because of this age difference, they are unable to awaken Snow White. This privilege is accorded to someone closer to her own age. "The story thus is about the awakening of the protagonist to adult life and marriage which the hostile mother-image has been trying to prevent" (33). Brewer also considers the more violent Grimms' version to reflect the German peasantry's harsh living conditions, justifying this theory by explaining that the entire German artistic tradition has "a marked vein of outstanding brutality" (33). He concludes that the tensions in the story also "partly represent (in so far as the Queen's hostility represents the protagonist's own attitude to self) a reluctance to grow up, a desire to stay as a child. But the dominant wish ultimately is to grow up" (34).

1980: Kay Stone addresses the "Disneyfication" of "Snow White," "Cinderella," and "Sleeping Beauty" and the effect some of these modifications in the movie had to the meaning of the tales to future audiences.

1984: Max Lüthi proposes that intensification, rather than contrast, is the focus of attention on Snow White's physical beauty (4). It is this beauty that sets the plot into motion, and it is irony that dominates the tale. Snow White is

> a sympathetically drawn figure . . . [who] harms herself . . . bring[ing] about her own death or apparent death . . . this "death" which then brings her the prince; and here contrary irony again comes into play: the clumsiness (stumbling) of the servants or, in other variants, their anger about the fact that they have to serve a dead maiden— one angrily strikes her—causes the bit of apple to come back up, and she wakes up (130).

1985: Maria Tatar examines the role of women in the tales. "Mothers in their various incarnations as stepmother, witch and mother-in-law stand as the chief source of evil in these tales even as they stand as the chief source of good when they make an appearance as fairy godmother, wise woman or Holy Virgin" (1985, 29). The ultimate function of the "evil" aspect is to banish the heroine from the safety of her home and to subvert her elevation to noble status. "To emphasize the definitive end to the stepmother's reign of terror, the fairy tale describes her demise in graphic and morbid detail" (1985, 32). She dies in both body and spirit and is no longer a threat to the newly formed royal family. To emphasize the cruelty of the stepmother, the role of the biological father is peripheral. Snow White, the "most chaste and guileless of fairy tale heroines," is frequently the focus of her father's sexual interest in some variants. The Grimms' version refers to the father only once and only to proclaim his second marriage. Agreeing with Gilbert and Gubar that the voice in the mirror is the voice of the father, "the patriarchal voice of judgment," Tatar maintains that the struggle between the heroine and her stepmother is motivated by rivalry for the attention and admiration of the absent father and husband (1985, 37).

1986:   Betsy Cohen uses the story of "Snow White" as a metaphor for "a woman liberating herself from her mother, and moving into the world of work and relationships by getting to know herself better" (1). Cohen coins the phrase "Snow White Syndrome" to designate a daughter who, in order to please her envious mother, does not become too successful and instead willfully limits her possibilities.

1986:   Sandra Gilbert and Susan Gubar feel the tale is essentially that of the relationship between the angel-woman and the monster-woman (1986, 201). Their queen is a "plotter, a plot-maker, a schemer, a witch, an artist, an impersonator, a woman of almost infinite creative energy, witty, wily, and self-absorbed as all artists traditionally are" (1986, 203). The three plots against Snow White, after the initial murder attempt, depend upon traditional female weapons for its force (1986, 204). The" kind" old peddler offers to lace Snow White properly and "suffocates her with a very Victorian set of tight laces" (1986, 204). The second attempt, involving a wise expert in female beauty, attempts to comb Snow White's hair properly with the siren's comb from classical mythology. The final attempt, by the farmer's wife, succeeds in the killing of the girl with the "female arts of cosmetology and cookery" (1986, 204). They also interpret the housework accomplished by Snow White as a disparaging attitude towards women's work and their place in society: "[T]he realm of domesticity is a miniature kingdom in which the best of women is not only like a dwarf but like a dwarf's servant" (1986, 205).

1987: Ruth Bottigheimer contemplates the silence of Snow White's biological mother, who "thinks to herself but never speaks and when her daughter is born, she dies" (53). Bottigheimer also speaks to the numerous illustrations of this tale in regards to the apparent age of Snow White who, at the time of crisis, is seven years old. Snow White's sexuality is stressed by illustrators who, reading backwards from the conclusion, realize that the young female in the glass coffin must be of marriageable age. Therefore, she is also portrayed as a young adult in earlier scenes such as serving the dwarfs at the table and fleeing the threat in the forest (164).

1987: According to Wolfgang Mieder, this "tale of narcissism, beauty, jealousy, competition, temptation, and eventually maturation" addressing basic conflicts of the socialization process can serve as a "parody of a society in which outside appearance is valued more highly than ethical convictions" (22). He demonstrates that this story is used by the mass media to both encourage and mock our society's preoccupation with an artificial ideal of external beauty (22).

1989: Joyce Thomas analyzes certain aspects of Snow White's step-mother, who operates on three simultaneous levels as the antagonist: stepmother competing with original mother and wife; mother competing with daughter who will eventually surpass her in beauty; and adversary-witch (70). The mirror is a natural symbol that "fully translates her obsession with her own beauty," but its glass component serves to connect the three female characters through the different uses of the material. The opening correlates the nature of the two queens: the good queen [mother] looking outward through the glass window and the evil queen forever looking inward at her looking glass. The glass coffin links Snow White with both women, reflecting both outward and inward visions. "Its glass serves as a window upon Snow White and simultaneously makes her part of the landscape as well as the focal point upon which all eyes are fixed" (70). But like the looking glass, the coffin is a framed, confined entity that has specific boundaries. "All the world may view Snow White, whereas the queen demands that her image be reflected throughout the world" (71).

1990: Shuli Barzilai contemplates various interpretations of this tale. According to Freudian theory (and Bruno Bettelheim), "Snow White" is about the Oedipal conflict of "being in love with the one parent and hating the other" (516). "Yet, in 'Snow White' the Oedipal rivalry is not evident in the narrative itself, and the object of contention—the father—is virtually absent from the story" (517). She continues her analysis of Bettelheim's "revision," stating that it reflects the culture of patriarchy by interpreting it as a story of repression and replacement (Bettelheim keeps the father at center stage although he is hardly mentioned in the tale itself) and by refusing to acknowledge that women may appreciate and value beauty for reasons unrelated to a paternal presence (518). She looks also at the feminist reading by Gilbert and Gubar, stating that they, like Bettelheim, are regarding the conflictual relationship between mother and daughter as determined by male rule and male influence (521). Barzilai's reading of the tale focuses on the differences inherent in the closest of female bonds. "It portrays relations gone radically wrong, or what happens when mothers and daughters cannot work out the problems created by the special intense bond between them" (523). The story is told from the daughter's perspective and is full of indications of her persepectival dominance: the repeated statements of the queen's jealousy; the fact that all the male figures instantly become enchanted by Snow White's own incomparative beauty, and her own concern about her mother's incapability to allow her to "grow up." Barzilai concluded that the story is one

> of two women, a mother and a daughter: a mother who cannot grow up and a daughter who must. Hate rather than love becomes the keynote of their story. The conclusion of this tale, like the narrative in its entirety, could be read as the product of two perspectives. From the mother's perspective, the wish she held most dear had turned into a tale of loss and fragmentation. . . . From the daughter's perspective, the old nurturing gestures—be it grooming or feeding—are threatening. . . . Snow White would like . . . nothing better than to get this interfering older woman, this deadly dragon-mother, out of her life (534).

1990: Steven Swann Jones notes "how folktales are cultural reflectors, how they mirror the values and the dreams of their audience. And we see how the values and dreams mirrored in 'Snow White' provide a revealing portrait of our culture and ourselves" (1990, 97). "Snow White" is a story that chronicles the three most crucial transitions in a female's life: menstruation, marriage, and childbirth. While the third instance is only found in extended versions of "Snow White," it is common to other tale types in this cycle. "Presumably the purpose of this patterning of the folktale to correspond to a woman's typical life crisis is that it attempts to assist the heroine in her passage through these major life changes by providing her with psychological, sociological and philosophical instruction along the way" (1990, 33).

Jones divides the story into nine episodes. *The Origin Episode* focuses on two main themes to answer the question "How did I get here?": the birth story of the heroine and how the natural mother was subsequently replaced. "By having a false and hateful stepmother replace the kind and benevolent true mother, the child can fully justify her [developing] resentment of the mother figure without incurring guilt" (1990, 41). Within this episode, the adolescent heroine becomes aware of human etiology, procreation, sexuality, Oedipal rivalry, menstruation, mortality, and cosmic regeneration, and, as they underlie the main anxieties facing a developing young adult, they provide the fundamental motivation for this tale (1990, 42).

The Jealousy Episode is told from the heroine's point of view as she innocently becomes the focus of a conflict between the mother figure and the developing child. (1990, 44). The fact that this is a one-sided narrative points to the function of this episode: It is "being told for the benefit of the growing child who either feels that their mother is really to blame and who wants external documentation of it or who is experiencing the envy herself and is projecting it onto her rival" (1990, 44).

The two themes within *The Expulsion Episode* are the dramatization of the heroine's abandonment and her becoming fully aware of the reason for this situation and the child's deep concern about her temporal existence as symbolized by the danger and her potential death at the hands of the huntsman. Now fully separated from her family and home, she must develop her own identity and value system (1990, 49).

The Adoption Episode delineates several important themes regarding the heroine's road to maturation, including the accomplishment of housekeeping chores that demonstrate socialization and self-control of appetites and the learning of social roles prescribed by the society. This "illustrate[s] the importance and value of the domestic arts for the developing adolescent, both for her assumption of an appropriate social role and for her acquisition of respect and appreciation from those around her" (1990, 52). In almost all instances of this story, the companions have been male and outsiders to mainstream society. They are all representations of the same character, who is somewhat uncivilized, sexually undeveloped, and supernatural (1990, 53–54).

> The Adoption episode documents the social, philosophical, and psychological development of the heroine, and the heroine's companions serve as mediators for the heroine in all of these areas: in the psychological acceptance of sexuality; in the philosophical struggle to comprehend the nature of life; and in the social acquisition of morality and the domestic arts (1990, 55).

The sexual rivalry between mother and daughter is still very active, but there is a second theme in *The Renewed Jealousy Episode* as well: Running away from issues is not a solution. "This episode reinitiates the persecution pattern of threat, hostility, expulsion, and relocation underlying the drama" (1990, 57). Death in *The Death Episode* is a metaphor for the psychological process of internally confronting her developing sexual maturation. The repeated attempts to kill the heroine represent the gradual process of the psychological acceptance of her development (1990, 61). From a social perspective, she is dying in her old role and is being reborn into a new role or status (1990, 62). The deathlike sleep philosophically represents "the existential tragedy that the heroine feels she is inevitably condemned to" (1990, 63).

Philosophically, the exhibiting of her body in a transparent coffin in *The Exhibition Episode* dramatizes the child's attempt to comprehend and confront death. From a sociological perspective, there is a reiteration of the structure of social rituals that are associated with maturation, and from a psychological viewpoint, this episode represents the child's sense of alienation and isolation (1990, 67–68).

The Resuscitation Episode suggests that because in most variants of "Snow White" the resuscitation is accidental, "it is life itself, the ongoing activity surrounding the heroine that ultimately brings her back to active participation after her inward psychological and philosophical journey" (1990, 70). The hunting prince is a metaphor for the male adolescent's adjustment to sexuality. While he is actively searching for a bride, he is really not sure what to do with her once he finds her and seems quite content with the idea of keeping her on display (1990, 71).

The main motif of *The Resolution Episode* is that of marriage for a heroine who is now sexually and emotional mature enough for this step. The wedding represents the social confirmation of her acceptance by her society and of her acceptance of them (1990, 74) Her mother is no longer a threat to her potential development, and the justifiable punishment, not by the heroine herself but by an agent of authority, demonstrates that society can be relied on to protect women and enforce moral principles (1990, 75).

1991: James McGlathery asserts that this is not a story of possessive love or envy but one of jealous envy. The stepmother is driven by the fear that Snow White's beauty will surpass her own. The means the queen uses for killing Snow White demonstrate her intense preoccupation with femininity, casting her "in the unflattering, comic role of the ugly hag who compensates herself for her lack of captivating charms by vicariously identifying with a blossoming maiden" (1991, 121). The fact that her jealous vanity is anticipatory (her rival is only seven years old) adds to the comedy. He quotes Jennifer Waelti-Walters, saying "Snow White" is "an overt commercial for marriage, carrying with it the message that all that matters in a woman is her appearance. It is preferable that in all other aspects she be dead" (1991, 151).

1991: Lutz Rohrich clarifies the queen's desire to consume Snow White's lungs and liver. "It appears that the queen's attempts to become more beautiful by consuming the beautiful Snow White's organs. . . . [We] could label . . . 'magic cannibalism' if both the Grimms' earlier texts did not completely lack cannibalism" (119). He also explores the cruel death of the stepmother: "[T]hese folktale punishments are reminders of past judicial systems. The punishments occasionally reflect reality (i.e., historical law) far more accurately than the fantastic folktales which house them" (129). Women were punished differently than men, often burned or drowned to purify the elements and to guarantee the total destruction of the witch's power and influence (130). Rohrich states that

> Germans can only half-heartedly accept an animated folktale film, such as Disney's *Snow White*, as an effective work because they are too familiar with "Snow White" through tradition and custom; she has become an almost sacrosanct figure. For the German, the dwarves playing jazz is not only an anachronism but also almost a sacrilegious desecration of the folktale (259).

1991: Kay Stone, perusing the story of "Snow White" in three distinct media, explores the concepts of text, texture, and context. Text is the basic story of "Snow White"; texture is the specific language used to tell the story (including visuals); and context encompasses any relevant personal, social, and historical influences on the telling of the tale. "This particular story in print and film is rigid in text and texture and has no inherent context except when actually created and received" (1991, 53).

1992: Maria Tatar cites this tale as an "example of murderous intentions masquerading as maternal goodwill: the three attempts . . . nearly all work because the heroine suspects nothing when an old peddler woman offers to lace her up 'properly,' give her hair a 'proper' combing, and to share an apple with her" (Tatar 1992, 218).

1993: Trina Schart Hyman interprets the "wicked queen" as someone who was slipping into madness, and while she was not evil, she did envy and hate Snow White's youth and beauty and her capacity for power. These were all elements that were of immense importance to the queen but, at the same time, diminishing as each year passed.

1995: Nancy Walker adopts Gilbert and Gubar's interpretation of this tale in her own examination of the writings of feminist writers. Walker states that "In Gilbert and Gubar's reading of 'Snow

White,' it is the unruly Queen who claims the ability 'to plot' Snow White's story; in the work of modern feminist writers, however, the mirror of the tale must be both examined and broken" (83).

1996:   Martin Hallett and Barbara Karasek state: "The tale ends with the celebration of marriage, denoting that the heroine had survived the loss of childhood innocence and is now ready for initiation into the privileged status of adulthood" (1996, 53).

1996:   In her research on witches, Diane Purkiss looks at folktales containing "clear traces of women's fears of and fantasies about the witch and her powers" and including warnings about the dangers of accepting a gift of food, particularly a luxury item such as fruit (277). The significance of the wicked queen using her magical powers to poison an apple in the final attempt on Snow White's life is lost to modern audiences and may have other interpretations assigned to the apple that is at variance with the meanings that operated in the older social contexts of the tales (280).

1997:   Christina Bacchilega considers the metaphor of the mirror as a natural extension of the heroine's exceptional beauty and the drama of jealousy. However, she maintains, what has been overlooked is the mirror's *magic*—"the makings of its power" (Bacchilega, 31). She discusses the effects of the mirroring process and various identifications of the voice of the mirror. While Bettelheim interpreted the voice as that of the daughter, to Girardot it is the voice of truth (self-reflection), and to Gilbert and Gubar, the voice is that of the father. Barzilai claims it is the voice of the mother, and Jones says that the voice is both Snow White's and that of society at large (Bacchilega, 33). Bacchilega also reflects on modern reworkings of the tale, including Angela Carter's short story "Snow Child" and Robert Coover's "The Dead Queen."

Reworkings of Snow White in Novel Form

While the tale of Snow White has enthralled many authors of short stories and poetry, it has not been the focus of many full-length novels. In fact only one young-adult novel to date has been a reworking of the tale. We will, however, introduce a contemporary Snow White, or Snohomish Quantrill as she is known in Elizabeth Scarborough's series of

"Godmother" novels. Although Sno is only one of the many folktale-based characters in these novels, she is a major character in the first two books, and the series will be discussed below.

Pictures of the Night

1992: Geras, Adèle. **Pictures of the Night**. San Diego, CA: Harcourt Brace Jovanovich.

This is the third book in the "Egerton Hall" trilogy. The first book retells the story of "Rapunzel," and the second volume of the series re-works the story of "Sleeping Beauty." These two novels are discussed in their relevant chapters.

Eighteen-year-old Bella, on her summer break from Egerton school, lives and sings with a small band in London and Paris during the summer of 1962. She is plagued with a series of mysterious accidents that she begins to believe are caused by her jealous stepmother, Marjorie. The novel opens with Bella recovering from the first "accident," the lacing of a belt by a supplier to one of Bella's favorite "junk shops." The supplier, visiting at Bella's commune, gives her a present of a "wide pink suede belt" and laces it for her at the back. Bella is convinced that something was familiar about this person but still trusts her. Still, once the woman leaves, Bella cannot remove the belt.

> The harder I pulled the tighter the belt became and the an-grier I felt. I'd seen a special chair in a museum once, long ago, into which they tied criminals, binding them to the back and arms by an intricate arrangement of leather straps. The more the prisoner struggled, the tighter the bonds grew, until they cut cruelly into flesh. This belt was like that (20).

She faints, but the band members find her in time, and they cut off the belt. Geras is faithful to the Grimms' version of the traditional story in almost every aspect. The other "accidents" also are closely aligned to the murder attempts of the traditional tale. Bella's memory of her mother is a story that her father told frequently about the woman who died while giving birth. While pregnant with Bella, her mother had slipped on snow after seeing the film *Gone With the Wind*. She grazed her finger tips, causing them to bleed. Her mother wanted her child to look like Vivian Leigh from the movie, "Hair like the night and skin like the snow and lips as red as the blood on this hankie" (24). The hairdresser looks in the mirror and comments to Bella's stepmother that the young girl (she is seven) is a beauty and in fact resembles her birth mother, who was quite beautiful herself. The hairdresser continues to comment on Bella's growing beauty each time she and Marjorie have their hair done. In a fit of pique, Marjorie "loses" Bella in the "forest" of Harrods department store, and when Bella connects with her father, arrangements are made to keep her safe at Egerton boarding school.

The next incident involves a comb that is placed in her hair by Margot, a dresser at the club. This elaborate comb and hairdo give Bella dizzy spells that also cause her to faint. This experience reminds her of an earlier one in which she choked on an apple given to her by her stepmother.

As in the picture-book version by Fiona French, *Snow White in New York*, the dwarfs are represented by musicians, and the prince (Mark) first sets eyes on her as a member of the audience during one of the singing gigs. It is during one of these gigs that Bella almost dies. Bella is to sing at a birthday party given at The Glass Menagerie. The club features hanging cages made of glass and thin gold wire, and in one of these cages is where Bella is placed after taking several pills given to her by Marjorie to calm her nerves. (And why, if she suspects her stepmother of being behind all the "accidents," does Bella take the pills?) "After she is gone, I turned to the mirror again. I suppose I must have had tears in my eyes, because the reflection I saw in the glass was fractured, as though my face had been broken up into tiny, glittering pieces" (172). Bella begins reacting to the medication and finds herself imprisoned, crushed, and unable to breathe (178). Fortunately for Bella, Mark, a medical student, is in the audience and manages to revive her with mouth-to-mouth resuscitation, "the kiss of life." Other than Marjorie having problems with her new shoes at a party ("I feel as if these shoes have been soldered to my feet with red-hot irons" [177]), there are no repercussions, consequences, or explanations to what happened before or to any of the other characters other than Mark and Bella, who ride off into the sunset (Boston) because they are meant for each other. The last line of the book makes implicit reference to the fact that this book, and the other two as well, are indeed retellings of the tales in novel format. The line? "Tonight, I thought, tonight my happy ending will begin" (182).

This book is much less a successful endeavor than the previous two novels, with many holes in the story that are never addressed. The almost exclusive audience for this novel will be females who have already read the previous two books in the series.

The Godmother

1994: Scarborough, Elizabeth Ann. **The Godmother**. New York: Ace.

This is the first in a series of stories about "fairy godmothers." The first two novels, *The Godmother* and *The Godmother's Apprentice* (1996), involve the same wide variety of characters from familiar folk and fairy tales, but the third novel, *The Godmother's Web* (1998), contains only passing references to these characters with the exception of further development of the character Cindy Ellis.

Familiar characters that populate the first two novels include: Snohhomish Quantrill (Snow White and Little Red Riding Hood), Hank and Gigi (Hansel and Gretel), Cindy Ellis (Cinderella), and Bobby the Henchman (and toad who is not quite the Frog Prince but "pretty close"). The story begins: "Once upon a time in a beautiful city by the edge of the sea there toiled a young woman who did not believe in fairy tales. Fairy tales, she said, had no relevance to her life and none to the lives of the children she knew" (1). This young woman, social worker Rose Samson, soon meets fairy godmother Felicity Fortune, who introduces her to a wide array of people and experiences. Sno, the daughter of an aging rock star, has as a stepmother a model who is facing a waning career. The plot accelerates when the model's agent wants to sign up Sno. The stepmother's henchman, Bobby, is sent to get rid of this 13-year-old threat but is defeated by Sno and her judo lessons. Sno runs deeper into the forest and into a camp of former soldiers who are part of the men's movement. Felicity assures Rose, when they are trying to find Sno, that "If she's following her archetype, she has protection and shelter" (160).

The lives of these various characters follow a broad outline of their respective folktale origins and eventually come together in a final search for the still-missing young heiress. Scarborough does not belabor the obvious with her references to the familiar tales. However, she is also up front about what she is doing. As Felicity explains to Rose:

> Sno . . . is not Snow White . . . bits and pieces change around depending on the time and the other people involved and *their* stories. If you read enough of the so-called folk and fairy tales, you'll see it happened in them too—partly because the original reports of these events became confused with time and telling and possibly because similar things keep happening—differently, depending on the circumstances. I think a lot of the trouble

you may have recognizing the archetypes comes from having stories set down on paper, instead of being transmitted orally, as they were originally. When things are told from person to person they're much more fluid. Set down on paper, it appears that if one version is right, that no others can be (160).

The references to "Little Red Riding Hood" mesh delightfully when Sno, wearing her red school uniform, dashes into the woods and first meets the shaggy soldier on the path. "Wild thoughts of werewolves skimmed the surface of her mind. . . ." (67). Hansel and Gretel's tale involves several urban flights into the mall culture just after Christmas. Seven-year-old Hank and his four-year-old sister Gigi are taken to Rose in her capacity as social worker, but Rose cannot keep them safe. At the gingerbread-house Christmas display, Gigi nibbles on the house. "Well, well it wasn't a mouse at the door at all. It's a couple of cookie monsters nibbling my house." "I'm not a Cookie Monster. . . he's on Sesame Street" (95). The children feel secure with the man who is taking down the display and go with him to his home. However, the man is much worse than a witch, and the danger they face is of a much more immediate concern.

Cindy Ellis works at the Lucky Shoe Stables and is constantly harassed by her stepmother and stepsisters. When Felicity asks for help in the search for Sno, Cindy cannot go as her horse Punkin is missing a shoe. Felicity steps in, magically repairs the shoe for 24 hours (it is not iron because the fairy folk cannot tolerate it) and transforms a motorcycle into a 4X4 and horse trailer complete with all the hiking gear that she could possibly need. Her character also follows the lead of her archetype with modifications and, by the end of this first book, she is managing the stables for the attractive "King of rock and roll, " Sno's father. The relationship deepens between Cindy and Sno's father in each of the successive titles of this series.

Sno is also a main character in the second book when she becomes the fairy godmother's apprentice in Ireland. She travels to the funeral of the King of the Cats; renews acquaintance with the talking toad, Bobby; and is beset by a variety of ancient spirits from Irish mythology. Reviewer Donna Scalon asserts that while this book also draws on folklore and mythology for characters and situations, Scarborough's "touch is much subtler and more effective. She does not attempt to force the contemporary plots to fit the tales" (110).

The format of this second volume is also different. Much of the tale is narrated through Sno's entries in a journal. The third book moves the story back into the United States, but in the southern region rather than the Seattle area of the first. The reader is introduced to a new godmother, a Native woman known as "Grandma" who intercepts Cindy's journey with a horse and takes her on a journey into another culture. Elizabeth Scarborough states that "Grandma" is based on "a very ancient being who appears as a Hopi Holy person long before the Navajos come to the Southwest and learned to weave from her" (*The Godmother's Web*, ix).

Short Stories

The tale of "Snow White" has certainly appealed to writers of short fiction, as the following "morsels" will attest. The themes of these stories are as varied as the interpretations of the tradition tale.

1973: Coover, Robert. **"The Dead Queen."** In *Spells of Enchantment: The Wondrous Fairy Tales of Western Culture*, edited by Jack Zipes. New York: Viking, 1973, reissued 1991, 704–11.

Narrated by the prince after his wedding night with Snow White and at the funeral of her stepmother, the story explores the function of the "dead queen." Coover describes, in great detail, the terrible punishment that caused the queen's death, and the prince ponders his wife's apparent lack of interest in anything beyond herself and her own pleasure. The dwarfs are caustic nuisances to the new marriage. The prince becomes more and more "bespelled" by the dead queen lying in the glass coffin that once contained her stepdaughter. In a final attempt to make sense of what is happening to him, he kisses her corpse trying to awaken her. For mature readers.

1979: Carter, Angela. **"The Snow Child."** In *The Bloody Chamber and Other Stories*. London: Penguin, 91–92.

This very short and intense story is about a count who, with his three wishes, fashions a beautiful child "white as snow . . . red as blood . . . black as that bird's feather," and the countess who wishes intensely to be rid of her (91). Carter's tale is for mature readers. While it focuses on the images of the "creation" of Snow White and the intense jealousy created in the "mother," the story digresses a great deal from the traditional tale, if not from some of the critical interpretations of the tale.

1983: Lee, Tanith. **"Red as Blood."** In *Red as Blood, or Tales from the Sisters Grimmer*. New York: DAW Books, 18–27.

In this Christian allegory Tanith Lee offers a mirror image of the traditional tale. The princess and her natural mother do not have reflections and are not seen during the daylight. When Bianca's mother dies and her father remarries the Witch Queen, the child refuses, as did her mother, to wear a crucifix or to take communion. She is also afraid of roses. At age 13, when Bianca's menses begin, a wasting disease envelops the kingdom. Her stepmother, afraid for the future of the kingdom, has her huntsman take Bianca into the woods. The plan was to merely frighten her to leave the area, but Bianca pretends to seduce the woodsman and kills him. She then takes refuge in the shade of "seven twisted dwarf trees" (24). The Witch Queen transforms into a hag and travels to the clearing with three gifts: a girdle, a comb from the sea, and an apple "red as blood" (a piece of the Eucharist). As in the traditional tale, the girl falls into a deathlike sleep for many years and is awakened by a prince, but this prince has a mark on his wrist. "It was like a star. Once a nail had been driven in there" (27). When she awakens she is transformed into a dove and given a chance to "Begin again, now" (27). The dove returns to the palace and her seven-year-old former self . . . but this time her reflection can be seen in the mirror.

1985: Crone, Joni. "**No White and the Seven Big Brothers.**" In *Rapunzel's Revenge: Fairytales for Feminists*. Dublin: Attic Press, 50–56.

In a world where the snow never melts and all women are forced to wear white to discourage any individuality, a young girl named Noreen wears a red knitted cap made by her grandmother. Upon the death of her grandmother, seven-year-old Noreen meets with the Seven Big Brothers, who banish her to the forest for seven years because she refuses to obey the no-color rule. In the forest she meets with Diana the Huntswoman who guides her for the duration of her exile. Other folktale characters, such as Hansel and Gretel, Rumpelstiltskin, and Tom Thumb, make their appearance as No White leaves the forest to rescue the Seven Sleeping Spinsters, who also refuse to wear white on their wedding day. With the melting of the ice coffins the summer solstice is freed, and serenity returns to the land.

This fast-paced tale, told in third person from the female character's perspective, introduces various issues but does not develop any of them effectively.

1985: Maher, Mary. "**Hi Ho, It's Off to Strike We Go!**" In *Rapunzel's Revenge: Fairytales for Feminists*. Dublin: Attic Press, 31–35.

Snow, a wealthy, happy young woman, is forced by her mother to get a job during a recession. Her only option, as housekeeper to seven short, gnarled miners, introduces her to the working conditions at "Prince Precious Jewel Mining Company." Snow informs the miners about the trade union movement and leads them to strike for better working conditions, including a job for herself as a miner. During Mr. Prince's offer of partnership, Snow saves him from choking on a piece of apple. This didactic version, told in third person from the female character's point of view, focuses on unions and working conditions, including equality of pay.

1986: Merseyside Fairy Story Collective. "**Snow White.**" In *Don't Bet on the Prince: Contemporary Feminist Fairy Tales in North America and England*, edited by Jack Zipes. New York: Methuen, 74–80.

An accomplished jewelry maker, Snow White, is kept prisoner by a power-hungry queen who uses a magic mirror to spy on the county. When the dwarfs help Snow White escape, the queen seals up the mine and all the miners within. When the people revolt and storm the castle, the mirror leads the queen to her death. This third-person narration focuses primarily on the queen's perspective. Jack Zipes, in his introduction to the tale, states that this version parallels the actual social conflicts in British society, and the ending points "to new beginnings in which underprivileged groups take destiny in their own hands with a new *political consciousness*" (Zipes, 19).

1991: Hessel, Franz. "**The Seventh Dwarf.**" In *Spells of Enchantment: The Wondrous Fairy Tales of Western Culture*, edited by Jack Zipes. New York: Viking, 613–14.

This dialogue by the seventh dwarf bemoans the fact, that while he was instrumental in Snow White's survival and resurrection, he is unknown and unappreciated. "She probably thinks about the seven dwarfs every now and then . . . But I'm sure that she has long since forgotten me, the last one, the seventh" (614).

1992: Brooke, William J. "**A Fate in the Door.**" In *Untold Tales*. New York: HarperCollins, 101–36.

The prince explains to Sleeping Beauty his tardiness in kissing her awake. He has made a second attempt because she is now a widow. He met with a detour last time because of a girl in a glass coffin who, upon his practicing his kissing techniques, awoke immediately. The bluebirds prepared a wedding, and the seven short men would not let him leave again. He and Snow White had lived happily until another prince arrived at the door. This tongue-in-cheek third person tale focuses on Sleeping Beauty rather than on Snow White. The four fairy tales within the book are interrelated through the reoccurring characters.

1993: Hirsch, Connie. "**Mirror on the Wall**." *Science Fiction Age* 3 (March), 59–61.

The narrator of this tale is the famous mirror itself, explaining to its listener the part it is forced to play in the drama involving Snow White and the Queen. It really isn't the mirror's fault but it does have a significant role in aiding the queen in her quest for beauty. "It wasn't merely hairstyle that we worked on, of course. There was skin care and makeup, wardrobe and accessories, diet and healthful exercise, and then we branched into deportment, flirtation, and charisma, the ineffable qualities of beauty" (59). Once the queen is secure about her beauty, she goes seeking a king to marry. She and the mirror get rid of an ailing wife, leaving a young daughter and grieving king to administer her charms (particularly her love charms). Soon the wedding is a thing of the past and Snow White a thorn in the side of the jealous young queen.

Snow White is soon done away with and languishes in her crystal coffin until Prince Charming happens by. In the words of the mirror: "I leave it to you to speculate on what impulse could drive a man to kiss a corpse, no matter how lovely. No matter why, the deed was done, and for whatever reason—a faulty spell, perhaps—the apple's bite lost its effectiveness and Snow White coughed up her bane" (61). After her wedding, Snow White puts the mirror out of harm's way, but today's listener . . . with a little bit of help . . . a new hairstyle, skin care and makeup, wardrobe and accessories . . . could be the fairest in all the land. Want to see?

1993: Lee, Tanith. "**Snow-Drop**." In *Snow White, Blood Red*, edited by Ellen Datlow and Terri Windling. New York: William Morrow, 105–29.

In this science fiction version of the tale, Cristena is haunted by a series of paintings created by her husband's first wife. The subject of all the paintings is a 14-year-old girl. "Her skin was white as that snow, and her long smooth hair was black as wood. She had a pale red mouth" (107). After having the portraits destroyed, Cristena sees the same young girl on a television advertisement; she is a circus artist performing with seven dwarfs. After deliberately seeking the performer out, Cristena brings her to her isolated house, where she employs a magic comb and a corset to seduce her and a poisoned apple to murder her. The body is later discovered in an ironic manner by Cristena's husband. Lee uses the major elements of the traditional tale in this dark retelling suitable for mature readers.

1994: Garner, James Finn. "**Snow White.**" In *Politically Correct Bedtime Stories: Modern Tales for Our Life and Times*. New York: Macmillan, 43–56.

The use of politically correct language, if not actual sentiment, renders this retelling a parody of the Disney version of the story. There is only the poison apple episode; the vertically challenged nasty men have no redeeming qualities, least of all a respect for cleanliness; and the story takes place over a few hours. The tale contains barbed references to both the men's movement and the concept of beauty as a commodity.

1995: Burch, Milbre. "**The Huntsman's Story.**" In *Ruby Slippers, Golden Tears*, edited by Ellen Datlow and Terri Windling. New York: William Morrow, 219–21.

Milbre Burch uses the role of the huntsman as metaphor in this powerful thought-provoking commentary on the murder of a child. The story was written "in response to the discovery of Polly Klass' body two months after the twelve-year-old's kidnapping" (219).

1995: Gaiman, Neil. "**Snow, Glass, Apples.**" In *The Year's Best Fantasy and Horror: 8th Annual Collection*, edited by Ellen Datlow and Terri Windling. New York: St. Martin's Griffin, 517–25.

This is the story of the stepmother, told in first person, of her dangerous and devouring stepdaughter, Snow White. The narrator loves her husband but soon realizes that his daughter is literally sucking his lifeblood from him and anyone else she can find. To aid the kingdom, the stepmother has the heart cut out of Snow White, but this does not stop her at all. The stepmother finally fixes a basket of poisoned apples and arranges for them to be consumed by Snow White, causing her to choke and fall. It is the stepmother who first meets and is attracted by the prince. But he cannot perform in bed if his partner shows any animation or response at all. Snow White, in her suspended state, is obviously the ideal partner for him! When Snow White awakens, she returns for her heart and places it back within her body. The prince arrests the stepmother and, after a great deal of humiliation, she is covered in goosegrease and placed in a kiln to burn to death. Like the Disney version, there is only one attempt on Snow White's life after the initial "heart-rendering" episode. For mature readers.

1995: Galloway, Priscilla. "**A Taste for Beauty.**" In *Truly Grim Tales*. Toronto: Lester, 97–106.

This is a first-person narrative of a young woman from an abusive home. She is encouraged to enter a beauty contest by her fellow employees in the abattoir where she works. Through a long year of training, the young woman meets Esmeralda, a fortune teller, who gives her a magic mirror and exacts a precise payment for her help. Upon winning the contest and the resulting marriage with the king, the young woman is to murder the king's daughter to help fulfill a curse. It is not until the story is almost complete that the reader realizes the actual identity of the narrator. An almost sympathetic look at circumstances behind a character's actions.

1995: Gould, Steven. "The Session." In *The Armless Maiden and Other Tales for Childhood's Survivors*, edited by Terri Windling. New York: Tor, 87–93.

Presented as a conversation between a therapist and an abusive young mother, the story offers subtle clues as to the identity of the therapist. The reader slowly realizes the identity of the patient as she gives background information: She met her husband when he saved her from choking on some fruit when she was doing housework for some miners after running away from home. While never actually naming any of the characters, Gould examines the cycle of child abuse within the framework of the familiar tale.

1996: Walker, Barbara G. "Snow Night." In *Feminist Fairy Tales*. San Francisco, CA: HarperSanFrancisco, 19–25.

After Lord Hunter's attempted rape of Snow Night is thwarted, he tries to turn her stepmother against her, but this too is to no avail. The stepmother realizes the danger that Snow Night is in when he reminds the stepmother of the old tale of the huntsman and the murder of the girl. She sends for seven of the dwarves to protect Snow Night from the man, which they do admirably, and Snow Night marries the very suitable Prince Charming.

Barbara Walker retold this tale to address two issues in the traditional version: "Snow White's stepmother seems to have been vilified because (a) she resented being less beautiful than Snow White, and (b) she practiced witchcraft. . . . [She] therefore seems to me a projection of male jealousies" (19).

1997: Donoghue, Emma. "The Tale of the Apple." In *Kissing the Witch: Old Tales in New Skins*. New York: HarperCollins, 43–58.

Told from the perspective of the heroine herself, the story sets forth a major reason for her problems with her father's new wife: there was only room in the castle for one queen! The girl's father is proud of both his beauties, but when time passes and his wife does not become pregnant, he becomes discontented with the situation. Soon the father dies, and his daughter leaves the castle and his jealous wife. She finds shelter with a band of woodsmen. When her stepmother finds her, she is propelled close to death through the aid of laces, a comb, and an apple.

Donoghue has prepared the reader for the natural acceptance of these items by the young girl from her stepmother—this is not the naive Snow White of the tales but a young woman who enjoys danger. When the tale finishes, although the reader has suspected all along that the narrator is Snow White, the actual identity of the teller of the tale may be a surprise. None of the stories in this collection actually end; they all flow into the next telling and the next voice. For sophisticated readers.

1997: Murphy, Pat. "The True Story." In *Black Swan, White Raven,* edited by Ellen Datlow and Terri Windling. New York: Avon, 277–87.

The story is told through the voice of the stepmother, beginning with her marriage at age 17. It was a marriage of convenience for both parties, and the new queen soon realizes that even at 17 she is too old to attract the attention of her new husband. Time passes, the king is busy at war, and the young queen tells her stepdaughter stories.

> I did not like the storytellers' tales. So I made up my own stories to tell to the child. . . . I told her of a peasant girl who planted a magic bean and grew a magic beanstalk. I told her of a little girl in a red hood who fooled a wolf and chopped off his head. In my stories, there were no wicked stepmothers, no helpless but beautiful princesses. In my stories, each princess was clever and kind and bold and strong—as well as beautiful (282).

When the young princess turns seven, the queen notices that she is upset about something and eventually, to her horror, discovers the cause of the young girl's distress. To protect her stepdaughter from further danger, the queen and the princess's nurse send her away from her home—and her father. "Over the passing years, the storytellers have made up lies about me . . . the world listened to these lies. After all, I was a woman and I was a queen, a powerful position. Everyone knows that women can't handle power" (284–85). The queen relates the rest of the "true story" and her reasoning behind the lies that have become associated with young Snow White. A plausible tale with an intelligent and personable narrator.

Feature Films

There are three feature film versions of "Snow White" discussed in this section. The first one, the prototype for all the Disney fairy-tale films that followed will be examined in great detail. It is interesting that the other two films are both recent and attempt to incorporate as many of the basic elements from the Grimms' tale as they can.

Snow White and the Seven Dwarfs

Walt Disney's Snow White and the Seven Dwarfs (1937). Directed by David Hand. Walt Disney Productions. Distributed by Buena Vista Pictures.

While the fairy-tale films of the Disney studio are now an established icon in the world of children's entertainment, Walt Disney was not taken seriously when he attempted this first full-length animated film. *Walt Disney's Snow White and the Seven Dwarfs*, labeled "Disney's folly," was released when the rest of the film industry in North America was concentrating on realism in contemporary life (Schickel, 211). However, Disney's reading of his viewing audience was soon vindicated both when *Time* magazine featured him on the December 27, 1937, cover a week after the world premier and when the film was awarded a special Academy Award of one big Oscar and seven little ones in 1939. The inscription on the Oscar read: "To Walt Disney for Snow White and the Seven Dwarfs recognized as a significant screen innovation which has charmed millions and pioneered a great new entertainment field for the motion picture cartoon" (Holliss and Sibley, 71). As a result, animation was now seriously considered an art form outside the immediate field. In a January 1986 *Variety* listing of North American "All Time Film Rental Champs," *Snow White and the Seven Dwarfs* placed fifty-eighth. A recent listing of the top 100 American films of the last 100 years includes Disney's *Snow White* at number 49. It is the only Disney fairy-tale adaptation to make the listing. Jack Zipes recognizes the importance of this film as the prototype for not only all of the subsequent Disney fairy-tale films but for most producers of folklore and family films since 1937 (1979, 113).

Disney's version was not the first time "Snow White" had been immortalized on film, however. The first moving picture version, in 1910, was a 15-minute French production titled *Little Snowdrop*. Three years later a longer version was produced with child actors portraying the dwarfs. This 40-minute film introduced the idea of Snow White being restored to life by a kiss from the prince instead of the dislodging of the poison apple as related in the Grimms' version. "The notion of the awakening kiss (borrowed from the fairy tale 'Sleeping Beauty') later formed a major element in the Disney version of the story" (Hollis and Sibley, 6). This kiss became the only antidote to the queen's poison (Zipes 1994, 89). In 1916, an hour-long silent film version staring Margurite Clark was released by Educational Films. It was this film that can be credited as the genesis of the Disney version when a young newsboy in Kansas City was invited to a special screening of it, shown simultaneously on four screens. This viewing became Walt Disney's "most vivid early memory of attending the movies" (Hollis and Sibley, 7).

The Disney Differences

Although the success of this film spawned an entire generation of animated reworkings of traditional and literary tales for young viewers, *Snow White and the Seven Dwarfs* faced heavy criticism at the onset about the appropriateness of the film for children. The traditional tale is a violent one, one felt to be difficult to translate visually in an acceptable manner for the proposed audience. Walt Disney was aware of this, and various methods were employed to soften or eliminate the effects of the huntsman's task of bringing the girl's heart to her stepmother, the agony of the three attempts on Snow White at the cottage, and the torture at the wedding dance. One solution was to emphasize the role of the dwarfs and animals and to reduce the footage devoted to the stepmother (Schickel, 216). While the plot, as first outlined by Walt Disney on August 9, 1934, closely followed the Grimms' version, there were obvious embellishments and changes that occurred during the process of transforming the idea to the medium of film. Besides the "borrowed" kiss already mentioned, Walt Disney borrowed various images from elsewhere. From the beginning he decided that each of the dwarfs would be individualized with their own personalities. This was different from any of the previous versions of this tale, with the exception of a picture book, published in 1921 in England and illustrated by John Hassall, where the dwarfs had their names (Stool, Plate, Bread, Spoon, Fork, Knife, and Wine) embroidered on their trousers. These names were inspired by the domestic scene of their first encounter with Snow White in their kitchen (Hollis and Sibley, 7).

Music was to be a strong component of the film from the very beginning. "It was Disney's objective that the songs would either offer exposition, develop characters and situations, or advance the plot, rather than be mere musical interludes inserted here and there. He wanted a fusion of story, character and music" (Behlmer, 55). This was accomplished, and three of the songs, "Whistle While You Work," "Heigh-Ho," and "Someday My Prince Will Come," became major hits with the public.

Snow White's flight through the forest offered the opportunity for a dramatic visual showcase by the studio artists. The chase is disturbing, establishing Snow White's vulnerability. "The anthropomorphic trees with scary eyes and branches that reach out like fingers recall the fairy-tale illustrations of Arthur Rackham, whose work had achieved great popularity in both Britain and the United States" (Hollis and Sibley, 18).

Richard Schickel points out that two other sequences in the movie version were controversial and considered by critics and parents as extremely frightening for children: the unclear course of the huntsman's knife as it plunged downwards and the transformation of the stepmother into the crone. He states "most children recall these scenes with a kind of delicious shudder—the sort of thing that, before psychology and do-gooding liberalism combined in an attempt to smooth the interesting edges off childhood, used to be the source of our best remembering" (221).

The result of Disney's embellishments and rearranging destroyed the balance of the traditional tale and fundamentally altered the mood in the film (Schickel, 217). However, while the story has been sentimentalized and reorganized, this movie "still preserves, unlike later Disney efforts, much of the dark ambiguous power of the original story—especially in the portrayal of the evil stepmother" (Girardot, 278). Zipes considers this refocusing to establish a different underlying ideological message from that of the traditional tale. The central themes of the film now revolve around cleanliness and order, and rather than the dwarfs offering protection for the young girl, Snow White becomes their surrogate mother. The queen, on the other hand, represents disorder, and although she dies "the social order is not changed but conserved and restored with youthful winning figures who will keep the realm and their minds spick and span" (1979, 114).

Hearne states that the re-visions of the story with current values being substituted for past traditions is what draws the ire of critics. This film "embroidered basic fairy tale formula with Hollywood romance, slapstick humor, and a utopian alternative to the harsh competition engendered by the Depression (witness the cooperative work ethic of the seven miners and of the heroine's menagerie of housecleaners)" (Hearne, 143).

But housework was not w-o-r-k, it was playful fun full of singing and cooperative effort from her animal friends. In reversed sequence from the traditional tale, Snow White cleans the house before meeting the messy dwarfs rather than using it as a bargaining tool, as the Brothers Grimm eventually made it. Reviews of the film demonstrate how the housecleaning sequence captured the imagination of the viewers, often singling it out as the film's high point (Tatar 1992, 234). The dwarfs in the Grimms' tale, however, were not in need of a housekeeper. Everything in their cottage is "indescribably dainty and neat." As Tatar comments, Snow White, in many post-Disney versions, is "represented as serving an apprenticeship in home economics" (1992, 234). Zipes points out that Walt Disney retained a key ideological feature of the Grimms' version: The home was the place where good girls remained. The film therefore was about the domestication of women (1994, 89).

The Names of the Dwarfs and Their Role

As mentioned earlier, one of the most obvious differences between the traditional tale and the Disney version is the individualization of the dwarfs, each having a name and a personality to suit. This was one of Walt Disney's original concepts at the onset of the Snow White project. The names have indeed become immortalized in generations of audiences since the characters were first introduced. Several of the names were decided immediately by Disney and his team and all were chosen to reflect a strong characteristic. "Doc" represented leadership and authority; "Happy" and "Grumpy" were counterpoints; "Sleepy" and "Bashful" lent themselves to endless gags; and both "Sneezy" and "Dopey" were inspired by real people (Hulett, 217). These secondary characters also serve to pad the content of the film, to make it possible to produce the story as a full-length feature film. Because each name represents an emotional state, Zipes contends that they suggest "the composite humors of a single individual" (1979, 114). If these healthy instincts are in order, they then become a powerful ally against evil.

The Use of Animals and Forest Scenes

The Disney trademark use of enchanting animal characters is featured prominently in this movie. They are employed whenever the studio is compelled to reduce dramatic tension for their potential movie audience. These characters become companions and champions for the young girl, entertaining and reassuring not only her but the audience as well. At this early point in animation history, it was also easier to bring these figures to life than the more realistic human characters. The reappearance of the animals throughout the film aided in establishing the continuity of the film as well as providing running gags, such as the slow tortoise who always arrived when everyone else was leaving and the fly who bothers Sleepy throughout the film (Holliss and Sibley, 23).

Age and Character of Snow White

Snow White has no time to grow older and mature in Disney's film world because the entire action spans a little more than 30 hours (Holliss and Sibley, 29). Compare this time frame with that of the traditional tale to understand why Disney's Snow White had to be older than any of her counterparts.

The traditional beginning scene depicting the mother wishing for a child "as white as snow, with ebony hair and lips as red as blood" is completely missing from the film. "There was never any material written or drawn and photographed for the film showing Snow White's real mother, who dies in childbirth, although references or drawings of this and other embellishments were made up for the authorized book versions and comic strips" (Behlmer, 59). Snow White is introduced as an adolescent "Cinderella" character who, while contending with a vain and wicked stepmother, is ready for romance and adventure.

Janet Ames explains her reaction to Disney's *Snow White* when she saw it again as an adult (and a mother of a daughter).

> The Snow White I remembered from my childhood was little more than a child herself. But, watching it three and a half decades later, I noticed with shock that Snow White was running through the forest, in fear for her life, wearing yellow high heels. She innocent, it's true, but at the same time seductive in a grown-up way. She coos and bats her eyelashes, flirting shamelessly with the dwarfs (92).

Snow White is an orphan in the film. Neither parent is alive, and she is depicted as a Cinderella-type figure at the onset of the film. Compare this to the royal heritage given to her by the Brothers Grimm. Their version contains the sentimental death of her mother, a live (if ineffectual) father, and a princess named Snow White.

The Prince

Because Snow White is not a blossoming seven-year-old but an adolescent yearning for someone to love, the romantic male lead is introduced at the beginning of the film. After her song and wish at the well, she sees the young man that will captivate her heart forevermore. The prince and her "happy ever after" ending is part of the story that Snow

White tells to the dwarfs before sending them all to bed the evening she arrives at their cottage. Beyond this early introduction however, the prince still has a limited role; he knows of her existence and therefore goes to look for her, arriving in time to kiss her awake. The original plan of using the prince as a major character never materialized in this film, but these ideas were not wasted; they were used in Disney's *Sleeping Beauty*. Beginning production difficulties made the realistic characters such as the Prince, Snow White, the Queen, and the Huntsman difficult to animate, while the cartoon styling of the dwarfs and animal figures had been perfected (Behlmer, 46). Ultimately, Disney had actors and models pose for the human characters. They were filmed acting out actual scenes, and these films were studied and brought to life by the animators. The model for Snow White was a young dancer, Marjorie Belcher, who became well known later as Marge Champion, the wife and dance partner of Gower Champion (Behlmer, 48).

Disney also downplayed the prince's royal background. This follows the pattern of traditional storytellers in North America who, when transporting the Old World tales, give them a different flavor. Heroines become more aggressive and active; the royal family of the castle are demoted to wealthy landowners; and the castle becomes a structure that would be recognizable and natural in the North American landscape. However, as Kay Stone reminds us, these changes do not affect the basic force of the tales, which "still must test against the materialism and cynicism of powerful antagonists often without the help of amusing dwarfs, fairies and friendly animals" (1980, 43). Zipes maintains that the prince may be symbolic of Walt Disney himself: It is the prince who frames the narrative; he is present from the very beginning, announcing his great love for Snow White, who can not be fulfilled until he arrives to kiss her (1994, 90).

The Queen

The Queen was not only jealous of Snow White's beauty in Disney's film but also envious, because after seeing and hearing the prince singing to Snow White, she realizes that her stepdaughter has such a handsome suitor (Zipes 1994, 87). Diane Purkiss, in her exploration of the witch in history, credits the use of the stock phrase "wicked stepmother" to a form of literary "contamination" engendered by Disney's *Snow White and the Seven Dwarfs* (279). Marina Warner credits this film and Disney's *Cinderella* (1950) as the chief movers in naturalizing "female-maternal-malignancy in the imaginations of children worldwide" (207). Disney concentrates on the wicked stepmother with glee and fails to offer anything beyond featureless banality and saccharine sentimentality to his heroines. Until recently, these images have maintained a leadership role in the public's perception of fairy-tale characters: passive princesses and vigorous but evil older women (Warner, 207). Maria Tatar states that Disney's portrait of Snow White's stepmother reveals

> in visual terms the monstrous nature of the wicked queen. While the Grimms' stepmother dresses up as an old peddler woman . . . Disney's stepmother transforms herself into a hag of such startling ugliness that she bears no resemblance whatsoever to the wicked queen. The images of this cinematic witch's physiognomy dominate the film and give us its most arresting, and controversial, moments" (1992, 138).

Tatar is concerned about the image of maternal evil in this tale, an image that had been constantly revised by the Brothers Grimm during their subsequent editions. The implication of the Disney revision, however, is that there is no longer a natural split between the good biological mother and the jealous evil stepmother. There is only one maternal aspect available to Snow White and the audience, and it is one of absolute evil. (Tatar 1992, 232). It was Disney's animation of the stepmother and her double face— "for she appears twice as an unsexed woman, endangering and destabilizing due order . . . as the raven haired queen . . . and the old beggarwoman"—that made her a familiar terror (Warner, 222). However, other critics do not agree in entirety. The wicked queen and her raven are less frightening than they could have been because of their joking conversation. The scene "had a fine touch for the sinister . . . the absurdly cute characters . . . overcame any sense of real evil" (Stone 1980, 43).

Although Walt Disney based his reworking of the tale on Grimms' version, he felt that the threefold repetition of traditional fairy tales would not appeal to his viewers. He immediately reduced the stepmother's attempts on Snow White at the dwarfs' cottage to the two episodes involving the comb and the apple, but the final product only featured the latter. This poisoned apple is represented as a wishing apple: one bite and your dreams will come true. Snow White, although warned by the dwarfs to beware of strangers, is consumed by her wish for her handsome prince and eagerly takes a bite of the apple, falling to her supposed death.

Snow White may not have taken the dwarfs' warning about strangers seriously, but her animal friends certainly do. When Snow White herself defeats their attempt to keep the transformed stepmother from her door, the animals set out for assistance from the dwarfs. After finally communicating their message to the dwarfs, all the rescuers chase and corner the old hag, who then falls to her death, never to dance at her stepdaughter's wedding!

Disney emphasizes romance rather than conflict with this change to the ending (not to mention the screen kiss and wishing and hoping for the prince). The red-hot iron shoes that are used to torture the queen in the traditional tale direct the audience's focus to the theme of justice done, while having the queen die before the wedding in the movie allows the focus to be directed on romance (Stone 1980, 44).

Influences of This Film on Future Generations

Since the movie's release in 1937, Walt Disney's reworkings of traditional fairy tales in animated form have changed the common perceptions of these tales among the world of moviegoers. Disney's technical skill and ideological proclivities were so consummate that his signature has obfuscated the names of Perrault, the Brothers Grimm, Hans Christian Andersen, and Collodi. For most people in Western society, the first and perhaps lasting impressions of these tales have emanated from a Disney film, book, or artifact (Zipes 1994, 72). The film has many of the elements that were part of subsequent Disney animated films: a damsel in distress, a wicked stepmother, a battle between good and evil, and a happy-ever-after ending (Nye, 1024).

The earliest films from the Disney studios perpetuated a male myth. Despite their beauty and charm, Disney's Snow White, Sleeping Beauty, and Cinderella are pale and pathetic compared to the more active and evil characters in the films. "Witches are not only agents of evil but represent erotic and subversive forces that are more appealing for the artists who drew them and for the audiences themselves" (Zipes 1994, 90). The heroines are much more like ornaments. This factor has drawn a great deal of criticism from feminists and other opponents to Disneyfication of folktales and did not go unnoticed by the Disney studios. According to Betsy Cohen in her examination of envy, Disney's *Snow White and the Seven Dwarfs* "presents a cultural ideal and stereotype of the passive housewife who comes to life only with the prince's kiss" (1). The story of Snow White is presented as overly sweet and romantic because Snow White spends a good deal of her time wishing and hoping for her prince to come. In contrast, the traditional character never anticipates a prince or a happy-ever-after existence (Cohen, 282).

> As it was sold and repackaged, through its songs,
> through plastic figures of Snow White and the dwarfs,
> and through books based on the film, it came to have a
> powerful effect on parents and children, impressing on
> everyone the image of a girl who makes her dreams come
> true through her flirtatious good looks and her effortless
> ability to keep a house clean (Tatar 1992, 235).

In subsequent (and much more recent) animated folk and fairy tales
such as *Beauty and the Beast* and *The Little Mermaid*, Disney Studios was
quick to promote the fact that these heroines were active and much more
involved with their own fate.

The Opies found it interesting that the film version, while attempting to obscure much of the violence in the tale, reestablishes the incident
of the huntsman's order to return with Snow White's heart as proof of the
accomplished deed. This incident had been glossed over by the earlier
translators and tellers of the story (Opie, 228). This film, and those that
followed, did indeed embellish many of the violent and terrifying scenes
for their young audiences. Wolfgang Mieder maintains that the movie
version gave, to the adult viewing audience, a broader version of the
dwarfs. They are seen by adults "as representing multiple concerns in
sexual or international politics" as demonstrated by their varied appearances in editorial cartoons as well as cartoons aimed at entertainment
(1987, 28). At the same time, Mieder is apprehensive. He states that

> the fairy tale of "Snow White" will continue to exist at
> least in printed or film versions, but judging by the de-
> creased knowledge of fables and other traditional lore in
> our society, one wonders if some day the allusions in
> these cartoons and other texts will no longer be recog-
> nized. It would certainly be a great loss to communication
> and understanding if that were to occur, for our modern
> children's stories don't even come close to the universal
> applicability to life's complexities that the traditional
> fairy tales have (1987, 32).

Zipes, in one of his discussions on Disney's film versions of traditional tales, enumerates a number of changes in the institution of the
genre. Technique now takes precedent over the story; the story is used to
celebrate technicians and their creativity. While the characters have been
fleshed out in order to fill the time frame of a feature film, they remain

one-dimensional. The characters do not develop because they are merely stereotypes. The thematic emphasis on cleanliness, control, and organized industry reinforces the industry and techniques of the film itself. Zipes's final point is that private reading pleasure is replaced by pleasurable viewing in an impersonal cinema where audiences are not brought together for the development of community but to be diverted and entertained. "Everything is on the surface, one-dimensional, and we are to delight in one-dimensional portrayal and thinking, for it is adorable, easy and comforting in its simplicity" (1994, 95).

Movie Trivia

- The movie earned $8,500,000 during the first release, at a time when children paid only a dime for admission to a movie theater (Ames, 92).

- It is estimated that at least one million drawings were made during the production of the film (Ames, 92).

- Suggestions for names of the dwarfs that were discarded included Gabby, Jumpy, Sniffy, Puffy, Lazy, Stubby, Shorty, Nifty, and Wheezy (Ames, 92).

- When the drawings were completed several of the painters were unhappy with Snow White's artificially red cheeks and harsh hairline. To solve the problem, they applied real rouge and other makeup directly to the cel (Ames, 92).

- Disney re-released the film theatrically during ensuing seven-year intervals after the premier release on December 21, 1937.

- It was first released as a video in 1994, becoming the most eagerly awaited release in video history. The print has been remastered, and the results are astonishing in their detail and rich color. The film was truly a remarkable achievement in an era when there were no computers to assist in the animation process (Nye, 1024).

- Disney also released a "Snow White" Deluxe Collector's Edition that included the video of the movie, a book about the film, ten limited lithographs of the film's original posters, and an extra video of the making of Snow White containing several animated sequences that were not used in the final release print (Nye, 1024).

Snow White: A Tale of Terror

Snow White: A Tale of Terror (1996). Directed by Michael Cohen and staring Sigourney Weaver, Sam Neill, and Monica Keena. Black Forest Films. Distributed by Buena Vista.

This film, in direct contrast to the version made by Disney studios, highlights the fact that the story is indeed an adaptation of the tale by the Brothers Grimm. This is not to say that the film does not take liberties with the Grimms' tale, as indeed it does. The story begins with a carriage accident involving a German nobleman, Frederick Hoffman, and his pregnant wife. As a result of the accident, the child is born at the cost of the life of her mother. The child, Lilli, has a carefree childhood until her father announces his marriage to Claudia, who arrives with her brother and a supernatural mirrored wardrobe. Life does not get too difficult until nine years later, when Claudia finally becomes pregnant but miscarries the child. Claudia asks her brother to kill Lilli, but she escapes and finds shelter in an abandoned mine inhabited by seven gold miners. Claudia discovers Lilli's whereabouts and, after several attempts to kill her, disguises herself as an old woman and offers Lilli an apple that performs its traditional deed. Lilli is buried but Will, one of the miners whom Lilli has fallen in love with, refuses to believe she is dead. He takes her from the coffin, dislodging the apple and bringing her back to life. They make haste to save Lilli's father, who has been injured in one of his wife's attempts on his daughter's life. Lilli ultimately kills Claudia by stabbing her reflection in the wardrobe mirror.

Claudia is not entirely unsympathetic. Her destructiveness stems from the traumatic confrontation with her own inadequacy. It is only after her miscarriage that the magic mirror becomes important, "reflecting back to Claudia her narcissistic ideal rather than the haggard reality" (Bruzzi, 54). However, the other characters are not developed as fully as they could be, and "Freud can only take you so far: goodness remains an inherently undramatic experience" (Bruzzi, 54).

The film was shot in Prague and starred Sigourney Weaver as Claudia, Sam Neill as Frederick, Taryn Davis as the young Snow White, and Monica Keena as the older title character. Although the story is that of Snow White, the film definitely belongs to the stepmother Claudia. *Time* magazine quoted Weaver as stating, "The whole thing for me was not about looks, it was about the father. Snow White wants to be first in her father's heart, and so does his wife. . . . As the stepmother suffers a series of misfortunes, she becomes overwrought and turns on Lilli. . . . It's a psychological thriller" (Luscombe, 81). The film is also known as "Snow White in the Black Forest."

Willa: An American Snow White

Willa: An American Snow White (1997). Directed by Tom Davenport. Delaplane, VA: Davenport Films.

This film was the winner of the 1998 Andrew Carnegie Medal for Excellence in Children's Video. It was also awarded the Parent's Choice Gold Seal Award for 1997. The video is targeted at preteens and adolescent girls and their families.

This adaptation by Thomas Davenport (part of his Brothers Grimm series and his first full-length film at 85 minutes) is set in rural Virginia in 1915. The jealous queen is Regina Worthington, an aging beauty whose stage career is sagging. Willa (Snow White) is her stepdaughter and the dwarves are represented by a failed Shakespearean actor, Dr. Alfonzo, and his two traveling medicine show companions.

Children's Video Reports comments that *Willa* "artfully interweaves the classic tales of Snow White and Romeo and Juliet, and throws in hints of the Wizard of Oz." The cast is from the American Shakespeare Theatre, the sets are elaborate, and the natural scenery is breathtaking. *School Library Journal* reviewer Barb White states that:

> It preserves the original tale's themes of death and resurrection, and betrayal and friendship. Cleverly incorporating the actual tale into its story, *Willa* is an excellent addition to the film series and proves engrossing and suspenseful. Families watching at home, and teachers and students in classrooms, will find the film of interest not only because of its high quality but because of the interesting comparisons to be made with its better known inspiration (62).

Short Films

Kay E. Vandergrift, in her gathering of cinematic versions of Snow White, briefly summarizes more than a dozen different titles. In this listing she includes the titles discussed in the previous section as well as several others worth noting here. Possibly the video version best known after Disney's version at this time is the 1983 film *Faerie Tale Theatre: Snow White and the Seven Dwarfs*. (Producer Shelley Duvall. Playhouse Video. 53 Minutes.)

Vincent Price is the witty and clever mirror and Vanessa Redgrave is the wicked queen in this satiric reworking of the tale. Costumes and set design were inspired by the work of illustrator N. C. Wyeth.

Other titles mentioned by Vandergrift include a seven-minute Betty Boop cartoon titled *Snow White* released in 1932. Vandergrift states that this piece is associated with Black jazz using Cab Calloway's "St. James Infirmary Blues" and is useful as a way to look at jazz history. Another interesting retelling of the story is *Snow White and the Three Stooges* originally released in 1961 and released as a video in 1985.

Poetry

"Snow White" images and themes also appeal to writers of poetry. The majority of these reworkings consider the stepmother, her mirror, and the dwarfs to be the most interesting aspects of the tale.

1971: Sexton, Anne. "**Snow White and the Seven Dwarfs.**" In *Transformations.* Boston: Houghton Mifflin, 3–9. Also in *Disenchantments: An Anthology of Modern Fairy Tale Poetry*, edited by Wolfgang Mieder. Hanover, NH: University Press of New England, 155–59.

Anne Sexton is obviously not very fond of the Snow White character: Her beauty is compared to inanimate objects, and she is referred to as a "living doll" who "maintains her purity even though she is beset by sexuality" (Hruschka, 46). She has no choices in her life, and her only refuge is in her innocence. It is the queen that draws sympathy from the poet. She is in the midst of a transformation, from a person of beauty replaced by a younger female to an old crone, but one that now has power. For this knowledge and power she is tortured to death. "Sexton transforms the story of Snow White, revealing the fact that women are made to suffer because men cannot resolve their conflict with their feminine side" (Hruschka, 46).

1977: Broumas, Olga. "**Snow White.**" In *Beginning with O.* New Haven, CT: Yale University Press, 69–71. Also in *Disenchantments: An Anthology of Modern Fairy Tale Poetry*, edited by Wolfgang Mieder. Hanover, NH: University Press of New England, 160–62.

Three generations of women sleep peacefully until the husband/father returns from war. Their peace is now destroyed, and Snow White realizes that her husband is an "alien instrument" while she and her mother are "two-halves of a two-colored apple." The conclusion of the poem imagines a return of the bride to her mother, and instead of a relationship based on jealousy, the relationship is based on an intimate mother-daughter bond. For mature readers.

1982: Dahl, Roald. "**Snow White and the Seven Dwarfs**." In *Revolting Rhymes*. New York: Albert A. Knopf, 11–17. Also in *Disenchantments: An Anthology of Modern Fairy Tale Poetry*, edited by Wolfgang Mieder. Hanover, NH: University Press of New England, 163–66.

This is a tongue-in-cheek retelling of the traditional tale using contemporary cant. The seven funny little men are ex-racehorse jockeys and terrible gamblers to boot. In order to help make ends meet, Snow White made her way to the palace where the king "was in the counting house" and the queen was "eating bread and honey" and stole the magic mirror, which "always got the answer right" and solved all their problems!

An inspired use of the mirror's magic. The focus of the tale no longer is on jealousy but on winning at the racetrack!

1982: Hay, Sara Henderson. "**One of the Seven Has Something to Say**." In *Story Hour*. Fayetteville, AR: University of Arkansas Press, 20. Also in *Disenchantments: An Anthology of Modern Fairy Tale Poetry*, edited by Wolfgang Mieder. Hanover, NH: University Press of New England, 150.

A lament from one of the dwarfs about the order and cleanliness that has invaded their home and lives with the arrival of Snow White. He does not want to hurt her feelings—she is just trying to help—but wouldn't it be grand if she got married and things returned to normal!

1985: Chute, Robert M. "**Snow White**." In *Disenchantments: An Anthology of Modern Fairy Tale Poetry*, edited by Wolfgang Mieder. Hanover, NH: University Press of New England, 152.

A commentary on the role of fairy tales and other fictions have in our modern society using the framework of the mirror, the apple, and the discontent that often marks our lives. This brief poem offers a contemplative look at the way society views and defines itself.

1985: Hall, Donald. "**Mirror**." In *Disenchantments: An Anthology of Modern Fairy Tale Poetry*, edited by Wolfgang Mieder. Hanover, NH: University Press of New England, 149.

A simple but powerful question and answer are conjured in four lines addressed to the mirror.

1985: Locklin, Gerald. "**The Dwarf.**" In *Disenchantments: An Anthology of Modern Fairy Tale Poetry*, edited by Wolfgang Mieder. Hanover, NH: University Press of New England, 151.

Another lament from a dwarf, but this one is dark and after the fact of Snow White's deliverance and departure.

1990: Strauss, Gwen. "**Confessions of a Witch.**" In *Trail of Stones*. New York: Alfred A. Knopf, 5–7.

The queen explains why it was necessary to make the various attempts on Snow White's life as she, the queen, "will not be outdone by her young Prince" (7).

1990: Strauss, Gwen. "**The Seventh Dwarf.**" In *Trail of Stones*. New York: Alfred A. Knopf, 8–10.

The poem contains the voice of the seventh dwarf as he dwells on melancholy memories and emotions evoked by Snow White's sojourn with them. He speaks of the three attempts on Snow White's life and the void left by her leaving the woods and the company of dwarfs.

1995: Sherman, Delia. "**Snow White to the Prince.**" In *The Armless Maiden and Other Tales for Childhood's Survivors*, edited by Terri Windling. New York: TOR, 40–41.

This first-person narrative by the protagonist of the tale addresses the despair that Snow White's beauty has caused her from the first time her mother realized that her beauty had been eclipsed by her daughter's. The mirror reflected both images: the mother was 40 and fair, but at 14, Snow White was much fresher and fairer still. Snow White recognized her mother in disguise all three times but played along with the charade so that she would be given the maternal love that had been withdrawn with that fateful glimpse in the mirror.

1995: Yolen, Jane. "**The Mirror Speaks.**" In *The Armless Maiden and Other Tales for Childhood's Survivors*, edited by Terri Windling. New York: TOR, 94–95.

The voice in the mirror "cannot speak lies—but each truth is half-told" (94). The mirror explains that the beauty and freshness of youth will always be fairer than that of those in their later years. This poem uses the image of the mirror's message from "Snow White" to address the prevalent issue of intergenerational jealousy and rivalry.

Picture Books

Only one reworking of this tale in picture-book format is likely to appeal to young adults at this time. But this one could be considered enough!

1986: French, Fiona. **Snow White in New York**. New York: Oxford University Press.

One of the most successful reworkings of a fairy-tale setting in picture-book format is French's "simple" parody. By moving the story to New York City in the 1920s, French incorporates the role of the queen (of the underworld), the mirror (the daily newspaper), and the wild forest (or urban center). Snow White survives not because of her beauty but because of her beautiful voice, which takes the town by storm when she first performs with her new benefactors, the seven jazz musicians. The prince, too, has a more active role in this reworking of the tale. He is the newspaper reporter who first makes her presence known to the world and reintroduces her to her stepmother. The Art Deco illustrative style fully complements the world and tale recreated by the author.

Although the text is simplistic, the cleverness of the adaptation and the creation of the "romantic" world of the gangsters appeal to the most sophisticated of young adults.

Graphic Novels

There is also only one example of the tale in a graphic novel format.

1995: Wenzel, David, and Douglas Wheeler. "**Little Snow White**." In *Fairy Tales of the Brothers Grimm*. New York: Nantier, Beall and Minoustchine.

The graphic novel follows the Grimms' tale faithfully but adds a few touches of additional drama as well. The viewer sees the huntsman dragged to the gallows as well as an additional scene between the queen in disguise and two of her guardsmen. When the queen discovers that her second attempt is unsuccessful, the illustrations show us her anguish along with the fear of her villagers as they witness it. The time between the second and the third attempt on Snow White at the home of the dwarfs has been extended, in this telling, to over seven full pages of illustrated panels. Time passes much more quickly when Snow White lies in her coffin. In three panels, the artists demonstrate that "Snow White lay motionless seven years, her body continuing to grow as that of any other child, while her clothes and the coffin lengthened with her." Faithful to the Grimms' tale again is the awakening scene. It is not a kiss but a stumble of the king's son and his servants when lifting the coffin that causes the apple to fall from Snow White's mouth and her to awaken. The final dance of the queen is agreed on by the prince, the dwarves, and Snow White's father upon hearing the truth.

Illustrations are realistic rather than comic, with several bows to other illustrators of this tale, including Arthur Rackham and Trina Schart Hyman. The setting of the castle and the village inhabitants is particularly successful.

Internet Resources

"Snow White" is the most accessible folktale on the Internet. This is due in part to the efforts of Professor Kay E. Vandergrift and her Snow White pages available at www.scils.rutgers.edu/special/kay/swteach. html. The website, created in January 1996 and updated regularly, is designed to incorporate information about the tale of "Snow White" and to encourage a variety of users to explore alternative paths for their own teaching and learning. It is aimed at adults and young adults who are interested in children's literature, folklore, cultural studies, or illustration. As stated on this page:

> Using an 1898 edition of the Grimm tale, the user can compare the highlighted text to over thirty editions of the tale representing more than a century of re-tellings. . . . On both the textual pages and the illustrations pages a number of questions have been inserted to prod the user into thinking creatively and imaginatively.

Vandergrift has included handouts prepared for her graduate students at Rutgers Universities as well as the following pages:

A. *Snow White: Context.* In this section she has provided selections of excerpts from scholars that help to form a context or frame for the study of this tale and others. These scholars include Jane Yolen from *Touch Magic*, James McGlathery, John Ellis, the Opies, Jack Zipes, Max Lüthi, and Kay Stone.

B. *Snow White: Issues.* Excerpts from scholars explore the issues of the nature of fairy tales and their "goodness" for children, morality in fairy tales, translation accuracy, Disney interpretations, and feminist interpretations.

C. *Snow White: Criticism.* In her introduction to this section Vandergrift states:

> When one includes historical renderings of *Snow White* with alternative contemporary visions, the varieties interpretations of a single text are powerfully demonstrated. . . . What has kept these stories alive over time and through many cultures is the ability of different peoples to recognize themselves and what is important in their lives within these very simple texts.

In this examination of the body of criticism on "Snow White," Vandergrift has included excerpts from Maria Tatar, Roger Sale, Barbara Keifer in *The Potential of Picturebooks* (which includes a sound analysis of the illustrations of Hyman and Burkert in regards to "Snow White"), Bruno Bettelheim, and a variety of articles focusing on Walt Disney's interpretation.

D. *Snow White: Illustrations.* This page allows the viewer to examine illustrations from a wide variety of retellings of the tale. The broad teaching focus of this site led to the inclusion of illustrations from both inexpensive mass-market picture books available at supermarkets to the more expensive and literary volumes found in bookstores and libraries. This section also includes several excerpts about illustrations as well as suggestions useful in a classroom setting. Thumbnail images as well as larger versions of the illustrations are available. The list of illustrations for viewing and comparison include the mother at the castle window, the stepmother before the mirror, the huntsman and the woods, the seven dwarfs' first meeting with Snow White, the creation of the apple, the death, Snow White in her coffin, the wedding, and the death of the stepmother.

E. *Snow White: Media.* This page offers cinematic versions of the story, including the Disney film and sites with information on or about "Snow White," including artifacts such as teapots, postage stamps, an advertisement for Child Advocates (an organization that helps abused children), and figurines.

F. *Snow White: Bibliography.* This is a selected bibliography of "Snow White" versions in chronological order, beginning with the 1882 edition of *Household Stories from the Collection of the Brothers Grimm*, translated by Lucy Crane and illustrated by Walter Crane.

G. *Snow White: Links.* This section includes a large number of on-line links to information about folklore, mythology, fairy tales, and children's literature.

Other Internet resources include a concise discussion of the tale in *Fairy Tales: Origins and Evolution* (http://www.easyweb.easynet.co.uk/~cdaae/fairy/swhite.htm); articles on the suitability of this tale for today, which include "Living Happily Ever After?" by Roy Zuck (http://www.fri.com/heritage/feb96/LivingHap.htm), "On Disney, Daughters, and Dads" by Michael J. Corso (http://www.fathermag.com/htmlmodules/jul96/xDisney.html), and "Is *Snow White* the Most Sexist of All?" by Jenny Sharp, which is a reprint from *The Oklahoma Daily* (http://www.daily.ou.edu/issues . . . eb-19/snowwhite.processed.html); the lyrics from all the songs in the Disney film of Snow White (http://arti.es/Disneymania/textos/blanca~1/lyrics/snowwhit.htm); a comparison of Snow White as illustrated by Nancy E. Burkert and Disney's animated film; and a parody of both the tale and the tabloid newspapers in the "Enchanted Examiner" (http://w3.macdigital.com/pcbs/snow/).

Classroom Extensions

On the Internet site provided by Kay Vandergrift, and of special interest to teachers, she has gathered assignments from a variety of folklore and children's literature specialists.

Jack Zipes's syllabus from his course on "The Grimms' Fairy Tales, Feminism and Folklore" includes the weekly topics and readings for this course. Several tales receive intense attention, including "Little Red Riding Hood" and 22 readings of this tale as well as a discussion of the transformation of fairy tales through film by looking at *Company of Wolves* and the Fairy Tale Theatre's production of *Little Red Riding Hood*; "Cinderella" with 19 readings; "Snow White" with 13 readings; "Rumpelstiltskin" with 14 readings; "Sleeping Beauty," 17 readings; and "Beauty and the Beast," 15 readings and three cinematic versions of the tale, including the television show. A bibliography for primary and secondary works is included.

Hilary S. Crew of Rutgers provides a specific assignment to "examine the representation of the mother figure, (including grandmother and stepmother figures) the witch (crone) figure, and the relationships between these figures and the daughter/protagonist in traditional tales."

Michael Joseph, Rare Book and Jerseyanna Catalogue Librarian at Rutgers and the owner of the listserv Child_Lit, offers an assignment based on illustrations and the interpretations offered by the artists. This would be a valuable exercise for those interested in exercises on perspective, visual literacy, and symbolism.

Ariko Kawabata, Assistant Professor of English Literature, Aichi Prefectural University in Nagoya-City, Japan, considers historical and cultural backgrounds of this tale and of "Little Red Riding Hood."

Sanjay Sircar from Australia offers four assignments comparing "Snow White" with other tales as well as Disneyfication of "Snow White."

Constance Vidor provides a detailed instructional activity for analyzing illustrations for use in grades 4 or 5 for use in the Language Arts Curriculum.

The following suggestions can be easily adapted for study with other folk tales.

Beauty

While beauty is an attribute that is common to many of the heroines in fairy tales, in this story it becomes the focus of a life-and-death struggle. What is the significance of beauty in "Snow White"?

The Influence of Popular Culture

Betsy Hearne, in her *Horn Book* article on Disney fairy-tale films, states:

> Disney's modifications originate from accurate readings of our culture. He got the address right. This is where we live. We who criticize Disney have seen the enemy, and he is us. We are mistaken to speak as a voice removed from the rest of the population, as eighteenth- and nineteenth-century educators did in criticizing fairy tales and fiction, or to condemn artists as gulling the rest of the population. Disney belongs to us and we belong to him. What he does to fairy tales and classics is, in a sense, our own shadow. We don't have to like it and we don't have to keep quiet about it, but we do have to understand our own society and the lore it generates. The alternative is

critical mystification. Popular culture and art are a vital dynamic. The past is always renegotiating with the present to become the future, and that requires the fresh air of our awareness (145).

What is Betsy Hearne saying? Do you agree with her statements? Has our society changed since Walt Disney provided us with his first full-length fairy tale in 1937? Does this change our interpretation of the film itself?

The Myth of Persephone

Steven Swann Jones claimed that there are many parallels between the classical myth of Persephone and the story of Snow White. In many versions of "Snow White" she is portrayed as picking flowers, as does Persephone before her abduction to the underworld. Both are separated from their familiar environment and family; both enter the world of the dead; and both are ultimately restored to the world of the living (1990, 63). Jones maintained that "Snow White" "teaches the adolescent about the wholeness of the cosmic life cycle, depicting both her existential anxieties and the philosophical answer to those anxieties" (1990, 64).

What does Jones mean by this statement? Compare the two tales to see if there are any other points of similarities. What is the significance of the myth of Persephone?

Picture-Book Versions of "Snow White"

Compare the illustrative style and rendering of traditional versions of the folktale. For example, Nancy Ekholm Burkert's illustrations for the retelling by Randall Jarrell emphasize a medieval setting. The queen seems to be well acquainted with the tools of the magic arts and the tarot. Look at the childlike innocent faces of the adult Snow White and her prince, and the adult faces on the child-size bodies of the dwarves. Look also at the placement of the illustrations in relationship to the text. Do these illustrations help tell the story, or do they ask more questions than they can answer? Now look at the illustrations by Trina Schart Hyman. She has used real faces for her characters: her daughter for Snow White and Jane Yolen's husband for the prince, and one dwarf is wearing the face of the artist herself. How do these illustrations and characterizations aid in telling the story? Are these two tales received differently because of the illustrative style? Find other picture-book versions of the tale and compare the characterizations, the setting, and the mood created by the placement of the illustrations and the illustrative styles.

Relationships Between "Snow White," "Cinderella," and "Sleeping Beauty"

Martin Hallett and Barbara Karasek put forth several pertinent questions regarding these tales in their first edition of *Folk and Fairy Tales*. Discuss and compare the following:

A. What similarities are there in the pattern of development each heroine undergoes in "Sleeping Beauty" and "Snow White"?

B. To what extent can the apple in "Snow White" be compared to the spindle in "Sleeping Beauty"?

C. In "Snow White," as in the Grimms' version of "Cinderella," nature seems to be important in regard to the protagonist. Both stories begin with the mention of the changing of seasons, and animals are important in both tales. What role does nature play in these two tales? (1991, 58)

The Role of the Witch

What is the role of the witch in history? In folklore? When did the wicked queen in "Snow White" become associated with the character of a witch? Is her role in this story different from the role of the witch in other folktales such as "Hansel and Gretel" and "Rapunzel?"

Snow White and "The Lady of Shalott"

In her essay, A. S. Byatt states that she has always associated ice and glass with Tennyson's "The Lady of Shalott." This tale and Snow White's story have many similarities for this author.

> The Lady has things in common with the frozen death-in-life states of Snow White and of the lady and her castle in the glass coffins. She is enclosed in her tower, and sees the world not even through the window, but in a mirror, which reflects the outside life, which she, the artist, then weaves into "a magic web with colors gay." She is not the Wicked Queen; she does not reflect herself. . . . The Lady was solitary and alive, even if the magic colors bright were only shadows and reflections. Once she steps out toward flesh and blood she suffers part of the fate of Snow White's mother who looked out, and desired a child. Her floating catafalque has a feeling of a glass coffin . . . (73-4).

Compare these two tales to see if you agree with the author's statement. If she is not the Wicked Queen, who is the Lady of Shalott?

Bibliography

Ames, Janet. "Snow White Revisited." *Ladies Home Journal* 110:8 (August 1993), 92.

Bacchilega, Christina. *Postmodern Fairy Tales: Gender and Narrative Strategies*. Philadelphia: University of Pennsylvania Press, 1997.

Barzilai, Shuli. "Reading 'Snow White': The Mother's Story." *Signs: Journal of Women in Culture and Society* 15:3 (1990), 515–34.

Behlmer, Richard. "They Called It 'Disney's Folly': *Snow White and the Seven Dwarfs* (1937)." In *America's Favorite Movies: Behind the Scenes*. New York: Frederick Ungar, 1982, 40–60.

Bettelheim, Bruno. *The Uses of Enchantment: The Meaning and Importance of Fairy Tales*. New York: Vintage Books, 1976.

Bottigheimer, Ruth B. *Grimms' Bad Girls and Bold Boys: The Moral and Social Vision of the Tales*. New Haven, CT: Yale University Press, 1987.

Brewer, Derek. *Symbolic Stories: Traditional Narratives of the Family Drama in English Literature*. Cambridge, England: D. S. Brewer, 1980.

Bruzzi, Stella. Review of "Snow White: A Tale of Terror." *Sight and Sound* 11 (November 1996), 53–54.

Burton, Sir Richard, trans. *The Pentamerone of Giambattista Basile*. London: Spring Books, 1952.

Byatt, A. S. "Ice, Snow, Glass." In *Mirror, Mirror on the Wall: Women Writers Explore Their Favorite Fairy Tales*, edited by Kate Bernheimer. New York: Anchor, 1998, 64–84.

Children's Video Reports. 11: 4/5 (1997).

Cohen, Betsy. *The Snow White Syndrome: All About Envy*. New York: Macmillan, 1986.

Datlow, Ellen, and Terri Windling. *Snow White, Blood Red*. New York: William Morrow, 1993.

Ellis, John M. *One Fairy Story Too Many: The Brothers Grimm and Their Tales*. Chicago: University of Chicago Press, 1983.

Gilbert, Sandra M., and Susan Gubar. *The Madwoman in the Attic: The Woman Writer and the Nineteenth-Century Literary Imagination*. New Haven, CT: Yale University Press, 1979.

———. "The Queen's Looking Glass." In *Don't Bet on the Prince: Contemporary Feminist Fairy Tales in North America and England*, edited by Jack Zipes. New York: Methuen, 1986, 201–8.

Girardot, N. J. "Initiation and Meaning in the Tale of Snow White and the Seven Dwarfs." *Journal of American Folklore* 90: 357 (1977), 274–300.

Hallett, Martin, and Barbara Karasek. *folk and fairy tales*. Peterborough, ON: Broadview Press, 1991.

———. *Folk and Fairy Tales*, 2d ed. Peterborough, ON: Broadview Press, 1996.

Hearn, Michael Patrick, Trinkett Clark, and H. Nichols Clark. *Myth, Magic, and Mystery: One Hundred Years of American Children's Book Illustrations*. Boulder, CO: Roberts Rinehart, 1996.

Hearne, Betsy. "Disney Revisited, Or Jiminy Cricket, It's Musty Down Here!" *Horn Book* 63: 2 (March/April 1997), 137–46.

Heuscher, Julius E. *A Psychiatric Study of Myths and Fairy Tales: Their Origin, Meaning, and Usefulness*. 2d ed. Springfield, IL: Charles C. Thomas, 1974.

Holliss, Richard, and Brian Sibley. *Walt Disney's Snow White and the Seven Dwarfs and the Making of the Classic Film*. [50th Anniversary]. New York: Simon & Schuster, 1987. (New edition published 1994).

Hruschka, John. "Anne Sexton and Anima *Transformations*: *Transformations* as a Critique of the Psychology of Love in Grimm's Fairy Tales." *Mythlore* 75 (Winter 1994), 45–47.

Hulett, Steve. "The Making of Snow White and the Seven Dwarfs." In *Walt Disney's Snow White and the Seven Dwarfs*. New York: Viking Press, 1979, 215–25.

Hyman, Trina Schart. "Cut It Down and You Will Find Something at the Roots." In *The Reception of Grimms' Fairy Tales: Responses, Reactions, Revisions*, edited by Donald Haase. Detroit: Wayne State University Press, 1993, 293–300.

Jones, Steven Swann. "The Pitfalls of Snow White Scholarship." *Journal of American Folklore* 92 (1979), 69–73.

———. *The New Comparative Method: Structural and Symbolic Analysis of the Allomotifs of "Snow White."* Helsinki: Academia Scientiarum Fennica, 1990. (FF Communications, no. 247).

Kolbenschlag, Madonna. *Kiss Sleeping Beauty Good-Bye: Breaking the Spell of Feminine Myths and Models*. San Francisco: Harper & Row, 1988.

Laurie, Alison. *Don't Tell the Grown-Ups: Why Kids Love the Books They Do*. New York: Avon, 1990.

Luscombe, Brenda. "Not Your Kid's 'Snow White'." *Time* 147: 5 (Jan 29, 1996), 81.

Lüthi, Max. *The Fairy Tale as Art Form and Portrait of Man.* Bloomington, IN: Indiana University Press, 1984.

McGlathery, James M. *Fairy Tale Romance: The Grimms, Basile, and Perrault.* Urbana-Champaign, IL: University of Illinois Press, 1991.

———. *Grimms' Fairy Tales: A History of Criticism on a Popular Classic.* Columbia, SC: Camden House, 1993. (Studies in German Literature, Linguistics and Culture).

Mei, Huang. *Transforming the Cinderella Dream: From Frances Burney to Charlotte Bronte.* New Brunswick, NJ: Rutgers University Press, 1990.

Mieder, Wolfgang. *Tradition and Innovation in Folk Literature.* Hanover, NH: University Press of New England, 1987.

Nye, Doug. "Disney Gives In, Releases 'Snow White' on Home Video." *Knight-Ridder/Tribune News Service* (24 October 1994), 1024K7937.

Opie, Iona, and Peter Opie. *The Classic Fairy Tales.* New York: Oxford University Press, 1974.

Penzer, N. M. *The Pentamerone of Giambattista Basile,* vol. 2. Translated from the Italian by Benedetto Croce. London: John Lane, 1932.

Purkiss, Diane. *The Witch in History: Early Modern and Twentieth-Century Representations.* London: Routledge, 1996.

Rohrich, Lutz. *Folktales and Reality.* Translated by Peter Tokofsky. Bloomington, IN: Indiana University Press, 1991.

Sale, Roger. *Fairy Tales and After: From Snow White to E. B. White.* Cambridge, MA: Harvard University Press, 1978.

Scalon, Donna. "Review of *The Godmother's Apprentice.*" *VOYA.* June 1996, 110.

Schickel, Richard. *The Disney Version: The Life, Times, Art, and Commerce of Walt Disney.* New York: Simon & Schuster, 1968.

Stone, Kay. "Fairy Tales for Adults: Walt Disney's Americanization of the Marchen." In *Folklore on Two Continents: Essays in Honor of Linda Degh,* edited by Nikolai Burlakoff et al. Bloomington, IN: Trickster Press, 1980, 40–48.

———. "Three Transformations of Snow White." In *The Brothers Grimm and Folktale,* edited by James M. McGlathery. Urbana-Champaign, IL: University of Illinois Press, 1991, 52–65.

Tatar, Maria. "From Nags to Witches: Stepmothers in the Grimms' Fairy Tales." In *Opening Texts: Psychoanalysis and the Culture of the Child*, edited by Joseph H. Smith and William Kerrigan. Baltimore, MD: John Hopkins University Press, 1985, 28–41. (Psychiatry and the Humanities, vol. 8).

———. *The Hard Facts of the Grimms' Fairy Tales*. Princeton, NJ: Princeton University Press, 1987.

———. *Off with Their Heads! Fairy Tales and the Culture of Childhood*. Princeton, NJ: Princeton University Press, 1992.

Thomas, Joyce. *Inside the Wolf's Belly: Aspects of the Fairy Tale*. Sheffield, England: Sheffield Academic Press, 1989.

Thompson, Stith. *The Types of the Folktale: A Classification and Bibliography. A Translation and Enlargement of Antti Aarne's Verzeichnis de Märchentypen*. 2d revision. Helsinki: Academia Scientiarum Fennica, 1964. (FF Communications, no. 184).

Vandergrift, Kay. "Snow White Media." http://www.scils.rutgers.edu/special/kay/swfilms.html

Walker, Nancy A. *The Disobedient Writer: Women and Narrative Tradition*. Austin, TX: University of Texas Press, 1995.

Walt Disney's Snow White and the Seven Dwarfs. New York: Viking Press, 1979.

Warner, Marina. *From the Beast to the Blonde: On Fairy Tales and Their Tellers*. London: Chatto & Windus, 1994.

White, Barb. "Review of Willa, An American Snow White." *School Library Journal* (November 1997): 62.

Zipes, Jack. *Breaking the Magic Spell: Radical Theories of Folk and Fairy Tales*. Austin, TX: University of Texas Press, 1979.

———. *Fairy Tales and the Art of Subversion: The Classical Genre for Children and the Process of Civilization*. New York: Methuen, 1983.

———. *The Brothers Grimm: From Enchanted Forests to the Modern World*. New York: Routledge, 1988.

———. *Fairy Tale as Myth, Myth as Fairy Tale*. Lexington, KY: University of Kentucky, 1994. (Thomas D. Clark Lectures, 1993).

Author/Illustrator Index

Motif Index

Tale Index

These references are to pages where the tales have been mentioned outside of their individual chapters or are mentioned in passing.

Title Index

from LIBRARIES UNLIMITED